The Copy Workshop Workbook

4th Edition

©2009 Bruce Bendinger

ISBN# 978-1-887229-39-5

Cover Design: Gregory S. Paus
Back Cover: Illustration, Mark Fredrickson;
Evolution Concept, David Bartels, Naked Branding
Production Editor: Patrick Guy Aylward

The Copy Workshop
2144 N. Hudson • Chicago, IL 60614
(773) 871-1179 FX: (773) 281-4643
www.adbuzz.com or thecopyworkshop@aol.com

This book is dedicated to:
Lorelei, Roy, John, Peter, Frankie, Ann, Adam, Mairee,
David, "The Bat," Sara, Jon, Judy, Eugenia, Pat, Aaron, Greg,
and Last-Minute Elizabeth. Year after year, you helped make
The Copy Workshop work.
Thank you.

Welcome to the Revolution

WOULDN'T IT BE BORING without a bit of evolution and revolution every once in a while?

Looks like we got some more.

FROM THE CREATIVE REVOLUTION TO THE MEDIA REVOLUTION.

When I was starting up – like you – the ad business was in the middle of The Creative Revolution. (It happened sort of right after *Mad Men*.)

Twenty years later, I wrote a book packed with all the good advice I'd picked up along the way.

Pretty good book, all things considered.

It became the #1 book on copywriting. Cool.

And now, if you go online, you can probably pick up used copies at a real nice price.

Do everything in that book and I promise that you'll have a successful career – if you can find a time machine and go back about 30 years.

Today? Well, it's a different world.

ADVERTISING & REVOLUTION.

They've been partners for a long time.

Though a business practice since earliest recorded history, advertising grew and prospered in the USA.

In many ways, the spirit of advertising is uniquely American.

"The First American," Ben Franklin, was an ad man, among other things.

A writer, Thomas Paine, helped "sell" the Revolution with *Common Sense*.

In general, advertising took hold in American society due to a number of unique forces:

The English Language.

Revolutions come easy in English. It's adaptable, democratic, and easy-to-use. It's now the world language of business.

Useful concepts and phrases are quickly adapted and adopted. It's a language made for a changing marketplace.

Economic Opportunity.

With an abundance of resources and opportunity, America had a population motivated to make the most of it and a government that encouraged and subsidized enterprise.

We attracted risk takers and innovators – and we still do. Even American consumers are eager to try new things.

Democracy.

Think about it – the marketplace is about choice and change.

Consumers vote every day.

America was the best place to have a new idea and make it happen.

From America to the World.

A key player has been the person who shaped these communications of commerce, writing with an entrepreneurial spirit – the copywriter – an American original.

As we move to a world economy, the need for effective communication is now a worldwide opportunity. It started here.

Alcohol and Tobacco.

Examples of ads for alcohol and tobacco products appear throughout the book.

Traditionally, they demonstrate state-of-the-art techniques. We've included examples to demonstrate the techniques – not endorse the products.

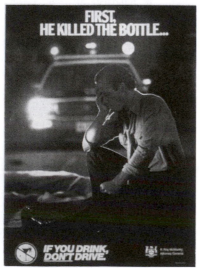

Cause-Related Advertising.

Many examples of exceptional ads for worthy causes are not featured.

Our focus is doing advertising that helps businesses stay in business.

Then, of course, you'll earn enough to support those worthy causes.

MAJOR MEDIA CHANGES = MAJOR CHANGES IN SOCIETY.

When Gutenberg invented the printing press five centuries ago, it was also a different world.

A narrow ruling class – mostly priests and nobles – owned all the information.

Then it changed. Suddenly – seemed sudden back then – there were books for everyone. Media evolved and the world changed. People learned to read.

Along the way, some of them decided to think for themselves.

So what happened?

You had The Reformation, The 30 Years War, and, pretty soon after that – as history goes – the American Revolution.

"THE FIRST AMERICAN" WAS AN AD MAN.

It was no accident that "The First American," Benjamin Franklin, was a printer.

He's also a member of the Advertising Hall of Fame. Yep, Benjamin Franklin. Ad man.

Now media evolution is in the process of giving us another Revolution.

Not only is the media world we swim in today dramatically different, it's a different business world, as well.

My college education was 100% paid for by my father. He worked at a newspaper.

One of his job titles was Classified Ad Manager. Classified Ads? Uh-huh. They were a "cash cow" for newspapers everywhere. But things can change.

Today, if you want a used car, or an apartment, or a puppy, your computer can connect you.

It's a different world.

THE GOOD NEWS.

The good news is that I have more than a few useful lessons to teach you.

Because even as the media is evolving, the core skills of effective communication still work – even if it's banner ads and e-mail instead of billboards and old-fashioned direct mail.

For you, the good news is, that even in this fast-moving digital world, there are basic principles that are still holding firm.

Not only that, but all the traditional stuff is still around. It's changing, but not disappearing. So you'll need to learn the old stuff as well as the new.

Companies still need effective communication – in all media, old and new. In fact, they need it more than ever. Good news for you.

BASIC PRINCIPLE #1 – IT'S A TEAM SPORT.

We'll start with this one.

Communication isn't something we do alone.

We have to connect. We have to understand who we're talking to and what "floats their boat."

And, if you get good at teaming up with others to make that happen, it can really be a lot of fun – it'll be a better world for you and for them.

So, now I'm going to give one of my very best friends a guest shot. He's Rich Binell.

Rich was the top copywriter at Apple Computer when all of this started to happen.

Then, it'll be time to roll up our sleeves.

See you in a few pages.

—Bruce Bendinger

Ethics.

Sad to say, this ain't no ethics book. (Or a grammar book, neither.)

One essential force of advertising and marketing is the search for advantage.

The "break the rules" spirit of the creative mind and the "bend the rules" history of many successful ad campaigns will continue to produce many examples of questionable ethics.

We've found that ethical questions are seldom bold moral choices – they just sort of sneak up on you.

Then you do the best you can.

Our best advice is to be of good heart and good intent in all you do.

In return, we offer our wishes for your good fortune and great success.

And this book.

An ad from P&G deals with the complex problem of diapers and recycling.

We like this book – AdCultUSA by James Twitchell. It won't help you write better ads, but it might help you understand the world in which you'll be writing them – and consuming them.

THE WRITER ON THE RIGHT.
He's Rich Binell. For many years, he was top copywriter at Apple Computer as they worked to change the world.

His biography includes graduating from Harvard, working with the very first laser printer, and replacing the entire wiring harness of a 1976 Ford F250 pick-up truck in the middle of a Wyoming fishing trip.

Today, he is CEO of Get Rich Quick. He writes for top companies in and around Silicon Valley – and beyond.

Some of them we can tell you about. Others we can't.

Periodically, Rich shares his skill and passion with young writers who want to be really good. Most of the survivors are glad they took his course.

(Note: The excellent photo on the right is by Bruce Ashley, www.phot.com)

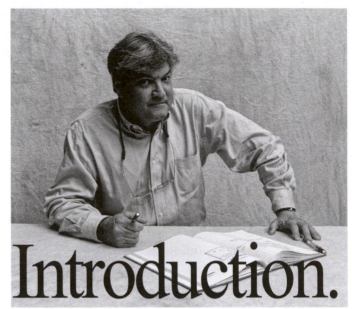

Introduction.

BRUCE WANTED ME TO WRITE THIS because I was around when the revolution began.

I was chief writer at Apple Computer in Cupertino.

I'd graduated from Harvard and was working in Boston at a terrific little ad agency named, Altman & Manley.

"HOW CAN WE MAKE THIS WONDERFUL?"

I worked with one of the most eager, passionate designers in the world, Bob Manley.

At the beginning of each project, he'd always ask, "How can we make this wonderful?"

I asked him why he asked that question.

He said, "Because nobody in charge of budgets or schedule, or any of that stuff will. And if you do ask, you can remind yourself that if you try, you can make things that solve the client's problem, AND are wonderful."

I always try to remember to ask that question when I start a project. Any project.

Because you never know what can happen.

YOU HAVE TO START SOMEWHERE.
The Harvard Mark 1 Calculator, 1944.

BAD SOFTWARE. GREAT COLLATERAL.

When Apple introduced the Mac, our agency got one, and I instantly monopolized it.

We had some high-tech accounts at the agency. One of them developed a software product for the Mac – the late, and not-so-great, Jazz.

Well, I guess I remembered to ask Bob Manley's question as I wrote the collateral, because one day my phone rang.

It was Apple. They liked my work. A lot.

Could they buy me a plane ticket? OK.

Even though I didn't think I'd want to relocate, I took the ticket. Then I walked into what seemed like the funnest place on earth a creative person could work.

And the funnest product since the VW.

That was over twenty years ago.

THE EARLY DAYS

Revolutions can be a messy business. We were giving creative people new tools and new power.

I remember how I felt looking at a print-out from one of the first laser printers. WYSIWYG* Wow.

But new tools don't come with common sense.

As one of Apple's designers observed, "Just because we give people 32 typefaces doesn't mean they should use them all on one page."

That might be the revolution's first lesson – just because you can, doesn't mean you should.

New power comes with new responsibilities.

AN ORGANIZATIONAL NIGHTMARE.

At Apple, we had to learn those lessons ourselves – and Bruce and his book helped.

We must have had fifty designers and project managers – each with a different way of starting a creative project.

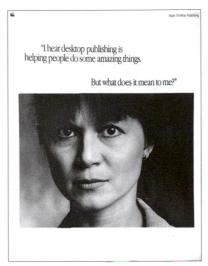

STARTING A REVOLUTION.
One page at a time.

Here's some of Rich's collateral damage.

AND DON'T FORGET
The bumper sticker.

* WYSIWYG = What You See Is What You Get. (This used to be a big deal.)

9

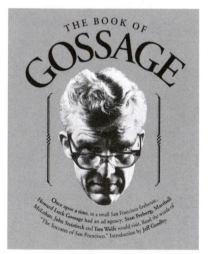

A Revolution is coming in your industry.

NOW IT'S YOUR TURN.

THE BOOK OF GOSSAGE

Once upon a time, in a small San Francisco firehouse, Howard Luck Gossage had an ad agency. Stan Freberg, Marshall McLuhan, John Steinbeck and Tom Wolfe would visit. Read the words of "The Socrates of San Francisco." Introduction by Jeff Goodby.

ONE MORE THING.

Rich also wants you to get this book.

Since we publish it, we're not going to argue. It was named one of the Ten Best Books on Advertising by *AdAge*.

However, it seems fair to mention that a lot of Howard Gossage's lessons will show up in the book you have now.

Then again, we hope that only makes you hungry for more.

** A version of Apple's Communication Work Plan is on page 269 of this book.

There was no consistent way of bringing a job in – no way of making heads or tails of what you had to do – so on each job you almost had to start from scratch.

Then I ran into Bruce's book – the first edition.

It showed systems for developing creative – it was exactly what we needed.

We brought Bruce to Cupertino to give us a hand, and he did. He helped us develop Apple's Communication Strategy system.**

NOW IT'S YOUR TURN.

I got to be part of a revolution – now it's your turn. You're lucky. You have this book as you start out.

I didn't.

The bad news? We succeeded.

Today, everybody has a personal computer with a keyboard – and everybody with a keyboard considers themselves a writer.

The good news? You have this book. So you have practical ways to begin your own writing in an organized, forceful, persuasive manner.

Now all you have to do is make it wonderful.

ONE MORE THING.

To get really inspired by a copywriter, I also recommend you read Bruce's book about the work of Howard Gossage – *The Book of Gossage*.

It is filled with Howard's passion, and amazing solutions to difficult communications challenges.

Now, I was thinking that I should wish you luck. But you don't need luck.

You have this book. Have a ball with it.

And good luck anyway.

Rich Binell
Los Gatos, California

How to Read This Book.

READ IT HOWEVER YOU WANT.

If you think you want to be a copywriter, use it like a good friend. Or a good boss.

If you're already in the advertising business, use it like a set of stretching exercises.

Do the exercises if you feel like it.

Or, just think about doing them.

Better yet, apply the principles to your latest assignment – the one that's due tomorrow.

If you're a student, do what your teacher says.

And, if you just picked it up because you're curious about advertising… enjoy yourself.

Because having a good time is one of the ways you make great advertising.

Bruce Bendinger

copywork@aol.com

A frame from one of Bruce's "Thought 4 The Day" videos.

See them on AdBuzz. Click on CAFÉ.

ABOUT THE AUTHOR.

"One of Chicago's creative superstars."

He was an award-winning copywriter – first at JWT, then with Dave Kennedy (co-founder of Wieden + Kennedy, the Nike agency).

Then he became the youngest-ever VP Creative Director at Leo Burnett.

As a "Creative Consultant," he helped Apple Computer with strategy systems, recorded with Rock & Roll legends, and was Creative Director for a President of the United States.

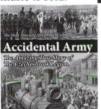

His CD, *Can't Sing Don't Care*, is available wherever mediocre lounge music is sold.

Recently, he wrote and produced an historical documentary – *Accidental Army: The Amazing True Story of The Czechoslovak Legion*.

ALL IN THE FAMILY.

Talent seems to run in the family. His daughter, Jessica, wrote teen hits *Bring It On!*, *First Daughter*, and *AquaMarine*, wrote and directed *Stick It!*, and has more movies, a book *(The Seven Rays)*, and a TV series in development.

She also wrote on *Sex & the City* (her father said she could only write on the "City" parts).

Bruce lives in Chicago's Lincoln Park with Lorelei, his wife, producer, and publisher. They have no spare time.

ABOUT THE COPY WORKSHOP.

It's a book, and it's a publishing company, specializing in "professional strength" books on marketing and advertising.

Find out more at www.adbuzz.com

#1 Warm-Ups

THE SEARS PAPER CLIP EXERCISE.

- Create a print ad for a paper clip.
- Make a rough sketch of the ad.

Write the headline(s) and body copy.

Exercise your imagination.

But, remember, the purpose of the ad is to sell the item.

Limit ad size to 8" x 10".

Speaking of Paper Clips...

Here's a classic copywriting assignment from Sears.

Do it now – and then see how you'd do it after reading this book.

Since this is a workbook, you might want to clip your ads to this page.

BEFORE WE START TELLING you how to do it, let's do it. Sometimes we learn by doing.

Here are four start-up exercises that don't need a lot of background. And they're fun.

The first is a classic that was used, for years, by Sears – once the largest retailer in the world. (We don't know what Walmart uses.)

The second is based on an award-winning ad for a Kellogg's cereal. The ad was done in Great Britain many years ago, but we think the format is one that really holds up.

Exercise #3 is based on something you've been familiar with since you were quite young. The zoo! Write/draw/create a piece of communication that you think would get someone to go to the zoo. Before you start, have it clearly in mind who that person is – a parent, a wealthy person who might donate money, or someone like you.

Finally, do a Classified Ad for something you want to get rid of – an old car, a guitar, a former boyfriend, whatever. Only you have to make that something attractive to others – or you won't be able to get rid of it.

And if you do a really great job, you might want to put it on eBay.

Good luck.

One more thing – something we'll tell you more than once – have fun!

#2: Your Name Here

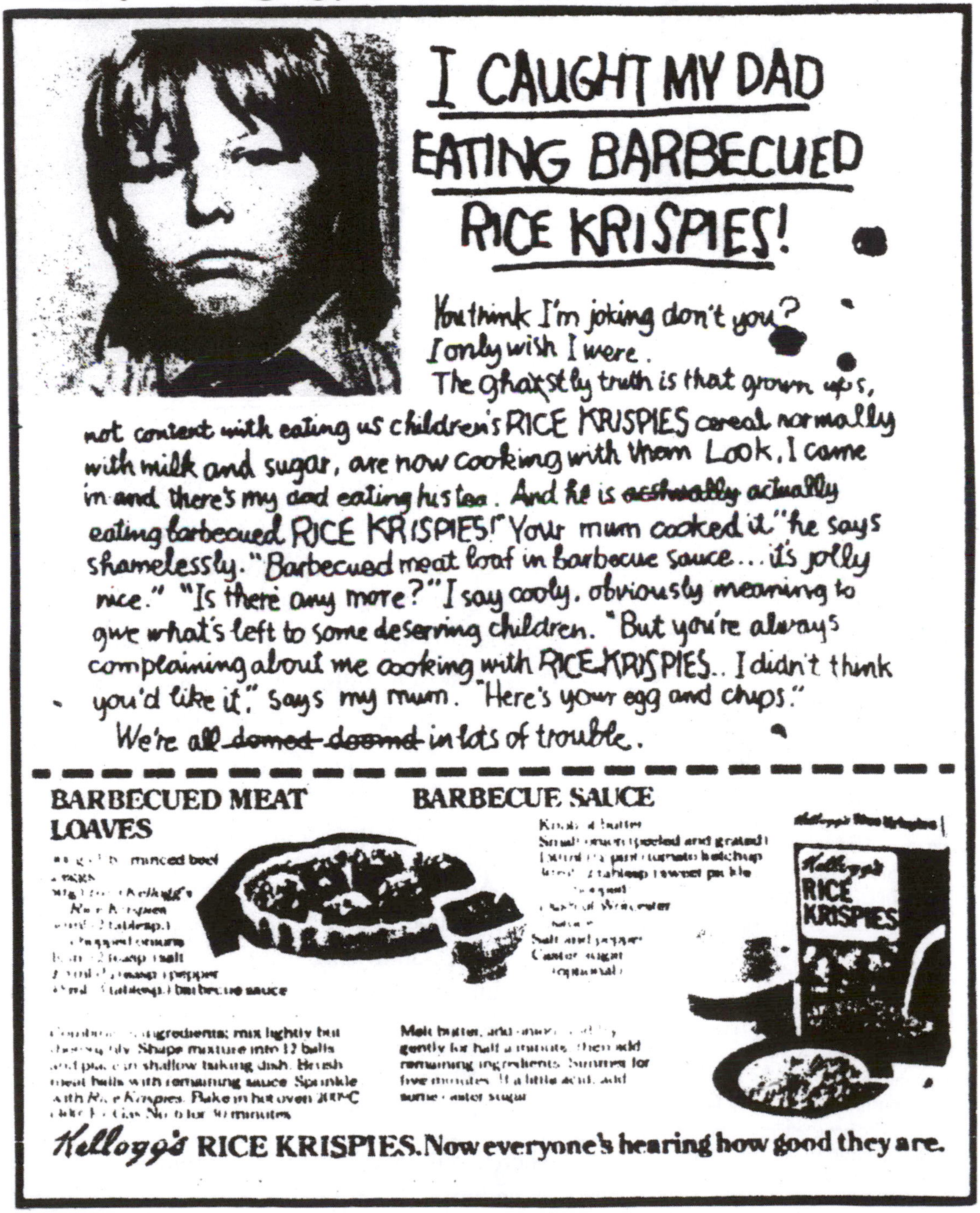
I CAUGHT MY DAD EATING BARBECUED RICE KRISPIES!
You think I'm joking don't you?
I only wish I were.
The ghastly truth is that grown ups, not content with eating us children's RICE KRISPIES cereal normally with milk and sugar, are now cooking with them Look, I came in and there's my dad eating his tea. And he is actually eating barbecued RICE KRISPIES! "Your mum cooked it" he says shamelessly. "Barbecued meat loaf in barbecue sauce... it's jolly nice." "Is there any more?" I say cooly, obviously meaning to give what's left to some deserving children. "But you're always complaining about me cooking with RICE KRISPIES.. I didn't think you'd like it," says my mum. "Here's your egg and chips."
We're all ~~domed doomd~~ in lots of trouble.
BARBECUED MEAT LOAVES
BARBECUE SAUCE
Salt and pepper
RICE KRISPIES
Kellogg's RICE KRISPIES. Now everyone's hearing how good they are.

MAKE
THE LAYOUTS
ROUGH
AND
THE IDEAS
FANCY.

STAVROS COSMOPULOS

WHAT ABOUT LAYOUTS?

This book's about writing good ads, not how to make them look good.

We'll show you examples of good-looking and effective design, but we won't try to show you how to do it.

However, we do have some advice.

LEARN TO PRINT.

First, get your handwriting together. Next, find a writing instrument you like. Then, develop a good strong hand.

I use a hard-to-find type of Pentel and make everyone crazy when I run out.

Find what works for you.

Then, practice your printing.

ABCDEFGHIJ
KLMNOPQRST
UVWXYZ123
4567890+?!

When you're in a meeting, you should be able to present what you write in a clear, confident hand.

Start Paying Attention to Good Art Direction.

Nothing makes a copywriter look better than a terrific art director.

Get a relationship going.

Find Out How Much Visual Talent You Have.

Find someone who knows what they're doing and see how you do.

You can probably learn how to do a brochure and newsletter.

Will you be able to do more?

Hey, you never know.

The ad on the left for "Barbecued Rice Krispies" won awards in Great Britain.

It sold a few Rice Krispies, too. Now it's your turn. Create an ad like this one.

First, pick your **product.** Throughout the book, you'll be asked to "pick a product."

Sometimes the categories are very specific and sometimes they aren't. In this case, your product is either:

A.   **A product you like –**
Cereal, peanut butter, whatever.

B.   **A service you might offer –**
Baby sitting, dog-walking, whatever.

C.   **An event** – party, picnic, lunch, whatever.

D.   **You** – think of it as a fun way to do a résumé.

HERE'S HOW TO DO IT:

1.   **Find an appropriate picture of yourself.** That's your **visual.**

2.   **Decide on your product.** Got it? Good. If you can find a picture of your product, maybe that should be in the ad, too.

3.   **Write a headline.** A quote, a story, a "true confessions" type of headline… whatever.

4.   **Write some copy.** Tell us things we should know about your product. Why is it a good product? What's the "benefit"?

5.   **Add an extra something at the bottom:** A coupon, your recipe for a great peanut butter sandwich, directions to the lunchroom… an offer… a contest … whatever.

6.   **Put 'em all together in a layout.** It should look sort of like the Rice Krispies ad. As you can see, neatness is optional.

There's only one absolute requirement.
Have fun.

#3: Do the Zoo

One. Communication Task.

What do you want your message to do?

Get people to visit? Who? Parents? Kids?

Do you want to raise funds?

Should you reinforce your Mission of saving endangered species?

Do you want to highlight a special attraction?

Maybe promote a rock concert to get people who don't usually come to the zoo to come to the zoo.

So, first, write down the Communication Task.

Two. Communication Tactic.

What bit of media is going to contain your message?

A poster? A radio commercial?

A handout from a person in a gorilla suit?

Three. Your Message.

Now that you know who you want to reach, why you want to reach them, and how you're going to do it, it's time to craft your message.

By the way, you've sort of written a Communication Strategy, something we'll be doing in more detail later on in this book.

But, for now, just try to do the best you can.

The good news is the Animal Kingdom is just full of great looking visuals – from cute little frogs to way big elephants. So you'll probably do a pretty good job.

"THUMBNAILS."

That's what we call small little sketches of ads. Write the headline and very roughly sketch the visual.

Then do another. And another.

Even in this day of computers, it's nice to work with a pen or pencil in your hand and connect with that piece of paper.

Try to make a habit of carrying a small pad – or packet of 3x 5 note cards – and something you enjoy writing with.

That way you won't have to take home the tablecloth.

ONE: COMMUNICATION TASK.

_____
_____
_____.

TWO. COMMUNICATION TACTIC.

_____
_____
_____.

THREE. YOUR MESSAGE.

_____
_____
_____.

A world of great visuals.

#4: A Classified Ad

THE CLASSIFIED ADS THAT CHANGED CHELSEA.

During the 50s and 60s, some creative, negative, and slightly outrageous, classified ads by British real estate agent Roy Brooks are given credit for single-handedly revitalizing the London neighborhoods of Pimlico and Chelsea.

He did it with small space all-copy ads.

A Cult Following.

His ads actually developed a cult following. Potential buyers literally queued up for the opportunity to view and buy his listed properties.

The neighborhoods were, at the time, crumbling, and Brooks' copy attracted upscale buyers – those with the resources to fix them up nicely.

This is one of his more notorious ads – with the curious but certainly attention-getting headline "Brothel in Pimlico."

Now before you go writing a classified ad about how ghastly your item is, think about what else Brooks did – he appealed to upscale potential home-buyers – with money to spend on renovation – and he worked in the fact that this "fixer-upper" was in Westminster, which provided an address of some quality. So there was both snobbery and reverse-snobbery.

The real lesson is Brooks knew his customer. And, in a subtle way, all of the negative mentions managed to scream the positive of "Bargain! Bargain! Bargain!"

Think about it. A 10 room house for £4650 (that's like under $10,000). Not bad. And then you can triple your money.

But notice he doesn't say "Triple Your Money." He lets you do the thinking… and kind of sell yourself.

Hey, bet you thought all classified ads were boring. See if you can help someone sell themselves.

OK, 150 words or less.

How appealing can you make something with just words?

As we said, your item is something you want to get rid of – a swing set, an old car, a guitar, a former boyfriend, an autographed photo of Paris Hilton, whatever.

But, if you want to sell that something, you'll have to make that something attractive to others – or you won't be able to get rid of it.

You might also consider the price you're going to charge. After all, it doesn't take much skill to sell a brand new car for $100.

As you select your item, give some thought as to how you can gain attention, overcome resistance, and make the reader desire your item.

Don't be afraid to be a little bit surprising. After all, we're not going to bore people into buying.

The ad below was written by a British Realtor.

Clearly, there are many ways to shape an effective and entertaining message.

See what you can do.

150 words. Or maybe 100 words. Better yet.

BROTHEL IN PIMLICO.

WANTED: Someone with taste, means, and a stomach strong enough to buy this erstwhile house of ill-repute in Pimlico. It is untouched by the 20th Century as far as convenience for even the basic human decencies is concerned. Although it reeks of damp or worse, the plaster is coming off the walls, and daylight peeps through a hole in the roof, it is still habitable, judging by the bed of rags, fag ends, and empty bottles in one corner. Plenty of scope for the socially aspiring to express their decorative taste and get their abode in "The Glossy" and nothing to stop them putting Westminster on their notepaper. 10 rather unpleasant rooms with slimy backyard. £4650 Freehold. Tarted up these houses make £15,000 – Roy Brooks.

Table of Contents:

THE FIRST SECTION.

The first step is to become a student of the craft of copywriting.

We'll look at early breakthroughs in advertising thinking.

Next, we'll look at forces shaping today's marketplace.

Then, we'll talk about how verbal and visual communication have to work together.

Finally, we'll talk about the new world of MarCom – that's short for Marketing Communication.

DO YOU KNOW WHO THIS IS?
You'll know by the time we're done. **Claude Hopkins** is one of the people who helped invent copywriting.

You don't have to thank him. He made $185,000 a year back when cars cost $1,000 and there were no income taxes!

THE VIZ BIZ.
Every once in a while, art directors and copywriters bug each other, but it's more important than ever that writers learn to think visually.

THE SECOND SECTION: BRAIN TRAINING.

The Second Section will introduce you to a few ways to think about the problems you have to solve.

We'll talk about how to have ideas and a number of ways to develop insights into the problems you're trying to solve and the people you want to persuade.

THIS IS A COOL GUY.
Alex Osborn – the "O" in BBDO (Batten Barton Durstine and Osborn) is the person who invented what we call "Brainstorming."

It's one of the fairly cool things we'll cover in this section.

THE THIRD SECTION: STRATEGIC DEVELOPMENT.

The Third Section – as advertised – deals with the development of Communication Strategy. We'll introduce you to the basic concepts and a variety of strategy formats.

You'll see how they're different, and, at their heart, very similar.

Strategy Selection Grid:			
Product Class Definition			
Target Group Selection			
Message Element Selection			
Rationale – based on information and/or judgement			

This is the Strategy Selection Grid. It can be very useful when you have to start from scratch.

PART TWO: CONCEPTUAL TOOL BOX

PART THREE: THE STRATEGY
Here's where we put it all together.

THE FUN SECTION!

We're going to write some ads – all kinds of ads – print, radio, and even TV commercials.

This section features approaches for print, radio, and television writing for the various media with Assignments and Exercises designed to put the principles you've learned into actual practice.

Finally, there's an introduction to con-temporary copywriting style, which varies from regular writing in a number of ways. Like sentence fragments.

Each media form has some additional considerations.

We'll spend a little time introducing them to you.

Then you can spend the rest of your life working to get better at it.

Outdoor in action.

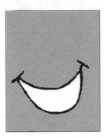
The Pitch. *One of the key formats you need to learn to create radio spots.*

Why are these dogs laughing?

19

THE LAST SECTION...
of this book is probably just the beginning of your communication career.

Because, whatever you do, communication is probably going to be a part of it.

You'll start by putting campaigns together, and we'll end up putting your career together – we hope.

We'll say more than once, "advertising is a team sport." So be generous with whatever it is you bring to the party.

Give Your Gift.

Good Luck.

CONGRATULATIONS.
You're on your way to a successful career helping think up the best ways to communicate.

Forewords.

THIS FIRST SECTION will provide you with some background on the business of creating messages.

It's a pretty interesting history. Advertising was a key partner in American economic growth.

And, as you'll see, that business keeps evolving.

You'll see evolution from the early success of those smart enough and lucky enough to be first to understand how things worked, and then a brand new revolution, as exciting opportunities open up in today's MarCom marketplace.

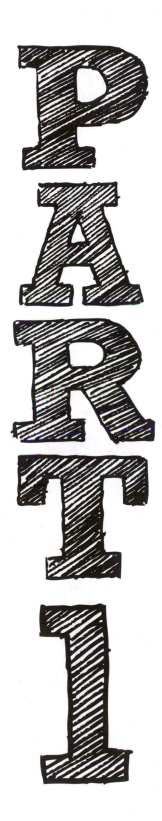

DRIVING PROGRESS

Advertising changes styles just like automobiles.

Here are classic ads from three of the eras we'll cover.

"Look at All Three" was an early success for Chrysler and demonstrated the power of advertising to build business.

"Think Small" was a classic example of "The Creative Revolution."

Today, work like that for the Mini is designed to drive through a new media environment – and it's steering us into new frontiers.

Advertising's Ages

Attention. Get noticed. *"You can't save souls in an empty church."*

Awareness. Be remembered. Early ad makers learned that consumers already aware of your brand name were more willing to buy and try your product.

Attitude. Your ads should make the consumer's attitude toward your product more positive. It helps.

Action. Ads should motivate action. Before you begin, you should have the desired consumer action clearly in mind.

AIDA.

Some call this sequence "AIDA."

Attention, Interest, Desire, Action – it's the same thing as our "Four A's."

ALBERT LASKER.
He not only improved advertising, he improved society. From medical research (Lasker Foundation) to the grass on your golf course to the tulips in Central Park.

IN THE BEGINNING, ad agencies were "agents." They sold advertising "space," primarily in newspapers and magazines, and collected a commission.

The idea – *"keeping your name before the public."*

After all, customers who know your name are more likely to buy your product or brand.

Today, we call that "awareness," and it's still a priority of almost all advertising.

Then, in the early 1900s, a young man named **Albert Lasker** at the Lord & Thomas agency (now Foote, Cone & Belding) had a revelation.

The advertising business was *not* about selling space – it was about creating and selling what was *inside* that space – the advertising itself.

Advertising was *"salesmanship in print."*

Getting Started.

Not every revolution involves guns, declarations, and riots in the streets. Sometimes they just happen.

Les Paul, a young guitar player from Waukesha, Wisconsin, started a revolution in music when he developed the solid body electric guitar.

We'll start with two young men at the turn of the 20th Century – a Jewish kid from Galveston and an ex-Mountie up in Canada.

They end up meeting in Chicago.

A BLOWN ASSIGNMENT.

Albert Lasker had a date one night. He was a 16-year-old cub reporter for a St. Louis newspaper assigned to review a play he'd already seen.

He skipped the play, wrote the story, and went on the date.

Next morning he found out two things.

First, the playhouse had burned down.

Second, his reporting career was kind of over.

His dad got him a job in advertising.

A RETAIL REVOLUTION.

Meanwhile, John E. Kennedy, ex-Mountie, was selling clothes in Manitoba, Canada.

He had become a star clothing salesman. A good salesman pays attention to the customer.

He noticed customers came in approximately three different heights and three body proportions.

From that insight, he persuaded a Canadian clothing manufacturer to totally re-make their suit line into essentially nine different sizes.

He called the line Fit-Reform.

He didn't stop there.

"Salesmanship on Paper."

Drawing on his experience, Kennedy developed what was then a new style of advertising. He called it "reason why."

He didn't stop there. He made the ad campaign a major feature of this new line of suits.

It was a great success all across Canada.

He followed that with another line – Semi-Ready.

Then, based on a new process for attaching shoe soles, he involved himself with Slater Shoes.

Again, Kennedy's advertising helped drive that brand into a leadership position.

In fact, Kennedy is given credit for not only developing Canadian retail (and retail advertising), but for making Canadians better dressed overall.

Then he headed south of the border.

KENNEDY MEETS LASKER.

By 1904, Kennedy was already established in many circles as a bit of an advertising miracle worker.

JOHN E. KENNEDY.
Canadian Mountie, copywriter, inventor of the modern definition of advertising.

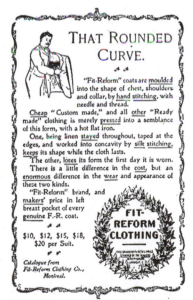

EARLY REASON-WHY.
Copy by Kennedy, to fit his concept – clothing with a built-in advantage.

What is Semi-ready?

Semi-ready is a new brand of gentlemen's clothes of the best custom tailor made quality.

So called because not quite ready made.

Only finished to that point where a suit may be tried on and afterwards completed to order.

That is to say :—

The cuffs of sleeves and bottoms of trouser legs are merely basted into position.

Outlets in coat collar, vest back, trouser leg and waist seams to let out or take in as desired.

It would be just as truthful to say " made to order."

But Semi-ready has this advantage, you don't have to guess at the effect of the color and style of the garments, but you see it before you order them.

"Semi-ready" is equal to the best custom tailoring.

The prices are:—Suits and Overcoats $10.00 to $25.00. Trousers $3.00 to $6.00.

Delivered two hours after ordered.

Your money back if dissatisfied.

22 King Street W. MANNING ARCADE
Toronto.
Montreal, Winnipeg and Ottawa.

KENNEDY DOES IT AGAIN.
His advertising and product concepts literally made Canadians better dressed.

Claude Hopkins. Copywriter. In 1908, Lord & Thomas paid him $185,000 a year! He was worth it. His copy made millions for his clients.

At a time when cars could be purchased for hundreds of dollars, he received $1000 for preparing ten advertisements.

His philosophy, in greater length, "*True Reason Why copy is Logic, plus persuasion, plus conviction, all woven into a certain simplicity of thought – pre-digested for the average mind, so that it is easier to understand than to misunderstand it.*"

He showed up at the offices of Lord & Thomas in Chicago, where Lasker worked. The two hit it off.

For Lasker, it was the keys to the kingdom.

He knew how to take that insight and make money. He made millions.

Lasker hired Kennedy for $60,000 – quite a nice salary at the time. However, his American career was fairly brief, though, I'm going to guess he enjoyed it to the fullest. Kennedy passed away in 1908.

His legacy – the modern definition of advertising.

COPY BY HOPKINS.

Claude Hopkins, a Lord & Thomas copywriter, was advertising's first great salesman.

In his book *Scientific Advertising,* he described the attitude a successful copywriter must develop:

"*Don't think of people in the mass. That gives you a blurred view. Think of a typical individual, man or woman, who is likely to want what you sell.*"

Hopkins continues…

"*The advertising man studies the consumer. He tries to place himself in the position of the buyer. His success largely depends on doing that to the exclusion of everything else.*"

Times have changed. The truth remains.

Talk *to* people.

One at a time.

PRE-EMPTION.

Hopkins is also credited with inventing an advertising technique known as "pre-emption." You take a product feature or a quality generic to the category, and, by pre-empting that feature, you make it yours.

Two early examples were "It's Toasted" for Lucky Strike and the claim that Schlitz beer bottles were sterilized with "Live Steam."

In fact, all tobacco was toasted and all beer bottles were sterilized with steam – "live steam" sounds more exciting. Hopkins knew how to add drama.

This advertising technique is still used today.

Can you think of some examples?

IDEA BY LASKER.

Drinking orange juice as a regular habit was Albert Lasker's idea.

He'd heard that growers were chopping down orange trees as a result of over-production.

At the time, oranges were mostly eaten.

The problem – how to dramatically increase orange consumption.

The answer – make orange juice a habit – one glass will use the juice of two or three oranges.

Today, Sunkist is still a client of Lasker's successor agency, Draft/FCB.

COPY BY HOPKINS.

Here's one of Hopkins' most famous ads – for Sunkist Oranges.

In 1916, this was a new idea for the average American – Orange Juice!

The headline was simple and, for the time, intriguing *"Drink an Orange."*

Benefits, Features, Support.

Now look at the first copy section.

First, Hopkins focuses on **consumer benefits** – good taste and good health.

Next, he focuses on **features** or **attributes** of the product, expressed as **product benefits** – such as "Nature's germ-proof package."

These function as **support** for the benefits of taste and healthfulness.

Note the use of informative captions throughout.

Closing Arguments.

Finally, he "Asks for the order" and closes with – an **offer.**

After Hopkins offered you good reasons to add orange juice to your diet, he offered you a "Juice Extractor" for *only 10¢.*

Hopkins and Albert Lasker actually had the juice extractor designed and manufactured.

They knew it would help increase the use of oranges. And it worked!

America's breakfast habits were changed forever.

"Onyx"
Hosiery

Lord & Taylor
Wholesale Distributors
New York

"Onyx" stamped on a Store, means "The Highest Expectation ever Fulfilled."

IMAGE ADVERTISING.

As Hopkins was proving the power of words and "reason why," other advertisers were having great success by *showing it* rather than *saying it* with advertising driven by visual impact.

The visual does most of the work.

Fashion ads are a good example.

Selling with Visuals.

Important selling points can also be communicated visually.

Below, the Uneeda Biscuit boy tells consumers (mostly mothers) Nabisco's packaging keeps their crackers dry.

It's a visual product benefit with an easy-to-understand reason why.

Palmolive

The successor to ordinary toilet soaps in Particular Homes. Made of Pure Imported Olive and Palm Oils skillfully blended and combined with Cocoa Butter. Palmolive is not merely a cleanser, it combines all the virtues of the wonderful ingredients from which it is made. It allays irritation and inflammation and supplies the necessary oils for harsh skins and dry scalps.

Palmolive exercises the skin in that it stimulates the action of the many tiny pores and glands. The removal of all obstacles allows free circulation of the blood, and the delicate nourishment embodied in **Palmolive** supplies just the necessary impetus to restore the skin to its proper condition after cleansing it. Continued use will produce a beautiful, healthy, rosy complexion. There is no complexion that **Palmolive** cannot improve. If your dealer cannot supply you, send us his name and 15 cents and we will forward, prepaid, a full size cake.

Send four cents in stamps, to cover cost of mailing, and the *names of your grocer and druggist*, and we will send one of our beautiful oriental photogravures without advertising upon it, suitable for framing, size 10 x 16 inches. Address,

B. J. JOHNSON SOAP CO., 318 Fowler St., Milwaukee, Wis.

Hopkins also did "image" advertising.

Here, he took an unknown soap made of palm and olive oils, and created what was, for a time, America's leading beauty soap – Palmolive!

Despite the "reason why" copy, the real impact of this ad is visual. This is often the case in image advertising.

Once again, Hopkins uses an offer.

This time, the art from the ad!

A $100,000 Dish

New-Type Baked Beans Which College-Trained Scientific Cooks Have Spent Years in Perfecting

It has cost us at least $100,000 to perfect Van Camp's Pork and Beans.

Modern culinary experts—men with college training—have devoted some years to this dish. Able scientists and famous chefs have co-operated with them.

856 Sauces

The zestful sauce which we bake with Van Camp's would itself give the dish distinction.

But these scientific cooks made 856 sauces before they attained this perfection. This ideal tang and savor came only through months of development.

A far greater accomplishment was to fit baked beans for easy digestion, while leaving them mealy and whole.

This Was Wrong

Old-style baked beans were very hard to digest. They were always under-baked. Yet the baking crisped them and broke them—made some hard and some mushy.

In the Van Camp kitchens each lot of beans is analyzed before we start to cook. They are boiled in water freed from minerals, because hard water makes them tough.

They are baked in steam ovens by live steam under pressure at 245 degrees. They are thus baked for hours—baked as beans should be—without bursting or crisping a bean.

This Is Perfect

The result is a new-type dish which will change your whole idea of baked beans. It will multiply their popularity. Above all, it will not tax digestion. And it costs you less—all ready-baked—than do home-baked beans. Please order a trial meal.

VAN CAMP'S
Pork and Beans
Baked With the Van Camp Sauce — Also Baked Without the Sauce

Your first shave

will prove, beyond all doubt, the claims men make for this unique shaving cream

Let us send you a 10-shave tube to try

WE'VE built Palmolive Shaving Cream to a national business success by making few claims for it. We let it prove its case by sending a 10-day test tube free to all who ask. In that way, we've gained leadership in a highly competitive field in only a few years.

130 formulas tried

Before offering Palmolive Shaving Cream, we asked 1000 men their supreme desires in a shaving cream. Then met them exactly.

We tried and discarded 130 formulas before finding the right one. We put our 60 years of soap experience behind this creation. The result is a shaving cream unlike any you have ever tried.

Five advantages

1. Multiplies itself in lather 250 times.
2. Softens the beard in one minute.
3. Maintains its creamy fullness for 10 minutes on the face.
4. Strong bubbles hold the hairs erect for cutting.
5. Fine after-effects due to palm and olive oil content.

Just send coupon

Your present method may suit you well. But still there may be a better one. This test may mean much to you in comfort. Send the coupon before you forget.

THE PALMOLIVE COMPANY (Del. Corp.), CHICAGO, ILL.

- 10 SHAVES FREE -
and a can of Palmolive After Shaving Talc

Simply insert your name and address and mail to Dept. B-1196, The Palmolive Company (Del. Corp.), 3702 Iron St., Chicago, Ill.

Residents of Wisconsin should address The Palmolive Company (Wis. Corp.), Milwaukee, Wis.

....

....

MORE COPY BY HOPKINS.

Note the similarities in these two ads.

Claims and Positioning.

Each has dramatic fact-based claims. "130 formulas/856 Sauces."

And, of course, "The $100,000 Dish."

Hopkins positions against competition. "Dish" positions against home-cooked beans. "First Shave" positions Palmolive against other shaving soaps.

"Asking for the Order."

For Van Camp's he says, *"Please order a trial meal."*

For Palmolive, a free sample. Each ad makes a small product important.

Famous Copywriters

HELEN LANSDOWNE RESOR.

"She had a dozen ideas to the minute… and kept them coming so fast you couldn't possibly keep up and had to sit down afterwards with a pencil and paper and try to sort them out."

"She had a brilliant feminine mind that darted and dipped and swooped with terrifying speed and accuracy."

She wasn't the only "brilliant feminine mind" to succeed.

Other Prominent Women.

There were a number of prominent women in the early days of advertising – at a time when women didn't even have the vote,

In 1903, the magazine *Profitable Advertising* profiled 40 women copywriters, advertising artists, agents, and advisers. Among the women from those early days were:

- copywriter-turned-author **Helen Woodward** ("Through Many Windows")
- **Louise Taylor Davis** (Y&R)
- **Jean Wade Rindlaub** (BBDO)
- the retail legend, **Bernice Fitz-Gibbon,** who wrote copy like – "It's smart to be thrifty" for Macy's and "Nobody, but nobody, undersells Gimbel's."

LET'S MEET A FEW OF THE COPYWRITERS

who had a big impact on the early advertising industry.

Some developed effective approaches, some helped develop successful agencies. Some did both.

HOW'S THIS FOR A STORY?

Smart, talented young copywriter meets up-and-coming young account exec. They work together and marry.

Together, they build the world's largest ad agency. Sound a bit far-fetched? It's true.

In the early 1900s, after graduating as her high-school valedictorian, **Helen Lansdowne** began writing retail ads in Cincinnati. First, she wrote for a newspaper and then for a local streetcar advertising company.

Then, she went to work with a bright young account exec who was making a name for himself developing ad strategies that appealed to the growing middle class. His name was **Stanley Resor.**

When J. Walter Thompson (JWT) hired Stanley to open a Cincinnati office, Helen went along.

At the time, many JWT clients had products that were purchased by women. Helen was the right person at the right place at the right time.

"I supplied the feminine point of view," she said.

"I watched the advertising to see that the idea, the wording, and the illustrating were effective for women."

Even then, understanding and insight into the consumer made a tremendous difference in advertising effectiveness.

Her ads for Woodbury's Soap increased sales 1000% with "A skin you love to touch."

She was the first woman to appear before the board of Procter & Gamble.

She explained advertising to a room full of men who marketed and advertised to women.

Together, Stanley and Helen ran JWT. He ran client service. She supervised the creation of the advertising.

She never really had a title. But she didn't need one.

Helen supervised the legendary JWT office decor as well as the advertising. She nurtured and supervised a creative staff where women were paid and treated well.

And they wrote advertising that worked.

Brands and Celebrity. If you want your brand to be famous, one way to do it is connect that brand with famous people. And vice versa. Appearing in advertising was not only a way to capitalize on fame, it was also a way to become more famous.

SOFT SOAP & HARD SELL. Here are two famous JWT campaigns.

Emotion and Poetry.

For Woodbury's, Helen Resor sold softness, romance, and sex appeal.

The line was simple and memorable, "A skin you love to touch," with an almost poetic rhythm.

Against that emotion, copy featured a skin-care regimen and an offer of product samples and the art from the advertisement.

The Art of the Testimonial.

For Lux, they sold glamor, luxury, fame… and sex appeal.

Helen Resor upgraded the testimonial format by getting famous people to endorse JWT products.

For Lux, the use of movie stars made a bar of soap glamorous.

Stanley Resor called it "the spirit of emulation." Helen called her friends.

Helen's Connections.

The first famous personage was Mrs. O.H.P. Belmont, a leader in New York society at the time – and a prominent feminist. She endorsed Pond's in exchange for a donation to her favorite charity.

Ads featured Mrs. Reginald Vanderbilt, the Duchess de Richelieu, and the Queen of Rumania.

Helen also invited a high-school chum to come work at JWT – James Webb Young. (Meet him in Chapter 5.)

Caples, Getchell & More…

John Caples. BBDO's direct response and copy testing expert.

READ ALL ABOUT IT.
You can understand Caples from the table of contents of *How to Make Your Advertising Make Money.*

HERE ARE SOME OTHER COPY PIONEERS – who invented and then improved the craft:

John Caples. He established some of the basic principles of successful direct advertising and shared them through books and an approach that applies to virtually all advertising.

Bruce Barton. He used his talent to grow one of the major advertising agencies… and more.

Ned Jordan. Here was a unique individual who combined copywriting and automobile manufacturing.

Stirling Getchell. His flame burned briefly and brightly. He pioneered techniques of positioning and photographic storytelling, which predated TV.

UNDERSTANDING WHAT WORKS.
Developing advertising is a learning process.

We learn about products, we learn about the competition, and we learn about people.

John Caples spent his career learning what works. Learn more about his legacy at www.caples.org.

For example, here are his thoughts on headlines:

"Headlines make ads work. The best headlines appeal to people's self interest, or give news. Long headlines that say something outpull short headlines that say nothing.

"Remember that every headline has one job – it must stop your prospects with a believable promise.

"All messages have headlines. In TV, it's the start of the commercial; in radio, the first few words; in a letter, the first paragraph.

"Come up with a good headline and you're almost certain to have a good ad."

"Can he really play?" a girl whispered. "Heavens, no!" Arthur exclaimed. "He never played a note in his life."

They Laughed When I Sat Down At the Piano But When I Started to Play!~

ARTHUR had just played "The Rosary." The room rang with applause. I decided that this would be a dramatic moment for me to make my debut. To the amazement of all my friends I strode confidently over to the piano and sat down.

"Jack is up to his old tricks," somebody chuckled. The crowd laughed. They were all certain that I couldn't play a single note.

"Can he really play?" I heard a girl whisper to Arthur. "Heavens, no!" Arthur exclaimed. "He never played a note in all his life...But just you watch him. This is going to be good."

I decided to make the most of the situation. With mock dignity I drew out a silk handkerchief and lightly dusted off the keys. I rose and gave the revolving piano stool a quarter of a turn, just as I had seen an imitator of Paderewski do in a vaudeville sketch.

"What do you think of his execution?" called a voice from the rear.

"We're in favor of it!" came back the answer, and the crowd rocked with laughter.

Then I Started to Play

Instantly a tense silence fell on the guests. The laughter died on their lips as if by magic. I played through the first bars of Liszt's immortal Liebestraume. I heard gasps of amazement. My friends sat breathless—spellbound.

I played on and as I played I forgot the people around me. I forgot the hour, the place, the breathless listeners. The little world I lived in seemed to fade—seemed to grow dim—unreal. Only the music was real. Only the music and the visions it brought me. Visions as beautiful and as changing as the wind-blown clouds and drifting moonlight, that long ago inspired the master composer. It seemed as if the master musician himself were speaking to me—speaking through the medium of music—not in words but in chords. Not in sentences but in exquisite melodies.

A Complete Triumph!

As the last notes of the Liebestraume died away, the room resounded with a sudden roar of applause. I found myself surrounded by excited faces. How my friends carried on! Men shook my hand—wildly congratulated me—pounded me on the back in their enthusiasm! Everybody was exclaiming with delight—plying me with rapid questions.... "Jack! Why didn't you tell us you could play like that?" ..."Where did you learn?"—"How long have you studied?"—"Who was your teacher?"

"I have never even seen my teacher," I replied. "And just a short while ago I couldn't play a note."

"Quit your kidding," laughed Arthur, himself an accomplished pianist. "You've been studying for years. I can tell."

"I have been studying only a short while," I insisted. "I decided to keep it a secret so that I could surprise all you folks."

Then I told them the whole story.

"Have you ever heard of the U. S. School of Music?" I asked. A few of my friends nodded. "That's a correspondence school, isn't it?" they exclaimed.

"Exactly," I replied. "They have a new simplified method that can teach you to play any instrument by note in just a few months."

How I Learned to Play Without a Teacher

And then I explained how for years I had longed to play the piano.

"It seems just a short while ago," I continued, "that I saw an interesting ad of the U. S. School of Music mentioning a new method of learning to play which only cost a few cents a day! The ad told how a woman had mastered the piano in her spare time at home—and *without a teacher!* Best of all, the wonderful new method she used required no laborious scales—no heartless exercises—no tiresome practising. It sounded so convincing that I filled out the coupon requesting the Free Demonstration Lesson.

"The free book arrived promptly and I started in that very night to study the Demonstration Lesson. I was amazed to see how easy it was to play this new way. Then I sent for the course.

"When the course arrived I found it was just as the ad said—as easy as A. B. C.! And as the lessons continued they got easier and easier. Before I knew it I was playing all the pieces I liked best. Nothing stopped me. I could play ballads or classical numbers or jazz, all with equal ease. And I never did have any special talent for music."

* * * *

Play Any Instrument

You, too, can now *teach yourself* to be an accomplished musician—right at home—in half the usual time. You can't go wrong with this simple new method which has already shown almost half a million people how to play their favorite instruments *by note.* Forget that old-fashioned idea that you need special "talent." Just read the list of instruments in the panel, decide which one you want to play and the U. S. School will do the rest. And bear in mind no matter which instrument you choose, the cost in each case will be the same—just a few cents a day. No matter whether you are a mere beginner or already a good performer, you will be interested in learning about this new and wonderful method.

Send for Our Free Booklet and Demonstration Lesson

Thousands of successful students never dreamed they possessed musical ability until it was revealed to them by a remarkable "Musical Ability Test" which we send entirely without cost with our interesting free booklet.

If you are in earnest about wanting to play your favorite instrument—if you really want to gain happiness and increase your popularity—send at once for the free booklet and Demonstration Lesson. No cost—no obligation. Sign and send the convenient coupon now. Instruments supplied when needed, cash or credit. **U. S. School of Music, 812 Brunswick Bldg., New York City.**

Pick Your Instrument

Piano	Harmony and Composition
Organ	Sight Singing
Violin	Ukulele
Drums and Traps	Guitar
Mandolin	Hawaiian Steel Guitar
Clarinet	Harp
Flute	Cornet
Saxophone	Piccolo
'Cello	Trombone
Voice and Automatic	Speech Culture Finger Control
Piano Accordion	
Banjo (5-String, Plectrum or Tenor)	

U. S. School of Music,
812 Brunswick Bldg., New York City.

Please send me your free book, "Music Lessons in Your Own Home," with introduction by Dr. Frank Crane, Demonstration Lesson and particulars of your offer. I am interested in the following course:

....

Have you above instrument?....................

Name......................................
　　　(Please write plainly)

Address....................................

City...............State...............

FROM COPYWRITER
TO CONGRESSMAN.
The AdMan Nobody Knows.

He was a best-selling author, confidante of presidents, and a U.S. Congressman.

He was Chairman of the United Negro College Fund and the American Heart Association.

He was a copywriter – a preacher's son named Bruce Barton.

His name's still on the door at BBDO – Batten, Barton, Durstine & Osborn.

In addition to his work at BBDO, he wrote continually – articles (he began as a magazine writer) and books.

He combined his background in religion and advertising to write *The Man Nobody Knows*, a book that combined classic parables of Christianity with those of modern salesmanship.

It was a bestseller.

In *The Seven Lost Secrets of Success*, author Joe Vitale lists some of Barton's classic principles. They include:

- **Discover your real business.** Lipstick or romance? Tires or safety?
- **"Story selling."** Use parables and stories to deliver your message.
- **The value of sincerity and honesty in effective selling.**

A preacher's son, he, and many others, wrote sermons for America's growing business community.

The PENALTY OF LEADERSHIP

IN every field of human endeavor, he that is first must perpetually live in the white light of publicity. ¶Whether the leadership be vested in a man or in a manufactured product, emulation and envy are ever at work. ¶In art, in literature, in music, in industry, the reward and the punishment are always the same. ¶The reward is widespread recognition; the punishment, fierce denial and detraction. ¶When a man's work becomes a standard for the whole world, it also becomes a target for the shafts of the envious few. ¶If his work be merely mediocre, he will be left severely alone—if he achieve a masterpiece, it will set a million tongues a-wagging. ¶Jealousy does not protrude its forked tongue at the artist who produces a commonplace painting. ¶Whatsoever you write, or paint, or play, or sing, or build, no one will strive to surpass, or to slander you, unless your work be stamped with the seal of genius. ¶Long, long after a great work or a good work has been done, those who are disappointed or envious continue to cry out that it can not be done. ¶Spiteful little voices in the domain of art were raised against our own Whistler as a mountebank, long after the big world had acclaimed him its greatest artistic genius. ¶Multitudes flocked to Bayreuth to worship at the musical shrine of Wagner, while the little group of those whom he had dethroned and displaced argued angrily that he was no musician at all. ¶The little world continued to protest that Fulton could never build a steamboat, while the big world flocked to the river banks to see his boat steam by. ¶The leader is assailed because he is a leader, and the effort to equal him is merely added proof of that leadership. ¶Failing to equal or to excel, the follower seeks to depreciate and to destroy—but only confirms once more the superiority of that which he strives to supplant. ¶There is nothing new in this. ¶It is as old as the world and as old as the human passions—envy, fear, greed, ambition, and the desire to surpass. ¶And it all avails nothing. ¶If the leader truly leads, he remains—the leader. ¶Master-poet, master-painter, master-workman, each in his turn is assailed, and each holds his laurels through the ages. ¶That which is good or great makes itself known, no matter how loud the clamor of denial. ¶That which deserves to live—lives.

Cadillac Motor Car Co. Detroit, Mich.

EMPHASIZING THE POSITIVE.

Bruce Barton referred to advertising as *"the hand-maiden of business."* He said, *"The advertisements which persuade people to act are written by men who have an abiding respect for the intelligence of their readers, and a deep sincerity regarding the merits of the goods they have to sell."*

The ad above, "The Penalty of Leadership," was one of the favorite ads of the period.

It was not written by Barton but by another well-regarded copywriter of the day, Theodore MacManus.

The tone is typical – positive and high-minded.

(By the way, MacManus had a young copywriter working for him named Leo Burnett.)

EMPHASIZING THE NEGATIVE.

Ads like the one above helped build Listerine into a major brand.

They "dramatized the problem" and pre-empted it by owning "halitosis," a semi-scientific word for "bad breath."

If your product solves a problem and you can, in some way, own that problem, your brand has a good chance of owning the solution.

Even today, agencies like Y&R are concerned with *"The Problem the Advertising Must Solve."*

PROBLEMS, PROBLEMS.

New levels of disposable income and a new concern with hygiene were driving forces in the success of many new personal products:

Cough Problems? *Smith Brothers Cough Drops dial up the social importance of not having a cough.*

Coffee Problems? *Postum, a non-caffeine hot beverage, positioned itself aggressively against coffee.*

Money Problems! *Correspondence schools used the promise of a better job.*

THE POWER OF LANGUAGE.

Is it prose, or is it poetry? The style and vocabulary are dated, but you can feel the appeal of this ad.

It tapped into classic imagery – The West– fast horses, fast cars, and, perhaps, fast women. "Word magic!"

THE POWER OF PRODUCT.

Here's a very restrained ad by Ford introducing their Model A.

This ad set a very different tone.

By not showing the car, or telling the price, interest was heightened.

An estimated 10 million people visited the showrooms and 800,000 ordered the car in the first weeks.

THE POWER OF MARKETING.

By doing a better job of paying attention to consumer needs – and providing services like financing – GM became the new leader in America's growing automobile industry.

Somewhere West of Laramie

SOMEWHERE WEST OF CLEVELAND...

The ad above was written by Ned Jordan – a copywriter who became an automobile manufacturer!

With ads like these, he literally created demand for a car which he had manufactured in Cleveland.

He sold thousands, and then he was smart enough to liquidate before the Depression.

This style of writing, sometimes called "word magic," helped start a whole new school of advertising, which lives on in ads for perfume and fashion.

The Campaign Concept. Once you have a winning idea, try to keep it going strong. Above, the first ad. Below, a follow-up for the next year's model.

GOT GETCHELL?

J. Stirling Getchell wrote one of the very first "Positioning" ads for Walter Chrysler – years before Avis.

Just one ad, "Look at All Three," established Plymouth as a major brand.

Somewhere East of Detroit.

The ad was part of a last-minute "pitch" by Getchell's new agency.

He did the work at his own expense and was able to photograph Walter Chrysler – before the ads he was writing were even finished…

"Look" was one of three ads – no one remembers the others.

The simple strategic appeal in the ad hit the public right.

Overnight, it made Plymouth a contender in the low-priced field.

Read the whole story in Julius Watkins' book *The 100 Greatest Advertisements.*

The Power of Change.

Important ads do more than sell products – they change the entire advertising environment.

The initial impact of each new style and each new approach changes the marketplace.

The Power of Continuity.

Notice how the first ad "positions" Chrysler as one of the three cars you should consider.

The second ad – which ran the next year – reinforces that position with Plymouth's new-found success.

Nothing succeeds quite like it.

Y&R: The First Modern Agency

RAY RUBICAM.

He proved you could do good advertising and be a good human being – good news for us all.

His agency set new standards for creativity and quality – more good news.

STEINWAY.

This classic ad is an early example of image advertising. And, at the same time, it was a very hard-working ad.

It was written by Rubicam before he started his own agency, and it solved a problem for Steinway – pianos had new competition – the phonograph!

Rubicam's advertising made the piano a status symbol as well as a home entertainment item.

Note the sense of proportion.

The ad is influenced by design considerations as well as copy.

CREATING ADVERTISING was mostly about writing copy. Then **Ray Rubicam** broadened the creative process at his agency – Young & Rubicam.

He involved research, hiring Northwestern professor George Gallup to study ad readership. Before writing the ads, they talked to consumers – at the time, a revolutionary change in agency behavior.

Most important, he involved art directors in the process, assembling the best team of copywriters and art directors in the industry.

Y&R set other standards, too, believing, *"Advertising has a responsibility to behave properly."*

Rubicam didn't like Hopkins' approach. *"You can sell products without bamboozling the public."* To him, a good ad was, *"An admirable piece of work."*

His philosophy? *"Resist the usual."*

NEW WAYS OF WORKING TOGETHER. Y&R was the first to institutionalize two processes that are critical to the modern advertising agency.

First, the visual/verbal interaction of writer/art director.

Second, **The Y&R Creative Work Plan.** It's the model for agency strategy systems used today.

It was an orderly way of gathering all the information available and distilling it down to a Key Fact and *"The Problem the Advertising Must Solve."*

LARGER CONCERNS. Rubicam showed a concern for more than advertising. Y&R was the only large agency to actively support consumer groups.

His was one of the first major agencies to initiate stock and profit participation plans for employees.

All in all, he had an advertising career that was most certainly *"an admirable piece of work."*

"Oh, Doctor, I bet you tell that to all the Girls!"

ADVERTISING BUILDS BUSINESSES. This period demonstrated the power of well-crafted advertising appeals to establish brand name products.

Many brands we know today were established during this period. Advertising was a key part of it.

Above, you can see the friendly approach Y&R used to establish Borden's dairy products – personifying the brand with "Elsie the Cow" (this predates the "inherent drama" approach of the Leo Burnett agency by decades) and "If it's Borden's it's got to be good." A simple memorable theme.

Ads had more copy – people read magazines cover to cover. How would you do this ad today?

IMPACT

ACCORDING TO WEBSTER: The single instantaneous striking of a body in motion against another body.
ACCORDING TO YOUNG & RUBICAM: That quality in an advertisement which strikes suddenly against the reader's indifference and enlivens his mind to receive a sales message.

YOUNG & RUBICAM, INCORPORATED • ADVERTISING
NEW YORK • CHICAGO • DETROIT • SAN FRANCISCO • HOLLYWOOD • MONTREAL • TORONTO • MEXICO CITY • LONDON

AN AD AGENCY ADVERTISES.
Few "house" ads are this memorable. Rubicam wrote it himself in 1939.
Art and Copy Work Together.
The visual/verbal approach was key to the '60s "Creative Revolution." Y&R did it first.

please do not lick this page !

Advertising then was different. Slower. But, gradually, the pace quickened. 20th Century technology was creating new consumer miracles: appliances, automobiles, filter-tips, and...

TV!

Unique Selling Proposition

Rosser Reeves. *Chairman, Ted Bates & Co. Author,* Reality in Advertising. *Inventor, USP.*

DEFINITION OF
USP:

1. Each advertisement must make a proposition to the consumer. Not just words, not just product puffery, not just show-window advertising.

Each advertisement must say to each reader, "Buy this product and you will get this specific benefit."

2. The proposition must be one that the competition either cannot, or does not, offer.

It must be unique – either a uniqueness of the brand or a claim not otherwise made in that particular field of advertising.

3. The proposition must be so strong that it can move the mass millions, i.e., pull over new customers to your product.

THE "USP" WAS advertising's child of the '50s.

Rosser Reeves was the father, and his book, *Reality in Advertising,* was the New Improved Testament.

The premise was simple. Find the unique benefit in your product. Hammer it home. Repeatedly.

"M&Ms melt in your mouth, not in your hands."

"Colgate cleans your breath, as it cleans your teeth."

In his Anacin TV commercial, heads full of hammers hammered home the Anacin USP. Repeatedly.

And Rosser Reeves' agency, Ted Bates & Co., sold carloads of Anacin, Colgate, and M&Ms.

Tools of the trade were: slogans, demonstrations, mnemonics, and repetition with an insistent rhythm.

And those tools built businesses. Repeatedly.

They demonstrated the power of television as an advertising medium. Repeatedly.

"The Most Hated Commercial." *This frame is from the classic Anacin commercial featuring "Fast! Fast! Fast Relief." "For headache, neuritis and neuralgia." (Whatever that is.) It cost $8,200 to produce. It made more money than* Gone with the Wind. *People hated it – but it worked.*

Some commercials were fun to watch and fun to hear. *"Use Ajax (Boom Boom) the Foaming Cleanser (Boom-ba-boom- ba-boom-boom-boom). Floats the dirt, right down the drain (Boom-boo-boom- boo-boo-boo-boom). You'll stop paying the elbow tax, when you start cleaning with Ajax (Boom Boom)..."*

THE POWER OF CADENCE AND INCANTATION. Reeves' USPs are almost magic formulas – ritual chants that are repeated over and over.

Note the rhythmic construction – words written to be said – over and over.

WONDER BREAD
Helps Build Strong Bodies 12 Ways

The Limits of Logic. The powerful TV commercials with their almost magical repetition and cadence didn't always make strong print. The incantation of "Wonder Bread Builds Strong Bodies 12 Ways" turns into psuedo-science. Still, the overall power of a proposition that turned a loaf of bread into a giant vitamin pill had its effect.

THE POWER OF THE PROPOSITION.

Reeves' influence was deeper with clients than creative departments – most creative people *hated* his ads.

But the discipline of the USP still remains with most package goods marketers. Though now you need to do a bit more than just say the same thing over and over.

In fact, Ted Bates & Co. added a new dimension to their USP. Now it's Unique Selling Proposition *plus* Unique Selling *Personality* – image. Time for the '60s.

Welcome to The Creative Revolution.

"Let's say you have one million dollars tied up in your little company and suddenly your advertising isn't working and sales are going down. And everything depends on it.

"Your future depends on it, your family's future depends on it, other people's families depend on it...

"Now, what do you want from me? Fine writing? Or do you want to see the God-damned sales curve stop moving down and start moving up?"

In his spare time, Reeves wrote short stories and poetry. But when it came to writing advertising, he was all business.

His only gauge was "will it work?"

His first lesson – *"You must make* the product *interesting, not just make the ad different."*

Copy: "Which hand has the M&M chocolate

candy in it? Not this hand– that's messy,

*but this hand... because **M&M Candies Melt in Your Mouth, Not in Your Hand.**"* This was a side-by-side demonstration with a "reason why." It worked.

The Creative Revolution

Leo Burnett and Bill Bernbach.

David Ogilvy. Copywriter. *Even after he retired to a French chateau, his agency kept growing with intelligent ads and intelligent management that built worldclass brands.*

The man in the Hathaway shirt

THE HATHAWAY "STORY."

What does the eye patch do?

First, it adds "story appeal," increasing interest and readership.

Second, it creates distinctiveness and memorability. (After all, a shirt is a shirt.) It gives the shirt "an image."

Third, it gives the campaign continuity.

Last, eye contact. People look back at people. And one is better than none.

THE '60S WAS THE DECADE of "The Creative Revolution." Three people were instrumental in shaping this dramatic change in advertising.

All three of them were copywriters: **David Ogilvy, Leo Burnett,** and **Bill Bernbach.**

David Ogilvy...

hired a model with an eyepatch for Hathaway shirts and created an ad for Rolls-Royce with a headline that the world of advertising will never forget:

"At 60 miles an hour the loudest noise in this new Rolls-Royce comes from the electric clock."

The title of his book was memorable, too – *Confessions of an Advertising Man.* It was a modest bestseller and a superb new business tool. He and his agency followed with more books, such as *Ogilvy on Advertising* and *How to Advertise.*

Ogilvy was a student of the craft of copywriting. His work combined the lessons of Hopkins, Caples, and Reeves with his own unique wit and style.

Here is Ogilvy's paraphrase of Hopkins: *"I don't write to the crowd. I try to write from one human being to another human being in the second person singular."*

AN INVESTMENT IN IMAGE.

Yet, Ogilvy's contribution moved beyond the rational.

It was emotional. Ogilvy had class. Image.

The style of the man in the Hathaway shirt.

The delightfully stuffy Commander Whitehead and "Schweppervescence," a tongue-in-cheek USP.

Rolls-Royce dignity with Brit wit as counterpoint.

Ogilvy did advertising that made you like and respect the advertiser. He believed *"Every advertisement is a long-term investment in the image of a brand."*

The Rolls-Royce Silver Cloud—$13,995

"At 60 miles an hour the loudest noise in this new Rolls-Royce comes from the electric clock"

What makes Rolls-Royce the best car in the world? "There is really no magic about it—it is merely patient attention to detail," says an eminent Rolls-Royce engineer.

1. "At 60 miles an hour the loudest noise in this new Rolls-Royce comes from the electric clock," reports the Technical Editor of THE MOTOR. Three mufflers tune out sound frequencies—acoustically.

2. Every Rolls-Royce engine is run for seven hours at full throttle before installation, and each car is test-driven for hundreds of miles over varying road surfaces.

3. The Rolls-Royce is designed as an *owner-driven* car. It is eighteen inches shorter than the largest domestic cars.

4. The car has power steering, power brakes and automatic gear-shift. It is very easy to drive and to park. No chauffeur required.

5. The finished car spends a week in the final test-shop, being fine-tuned. Here it is subjected to 98 separate ordeals. For example, the engineers use a stethoscope to listen for axle-whine.

6. The Rolls-Royce is guaranteed for three years. With a new network of dealers and parts-depots from Coast to Coast, service is no problem.

7. The Rolls-Royce radiator has never changed, except that when Sir Henry Royce died in 1933 the monogram RR was changed from red to black.

8. The coachwork is given five coats of primer paint, and hand rubbed between each coat, before *nine* coats of finishing paint go on.

9. By moving a switch on the steering column, you can adjust the shock-absorbers to suit road conditions.

10. A picnic table, veneered in French walnut, slides out from under the dash. Two more swing out behind the front seats.

11. You can get such optional extras as an Espresso coffee-making machine, a dictating machine, a bed, hot and cold water for washing, an electric razor or a telephone.

12. There are three separate systems of power brakes, two hydraulic and one mechanical. Damage to one will not affect the others. The Rolls-Royce is a very *safe* car—and also a very *lively* car. It cruises serenely at eighty-five. Top speed is in excess of 100 m.p.h.

13. The Bentley is made by Rolls-Royce. Except for the radiators, they are identical motor cars, manufactured by the same engineers in the same works. People who feel diffident about driving a Rolls-Royce can buy a Bentley.

PRICE. The Rolls-Royce illustrated in this advertisement—f.o.b. principal ports of entry—costs **$13,995.**

If you would like the rewarding experience of driving a Rolls-Royce or Bentley, write or telephone to one of the dealers listed on opposite page. Rolls-Royce Inc., 10 Rockefeller Plaza, New York 20, N. Y. CIrcle 5-1144.

STUDY THE AD ABOVE.

First, it's smooth as a ride in a Rolls. Though long, it's still tightly written. And rewritten.

Second, it's filled with interesting facts. (By the way, the headline came from a review in a British car magazine.)

Third, note the witty counterpoint – technical facts with a human touch. *"The engineers use a stethoscope," "No chauffeur required," "People who feel diffident about driving a Rolls-Royce can buy a Bentley."*

Finally, he ends with an offer. Just like Hopkins.

The Man from Schweppes Arrives!

SCHWEPPES PERSONIFIED.

"Personification" is an interesting advertising technique – a person represents the product or brand.

Here, Ogilvy used Commander Whitehead, an executive with the company that introduced Schweppes to the US.

In many ways, Whitehead *became* the product. Sophisticated. Attractive. Sociable – someone who mixes well at parties. Just like Schweppes.

Note the similar layout styles of the Schweppes and Hathaway ads – even the headlines are similar.

Ogilvy studied readership results and determined what he believed to be the best layout approaches.

Ogilvy did not believe in…
Periods.

He believed that they stopped readers.

By eliminating periods from headlines, he felt it was easier for readers to continue into the copy.

AN OGILVY USP.

"Dove is 1/4 cleansing cream."

By the way, did you know that Rosser Reeves was Ogilvy's brother-in-law? It's true – they were married to sisters.

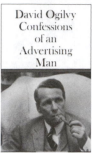

These two are classics. They should absolutely be on your bookshelf. You might also want to get *How To Advertise* (or *The New How to Advertise*) by Ken Roman and Jane Maas – Ken Roman was a top Ogilvy exec for years.

David Martin's agency, The Martin Agency, in Richmond, VA, became part of the O&M network. *Romancing the Brand* is another book that you'll enjoy.

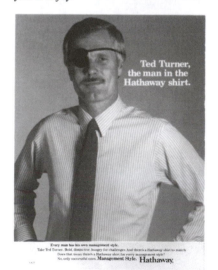

THE OGILVY INFLUENCE.

The account went to another agency – it had become too small for O&M, but the heritage stayed – here's an example using media mogul Ted Turner.

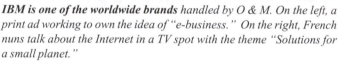

IBM is one of the worldwide brands handled by O & M. On the left, a print ad working to own the idea of "e-business." On the right, French nuns talk about the Internet in a TV spot with the theme "Solutions for a small planet."

THE OGILVY HERITAGE.

Most important, David Ogilvy created an agency.

Today, Ogilvy & Mather is one of the world's largest. Much of their success is a result of Ogilvy's philosophy.

Today, his agency abounds with rules and guidelines, which will surprise no one who reads his books.

But Ogilvy himself says, *"I hate rules."*

In the beginning, Ogilvy's image-making was rule-breaking and helped create a whole new style of advertising.

Now O&M is part of a large agency conglomerate – WPP – a result of what Ogilvy says is his one regret – going public.

But his spirit and individuality are still a part of their heritage. They're still going like sixty.

And the loudest noise is the electronics.

A Brand-Building Partner. That's what Ogilvy's agency became. Above, two examples of the range of work they do to build the American Express brand.

A niche ad, saluting a well-known tennis player as part of a sports marketing program, and a local newspaper ad, saluting restaurants that honor the card.

SOMEWHERE WEST OF OGILVY. Above and below, two examples of some Western Ogilvy work – Hal Riney ran their San Francisco office, which then became Hal Riney & Partners.

That's just one example of agencies started under the Ogilvy influence.

Above is Bartles & Jaymes, wine cooler *personifications.*

Below, some Riney long copy – note the rhythm and rhyme.

Leo. *Leo Burnett was influenced by the philosophy and writing style of an early boss. He worked for Theodore MacManus ("The Penalty of Leadership") in Detroit during the first wave of image selling.*

He knocked around the Midwest, ending up in Chicago in 1935 – the middle of the Depression. When he started his agency, people told him he'd be selling apples on the street. From then on, there was a bowl of apples in the lobby.

They represented "the agency's commitment to simple, honest communication and an optimistic vision of the future" (Morrison in The Ad Men and Women). *Slowly, this vision grew.*

RED MEAT. RED BACKGROUND.
This was one of Leo's earliest ads and his first million-dollar account.

The power is Image. This small black and white rendition doesn't do it justice.

The selling idea is *Red!*

The "inherent drama" in meat.

Leo Burnett

MEANWHILE, Leo Burnett was building an agency in Chicago, Illinois.

Leo, a loveable man in a freshly rumpled suit, had bowls of apples in the lobby, peas picked in the moonlight, and a slogan that was pure Leo:

"When you reach for the stars, you might not quite get one, but you won't come up with a handful of mud either."

Everyone loved Leo.

And they loved his advertising.

Leo put red meat on a red background. *Leo's Logo.*

He took a little canned vegetable company in Le-Sueur, Minnesota, and grew the Jolly Green Giant.

His Chicago agency took a New York cigarette with a British name and moved it to Marlboro Country.

Charlie the Tuna, Morris the Cat, the Pillsbury Dough-boy, the Keebler Elves, Tony the Tiger, and all the other cute cartoon critters of Kellogg's were born at Leo's.

INHERENT DRAMA.

Leo believed in "inherent drama." He believed it existed in almost every product or service.

Leo believed in Middle America.

His "Chicago-style" advertising showed love and respect for people.

It felt homegrown and authentic.

It was. Leo called it *"The glacier-like power of friendly familiarity."*

That friendly strength, and the hard-working Middle Americans who thought the way Leo did, grew his agency into one of the largest in the world.

Now there's a big, brawny building in Chicago with his name on it, where thousands work every day.

And the apples are still in the lobby.

THE BURNETT STYLE.

The agency was built on strong, simple instinctive imagery. Each with its own "inherent drama."

Let's look at some of the long-term advertising ideas that were born at the Leo Burnett Company.

Kinda Corny. *Burnett's brand images provided built-in story value.*

New Kid on the Block. *Altoids. Another long-term campaign.*

Even Little Ideas Can Grow into Big Ideas. *The Keebler story is simple – they're made by elves. Suddenly the brand has a unifying idea that provides continuity at the same time it gives Keebler the flexibility to advertise a wide variety of cookies. Magic in action.*

Strong Simple TV Ideas. *Burnett's heritage of visual impact also translates into television. Here are two frames from a long-term campaign for All-Temperature Cheer. A stain is removed with musical accompaniment.*

THE MARLBORO STORY.

When the agency first received the assignment from Phillip Morris, everyone gathered around working to have the right idea – a "Big Idea."

Leo walked in with a copy of *Life* magazine. There was an article about the King Ranch in Texas – and it featured cowboys.

That's it, he muttered, and he insisted that a cowboy be one of the original ads – they had featured men with tattoos.

Like this one.

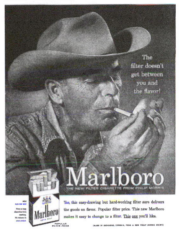

The Original Marlboro Man.

Early ads featured a range of models and TV commercials. The sexy voice of Julie London crooned, *"You get a lot to like from a Marlboro. Filter, flavor, Flip-Top Box."*

But the cowboy concept took hold and the "glacier-like power" kept building.

Today, it's the largest cigarette brand in the world – whatever your feelings about smoking, Marlboro is a huge advertising success.

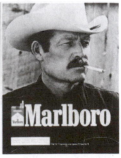

It has maintained and extended that imagery.

And it all began with Leo's instincts about "inherent drama" when he saw that article in *Life*.

Blessings on thee, little man,
barefoot boy with cheeks
full of *Kellogg's* CORN FLAKES

Classic Work for Kellogg's.

NOT SO LONG AGO...

Leo Burnett leveraged early feminist issues for this Philip Morris brand with "You've Come a Long Way, Baby."

Yes, we have come a long way.

The Burnett Secret

Here are what I believe were the four main reasons for the Leo Burnett agency's long-term success:

1. AGENCY TEAMWORK.

The people at Burnett worked together.

Creative and account people worked as equals.

They listened to each other and respected each other.

The creatives were smart. So were the suits.

2. CLIENT PARTNERSHIP.

The agency operated as a dedicated business partner.

They had the client's best interests at heart. Always.

This was not an act, it was a rock-solid belief.

This builds client respect and trust and unifies the agency around a single-minded goal – build the client's business.

3. LONG-TERM CAMPAIGNS.

Burnett knew how to stick with an idea. Eventually, this becomes a tremendous competitive advantage.

But the cumulative power takes time to build.

Of all advertising agencies, Leo Burnett has more long-running campaigns than any other. By far.

They could take a simple idea, like "fly the friendly skies" for United Airlines, and make it last for 20 years. Make that 30.

In fact, even after United left for another agency, some of that long-term equity is still being used.

They may or may not have had better ideas first year.

But, over time, Burnett really knew how to keep a campaign fresh.

They didn't change campaigns just because there was a new creative team or a new brand manager.

They knew that building the equity and image of a brand is a long-term job. And they did it.

Year after year after year.

4. HARD WORK.

Nobody outworked Burnett.

It was only possible to work as hard as the people at Burnett. It was impossible to work harder.

Some successful new agencies, such as Chiat/Day, have this same work ethic.

Once upon a time, when I worked at Leo Burnett, I received a compliment from The Creative Director of the World. *"You know why you're good?"* he asked.

"Why, no," I said, puffing up for some flattery about my unique talent or, perhaps, my keen intelligence.

"You've got stamina," said The Creative Director of the World. Nobody out-worked the Leo Burnett Company.

CRITTER POWER.

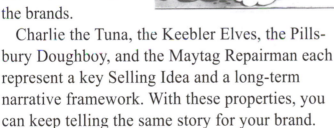

Leo Burnett built long-term advertising properties which captured the inherent drama of the brands.

Charlie the Tuna, the Keebler Elves, the Pillsbury Doughboy, and the Maytag Repairman each represent a key Selling Idea and a long-term narrative framework. With these properties, you can keep telling the same story for your brand. Brilliant.

Burnett knows *how to keep P&G smiling. A long-term relationship.*

Dewar's Profiles *ran for decades. Another long-term relationship.*

YOU CAN'T WIN 'EM ALL.

The Oldsmobile brand is one that could not be saved with the Burnett magic. Despite years of effort, the brand kept losing share, and GM decided to terminate the brand.

Some blamed the cars, some blamed the advertising. It certainly wasn't lack of effort.

William Bernbach – Creative Director.

DDB'S FIRST CLIENT.

Ohrbach's was outspent by ten other retailers, but their advertising gave them greater awareness than the competition, as DDB won awards for Best Retail fifteen years in a row!

This ad is a surprise, but you understand it instantly. Art direction was by Bob Gage, a disciple of Paul Rand.

Bill Bernbach

Meanwhile, a copywriter started a New York agency that set new standards for the entire industry. Bill Bernbach (Pronounced Bern-*back*).

His agency, Doyle Dane Bernbach, set the tone for advertising in the '60s.

Some people called it "soft sell," but it wasn't. It sold hard. It just wasn't rude.

Bernbach's work was smart. Intelligent.

It didn't talk down to people.

It was honest. Admitting faults and winning sales ("We're Only #2." "Ugly Is Beautiful.").

It was funny. It was classy.

And the graphics knocked you on your you-know-what.

Though started years ago at Y&R, it was DDB that made the writer/art director team the industry standard. The latest graphics, typography, and film techniques were used to create advertising that raised the craft to the level of art.

As Bernbach said, *"I warn you against believing that advertising is a science. It is intuition and artistry, not science, that develops effective advertising."*

Yet it was not art for its own sake.

"You must have inventiveness, but it must be disciplined. Everything you write, everything on a page, every word, every graphic symbol, every shadow should further the message you're trying to convey."

He wasn't just a leader, he was a teacher who seemed to know how to bring out the best in others.

His people created advertising and agencies in DDB's image: Julian Koenig, George Lois, Mary Wells, Helmut Krone, Ron Rosenfeld, and many others were part of the DDB Creative Revolution.

Today, his influence is still felt in every award show and almost every agency creative department.

What was it exactly?

He never wrote a book about it, and many of the best DDB ads were written by others.

Bill Bernbach broke the rules but never felt obliged to write new ones.

His philosophy was quite simple, really.

"Find the simple story in the product and present it in an articulate, intelligent, and persuasive way."

It was all based on an even simpler belief:

"The power of the idea."

Lemon.

This Volkswagen missed the boat.
The chrome strip on the glove compartment is blemished and must be replaced. Chances are you wouldn't have noticed it; Inspector Kurt Kroner did.
There are 3,389 men at our Wolfsburg factory with only one job: to inspect Volkswagens at each stage of production. (3000 Volkswagens are produced daily; there are more inspectors than cars.)
Every shock absorber is tested (spot checking won't do), every windshield is scanned. VWs have been rejected for surface scratches barely visible to the eye.
Final inspection is really something! VW inspectors run each car off the line onto the Funktionsprüfstand (car test stand), tote up 189 check points, gun ahead to the automatic brake stand, and say "no" to one VW out of fifty.
This preoccupation with detail means the VW lasts longer and requires less maintenance, by and large, than other cars. It also means a used VW depreciates less than any other car.
We pluck the lemons; you get the plums.

The original headline was "This Volkswagen missed the boat." It became the first line of body copy. Julian Koenig started it (then he went to the track) and Rita Seldon finished it. Helmut Krone made it all work (you can read more about his contributions at the end of Chapter Six). Many DDB print ads featured a "klitchik," a clever last line of copy that tied to the headline. Check out the last line of this ad.

THE DDB PHILOSOPHY.

• Nobody's waiting to hear from us.

• Advertising that nags its way into people's consciousness does only half as much as advertising should.

• Genuinely entertaining, involving, or dramatic advertising not only gets people's attention, it gets their affection.

• This kind of advertising multiplies every dollar an advertiser spends.

DDB CREATIVE APPROACH.

• Creativity is as important in developing a strategy as it is in communicating it.

• Creativity that doesn't reinforce the proposition in an ad or commercial isn't creative, it's disruptive.

• Execution isn't a vehicle for delivering a selling message, it *is* a selling message.

SOME DDB QUESTIONS.

• Does it communicate a message that is motivating?

• Is it fresh, appealing, intrusive?

• Is the style and tonality appropriate to the product and the point?

• Do you like the company that manufactures/sells this product?

• Will it help build a long-term personality for the product?

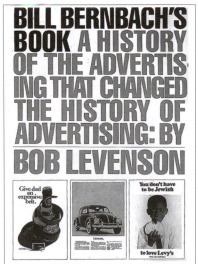

READ ALL ABOUT IT.

An excellent summary of the DDB legacy with terrific reproductions of the classic campaigns and the stories behind them.

to love Levy's
real Jewish Rye

THE POWER OF SURPRISE.

Surprise! DDB made bread exciting – Levy's Jewish Rye, to be exact.

Instead of backing away from the ethnic nature of the product, they met it head on.

As a result, they managed to say "The rye bread for everybody" in a tremendously arresting and distinctive way. There is also a powerful but subtle logic at work.

Since Jewish people eat (and bake) a lot of rye bread, naturally they'd be the rye bread experts.

Another facet of DDB style. Taste.

This approach could have been offensive, but it wasn't.

You don't have to be Jewish
to love Levy's
real Jewish Rye

Or buy a Volkswagen.

__News as Product News__. Bernbach believed in using the timeliness of today's newspaper to make a point for his clients – he believed that advertising should be a bit sociological. Look how they did it. When New York had a water shortage, VW was there with an ad that humorously leveraged the fact that a Volkswagen had an air-cooled (rather than a water-cooled) engine. When the US had a gas shortage, Volkswagen capitalized on the event with this ad. They ran the art director's rough as the illustration. When the economy took a bit of a bump, they used it as an opportunity to advertise an economy car.

Think small.

"It was the only thing to do after the mule died."

IBM's "Think" and "Think Big" were common slogans of the times. DDB bucked the trend… just like Volkswagen. The "Think Small" ad was originally a "one-timer" for *Fortune*. It was so well received that consumer versions were written.

Not as fact-filled as Rolls-Royce, but, there was less to say.

And less to pay.

A dramatically different layout approach by Helmut Krone (who also wrote the last lines of copy). It said, "Read Me." People did.

The "mule" ad shows how delightfully extendable the whole campaign was, with an understated humor that brought warmth, charm, and humanity to almost every situation where there was a Volkswagen.

Avis is only No.2 in rent a cars. So why go with us?

We try harder.
(When you're not the biggest, you have to.)
We just can't afford dirty ashtrays. Or half-empty gas tanks. Or worn wipers. Or unwashed cars. Or low tires. Or anything less than seat-adjusters that adjust. Heaters that heat. Defrosters that defrost.
Obviously, the thing we try hardest for is just to be nice. To start you out right with a new car, like a lively, super-torque Ford, and a pleasant smile. To know, say, where you get a good pastrami sandwich in Duluth. Why?
Because we can't afford to take you for granted. Go with us next time.
The line at our counter is shorter.

The writer of this ad rented an Avis car recently. Here's what I found:

I write Avis ads for a living. But that doesn't make me a paid liar.
When I promise that the least you'll get from Avis is a clean Plymouth with everything in perfect order, I expect Avis to back me up.
I don't expect full ashtrays; it's not like them.
I know for a fact that everybody in that company, from the president down, tries harder.
"We try harder" was their idea; not mine.
And now they're stuck with it; not me.
So if I'm going to continue writing these ads, Avis had better live up to them. Or they can get themselves a new boy.
They'll probably never run this ad.

EL AL.

Here's another DDB trademark – *visual surprise!* DDB's art directors gave us a new way of looking at the same old page – like this. Surprise! A new way to say faster.

What a wonderful theme. *"We Try Harder!"*

It communicated the benefit of being better without over-promise. And, it motivated personnel – an important and often overlooked function of advertising.

This was one of the first modern "positioning" campaigns. A marvelous piece of logic. It made you believe you got a better deal and better service.

It's an excellent example of '60s style copywriting by Paula Green, with help from Helmut Krone. Tight and delightful.

Are you working like a dog to get to the top? Shake hands with Avis.

When you're not top dog, you try harder. You work more hours. You worry more. You eat much too fast.
You go through the same thing Avis is going through. We're only No. 2 in rent a cars. We have to knock ourselves out to please people.
By not giving them anything less than fine cars like lively super-torque Fords. By worrying that one of our people might forget to empty an ashtray. Or clean a windshield. Or fill a gas tank. We try harder. But you'll never know how hard we try until you try us.
Walk up to our counter.
And give us some growing pains to keep our stomach pains company.

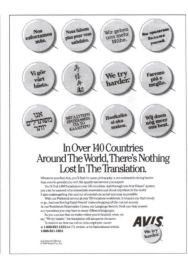

In Over 140 Countries Around The World, There's Nothing Lost In The Translation.

KNOW WHO THIS IS?

He's Paul Rand – one of the major influences on 20th century design. See more at www.paul-rand.com.

Know who his favorite copywriter was? It was Bill Bernbach.

They worked together early in Bernbach's career on accounts like Ohrbach's – which became DDB's first account. Paul Rand was primarily a graphic designer.

Rand disciples like Bob Gage went to DDB and applied Rand's graphic design approach to advertising.

Find The WO

YOW!

For Naugahyde, George Lois created inherent drama in The Nauga!! An idea that *"bristles with visual imagery."*

What makes a great ad?

Ogilvy had guidelines.

Burnett had a feeling.

Bernbach had an idea.

We'll talk about ways to develop ideas and strategies later, but here's a quick review of some of the techniques that the '60s pioneers used.

REDEFINE THE PROBLEM.

Beginning with Y&R and refined at DDB, they were constantly turning the problems over in their minds.

This was a lot of the "creative" work done. While a lot of headlines were written along the way, the real job was articulating the underlying marketing issue the advertising had to address.

DRAMATIZE VISUALLY.

George Lois looks for *"words that bristle with visual imagery."* He's an art director who looks for *"the blending of verbal and visual imagery… that inexplicable alchemy which causes one plus one to equal three."*

Even much of David Ogilvy's work had strong visual elements: "Dove is 1/4 cleansing cream," Commander Whitehead, and the Hathaway eyepatch.

Writers thinking visually. Art directors looking for the right words – two things into one bigger thing.

LOOK INTO TODAY'S WORLD.

Though many of the ads now seem dated, they were contemporary when they ran.

They all featured contemporary language and a contemporary graphic style – whether cutting-edge or straight down the middle.

UNDERSTAND THE CUSTOMER.

The creative work of the '60s had a genuine understanding of how people felt. About their lives. About products. About advertising.

Whether it was Ogilvy's intellect generating a tour de force on Rolls-Royce, or Leo's instinct putting red meat on a red background, *an understanding of the person who would respond to the ads* was a key part of their creation.

DDB's Avis campaign had this deep understanding of the customer. Think about it. The key customer for rent-a-cars is usually a salesman on the road – who probably has a bigger competitor. Like Avis!

That person knows in his own life exactly what it's like to "Try Harder." So while it was interesting that Avis admitted "We're only #2," the Wow connected with people in a very powerful way – because it was also about them!

The strength was not just the brains of clever copy or the beauty of brilliant art direction.

It had heart. It understood and respected the people it was talking to. So should you.

POW!

Campbell's visualizes a simple but meaty proposition for Chunky Soup – a soup aimed at men.

These memorable visuals introduced Trout and Ries's classic *Advertising Age* article. The visuals made the point that advertising had evolved from repeating a USP-style message ad infinitum or adding

memorable, but not always relevant, imagery. There were too many messages. In this new mental environment, the first step was understanding what was going on inside the mind of consumers you were trying

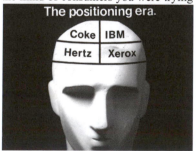

to reach. Their timing was perfect – their book became a business bestseller.

Positioning

"The Positioning Era Cometh," was the headline of Jack Trout and Al Ries's *Ad Age* article.

The premise was simple, and its promise of profit in the age of product proliferation was irresistible.

The key to success was *positioning* your product properly in the consumer's mind.

Positioning was a product of product proliferation. The '70s marketplace was a teeming pool of products and messages. Consumers were on overload.

P&G was an early practitioner, marketing detergents with distinct positions: Tide for clean, Bold for bright, and Cheer, renamed and repositioned as All-Temperature Cheer, for all-temperature washing.

ADVERTISING THINKING FOR MARKETERS. Positioning was tailor-made for the brand management organizations that had become standard in the major advertisers' marketing departments. And, in fact, Trout and Ries began as brand managers at GE.

Did it work? Sure. But remember, much of the analysis came after the fact – it described campaigns that were already successful.

Positioning helped us understand why the DDB Avis campaign was effective, with a classic "Against" position featuring "We're only #2."

It also explained Burnett's instincts – capturing core category values with advertising that was full of inherent drama.

Finally, it was a helpful way of thinking for both clients and agencies. Whether they happened to believe in USP or image, it didn't matter.

It helped everyone involved find a common conceptual framework based on an eternal truth of advertising – understand the consumer.

HOW TO GET STARTED.

First, you must develop a "conceptual map" of your category inside the mind of the consumer. You need to find out what's important and what's already there.

While earlier advertising approaches worked to put new thoughts and concepts into consumers' minds, positioning works to understand what's in there already.

The search moves from "within the product" (USP) to "within the ad" (image) to "within the prospect's mind."

That's where you create your position.

MARKETING THINKING FOR ADVERTISERS.

Since positioning is rooted in both marketing and creative advertising thinking, making it work demands cooperation between "creatives" and "suits."

It can help marketing and creative people find a common ground and a clear path of development.

By the end of the '70s, positioning was part of every major agency's vocabulary and part of how most agencies and marketers worked to solve their problems.

Trout and Ries continued to maintain their own leadership position in marketing thinking with more popular marketing books like *Marketing Warfare* and *Bottom-Up Marketing*.

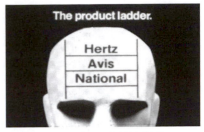

A CONCEPTUAL MAP.

Where is your product "within the mind of the consumer?"

That's the first question.

Often, the product category is already occupied by information, brands, and pre-existing attitudes.

For example, a car rental brand might have to deal with something like this. Is there room for another?

Yes and no. You have to find a way to establish a new position in the consumer's mind. That's what Budget did.

**SUCCESSFUL POSITION.
WINNING PROPOSITION.**

A distinct positioning and a new proposition for Lite Beer from Miller succeeded in a market where many (including DDB) had failed.

They solved the problem of trying to market "diet beer" to beer drinkers.

Their proposition, "Great Taste. Less Filling" provided a reason why – since it was less filling, you could drink more.

That, plus the fun use of ex-jocks in their TV spots, helped Lite to become the #2 beer brand – at least for a while…

FIRST THOUGHTS...

At the very beginning of a project, a copywriter needs to think about what position is right for the product.

THE BEST POSITION.

Be first in the consumer's mind in a meaningful way. Dominant share of mind usually results in a dominant share of business. And vice versa.

MCDONALD'S.

Some of the best work of the '70s was Needham's work for McDonald's.

In many ways, a version of the Burnett/Kellogg's school of advertising, with "You Deserve a Break Today" and "We Do It All for You."

Great music, warm, human TV production, and, most important, a company totally committed to QSCV: Quality, Service, Cleanliness, and Value.

FOUR BASIC TYPES OF POSITIONING:

1. The Best or Leadership Position

2. The Against Position

3. The Niche Position

4. The New Category

Naturally, there are some combinations and variations. First, the basic positions:

The Best Position

Become first in the mind of the customer.

Once you're there, it's hard to beat.

Just ask IBM's competitors.

Many beat IBM to the punch with better products. But, in the customer's mind, IBM held onto #1 for quite some time. They still maintain that position in the minds of many.

Hertz and McDonald's are two other excellent examples of this position. But wait, it gets better.

THE POWER OF LEADERSHIP.

From that leverage point, you can do things that no other brand in the category can really do.

Tide, Chevrolet, Budweiser, and McDonald's have a power in their messages that comes not only from what's being said, but from who's saying it.

OTHER WAYS TO BE #1.

As you can see by the Acura ad, you can say you're #1 without necessarily being the biggest seller.

That's why two other types of positions are important – Niche and New Category positions.

We'll cover them a few pages from now.

The "Against" Position

It can be a tough road. But sometimes you don't have a choice. You suck it up and take 'em on.

Avis had the right idea. You do have to try harder.

SOME EXAMPLES:

Remember Plymouth's "Look at all Three?"

Sometimes, just by adding yourself to the competitive set, you accomplish an important task.

That's what "UnCola" did for 7Up.

Burger King and Pepsi are examples of really going at it. If you're going to sell more burgers or cola, you've got to go after somebody else's customers – and they've got more than anyone else.

The Pepsi Challenge – an Against position that became an entire marketing effort – included taste tests at malls across the country.

Apple Computer, with a unique operating system, positioned itself against the entire world of PCs.

Today it continues with "Mac vs. PC."

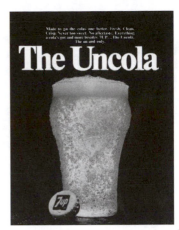

7UP VS. THE COLAS.

In the '60s and into the '70s, 7Up positioned itself against the brown cola drinks. Their research discovered that in the mind of the consumer, soft drinks meant colas.

The UnCola worked because it related to something already established in the consumer's mind.

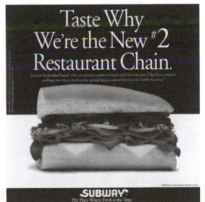

#2 AS LEADERSHIP CLAIM?

Positioning is a way of thinking, not a set of hard and fast rules.

Here, Subway uses its large number of outlets to build its image in the mind of the consumer.

In the mind of the consumer, Subway is much farther down the ladder.

So the #2 claim actually raises it a few notches in your perception, and it works to improve their position in your mind.

But, of course, just saying it isn't enough. So it shouldn't be surprising that this ad also came with a coupon.

When you're only No.2, you try harder. Or else.

Little fish have to keep moving all of the time. The big ones never stop picking on them.

Avis knows all about the problems of little fish.

We're only No.2 in rent a cars. We'd be swallowed up if we didn't try harder.

There's no rest for us.

We're always emptying ashtrays. Making sure gas tanks are full before we rent our cars. Seeing that the batteries are full of life. Checking our windshield wipers.

And the cars we rent out can't be anything less than lively new super-torque Fords.

And since we're not the big fish, you won't feel like a sardine when you come to our counter.

We're not jammed with customers.

No. 2ism. The Avis Manifesto.

We are in the rent a car business, playing second fiddle to a giant. Above all, we've had to learn how to stay alive.

In the struggle, we've also learned the basic difference between the No.1's and No. 2's of the world.

The No.1 attitude is: "Don't do the wrong thing. Don't make mistakes and you'll be O.K."

The No.2 attitude is: "Do the right thing. Look for new ways. Try harder."

No. 2ism is the Avis doctrine. And it works.

The Avis customer rents a clean, new Opel Rekord, with wipers wiping, ashtrays empty, gas tank full, from an Avis girl with smile firmly in place.

And Avis itself has come out of the red into the black. Avis didn't invent No. 2ism. Anyone is free to use it. No. 2's of the world, arise!

AVIS. Classic Against. Among other things, it can leverage off natural sympathy for the underdog and resentment of the big bully. Can be difficult to defend.

FROM NICHE TO NEW CATEGORY.
Product positions can migrate.

Red Bull began as a niche soft drink – with the unique characteristic of providing a bit of a lift.

From there, its sales growth – and the emergence of other competitors – turned it into the leader brand in a New Category – energy drinks.

They've kept that leadership position with good distribution and smart marketing.

SOME "NEW CATEGORIES."
In the relatively recent past, each of these has been a New Category:
- CDs • DVDs • PCs • VCRs
- Mini-Vans & Minis
- Granola Bars & Energy Bars
- Overnight Delivery
- Lap Top Computers
- Smart Phones & Touchscreens
- "Gourmet" TV Dinners
- "Light," "Lite," or "Low Carb" Anything
Can you name a new New Category?

Niche Positions

If you can't have the whole pie, how about a slice?

That's the Niche position.

In general, this position establishes leadership in one aspect of a product category.

When it's the right match with a segment of the marketplace, you can be #1 with some of the people all of the time!

Many New Category products and "flanker" brands can also be viewed as Niche positions.

Success depends on identifying a target and doing a better job of matching your product to the needs and preferences of that target.

"Market segmentation" is one of the techniques used to help discover a profitable niche in the marketplace.

The New Category

By establishing (or inventing) a new category, you give your brand a brand new opportunity to be #1 and take a leadership position.

It may be totally new, like FedEx, or, a new definition, like Red Bull (energy drinks).

SOMETIMES NICHES TURN INTO CATEGORIES.
The marketplace is always changing.

SUVs were a niche, with just a few players.

Now it's a category.

FedEx was a new category – soon, there were lots of competitors – including things you might not think of as competitors – like the fax machine.

FedEx's original business involved moving a lot of documents. But soon, everyone had one of those strange little machines spitting out rolls of fax paper.

And soon there was another new category – and a whole new category of retailer as well – office supply superstores!

RePositioning

IF YOU DON'T LIKE YOUR POSITION, you may want to change your position – from one you have to one you want. That's "re-positioning."

During the '70s, marketers like Pontiac and 7Up, revitalized their products by repositioning.

ALL-TEMPERATURE CHEER.

The All-Temperature position took Cheer from #5 to #2 in the very competitive detergent category.

Cheer moved from a "white-ness" position ("New Blue Cheer") to a position that was associated with a new laundry practice – washing in all temperatures.

P&G repositioned (and reformulated) the product to match the change in laundry habits caused by new fabrics and brighter colors.

Contemporary "slice of life" commercials reflected new habits and new values.

Earlier spots, with the same basic strategy, had marginally competent women confused by their laundry. They were then told to use Cheer by a male authority figure. The commercials didn't work, even though they did "Burke" (a type of "day after recall" research).

MORAL: The right positioning isn't everything. You need the right advertising!

Then, they shifted to a new approach. Using a demo from a P&G sales meeting, Leo Burnett developed a long-running series of commercials that used the same proposition over and over – Cheer got out spots in cold water.

Rolling Stone *works to reposition itself from its initial "hippie" reputation with this classic trade campaign.*

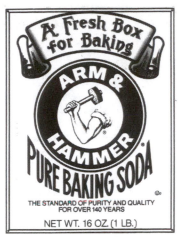

Arm & Hammer Repositioned Itself into the refrigerator – turning baking soda into a refrigerator deodorant!

VOLVO'S FIRST POSITION.
Originally, Volvo positioned itself for durability, based on the fact that they were longer-lasting than, at the time, less-durable US brands.

Later, they evolved that position into a different niche – safety.

READING LIST.
Some books you might like:

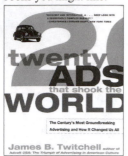

Twenty Ads That Shook the World
James Twitchell
   I love this book. Highly recommended. Takes you from P.T. Barnum to Apple Computer.

BEFORE THE '50s.

Scientific Advertising
Claude Hopkins
Chelsea House Publishers

100 Greatest Advertisements
Julius Watkins
Dover Publications

**Tested Advertising Methods
& How to Make Your
Advertising Make Money**
John Caples
Prentice-Hall

They Laughed When I Sat Down
Frank Rowsome, Jr.
Bonanza Books
(A great book if you can find it.)

**The Mirror Makers:
A History of American Advertising and Its Creators**
Stephen Fox
William Morrow & Co.
(A terrific book! Now available from University of Illinois Press)

The '50s.

Reality in Advertising
Rosser Reeves
Alfred A. Knopf

Madison Avenue, USA
Martin Mayer

The Benevolent Dictators
Bart Cummings

#5: Copy the Copy

THESE ASSIGNMENTS are designed to help you get in touch with some of the historical lessons we've covered. Some are pretty easy, and some are pretty tough.

A. DO A PARODY OF AN AD IN THIS CHAPTER.
   Use the product of your choice. This one's fun!

B. FIND ADS THAT REPRESENT THE DECADES.
   See if you can find ads that represent principles or techniques from the different periods. Start with some favorite magazines and the Sunday paper. Then, if you can find some old magazines, see what you find there.
   • Hopkins-style (person-to-person and pre-emption with some product-based news).
   • '50s-style USP. (Pay attention – you need a clear proposition.)
   • '60s-style Image.
   • '70s-style Positioning.

C. HISTORY EXERCISE.
   Pick a product, any product. (I've done this exercise a few times, and I just pick something close at hand.)
   Do ads that demonstrate basic techniques from each period. It's a little tough, but it can be a lot of fun! And, you'll be amazed at how much more facile you become.
   Try it now and then try it again in a month or two.
   • Do a Hopkins-style ad.
   • Do a '50s-style ad. What is the USP?
   • Do a '60s-style ad. What is the Image?
   • Do a '70s-style ad. What is the Position?

They laughed when I sat down at my Macintosh keyboard.

They snickered. "He can't run a Macintosh IIci. He knows nothing about Quark. Aldus Freehand will make a fool of him."

Then I booted up. And they shut up. Because they didn't know I had visited NovaWorks for some intensive training. I heard gasps of amazement as I produced letter-perfect layouts, meticulous mechanicals and powerful presentations. With NovaWorks, I turned into a Macintosh virtuoso virtually overnight. You can, too, by calling (212) 557-9199.

NovaWorks
COMPUTER SYSTEMS, INC.

"They laughed when I sat down at the piano. So I sold it."

They laughed when I sat down to write this assignment.
Here are some examples that people sent in.

They laughed when I sat down at the piano. They stopped when I picked it up.

Let's not play around. Whether you're into Schwarzenegger or Shostakovich, no one gives you a better workout than Gold's Gym.

GOLD'S GYM
AND FITNESS CENTER

Land-Rover 109 Station Wagon with Heat Shield Roof.

"At 60 miles an hour the loudest noise in this new Land-Rover comes from the roar of the engine"

What makes Land-Rover the most conspicuous car in the world? "There is really no secret," says an eminent Land-Rover enthusiast.

1. "Except for rattles, I am against silence in a car," writes John Steinbeck, a Land-Rover enthusiast, "and I don't know a driver who doesn't want to hear his engine."

2. If this is so, then you may like the Land-Rover very much indeed.

3. Our 4-wheel drive (8 speeds forward, 2 in reverse) masterpiece is not mousey. Its throaty authority is assuring in times of stress; which nowadays is usually.

4. Nor is this claim true only at 60 miles an hour. A Land-Rover is more conspicuous even when it is standing still. With the ignition off.

5. The Land-Rover stands nearly seven feet tall. All its features tend to heroic proportion.

6. Therefore, when driving, you will simply loom over traffic which previously had scared the devil out of you.

7. This is not only safe and enjoyable, but you will exult to observe how other

drivers, awe-inspired by the Land-Rover's casual might, yield in deference.

8. (Small wonder that women are enormously fond of driving Land-Rovers. The easy command of such massive, maneuverable masculinity is heady stuff.)

9. You may have read of tests where "imported cars" fared badly in collisions? It's a pity we weren't in there to help out the side. The Land-Rover is built to resist the charge of a bull rhinoceros; or a bull Lincoln for that matter.

10. The Land-Rover's sturdiness of construction (the under-frame resembles a reinforced section of railway track) makes it ideal for trackless wastes, car pools of small children, wretched ordeals, et cetera.

11. There are perhaps 14 Land-Rover hardy perennials ranging from safari cars and campers to police vans and getaway cars. Our most popular passenger models are the 7-seater Model 88 and the 10-seater Model 109 Station Wagons.

LAND-ROVER WITH & WITHOUT
TIRE ON HOOD

11-A. An attractive feature of the '66 Land-Rover is that it is precisely as attractive as the '65.

12. Both of these have capacious rear doors for unloading bulk or people. The unathletic may use the fold-down step.

13. The after compartment has facing seats. This arrangement, although somewhat reminiscent of riding in a paddy-wagon, is extremely sociable. Late at night, it is hilarious.

14. The Land-Rover is available with a spare tire either mounted on the rear door or on top of the hood. The tires are identical in every respect save that it costs $7.40 more to have one on the hood.

15. People who feel diffident about driving a Land-Rover with the spare tire on the hood can buy the conventional Land-Rover and save $7.40.

PRICE: The Model 109 Station Wagon illustrated in this advertisement costs $3,906 on the Atlantic Coast, $4,092 on the Pacific Coast; at places in between, it costs in between. The Model 88 Station Wagon (shorter by 1 door) costs about $600 less.

If you would like to listen to the Land-Rover, or to the embarrassingly quiet Mark II Rover Sedan, or to the Rover 2000 Sports Sedan (which has "a little panty matter when idling that rises to a whispering roar in the lower gears," according to Mr. Steinbeck), please ask any dealer here listed. (LR) signifies a Land-Rover dealer; (R), a Rover dealer; (R & LR), both.

Thank you.

©1965 Rover Motor Co. of North America, Ltd., Chrysler Bldg., New York 17.

A Rolls-Royce ad parody done by Howard Gossage (Ogilvy was amused).

SLAM-DUNK MARKETING!

In 1992, the back page of *Rolling Stone* announced the premiere of the Charles Barkley vs. Godzilla commercial on the MTV Music Awards.

An ad promoting another ad?

Was it a promotion? Was it an event?

Was it the shoes?

It's an excellent early example of the thinking that turned the idea into more than a TV spot.

Stations received PR footage, which sports shows featured along with the latest scores.

There was even a "teaser" TV ad.

Charles Barkley was interviewed and asked about Godzilla. It was all in fun, but there was serious marketing going on.

Meanwhile, posters and promotional materials made it an event in stores as well as in the media.

That's how Nike and their agency, Wieden+Kennedy, turned a single TV spot into a multi-dimensional media event – including a monstrous amount of free media coverage.

You can still see the spot and the teaser on YouTube.

Current

THE PREVIOUS CHAPTER was about progress. This chapter is about change.

Progress usually makes everything better. Change has winners and losers.

We'll start with changes in the '80s and '90s and work our way up to today, with even bigger changes kicking in.

In his book *PowerShift,* Alvin Toffler made an important point about today's economy – the value of information is approaching and surpassing the value of things. Think about it.

Cars, computers, and your new phone that now takes photos, sends text, and remembers your class schedule each contain a lot of information – it's not just the metal, plastic, rubber, and silicon.

Think about it. It's not just metal, it's *mental.*

It means information content is more important than ever. It means people who produce useful information will be more important than ever.

If you can do that, whether it's creating ad messages, marketing plans, or websites, there's a need for you somewhere in this fast-changing marketplace.

THINKING INTEGRATED.

Today, marketers have to develop a whole new way of thinking. So do copywriters.

There are more options. Messages can go through a wider range of channels. Think of all the different places you can see a Nike logo – or an Apple logo.

With all those options, you have to pick the right ones, and then make them work together. It's "IMC," **Integrated Marketing Communication.**

Events

An excellent example of this integrated thinking was Apple's 1984 introduction of the Macintosh.

A LOT MORE THAN "1984."
There was a lot more to Apple's introduction than their spectacular "1984" commercial.

The commercial ran *once* – during the Super Bowl.

Here's what else was going on:

For months, PR people had been briefing the technical and business press. Stories were timed to break in newspapers and magazines.

They prepared informative print ads, multipage "FSIs" (Free Standing Inserts), and even sponsored entire magazines. Other TV spots highlighted specific product features and benefits.

Three magazines were born – two monthlies, *MacWorld* and *MacUser,* and *MacWeek* – a trade weekly.

Other important groups, from retailers to software developers, were involved in special Apple programs. They were reached through: direct mail, events (such as demos and sales meetings), advertising in specialized media, and "Evangelists."

In-store posters, brochures, banners, and T-shirts were created. So were special interactive software programs that allowed customers to walk into a store and immediately interact with a Mac.

After the introductory period, a "test drive" sales promotion event even let you walk out with one.

Apple's agency, Chiat\Day, and their own in-house creative department worked together.

On January 24th, Apple Computer will introduce Macintosh. And you'll see why 1984 won't be like "1984."

[QuickTime version @ www.adbuzz.com]

They even developed a common typeface…
"Apple Garamond" (Garamond condensed to 80%).

Ad for In-store Promotional Event.

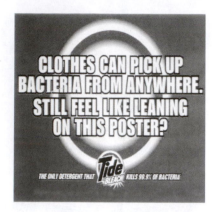

LEADERSHIP BRANDS:
CAPITALIZING ON
BRAND EQUITY.

In today's economy, leading brands are more valuable than ever.

Years of advertising and consumer familiarity build equity in the marketplace.

For that reason, many of the mergers and buyouts you've read about involved high values being paid for existing brands.

After all, what would it cost today to establish a brand with the same awareness and familiarity of one that had been around for decades?

A Change in Philosophy.

Previously, marketers like P&G would establish a new brand – with its own unique benefit and position – every time it introduced a new product.

Now, it makes more sense for brands to become families of related products.

Changing Channels.

Established brands have a huge advantage.

They're already familiar. So you don't have to say as much or work as hard to get inside "the mind of the consumer."

That's why a brand like Tide can have good results with short, relatively inexpensive messages on billboards using their familiar graphics and their familiar brand image.

Major Changes...

YOU CHANGE every ten years. So did advertising.

Marketing became firmly established as the most important business function. Apple consultant Regis McKenna noted, *"Marketing is everything."*

Once, ad agencies were the top marketing organizations. Now, it was client marketing organizations, though ad agencies were still valued for ideas and innovations.

Advertising also changed because of:

• Changes in the marketplace.
• Changes in the media environment.
• Changes in our lives. Yours and mine.

Traditional advertising became less effective. Here's what happened:

1. CHANGING MARKETS: "MATURITY." Fast food and VWs aren't new anymore.

Today, you expect more than one kind of Tide.

Not that long ago, cell phones, PCs, VCRs, CDs, DVDs, and e-mail were new technologies.

Now, we take them for granted.

We've moved from growing categories, where almost every sales curve went up, to "mature" categories, where, whatever you're selling, most people already have one. Think about it.

That's a big difference – a huge difference.

In mature product categories, the growth that comes from people adopting new habits is essentially over.

Sales are "flat"– our purchase habits and brand choices are more established.

After you've decided on a brand, it takes more than a clever TV spot to get you to change.

It also means that people like you – younger and still in the process of making major brand decisions – are very desirable to marketers. (How many credit card offers have you received?)

In mature categories, advertising has a much more difficult task to accomplish – it's a tougher job.

When Volkswagen established itself in the '60s, with a unique car and unique advertising, they pretty much had the field to themselves.

Then, VWs were better built and more reliable than most other foreign cars. Times change.

A unique car, like the Mazda Miata, quickly found itself competing with other nifty convertibles.

These days, a new category can mature in a startlingly short period of time.

"A Zero-Sum Game."

In a mature category, it's a "zero-sum game."

For each winner, there's often a loser.

It's *Marketing Warfare.*

As a friend said, *"Advertising today is selling corn flakes to people who are eating Cheerios."*

The Growth of Sales Promotion.

This more competitive "mature" marketplace is a major reason for the tremendous growth of sales promotion – the use of incentives to stimulate purchase behavior.

That's the first big change – mature categories.

The next big change is in the world of media.

FAST COMPETITION.
In the '90s, way before the Mini, Mazda drove into an open niche in the marketplace – with a nifty small convertible – designed to be profitable with a small production run.

The result – a unique new car that was like nothing else available.

Guess what? The ads worked.

In about a year, other car makers had their own small convertibles. From niche success to a New Category.

SALES PROMOTION.
Adding an incentive – like special savings, an intriguing sweepstakes prize, or something extra – can increase sales on the short term.

This is particularly important when just an ad message may not be enough.

More media choices *often mean smaller audiences – that's "fragmentation."*

TRADE AD OF THE '80s.
Often, the challenge is to change minds.

This campaign repositions *Rolling Stone* by cleverly challenging the target's mindset – by first agreeing with it.

In this case, the target consumers are potential advertisers in *Rolling Stone*.

FREQUENCY PROGRAMS.
Tobacco marketer Marlboro worked to make the most of its most valuable asset – current Marlboro smokers.

2. CHANGING MEDIA: "FRAGMENTATION."

There are more media choices. And, with one exception, each media choice costs more.

CPMs (Cost Per Thousand) in mass media have generally risen much faster than the rate of inflation.

It can cost well over twice as much to reach the same number of people as it did ten years ago.

So, unless your new ad is over twice as effective, it simply won't work as well.

The Internet is an exception, but how often do you click on those web ads?

That's why advertisers and agencies are always looking for "breakthrough" concepts – ads that are many times more effective.

That's also why strong programs, like the Charles Barkley vs. Godzilla example and the Mac intro, were built to communicate across media forms.

But mass marketing still needs a mass audience.

From Mass Marketing to Target Marketing.

As audiences fragment, marketers and agencies are looking at alternative media channels, alternative media delivery strategies, and alternative targets.

Finally, since it now costs more to reach (and persuade) new customers, why not increase effort against *current* customers? Why not indeed.

In many ways, fragmentation has stimulated the growth of direct-mail, "frequent-user" programs, niche media (like special interest magazines), and various forms of database marketing.

Why are we talking about this? Because anyone who creates media messages needs to know about the environment they work in – an environment that's changing dramatically.

3. CHANGING CONSUMERS: "OVERCHOICE."
We've changed, as customers and as receivers of the messages. Remember all the copy in those ads in Chapter One? Back then, people took the time to read those ads.

As the number of messages increases, we have to deal with "overchoice." Too many messages.

We become less responsive and more selective. It's impossible for us to respond to every message.

As a survival mechanism, we learn to ignore, or, more accurately, we learn to not pay attention.

We all do it. We have to. Moreover, as a top ad exec noted, *"Too much of advertising isn't simply bad, it's simply irrelevant."*

The good news? We're very good at selecting information when we need it. If your car starts slow on a winter morning, you start to pay attention to those car battery ads you usually ignore.

We're all smarter consumers of advertising.

We use it when we need it. When we don't, we don't.

And, of course, we've made a lot of choices.

Our choice of car, cola, fast food, laundry detergent, and concert tickets is based on our own real-world experience and our own personal taste.

We use advertising for information, entertainment, and to pay for the media we enjoy. But we're not that easily influenced or persuaded.

Today, effective communication has to overcome:

- Mature product categories.
- Media fragmentation.
- Consumer overchoice.

And the changes keep on coming.

Here are a few more…

HOW ABOUT NO COPY!
Jeff Gorman and Gary Johns "wrote" the billboard above and the print ad below for Nike.

They knew that, done right, no words could create a stronger communication!

HARDERFASTERBETTERMORE!
Visual communication is faster.

You can say more in less time.

And just in case you didn't think there was enough to worry about, it's all happening faster than ever, too.

FASTER THAN A SPEEDING CIVILIZATION.
Computer-based technology accelerated the pace of business.

For example, during the '80s, major amounts of business moved from FedEx to fax machines in less than a year.

That's just one example.

There's no time for all of them.

BIG CHANGE. SMALL CHANGE.

Two other things happened to advertising in the '80s:

First, the effect of the stock market.

Second, an exciting change in what used to be called "secondary markets."

1. Stock Markets.

The first major change was due to price differentials between the New York and London Stock Exchanges.

The London Exchange valued agency stocks more highly. The P/E ratio (Price to Earnings) was twice that of the New York Exchange!

This meant Saatchi & Saatchi, based in London, could offer US stockholders almost twice as much.

They bought Ted Bates, Compton, Campbell-Mithun-Esty, Dancer Fitzgerald Sample, and others.

Can anyone do this trick? Yes.

Saatchi's accountant, Martin Sorrell, bought a small shopping cart company – Wire Plastic Products (WPP), listed on the London Stock Exchange.

In a startlingly short period, he bought Ogilvy & Mather and JWT, two of the world's largest agencies.

Other agencies merged as well.

And it changed the agency business.

2. Smaller Markets.

The business changed in another way.

There was tremendous improvement in advertising quality in smaller cities. Austin, Miami, Minneapolis, Portland, Richmond, and more.

Production technology was no longer limited to large markets.

You no longer have to go to New York to get a good job in advertising – or to do good advertising.

SOME ADS CHANGE HISTORY.

This advertising for Margaret Thatcher and the Conservative (Tory) Party in Great Britain was one key to their victory.

This change in government not only put Great Britain on a new political path, the Labour Party's response to that success resulted in that party repositioning itself. The result? Tony Blair.

The tactics and techniques of advertising became a key part of the politics of a major industrial nation.

JESSE VENTURA, GOVERNOR.

Entertainment and politics are mixing it up more than ever. For a while, the Governor of Minnesota was an ex-wrestler named Jesse Ventura.

A key part of his campaign was ironic, humorous, and very "po-mo" (post-modern) advertising that appealed to a turned-off electorate.

Ads featured Jesse Ventura action figures and Jesse "The Body" Ventura posed as "The Thinker."

A huge last-minute youth vote was one key to his victory. Now, successful politicians have to be successful media personalities.

TWO FOR ONE.
The Pink Bunny interrupts a phony TV commercial for deodorant soap. It even interrupted a real commercial – for Purina Cat Chow. (Both brands had the same parent company – Ralston-Purina.)

ADVERTISING ENTERS THE IRONY AGE. Now advertising makes fun of advertising with irreverent and ironic humor.

The charming Energizer "Pink Bunny" ads established the ironic style as part of a very tough-minded business decision.

The Energizer agency, Chiat/Day, discovered that durability was not only the most important claim for batteries – it was the *only* meaningful claim.

The leading brand, DuraCell, was making exactly that point in their advertising – with a larger budget.

Client and agency made a tough decision – compete with category leader DuraCell on durability. The challenge wasn't do it different, but do it better.

When the ads first broke, research showed a high level of confusion. Energizer's Pink Bunny was being confused with DuraCell's ads that also featured battery-powered toys. Client and agency stuck with it.

Over time, it worked, building Energizer's reputation for durability. And the Bunny became one of America's favorite ad icons.

Tough marketing. Charming advertising.

That kept on going. And going…

TOUGH PROBLEMS.
TOUGH DECISIONS.
Deciding to take on a bigger competitor with a smaller budget and "me-too" advertising was a tough decision.

After that decision was made, client and agency still had to endure research and trade magazine articles that reported consumers confusing Energizer advertising with Duracell.

BUD LIGHT EVOLVED...

with "Party Animal" Spuds McKinzie.

The pleasantly goofy ads grew along with the brand – until Spuds T-shirts were even merchandised in two-year-old sizes. Hey, wait a minute!

Two-year-old sizes? For beer?

Suddenly, Spuds disappeared and beer advertising changed dramatically.

Cutty and denim.

The day was all business. The evening is all yours. It starts with your favorite jeans, an understanding friend, and the smooth, mellow taste of Cutty Sark. A taste to savor. Cutty Sark. You earned it.

THE PICTURE STORY.

With fewer words, you read in your own feelings and your own experiences.

The Viz Biz!

TELEVISION HAS TRANSFORMED SOCIETY. Some might argue it has transformed many of us neurologically, but we'll leave that to pediatricians and neurophysiologists. We'll observe the obvious.

We watch a ton of TV. And, more and more, advertising has become visually driven.

Doug Warren, an agency president who'd left the business, made this observation on his return.

"We now live in a nonverbal society. Impressions are made on a visual basis. Language mainly serves to reinforce preconceived stereotypes.

Nothing new you say? I disagree.

The change over the past ten years is extreme and will grow stronger...

We respond in an ever-increasing degree on a strictly emotional level triggered by visual stimuli.

Talk all you will about your product's advantages, but the verbiage had better conjure up acceptable visual recall. People no longer have time (and there's growing inability) to isolate or critically examine facts."

He's right. Successful advertising is now more visual.

It's a move from verbally dominant to visually dominant communication... from logical left-brain "perception" to right-brain "reception."

Words became less important overall. Headlines became shorter – or even nonexistent.

More and more, readers "viewed" print.

We are also a more visually sophisticated audience, with TV as our dominant input mode – experiencing ever more intense and condensed visual input.

Scrapbook

DURING THE '80s AND '90s, computer-based visual assembly made a wider range of visualizations possible.

As computing power increased, a similar evolution happened in film and video.

Another example of the computer's impact.

Advertising as Art. Art as Advertising.

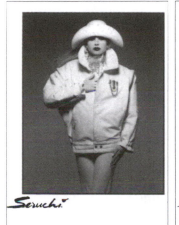 

The Passionate Eye of Fashion. *The benefit is both the look of the clothes and the feeling of knowing that one is wearing something special. Building equity in the brand name is critical – and often visual.*

Some of us have more finely developed nesting instincts than others.

The Surreal Vision. *Schools of art re-emerge in advertising styles – with an assist from technology. Digitized photography expands the range of possibility.*

COMPUTER POWER.
Early TV spots like this one for Levi's used computerized motion control and film assembly to open new visual vistas.

THE POWER OF ROCK 'N' ROLL.
Popular music has a deep and positive connection.

It was demonstrated by the California Raisins dancing to *I Heard It Through the Grapevine.*

Viz Biz Video

WE'RE NOW A VISUAL CULTURE. From *Sesame Street* to music videos to high-tech TV commercials, we've become ravenous consumers of the newest video techniques.

Today, the "channel-changer mentality" zips and zaps through the media environment. It continues as our computers become an increasingly common part of our viewing behavior.

Today we receive and perceive at an ever-increasing speed through an ever-wider range of media choices.

Here are some of the trends that kicked in:

THE ROCK VIDEO INFLUENCE. Aggressive and surreal quick-cut imagery driven by a powerful music track. A shorthand symbolic language – heavy on the attitude.

This is both cause and result of an improved ability to receive and interpret visual information.

In addition, marketers now perceive rock 'n' roll as part of our contemporary cultural heritage and use it as a marketing tool.

Want to reach a target? Check out what they were listening to when they were about fourteen and you won't be too far off. The same goes for old TV shows. Notice the little twinge you get when you see something from your younger days.

THE GROWTH OF TECHNOLOGY. Computers and video technology expanded the techniques available in video production.

What was once state-of-the-art is now available at most TV stations and video houses, or on your desktop. Complicated video effects are now easier and more affordable – and the trend will continue.

CELEBRITY.

The media adds its own aura to those who stand center stage in our electronic window.

From nationally recognized supermodels to the celebrity status generated by local retailers and advertising spokesmen. It's electronic sizzle.

While the use of celebrities has been a common advertising technique, the game of fame in marketing has grown stronger.

The lines of celebrity blur – public figures do commercials, commercial stars become public figures.

For example, a key part of Nike's strategy to create a major golf brand was Tiger Woods.

It's all part of the growth of our visually driven media culture. Viz biz!

Two celebrities team up – not a big hit – but you know who they are without us telling you. You can see the spots on YouTube.

DONNA: *Looking for a job, Mom?*
FERRARO: *Very funny.*
LAURA: *Well, I am.*
DONNA: *So what's it this week Laura, marine biology?*
FERRARO: *Are we still hoping to be a star of stage and screen?*
LAURA: *Come on, Mom, it's a tough choice.*
FERRARO: *Sure, it's tough when you can be anything you want to be.*
VO: *When you make a choice, what's right is what feels right. Diet Pepsi.*
FERRARO: *You know, there's one choice I'll never regret.*
DONNA: *Politics?*
FERRARO: *No, being a mother.*
VO: *Diet Pepsi. The one-calorie choice of a new generation.*

FEATURE ATTRACTION.

This Nike spot became the movie *Space Jam,* featuring Bugs Bunny and Michael Jordan. And ads become pop culture.

WHO IS THAT LADY?

Today, you might be used to politicians doing advertising pitches. But when this TV spot ran, it made quite an impact. It featured Geraldine Ferraro, the 1984 Democratic vice-presidential candidate.

This commercial was done in the "hyper-realism" mode – featuring tight framing and intimate communication.

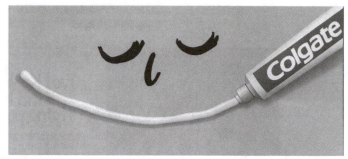

A New Brand World

THE POWER OF GLOBAL COMMUNICATION.

See how quickly Colgate communicates their benefit – white teeth and a happy mouth. Smile.

This is communication that works in any language – since it's all *visual*.

THE EUROPEAN TRADITION.

Advertising posters are a more dominant media form in this multi-lingual environment.

Simple visuals communicate powerfully in a language everyone understands.

ich liebe es

A WORLD BRAND. McDonald's implements the same theme worldwide.

NEW BUSINESS INITIATIVE.

Nike took a swing at a huge new business opportunity – golf. A major part of their strategy to establish themselves as a winning brand was hiring the winningest golfer – Tiger Woods.

THE BRAND AGE BEGAN IN THE '90s. A maturing marketplace, more expensive media, and more experienced consumers made a big change.

As alternative marketing communications options grew, and as the impact of individual ads lessened, marketers looked for ways to accumulate impact.

One of those ways was to refocus on the brand itself. And, as it cost more to establish a new brand, the value of existing brands grew.

THE GROWTH OF BRAND VALUE.

Here's another way to look at it. As we experience a shift in value from tangible things to information, we discover that the name and reputation of the product – the brand – is hugely valuable.

It has become very important to consumers, marketers, and investment bankers.

In many ways, the brand is the organizing concept of business. Though each business has its own way of marketing products and making money, virtually every business is, in some way, building the equity of its brand.

Today, brands rule.

That's a rule.

Iconic Communication

In a complicated world, simple can be powerful.

Look at that Volvo image – a safety pin. Wrapped around years of heritage and product design concerned with safety, it's a powerful image and a powerful advertising message.

Without all that went before, it wouldn't be.

It connects with something already inside your mind – with some history in the marketplace.

So – how do we build brands and accumulate that power and simplicity?

Time helps. So does keeping it simple.

Remember Tony the Tiger? Sugar Frosted Flakes are "G-r-r-r-eat!"

I know an art director who was there at Tony's creation – many years ago. I asked him about it. "*Well,*" he said. "*We drew up an animal for each of the Kellogg's cereals. Sugar Frosted Flakes had sugar, and that meant energy, and we thought the best energetic animal imagery was a tiger.*"

There you have it.

Not rocket science – but connections that make sense on a simple, basic level. When you combine that with over fifty years of keeping at it, you get a powerful bit of brand communication.

So what does that mean for you?

FOUR GUIDELINES.

First, respect what's already in place.

It took a long time to build and maybe it's not perfect, but it's something.

Crispin Porter + Bogusky took a kind of goofy, not that effective, bit of iconic work from an early Burger King project (it was a "Kids' Club" – they were trying to compete with Ronald McDonald).

STRONG, SIMPLE ICONS…
can build into something meaningful. Sometimes it takes time – decades.

RESPECT WHAT'S IN PLACE.
A brand's history gives you something to work with – even if it's kind of goofy and not successful – yet.

VOLVO
A car you can believe in.

YEARS OF HERITAGE…
can pay off in strong, simple brand reputations in the mind of the consumer.

A REASON FOR BEING.

It gives leverage – Archway was already the #1 oatmeal cookie (in an Oreo and chocolate chip world) – and you had a strong simple bit of communication that just plain made sense.

FOUR GUIDELINES:

1. Respect the past.
2. Keep it simple.
3. Make it meaningful.
4. Make it easy.

MEANINGFUL TO THE CONSUMER.
The rich heritage of the West and cowboys added richness to Marlboro cigarettes Even though the brand name's British heritage was a bit of a disconnect – at first.

EASY TO RECOGNIZE.
The familiar Snickers typography tells you the brand without having to say it.

And, with a nice contemporary sense of humor, they leveraged this icon into some fairly powerful communication. Ironic. Iconic.

Second, try to keep it simple – with an actual reason for being.

The Good Food Cookie position – one that helped the Archway brand achieve solid growth in a crowded market – was based on a very simple Attribute of oatmeal cookies – they were made of oatmeal.

Use "reductionist" thinking. Get it boiled down into one easy-to-remember statement.

That's the second thing – simplicity.

Third, even though it's about the product, it also has to be meaningful to the customer. Safety is meaningful to car buyers. Tigers are kinda cool – you don't mind being a bit of a tiger.

Same with cowboys and Marlboro cigarettes.

Fourth, remember that the world is noisy – a lot noisier than your office.

You're giving your message a lot of attention – getting all the bits and pieces exactly right – but the world is driving by at slightly above the speed limit with other things on their minds. So make it easy to understand in a noisy, complicated world.

Take a quick look at Snickers. They used their well-known typography to deliver simple messages related to characteristics of the candy bar. It's simple reminder advertising, just a notch more complex than just showing the package.

 Target's little target and McDonald's arches... and more.

THE NEW PEPSI CAMPAIGN.

As this book was being written, a new Pepsi campaign kicked in. Did you notice?

Bet you did – pretty simple.

This was big news in advertising. Pepsi had been with the same agency (BBDO) for nearly 50 years.

And their advertising was generally regarded as above average.

So why the change? My guess is that, sometimes, "above average" might not be enough, and it was time to shake up the Pepsi.

Our guess is, the things we just talked about had a lot to do with the thinking behind the Pepsi campaign done by Lee Clow and the smart people at TBWA\Chiat\Day. We're guessing the Pepsi people agree – since they're spending their money on simple iconic messages like this – with the round logo in place of the "O."

With iconic communication, you give the audience just a little bit to process, and, over time, a lot to think about.

As media becomes more fragmented, the move to iconic messaging will continue. Now, simple symbolism can do the work that used to be done by more complex narratives.

Icon? Yes we can!

ICONIC AND ENVIRONMENTAL.
Simple, iconic communication allows the messaging to become a part of the simple graphic environment of street signs and signals.

WORLDPLAY.
That's the name of the kick-off commercial for the new Pepsi campaign.

Right now, it's all over the 'Net and you should be able to find it.

Take a look. See the minimal/maximum strategy they developed.

The messaging is minimal, yet the scope is maximum – leading to their all-encompassing theme – Refreshes Everything.

East, West, & Out There

THERE ARE A LOT OF GOOD AGENCIES doing a lot of good work.

And, as you become more familiar with the business, you're going to have some favorite campaigns, favorite agencies, and maybe even favorite creative teams.

Here are six snapshots of six agencies doing consistently interesting work.

Some of it you may recognize and others are campaigns you may only find in small venues and award books.

The six agencies are… the envelope please…

EAST:

BBDO – one of the original major agencies, still doing important and effective work for big clients like FedEx, GE, and Campbell's Soup.

Big clients. Smart work.

Until recently, they did many years of award-winning work for Pepsi.

The Martin Agency – down the coast in Richmond, Virginia, this agency has grown into one of the big and important agencies in America. They're a good example of how the business has changed. Once, all the important agencies were in New York (plus Leo Burnett in Chicago). Today, they range across the country. Originally, strong local or regional agencies were connected to nearby clients – like Nike with Wieden + Kennedy in Portland. Now, these agencies draw clients from all over.

For the last few years, the Martin Agency has been working on Walmart – America's biggest retailer. Their campaigns for UPS and Geico are certainly ones you're familiar with.

One of my favorites is some delightful work for a brand of baby clothes.

WEST:

In LA, **TBWA\Chiat\Day** – has been one of America's best agencies for the last 30 years. Not bad for an upstart with a pirate flag flying. Led by Lee Clow, a surfer turned to art direction, the agency collected top talent and numerous Agency of the Year awards.

Their founder, Jay Chiat, helped introduce the practice of account planning to US agencies and dedicated himself to being an agency with the highest creative standards.

Their work for Apple Computer, Energizer (that Pink Bunny), Nissan, and now Pepsi is well-designed and memorable.

San Francisco is home to a number of very interesting agencies. One of the finest is **Goodby Silverstein & Partners**.

You'll recognize their famous "Got Milk" campaign as well as state-of-the-art work for H-P, and some crazy ComCast stuff.

In one of those curious things that can happen in the ad industry, they've done excellent work for a number of car companies: Porsche, Isuzu, Saturn, and, most recently, Hyundai. (Seems like they get traded in every three years. Go figure.)

FIFTEEN MINUTES.
The Martin Agency knows how to keep a campaign fresh and growing.

Here, the corporate spokes-Gecko provides name recognition and an amusing personality.

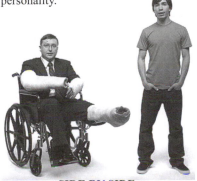

SIDE BY SIDE.
Compare TBWA\Chiat\Day to most agencies and you will be impressed by the consistent excellence of their work.

Their clever PC/Mac comparisons have helped grow the business and forced Microsoft to respond.

POP CULTURE #1.
Their iconic work for the iPod has helped build a dominant business for the iPod and iTunes.

EARLY CP+B.

Their "Body Bags" ads for the "Truth" anti-tobacco were part of an effort that shifted the tone of voice from adults saying "don't smoke until you're an adult." (Think about that.) To young men and women who said, "Stop lying. Stop killing us!" They have unique and effective insights into contemporary culture.

READ ALL ABOUT IT.

Wexley School for Girls is featured in *Inc. Magazine*.
http://www.inc.com/magazine/20090301/the-wexley-way.html

5 SECRETS TO GREAT ADVERTISING.

Here's Wexley's state-of-the-art advice.

Secret No. 1: Look beyond the obvious

The agency's first rule of thumb? Just because you're a fast-food joint doesn't mean all your ads have to feature a burger and fries.

They practice cognitive dissonance.

"*People are spending more time getting branding messages than ever before,*" says Cal McAllister, Wexley's co-founder. "*To reach them, think entirely differently.*"

Secret No. 2: Customize your message

A one-size-fits-all approach won't do much to grab people's attention. A small core audience is "*a whole lot more valuable than a bunch of people who really don't care about the product.*" Wexley conducts research to find out how its clients' customers tick.

(Continued on Next Page.)

OUT THERE…

Certainly everyone will mention Wieden + Kennedy, the Nike agency in Portland, OR. Nike work is featured throughout this book as one of the leaders in effective advertising and marketing that crosses traditional boundaries and sets new standards.

We'd like you to know about two others…

Crispin Porter + Bogusky – currently the "hot" agency, with offices in Miami and Boulder – and a little shop in Seattle you probably never heard of… **Wexley School for Girls**. No Kidding.

Nobody has captured the "Po-Mo" spirit better than CP+B.

They have the right touch to cut through the noise and engage a young, modern audience with irreverent but strategically effective work that crosses traditional media boundaries. So they will do ads that are more like art installations, mock documentaries that find a place on the Internet, and grab a momentary moment in our fast-changing media culture.

The effectiveness of their work has attracted (but did not always keep) big-time brands such as American Express, Microsoft, VW, Miller Beer, the Mini, and Burger King. Their cutting-edge "Truth" campaign broke barriers in anti-tobacco advertising and was uniquely effective.

In their work, they look for "social tension" and "talk value." They seek controversy, which is quite different than the usual controversy-averse nature of most ad agencies.

And then there's Wexley. Located in Seattle, they've been given projects by brands you've probably heard of – such as Microsoft, Bath and Body Works, Nike, and Virgin Mobile.

For Virgin Mobile, they designed a Miss Virgin Mobile competition – an online beauty pageant using photos taken on mobile phones.

Crazy like a fox, Wexley owned the trademark and, from the beginning, was an equity partner.

With a youthful sensibility combined with a surprisingly business-like strategic sense, they're finding new ways to create impact for marketers.

As they say, "*the worldwide web just got a whole lot worldwider.*"

"Even squirrel races, done properly…"

Wexley has a broad view of what is possible.

As they say in the "not funny" part of their site, "*we believe everything is advertising: Traditional media, design, packaging, PR-generating ideas, video games, branded entertainment, short films, guerilla tactics and events, even squirrel races, done properly, can be advertising.*"

A NEW WORLD OF POSSIBILITIES. As McLuhan observed, when media evolves, it doesn't necessarily eliminate what has gone before, it encompasses.

This, for some strange reason, is why antiques will look OK in a room full of modern furniture, but a bit of modern furniture among antiques would look strange.

Our new media world encompasses all the media that has gone before. It ranges from the big brand traditions of BBDO to the post-modern bomb-throwers at CP+B and Wexley School for Girls.

Got it?

OK, time to develop a fairly wide range of skills.

5 SECRETS (CONT.)

For example, Microsoft's college recruiting campaign, "Hey, Genius!"

Secret No. 3: Take it to the streets

Getting in front of your customers live can pack a powerful punch.

Copper Mountain Ski Resort wanted to push its marketing beyond print ads featuring pretty scenery. In a campaign called National Snow Day, the agency brought snow to Austin, Texas, literally, by spraying it onto the streets.

Secret No. 4: Preserve a little mystery

Plastering your company's name all over your advertising might seem like a good way to gain brand recognition, but maintaining some subtlety is often the more effective approach. To promote Microsoft's Live Search Maps, Wexley placed giant pushpins on buildings throughout Seattle. The only clue was a web address displayed in window signs.

Secret No. 5: Always remember to have fun

Wexley applies offbeat creativity even to the most sober of products.

"*We look for something smart but a little ridiculous.*"

Mission accomplished.

IMC. NOT NEW.

As Don Schultz of Northwestern University pointed out, one group of marketers practiced IMC (Integrated Marketing Communication) for years.

Small companies. Smaller business-to-business marketers have been "thinking integrated" since marketing began.

The small business-to-business marketer knows how to integrate his communications all by himself:

- **Advertising in trade journals**
- **Direct mail to customers**
- **Conventions and trade shows**
- **Press releases to trade press**
- **Incentives for the sales force**

Whether or not all the right decisions are made, these marketers are fairly familiar with the marketing and selling options available to them.

Their ad agency often supplies a full range of IMC services:

- **Advertising • PR**
- **Brochures & Catalogs**
- **Sales Meetings • Trade Shows**
- **Newsletters • Corporate ID**
- **Package Design**

Other smaller businesses, such as single-store retailers, practice their own brand of IMC:

- **A sale (promotion)**
- **A newspaper ad**
- **A mailing to customers**
- **"Co-op" advertising**
- **Incentives to sales people**
- **Telemarketing**
- **Bus bench backs**
- **Flyers handed out in the mall**

All are IMC tactics appropriate for a small retailer. Without even knowing it, they already "think integrated."

Bigger brands. Bigger problems.

For larger marketers, it's more complicated. Budgets are bigger, and so are organizational problems.

One person runs sales promotion, another runs PR, and someone else handles the advertising agency.

Simple things become complicated as larger marketing organizations try to "think integrated."

FROM ADVERTISING TO MARKETING COMMUNICATIONS.

Once, advertising was almost the only way a brand talked to consumers. Today, there are many options.

The same kind of thinking used to create great ads is now used to develop sales promotion, PR, direct marketing, events, and web-based programs.

Now marketers are looking everywhere.

Nike, who first signed Michael Jordan, now signs up leading universities. Is it an ad? Not really.

Is it effective? What do you think?

We'll cover this in more detail in the next chapter.

CONTRADICTORY PRESSURES.

Change isn't easy.

The pressure to solve problems with a breakthrough is constant and intense – so's the pressure to play it safe.

The challenge to reduce risks and conserve resources in a less effective environment competes with the challenge to break through the clutter and make an impact.

Often, that means risk. It's riskier than ever to change. It's riskier than ever *not* to change.

That's why advertising – and all marketing communications – has become a much tougher business.

That's bad news. But the good news is we need people who can think and communicate effectively.

MANY TARGETS, MANY CHANNELS.

Since the beginning, talking to your target as a single individual has been critical. But now you may have multiple targets.

For example, software developers were critical for Apple Macintosh's success – even though they're not exactly customers.

You may have to reach large important target groups who don't have much in common with each other – including their use of your product.

Now let's talk about one more target group – you.

Yo! It'sPo-Mo!

THIS IS ABOUT POST-MODERNISM – or "Po-Mo."

It's one more change – a change in you.

There are po-mo movements in art, architecture, philosophy, literature, history, and sociology.

And, there's one in advertising. Sort of.

Post-Modernism began as *"a revolt against modernism* (duh)*, a rejection of progress, the power of reason, and the dominance of science and technology..."* (From "The Chaos of Meaning" by Ian Forth, BMP/DDB)

You'll find this sensibility in art galleries, rock lyrics, and even physics lectures on "chaos theory."

MARKETING MODERNISM.
Meanwhile marketing, which pays for advertising, is essentially "modernistic" and "positivist."

Marketers view their activities as "progress." They offer you products that solve problems, fashionable fashions, specials this week only, and generally work to keep business in business.

Marketing tries to be logical – there's a lot of money at stake. Marketing works to discover objective "truths" about the best way to do things – whether it's how to introduce a new running shoe, sustain consumption of a breakfast cereal that's been around for fifty years, or sell you a beer as soon as you're old enough to buy one.

On the Other Hand, It's Not a Simple World.

One person's progress may be another's environmentally unfriendly behavior.

One person's "better" may be sexist, racist, classist, exploitative, or worse yet, unfashionable when viewed from another perspective.

Addendum:

At the end of some chapters, we may add a few more things we think you need to think about.

Ad for a "po-mo" brand – Doc Martens.

#31070

subscription holder, reporting for duty! Is that what you want, for me to become another faceless entity that you can anonymously slip your paper to? Maybe I'm an antique, but I don't mind going down to a real newsstand, paying with real money, flashing a real smile, and heck, maybe even slipping in a "Thanks, 'preciate it." What human contact do we have left? Computo-bank tellers, TV diplomas, "Personalized" bulk mail, blow-up dolls, push "1" for this - push "2" for that. How 'bout I come down there, push "3" and blow your whole operation to bits? Listen here, you... you...personality leeches, I'm a real person! I have a name. I am not, I repeat, NOT, a credit card number!

A SIDE-BY-SIDE COMPARISON.

Time for a chart. On one side, we'll list some "modernist" and "progressive" values, and on the other, we'll list some post-modern perspectives.

Modernity	Post-Modernity
Order/Control	Disorder/Chaos
Certainty	Ambiguity
Content	Style
Tomorrow	Today
Similarities	Differences
Commodification	Customization
Universality	Individuality

See what's going on here?

Marketers are usually modernistic.

They pretty much have to be. Because there's a lot at stake if you own a cereal factory.

But consumers nowadays, and young people in particular, may not be. After all, if you're just buying one box of cereal, what's the big deal.

Meanwhile, advertising is usually in the middle –working for the cereal manufacturer, trying to sell one box at a time to individuals.

Now let's talk about those individuals.

GENERATION PO-MO.

Today, most younger people understand and empathize with the chapter title from Doug Coupland's book *Generation X.*

That chapter was titled "I Am Not a Target Market."

Well, actually, you are a target market – we all are.

But that awareness, and that dissonance, changes things. And this awareness can be very different for different generations.

For example, even though I know I'm a target market, I don't have those feelings.

I can remember a time, as a child, when I was

only occasionally a target market. For only a few hours a day, we could see TV for kids. Yay!

We'd plant our little blue-jeaned fannies in front of *The Howdy Doody Show*.

But, just like you, I discovered that you can eat just so many boxes of cereal – no matter what cool prize is inside. And we all discovered that the cool prize maybe isn't as cool as you thought it would be.

But you… Can you remember a moment when you didn't have a channel changer full of KidVid?

I'm guessing probably not.

You have a different attitude about the marketplace – very aware – but with very mixed feelings. Yes?

Well, that's po-mo.

TARGET MARKET AWARENESS.

So now let's look at the problem of advertising – the major way marketers speak to their target market.

The target is onto the game. They "get it." Don't you?

It isn't that you don't want to see an ad for something that might interest you – it's that you're aware of the fact that the marketer is doing what they're doing.

And, if advertisers don't send some sort of signal that "they know that you know," you may think they're pretty dim – or you may give them no thought at all.

You may buy the product, you may not, but the connection with the brand won't be as strong.

This awareness of being the target of marketing efforts is at the center of post-modern advertising.

CLAUDE HOPKINS RIDES AGAIN.

Remember Claude Hopkins? Remember his lesson?

It was to make that one-to-one connection.

It's still all about connecting with the consumer.

And the post-modern movement in advertising, which tends to be limited to certain specific types of products – those that appeal to younger consumers – is simply applying that lesson.

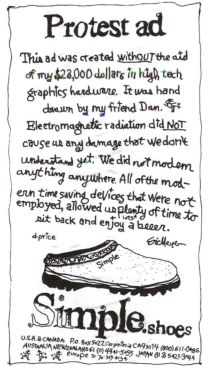

Po-Mo Promo. *Here, ABC uses an ironic po-mo attitude to promote their "brand."*

Po-Mo Attitude. *Here, Simple.shoes takes a stand against modernity. Wonder if they have a website?*

WHEN DO YOU PO-MO?

For certain products, in certain circumstances, good po-mo is critical for making a successful connection.

It's Claude Hopkins' one to one – with attitude.

Above is a good example – a frame from a Sprite TV spot. They made up a phony soft drink, Jooky, and made fun of the claims and attitude.

It positioned Sprite as a more "honest" drink and more in touch with younger drinkers. Sprite sales grew.

Below is a not-so-good example. The cutting-edge work for Subaru by Wieden + Kennedy didn't work.

Then again, the cars weren't much.

Better cars and more traditional advertising helped them get traction again.

And, at this point, it depends on the type of product.

You may have a po-mo mindset picking out Friday night's entertainment or the clothes you wear when you go out – but when you're figuring out the best way to finance a car – or pricing a trip for Spring Break – you're probably all business.

In the Chapter Six, "Conceptual Models," we'll spend a little more time on the idea that we can be very different people depending on what types of products we're thinking of purchasing.

"WHASSUP" WITH PO-MO?

The post-modern attitude tends to be ironic, knowing, and often self-referential.

It's the "we know that you know" syndrome. Done right, it's a shared joke.

"We know you get it. Wink. Wink. Nudge. Nudge." And you do – when it works.

This is the road that logically leads to "Whassup?", the classic Bud commercial. "Whassup?" is about camaraderie and connection.

Good po-mo creates a loop of shared understanding.

Nike, because of its concern for the "personal truths" and values of its audience, contains aspects of po-mo.

It's also probably true that the crew at Wieden + Kennedy in Po-Mo, Oregon, is more in touch with these values than most.

PO-MO STYLE.

As Stephen Brown said in his very clever little book, *Post-Modern Marketing, "Post-modernism is characterized by style rather than by content."*

Getting the style or attitude right is critical.

Make it a night she'll never forget with **JOHN SMITH'S.**

JUST WATCH HER FACE WHEN SHE FINDS OUT **THE LADS ARE COMING 'ROUND.**

What is that style? It's often a bit wry, or ironic, or cynical – but not always.

It's often "deconstructed" so that the audience can be involved in filling in the missing puzzle pieces.

This proves that you know that they know – or is it they know that you know?

And, since it's about style, not content, the critical ingredients in getting the recipe right are subjective –like art, attitude, and awareness.

So, how do you use po-mo? And when?

You use it like the beer they want you to buy when you're old enough – with moderation and when it's appropriate. Too much at the wrong time tends to have an unhappy result.

Because if you do it wrong, it shows that you don't know, you know?

Still, now you know po-mo.

But then again, we already knew that you knew.

A VERY FUNNY CAMPAIGN.

The billboard on the left, for John Smith's Bitter, a British beverage, uses a number of po-mo devices.

It deconstructs a billboard, showing part of a John Smith's billboard over what looks like someone else's old billboard – with a very humorous result.

It's ironic and makes fun of ad cliches as it builds its own humor on top of it.

Get it?

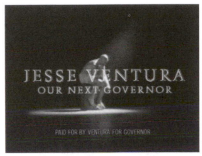

JESSE VENTURA
OUR NEXT GOVERNOR

PAID FOR BY VENTURA FOR GOVERNOR

GOVERNOR PO-MO.

Ironic, satirical commercials that made fun of establishment values and rhetoric were key ingredients in ads for Jesse Ventura's run for governor of Minnesota.

Young voters, who responded to those appeals, were the key to his victory.

READ ALL ABOUT IT.

The book *Where the Suckers Moon* tracks the history of a Subaru new business pitch and the subsequent advertising by Wieden + Kennedy, who won the business.

Their innovative work had many po-mo aspects – such as deconstructed typography. One presenter mentioned punk music in the context of one of the Subaru models. It didn't work.

It can also be argued that the Subaru product that Wieden + Kennedy had to sell at the time wasn't all that terrific.

Then again, some have observed that the most popular car brand with younger consumers is "used," which is, after all, a po-mo brand.

WHOPPER VIRGINS.

The "mock-umentary" is a new device used by many marketers with a "po-mo" target. You get added YouTube viewership with these entertaining send-ups.

PO-MO TO GO.

A po-mo attitude adds an ironic overlay.

It's the 'tude, dude.

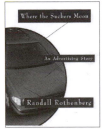

I like this one.

#6: Thinking about Change

MAKING THE MOST OF CHANGE.
Wrigley's Spearmint Gum saw a problem as an opportunity, taking advantage of increased smoking restrictions by positioning their product as an alternative for smokers.

With a strong simple visual device (substituting the No Smoking symbol for the "O"), they quickly communicate the thought "When You'd Like to Smoke But Can't."

The brand had been on an eight-year sales decline – until these ads.

The first year, sales *increased* 5%.

Gum was a "mature category," but they found new growth. Can you do that?

EXAMPLE:
Healthy Joints tablets (helps fight arthritis in older dogs).

Growing Category – Dogs living longer, pet food superstores, growing pet health knowledge.

Best Ways to Reach – Pet store point of purchase and visit to vet. Look for places w. high dog concentrations – particularly larger dogs.

Best Way to Sell – Sampling w. coupons at vet office. Or…

Selling Thought – "Every dog 8 or older needs Healthy Joints every day."

THE OBJECTIVE of this assignment is to get you thinking about the dynamics of today's marketplace –and the problems you'll have to solve.

1. DEALING WITH CHANGE.
   A. Pick a Product. It doesn't matter what.
   The objective is to develop the right kind of mental muscles for thinking about change.
   B. Think about the Category.
   Is it growing or is it mature?
   Are potential customers using something else?
   Do you already have a loyal customer base?
   Why do people buy?
   Briefly, describe the category and competition.
   C. What's the Best Way to Reach People?
   What are the best communication channels?
   Write down your top choices.
   D. OK, What's the Best Way to Sell Them?
   Based on your initial instincts, what's the best way to get the job done?
   E. Selling Thought.
   Write your general approach in a few simple sentences.

2. VISUALS:
   A. Bring in a Visual that you think works.
   B. Start a File of visuals you think are strong.
   C. Think Visuals First. See it before you write it.

3. ICONIC COMMUNICATION:
   Start collecting examples of communication condensed into minimal visual information.
   Take a photo with your cell phone if it's outdoor.

#7: Mo' About Po-Mo

OK, we know that you know that we know.

But let's burn a few more brain cells on this "po-mo" thing.

A. Po-Mo Products.

Describe the types of products where you think a po-mo appeal might be effective.

B. Po-Mo? No.

Describe people and products that are not po-mo.

C. Yes-No.

OK, let's make a list:

First, categories that are po-mo and not po-mo.

Then, brands in categories that are and are not.

D. Got Po-Mo?

Look for some examples of advertising you think demonstrates good po-mo. How did they do it?

E. Po-Mo or Just Plain Mo?

When are you a bit po-mo?

When are you a modernist who believes in progress?

POSTMODERNISM IS THE NEW BLACK.

An article in the *Economist* cited a once failing British retailer, Selfridges, which was revitalized by embracing consumer anarchy in a retail environment.

The result? They were voted "Britain's coolest brand."

It's po-mo in action.

So even though the philosophy seems anti-commercial, po-mo entrepreneurs like Sir Richard Branson of Virgin and Anita Roddick of the Body Shop have had great success even while having "an emancipatory, anti-corporatist tilt to their business."

The rebellious po-mo attitude shows up in the messages of marketers like Nike, and for smaller "entry-level" car models – aimed at younger po-motorists.

Scratch That Niche.

The fragmentation of narratives and the shattering of the mainstream is reflected in the media environment. Old mainstream narratives, such as your daily newspaper and network TV, fly apart into a world of blogs and YouTube.

In "The Long Tail," Chris Anderson observes, "When mass culture breaks apart, it doesn't re-form into a different mass, instead it turns into millions of microcultures…"

What does this mean for mass marketing? Certainly, there will still be large mass marketers broadcasting a single message to as many as possible.

But there will be more specialized messaging as well, as marketers and markets seek each other out in a postmodern world.

For those involved in the art of commerce, there may be a surprising abundance of opportunity.

We think that's good news.

(From "Post-Modernism is the new black." *The Economist* – 12/28/2006.)

If You Want Fiber. Eat the Box. Krispy Kreme DOUGHNUTS

Evolution = Revolution!

AGENT OF CHANGE.

The printing press did more than make books available.

It ended a way of life where truth and power were held by a small priestly class claiming ownership of all knowledge.

It was a revolution – and revolutions, as a rule, are not orderly affairs. The printing press changed religion – no longer was the Bible only available in Latin.

It brought us literature in contemporary languages.

Experiments occurred that only in retrospect were revealed to be turning points. For example, Aldus Manutius was an Italian printer and publisher long before he was desktop publishing software.

He invented smaller books and italic type. It may have seemed like a minor change — take a book and shrink it. But, in retrospect, it was a key innovation. As books became cheaper and more portable, it expanded the market.

Newspapers were started – not necessarily by truth-loving reporters, but by political parties dedicated to their own point of view. The American Revolution was as dependent on printer's ink as it was on patriot's blood.

Revolutions are a curious business. Old stuff gets broken faster than the new stuff is put in its place. It's a messy business. Small changes spread. Unlikely heroes emerge. Even revolutionaries can't predict what will happen.

That's how it is today. Newspapers are a classic example. They powered that earlier revolution and now they'll be changed dramatically by this one.

HANG ON! The changes keep on coming.

Thomas Jefferson observed, "*Every generation needs a new revolution*." Well, we got one.

This one's big – even if you didn't notice it.

When media forms change, a lot of other things change as well. Gutenberg's printer was a major force for social change.

In Chapter One, we saw how an evolution of media forms – newspapers to magazines to radio to television – changed advertising in major ways.

In Chapter Two we discussed how media fragmentation had its own impact.

A NEW MEDIA FORM.

This time The Big One is a whole new media form – the computer.

Your computer is *The Media Channel That's Changing Everything*. It's a change as profound as the invention of the printing press.

And many of you take it for granted.

You do e-mail, connect with your Facebook friends, cruise the 'Net, maybe download some music, and look at a few YouTube videos, Google something for a homework assignment, and… and… and…

See what's happening?

Now add in your computerized cell phone, text messaging, maybe a built-in digital camera or video gizmo in your pocket, and then, if you're a bit of a Gamer…

See what's happening? Can you feel it?

Well, this change is causing more change.

FOUR MORE CHANGES.

As this new media channel becomes a more dominant part of everyone's life, it's kicking in a few other big-time changes.

Now let's take a look at what's happening to marketing and advertising. Here are four changes we think are huge:

- **Growth of interaction**
- **Loss of narrative control**
- **Explosion of opportunity**
- **Dilution of traditional media business models.**

These four changes are simple, but profound.

You already understand them instinctively, but let's think about them in the context of effective commercial communication.

Growth of Interaction.

Up 'til now, most communication has been one-way. Sure, you could clip a coupon or enter a contest, but, for the most part, you either sat through the message or changed the channel. Now you can react – if you want. It's a big difference.

Even though we don't react to all that many messages, we have the power to react to virtually every message. Big change.

Loss of Narrative Control.

Up 'til now, with most traditional messages, the narrator has been in charge. We organize the words and the receiver follows the path we set.

EVOLUTION IN ACTION.

Before we look at the areas of advertising and marketing communication, let's look at how business is changing.

Amazon Blows Up the Book Biz.

Your computer is a lot of things – one of them is – thanks to Amazon – the world's largest book catalog. Now every book author has a distribution channel.

And, of course, we get a bit of "creative destruction" as smaller local bookstores go away. Hmmm… what's happening at the local library?

eBay & CraigsList Change Commerce.

Now we can all be in business.

Whether it's selling Grandpa's beer can collection or hiring out your own special talents for cleaning refrigerators, web-based providers like eBay and CraigsList offer easy to execute opportunities.

A Brand New Business.

Video gaming. It's huge – in the US alone, combined hardware, software, and accessories sales reached $21.33 billion in 2008 – and these brands also grow into movies and books for brand-loyal consumers who enjoy the experience.

What about the Music Industry?

More changes. Sharing music files destroyed stores that sold CDs. Portable players like the iPod have helped somewhat, but, like so many things, the mass marketing business model is collapsing and it is not being replaced by one simple business model.

MCLUHAN ON "EXTENSIONS."

To help us understand his concepts, McLuhan developed a not-so-easy-to-remember acronym – E.O.R.F.

Here's what's going on as media forms evolve.

E= Extension.

First, here's how McLuhan thinks.

Things (not just media) are Extensions. They extend or amplify.

Clothes are an extension of your skin. A car extends your legs and amplifies your ability to move.

Media extends our brains and amplifies our nervous system. Radio extends our ears. TV extends our eyes. Books extend our brains. Got it?

Now it gets a bit weirder.

That extension is kind of an amputation.

A car is like a big wheelchair.

We extend into TV land or computerland, but other things around us (like family and relationships) are often cut off – at least temporarily.

Go totally couch potato, and the effects are larger and more permanent. Obesity and a general lack of cardiovascular fitness are not inconsequential effects. Next.

O = Obsolete.

When media forms evolve, we get a bit of "creative destruction." Things previously amplified may go away.

It could be newspapers' once profitable business model – with classified ads going away.

The telephone made letter-writing obsolete. Get the idea?

(Continued on Next Page.)

Another big change. In the computer environment, we can navigate pretty much any way we want.

If the message holds our attention, we go along – and, if we like it, we can even notify our friends. But we can click to stop, go off on a tangent, or concentrate on a small aspect.

With traditional media, the author kept control of the message sequence. Now, more and more, it's up to the receiver. Take a breath. Think about it.

OK. Good news coming up.

Explosion of Opportunity.

We can do whatever we want. Wow.

Music videos. Photos. Dancing hamsters.

Our time, our imagination, our technical skills, and our website give us the keys to the kingdom.

Whether it's your Facebook page, your own site, a project you put together with a few friends, your new job for a brand new "dot-com," or a traditional marketing firm growing into this brave new world, it's like, "anything we can imagine, we can do."

We'll loop back to this point later on.

Dilution of Traditional Media Business Models.

One thing we can't always do is make a lot of money at it. Unless, of course, we create it ourselves and sell it to a big media company.

Overall, the good news has been a dramatic lowering of cost: cost of entry, cost per visit, cost of development.

But the fragmentation, the loss of mass, has been part of a general fragmentation of business models. When the mass in mass marketing leaves the room, so do big profits.

It may be true, as they said in the baseball movie, *Field of Dreams*, "*if you build it they will come.*" But when only nine people show up, you may have a baseball team, but not much of a business model.

So, while a few people have been making money – like Google and eBay, it's been a tough road. It could stay that way for a while.

Until a relatively practical, reasonably easy-to-execute business model comes along, all this revolutionary change may not be the road to riches.

But it sure is one heck of a ride.

The Rise of Design

As we move across media forms and types of marketing communication, we need to be thinking less as art directors, concerned with designing an ad for optimum effectiveness in traditional media, and more like designers – concerned with the graphic rhythm of the brand in the overall environment.

If you've ever seen a graphic standards book – where designers look at everything from letterhead to retail environments to corporate communications, you see how this approach is a more natural fit with the multi-media needs of today's modern brands.

It's interesting that two of the most successful advertising art directors today – Rich Silverstein and Alex Bogusky – actually think of themselves more as designers.

Rich Silverstein.

Rich takes a classic craft-based approach. He calls himself a designer trapped in an advertising body. He'll often work to get the logo right before he worries about the advertising.

He tries for solutions that are *"brilliantly created and brutally simplistic."*

Silverstein came to advertising with a design background that included everything from logo design to pasting up type mechanicals for magazines.

His dedication to the craft continues, even in a high-tech world.

MCLUHAN (CONT.)

It might be good exercise for your brain if you think of a few examples.

R = Retrieval.

Sometimes things come back.

E-mail helped recover letter-writing.

Text messaging is a curious new reductionist version. OMG, LOL, FYI.

As equipment improves and bandwidth expands (thanks to Moore's Law), video connections will expand and we may have new forms emerge – which will retrieve old forms in brand new ways.

F = The "Flip."

When things go far enough they can sometimes "flip." They almost become the opposite... or something else entirely.

In my view, this happened to advertising.

Instead of viewing commercials that get us to consume the thing advertised, we merely consume the advertising!

How many car and beverage commercials do we consume in a weekend?

Too often, these calorie-free bubbles of entertainment leave no permanent impression on our over-stimulated brains.

Give this some thought.

E.O.R.F.

It's a useful anagram, even though it's not very memorable.

(By the way, we've posted a little bit of McLuhan himself talking about this in the AdBuzz Theater. Thanks to Stephanie McLuhan. If you want to see more, seek out "The Video McLuhan.")

Das Auto.
Classic European design.

got milk?

Classic Silverstein.
Brilliant type choice.

UNLIMITED HEADROOM.

THE ALL-NEW MINI CONVERTIBLE. ALWAYS OPEN.

MEDIA IN ACTION.
Bogusky's influence holds, even though they no longer handle the account.
  Here is a vertical layout.

ARE YOU MEDIA AGNOSTIC?
Be sure to read the sidebar story about Boots and Naked Communications.

Alex Bogusky.
  Alex has more of an extra-environmental view – he and his crew are looking for "social friction points" and "talk value."
  Alex was almost born to design.
  Both his parents were graphic designers. "*It's the family business. It's what we Bogusky's do.*"
  Alex really wanted to be a motocross racer, and then a professional windsurfer.
  Instead, he chose something riskier and more dangerous – advertising.
  You can see the Bogusky design heritage in campaigns like Mini, where the design vision is maintained from the sticker on the car in the dealership all the way through to the billboard. Now you can see that same sense of design in their work for VW.
  CP+B brings that total design commitment to all their accounts.

DESIGNERS FIRST.
Rich Silverstein and Alex Bogusky are two of the industry's top advertising art directors, but they both think of themselves as designers first.
  And, just as the first Creative Revolution was, in many ways, led by the designer Paul Rand, this one may also find many designers leading the way.

Job Evolution
It's not just media that's evolving.
  Jobs are evolving, too.
  Just as the scope of many jobs is moving from traditional advertising to new media forms and op-portunities, other jobs are evolving as well.

FROM RESEARCH TO ACCOUNT PLANNING. Market researchers are still around – but you will more and more deal with an interesting new breed called Account Planners.

They work to help you understand your communication task by giving you insights into the product category and the target consumer.

This evolution started in England – though many of the planners were Scottish (long story) – and migrated to the US thanks to Jay Chiat at Chiat/Day.

Today, most agencies use account planners – but, in some cases, the job has evolved further.

FROM MEDIA PLANNING TO CONNECTION PLANNING.

Big agencies used to have Media Departments. Creatives seldom saw them – maybe in a big meeting where they gave the Media Plan before or after you presented "the creative."

They didn't miss us, though. Some Media Rep was always taking them to lunch or a golf outing.

Today, the wide range of media options makes the media decision a creative decision.

And, since media effectiveness overall has deteriorated, it's now more important to build a synergy between creative and media – to get traction in an overcrowded media environment.

That's why media planning has evolved.

New kinds of planners are examining how we relate to our media environment.

Their concern – the "message windows" that allow us to avoid the noise and achieve some sort of effective communication.

That's the basic thinking behind CP+B having "Creative Content Distribution" as a key function.

But whatever you call it, the new creative task is often not only "what's the message?" but "where does it go?"

NAKED COMMUNICATIONS AND BOOTS.

The classic example of this shift comes from a British consultancy known as Naked Communications – a group claiming to be "media agnostic."

Naked was hired by Boots, a major British drugstore chain. The project – implement a program related to fulfilling prescriptions. Much had been spent on advertising to little effect.

Kill the Advertising.

Naked examined the problem and recommended that Boots eliminate all advertising.

Instead, they told Boots to implement a training program for their personnel – and to approach customers waiting for prescriptions to be filled, and tell them about Boots' new service.

Guess what? The program was very successful – for far less money.

Old formulas and business practices that may have worked in the past, have to be re-examined.

The new belief is "media agnostic."

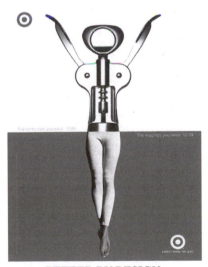

BETTER BY DESIGN.
Target has built a strong position by adding a few nicely designed items to their very basic offerings.

Their stylish advertising also adds value. So people feel better shopping for their everyday items at "Tar-gét."

DEAR DIARY...
Track yourself through a typical day.
What's your "personal media network?"

Me
WAKE UP

LUNCH

DINNER

SLEEP

The You Network.

TO STATE THE OBVIOUS, your media behavior has changed. And you, multiplied by everybody else, is making it a brand new media world.

Before we think about everybody else, let's think about you.

At the end of this chapter, we're including an exercise that has you keep a media diary – for a day and for a week.

A WORLD OF MEDIA OPPORTUNITY.

As you keep your media diary, remember that almost everything is a media opportunity.

The aisles of the store where you shop and make purchase decisions.

The place you go for entertainment on Friday night, whether it's a movie, a concert, or a comfortable couch. The place you looked for that Friday entertainment: online, or a newspaper, or a friend's recommendation. Remember, word of mouth is one of the most powerful and persuasive media channels.

WHERE ARE THE "MESSAGE WINDOWS?"

During your busy media-filled daze – excuse me, that's days – what and when are the moments it's best to connect with you?

Remember, the world is a media opportunity. What are the best opportunities to reach you?

You also need to realize that this can vary by purchase category.

The Friday paper or an alternative weekly might be the right window for weekend entertainment.

What screen is the best way to connect with you. How? When? How do I get a pizza or sandwich coupon in your hands?

Is there anyplace where you're in a purchasing mode and might like some help?

A store aisle? The mall? Doing a map search for the nearest shoe repair?

See what we're driving at?

And, if you're driving, is there anything else we can do to help steer you?

Aperture.

There's another word for "message window." "Aperture."

DDB defines it as *"When, where, and under what circumstances will the target be most receptive to the message?"* Obviously, breakfast specials and spicy pizza will fit best in different dayparts. But when? And where?

There's time of day and time of year.

For example, you might notice more weight loss ads right after the holidays.

Brand Contact Points.

Another concept is the "brand contact point."

It's those moments in which the brand touches you (and vice versa), whether it's an ad in traditional media, a package on a shelf, or a logo on a T-shirt.

Don't underestimate environmental presence. Now the whole world is a media opportunity, remember?

IMC gurus Don Schultz and Beth Barnes remind us that brand contacts *"occur whenever customers or prospects have contact with a particular brand or organization over time.*

"Every exposure has the potential to provide some new information or message to the consumer about what the brand is, how it is used, who uses it, when it is relevant, and on and on."

Brand awareness is, in the main, a cumulative function. In theory, the more appropriate brand

You're just 5 minutes from Cathedral Ridge
TURN RIGHT .8 MILES • COUNTRY CLUB RD.

DIRECTIONALS.
Still a great way to use outdoor.

HOW MANY SCREENS?
Now your personal media network has multiple screens.

The First Screen.
That's your television. Many homes have more than one. They're getting bigger, and with the shift to digital television, capabilities will expand further.

The Second Screen.
That's your computer. Online searching, e-mail, Facebook updates, a bit of music downloading (hopefully, legal – you really do need to give your support to those whose music you care about), and maybe a viral video on YouTube.

As we've discussed, this part of your life has grown into a greater and greater share of your media consumption. Might be interesting to keep track of it for a bit.

The Third Screen.
What's that? It's the growing-ever-larger screen on your mobile communication device. Cell phone, BlackBerry, iPhone, whatever… this increasingly important bit of digital connection is having its own impact.

How do you use yours?

And Everything Else.
How about other traditional media?
Did you listen to some radio?
When? Why?

What have you been reading? Magazines? A newspaper? What kind of newspaper? Was it the traditional daily or an "alternative" weekly. When did you read it? Every day or just on Friday to check the movie times?

And then there's the movie screen…

**ALL THE WORLD
IS A MEDIA BUY.**

Today, there are more and more messaging opportunities. The good news – more chances to be unique and creative.

The bad news – more clutter.

**OFF-ROADING ON
TIMES SQUARE**

This multi-billboard spectacular climbs up the walls of a Times Square building to dramatize Land Rover's off-road capabilities. With the growth in unique sites for messaging, there is more attention to design that relates to the specific environment.

contact points you can place in the environment, the more effective your program will be.

PERSONAL MEDIA NETWORK. When we first heard this phrase, it was trademarked by DDB.

They defined it as "*the combination of media vehicles a customer individually selects to satisfy his or her individual needs.*"

With our thanks to DDB, let's really start to think about how we use media.

So, what are you waiting for?

Time to start your media diary, isn't it?

And for those who sincerely say, "Hey, I want to be a copywriter, not a media research analyst," we'd note that the really good agencies are sliding into this space – like CP+B's Creative Content Distribution and the work that is being done by Connection Planners.

More and more, we not only need to say the right thing, we need to say it at the right place and the right time.

And now, there are more and more unique places to place those messages.

All of this adds up to exciting new challenges for everyone who crafts messages.

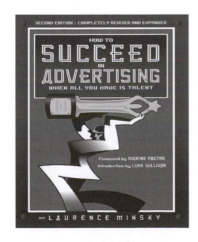

**FOR EVERYONE WHO
CRAFTS MESSAGES.**

An amazing collection of interviews with eighteen of the top creatives in the history of advertising: Ed McCabe, Roy Grace, Lee Clow, Rich Silverstein, Alex Bogusky and more. You must have this book. From The Copy Workshop. (Of course.)

Media Evolution

NOW LET'S TAKE A LOOK at the impact media
evolution is having on traditional media forms.

Traditional Media	Traditional Skills	New Media	New Considerations
Basic Brand-Building	Environmental Strategy Design (Logo/etc.)	Domain Name(s) Online Presence	Digital Strategy Engagement, Memorability Relevance, "Stickiness" SEO + Google Ranking
Posters/Billboards	Clear and clever Local Customization (Directionals)	Banner Ads Video Boards	Simple Animation Plus Click-through Response. Animation Interactivity
Brochure/Catalog	Complete Information Good Organization Clear and Involving Copy Easy Ordering (if Appropriate) 800#s and Order Forms	Website	Menu/Navigation "Sticky" Involving E-Commerce (if Appropriate) Database Capture
Print/Direct Response	Headline + Opening Sentence + Offer Generate Response Not Perceived as "Junk Mail"	E-mail	Subject Header Initial Impression Click-through Response Not Perceived as "Spam"
Print/Brand Building	Reinforce Brand Values Build Awareness to Influ- ence Purchase Decision	Online Display	Generate Online Involvement SEO – Search Engine Optimization
Radio	"Theater of the Mind" "Write for the Ear."	Podcasts HD Radio	Podcast Programming Add Interactivity to Radio
Television	Audio/Visual Integration Involving "Cut through Clutter" **Infomercials** Long-form Video Using Classic Direct Marketing Techniques w/ 800 #s	Video/Viral	Generate Online Interest Turn Interest into Commerce Drive Traffic to Site **Infomercials** Long-form Video with New Interactive Capabilities

After looking at the brief summary chart on the previous page, let's take more of an in-depth look.

DESIGNING MINDS.

Basic Brand-Building	Environmental Strategy Design (Logo/etc.)	Domain Name(s)	Digital Strategy
		Online Presence	Engagement, Memorability Relevance, "Stickiness" SEO + Google Ranking

RETAIL BRANDS.

Design wall to wall.

In the beginning, we will all need to think like designers as we build our brands.

Design considers the brand and its graphic presence within the entire relevant environment – ranging from internal communication, to the retail environment, to final usage. There is a consideration of "touch points" or "brand contact points" Today, those contact points extend into New Media.

And every brand needs to have an appropriate digital strategy as part of its branding strategy.

OUT-OF-HOME EVOLUTION.

Posters/Billboards	Clear and Clever Local Customization (Directionals)	Banner Ads	Simple Animation Plus Click-through Response.
		Video Boards	Animation Interactivity

SEE HOW THIS WORKS?

Mom is taking a picture of her daughter in front of a McDonald's in Piccadilly Circus – a major tourist location.

See the little billboard with the bowler hat? It's kind of up and in back.

Now, the photo will have the bowler hat on the little girl's head – cute.

The McDonald's board rotates a number of images that allow tourists to snap a fun (Continued on next page.)

Outdoor, or, more accurately, out-of-home is undergoing revolutionary change due to two complementary trends: media fragmentation and technology.

Traditionally, low-cost outdoor impressions were discounted somewhat by media planners since the impression was "low-quality" compared to print and television.

But, with media fragmentation, the quality of impressions in all those other media options has been reduced, so the relative quality of an outdoor impression has improved.

Second, the rise of a variety of large video screen technologies has turned once passive and difficult to change outdoor displays into giant TV screens. In smaller venues, smaller units are now affordable: in office elevators, movie lobbies, bus stops, taxicabs, bars, and anywhere an argument can be made for the delivery of a profitable audience.

SEE HOW THIS WORKS (CONT.).
photo or a short phone video. Thought balloons… steam coming out of ears… it's pretty neat.

To see the video, search McDonald's Piccadilly Circus on YouTube.

As they say, "When designing a mouse-trap, leave room for the mouse."

FROM BROCHURE TO WEBSITE.

Brochure/Catalog	Complete Information	Website	Menu/Navigation
	Good Organization		
	Clear and Involving Copy		"Sticky" Involving
	Easy Ordering (if appropriate)		e-Commerce (if Appropriate)
	800#s and Order Forms		Database Capture

Traditionally, every business needs some sort of brochure. Whether a bank with a brochure for virtually every financial product, a bit of real estate, a hotel or tourist destination, a piece of high-tech hardware, or a low-tech item that needs a piece of material for the sales force, there always seems to be a need to say everything somewhere.

The addition of new media forms has also caused the evolution of this bit of marketing basics.

Sometimes it's total replacement – the brochure is turned into a pdf that can be downloaded and printed out on the printers of those interested.

Other times, the website becomes a whole new communication channel.

In either case, there are new considerations – primarily those of navigation.

One seldom needs navigational help with a traditional brochure or catalog. But, when online, even when things are fairly obvious, we are obliged to put in clear and engaging navigational cues to assist those who come to our website – some come on purpose with a clear mission, but others are just wandering through and we need to provide them with as much help as is practical to optimize the value of their visit.

WORKING TOGETHER

Lands' End has evolved from a traditional mail order marketer to e-commerce. They were an "early adopter," launching their site in 1995. In business volume, they are the world's largest apparel website. They have also pioneered new ways to enhance the online shopping experience and foster one-on-one relationships with customers.

NOW ALL PRINT IS DIRECT RESPONSE.

Print/Direct Response	Headline + Opening	e-mail	Subject Header
	Sentence + Offer		Initial Impression
	Generate Response (Purchase or Donation)		Click-through Response
	Problem: "Junk Mail"		Problem: "Spam"

SIMPLE MESSAGING.

With a URL address, you can focus your print on a strong, simple message, and let those interested find out more by going to the site.

But be sure that the site delivers once you get there.

Before Google, an easy-to-remember URL was necessary. Now you just need to be easy to find.

As McLuhan observes, when media evolves, often older forms are "retrieved."

New Media has "retrieved" classic direct, as the essence of interactivity is response.

While individual response levels remain low – often just a percentage point or a fraction of a percentage point – when the opportunities expand dramatically and the delivery costs plummet, the result is still quite profound.

Now clients that might never have considered a direct response effort due to the cost barriers of traditional direct can jump right in.

In addition, the cost and speed of learning which direct response approach was most effective were quite high with traditional direct. With websites and other new media tactics, the costs are low. Plus, you can get response rates much faster.

That's a recipe for revolutionary change.

Now all marketing is direct response marketing – just remember to include a URL.

Print/Brand Building	Reinforce Brand Values	Online Display	Generate Online Involvement
	Build Awareness to Influence Purchase Decision		SEO - Search Engine Optimization

Traditional print advertising is evolving as well.

Now, many print ads are turning into page-size outdoor boards. You will see a lot of dramatic poster-like ads and very little copy.

But, sometimes, copy is still needed.

An example is the "considered purchase," where consumers want more information before buying. For products like drugs and financial services, there are legal requirements.

Other traditional print categories remain. You may need retail information like price and location, short summaries of benefits, or a reminder that the company is still in business.

Most print ads now include New Media information – usually a URL.

And cars brag about their computing power.

THE SOUND OF "CREATIVE DESTRUCTION."

Radio	"Theater of the Mind"	Podcasts	Podcast Programming
	"Write for the Ear."	HD Radio	Add Interactivity to Radio

Audio has taken a dead center hit from the "creative destruction" of new media and has yet to emerge with a viable business model.

Destruction seems to have the upper hand.

But let's take a quick look at what has happened in the larger world of radio and music.

First, individuals – including you – are listening to just as much music, but less radio.

Your iPod, or other music delivery system has replaced a large chunk of that media time.

The radio industry has been hit by declining audiences and declining responsiveness to the ads they depend on for revenue.

At the same time, the music industry has taken its own hit – non-compensated music copying has been a financial disaster.

As individuals, you may be enjoying as much music as ever, but loss of control over Intellectual Property has had a devastating impact.

If you enjoy music, we might pause to remind you that it will be a better world if you provide

HD RADIO.

Soon, this sidebar will be old news.

But since a lot of you reading this are just entering the media world, it'll still probably be news to you.

Here's what's going on.

MultiCasting.

Radio channels are now broadcasting digital signals.

Basically, that means they can pump more information into the airwaves.

They can broadcast more than one channel. So the smooth jazz channel, which I don't like much, can add a real jazz channel. I might like that.

They can broadcast more information, with visuals on your computer screen.

What's that song? With the right digital receiver, you can see what the song is.

Even tag it to download later.

For a small fee.

Advertising Evolution.

Radio ads will have new dimension as well.

That pizza special? Click here and download a coupon for extra pepperoni.

Those concert tickets? No problem.

(Continued on next page.)

HD RADIO (CONT.).

Thanks to a fanbase/database, everyone who's into Punk Country can download the new band CowKiller, along with the optional tattoo.

Hit the Buy button and order the T-shirt, video game, and Guitar Hero Play-Along.

Radio is getting more interactive.

Additional Improvements.

Surround sound? Sure.

Store-and-replay features will probably become standard on the better HD radios – though we don't know how we feel about fast forwarding the commercials.

Text capabilities will provide song and artist names, on demand retrieval of weather, traffic, and sports scores.

Tune in to Opportunity.

Somebody is going to make money on this new technology.

Though, not always the ones you think.

But, if you're interested in radio and all the interesting ways we can communicate in audio, pay attention to an exciting media in the middle of a little revolution of its own.

appropriate financial support to the musicians who make the music you like – and the companies that work for the musicians you like.

You might not feel like a criminal as you dance to the latest album you downloaded, but those who made that music are being robbed of their livelihood if you don't pay for it. End of public service announcement.

As this edition was going to press, major upgrades, such as HD radio, were being implemented, with useful features and applications, such as being able to order the song you just heard or the ability to respond online to the radio commercial you just heard. This will add new levels of interaction. Meanwhile, we will be seeing and hearing important improvements in this media form.

If you enjoy music and creating audio messages, pay attention to the changes going on.

"NOW WE'RE ALL BROADCASTERS."

Television	Audio/Visual	Video/Viral	Generate Online Interest
	Integration		Turn Interest into Commerce
	Involving "Cut through Clutter"		Drive Traffic to Site
	Infomercials		**Infomercials**
	Long-form Video Using Classic Direct Marketing Techniques w/ 800 #s		Long-form Video with New Interactive Capabilities

THE EIGHMEY BLOG.

One of the hidden treasures on the 'Net is http://eighmey.blogspot.com/ – containing the observations of John Eighmey, a former Y&R exec, now an ad professor at the University of Minnesota.

His blog posts observations about advertising and helpful sources for thinking about advertising.

John consistently comes up with thought-provoking examples of work that is both effective and an outstanding representation of the use of contemporary techniques.

(Continued on next page.)

It's a profound evolution. With the Internet, we've all become broadcasters.

But this evolution is still in process.

Here, the evolution is, in many ways, a function of bandwidth with a related factor being the increasing availability and ease of use of video production technology, such as HD video, and editing programs, such as FinalCut Pro.

In addition, the evolution is spreading out past traditional advertising formats like 10/30/60.

Moore's Law has resulted in relatively low-cost, high-quality, and easy-to-use video tools. Growing bandwidth and storage capacity is making relatively large video files easier and easier to transmit.

This is something that you may take for granted.

However, in the course of history, this is an absolutely profound and paradigm-shattering situation.

The erosion of the traditional broadcast model and the growth of new forms and new channels is all a part of it. This situation is so volatile that it would be foolish to even attempt a prediction.

But the good news is the basic principles of creating interesting video messages still work.

THE GROWTH OF THE INFOMERCIAL.

One more note – as video channels expand, there will be additional opportunities for the "Infomercial" format – program-like video presentations for some unique product or service.

Here, the lowered barriers to entry and lower video production costs will expand opportunities.

What's more, a longer form may be a better way to sell – particularly with complex products and those with features that do not lend themselves to short-form communication.

Another thing to consider – your own communication skills. Keeping yourself tied to short-form communication may also limit your perception of the possibilities that are now available.

BUT WAIT, THERE'S MORE.

You might want to pay attention to how these long-form videos work. If you see certain techniques being repeated, it's probably because they're effective.

You may not like 'em, but remember… if you see 'em a lot, they're probably working.

#8: Evolutionary Thinking

EXTEND YOURSELF.

As the Media Revolution rolls, here are three ways to upgrade your brain into a bit of McLuhanThink.

1. Everything is an Extension. This is McLuhan's "fits all sizes" concept. Shoes are extensions of our feet, the car is an extension of our legs, media is an extension of our sensory awareness. (A travel brochure extends your awareness onto a cruise ship.)

2. The Medium is the Message. Here, he means that the medium itself has a profound effect on human behavior. It's not the phone call, it's the fact of the phone – connecting us all – and, now, with mobility added, society and our behavior will be affected further.

3. Hot/Cool. If you're a bit removed from the medium, it's cool. If you're immersed, it's hot. And don't be overly simplistic about any one type of media. Background music is one, and an iPod pounding into your brain at top volume is something else. It's a measure of the degree to which you are engaged. And, while some media forms may be inherently "hotter" or "cooler" than others, we also help set the temperature.

Now you have a basic grasp of the concepts.

Let's use them to notice the continuing change in the media environment that surrounds you.

Very often, the cutting edge of technology will offer you some new opportunities to make those fresh connections.

OK, let's give those brand new brain cells a bit of exercise with McLuhan's E.O.R.F.

1. E = Extension.
Start by choosing an important part of your life. First, your cell phone. Then, something else. Think. What is being extended? What is amplified?
For your cell phone: _____
For _____: _____

2. O = Obsolescence.
What is now becoming obsolete?
For your cell phone: _____
For _____: _____

3. R = Retrieval.
What is being retrieved or brought back?
By your cell phone: _____
By _____: _____

4. F = "Flip."
Where is "The Flip?"
How might the cell phone be transformed?

_____
_____

#9: Personal Media Network

Here's a "stretching" exercise to help you think about the range of IMC opportunities.

Discover your own "Personal Media Network."

1. Track yourself through a typical day – what "media" are part of your network?

Me
WAKE UP

LUNCH

DINNER

SLEEP

2. When and where were the best opportunities to reach you? What's your Aperture?

3. How does your Personal Media Network differ on the weekend?

A BIT MORE ON THE PERSONAL MEDIA NETWORK.

Keith Reinhard, former head of DDB, wants you to think about your "Personal Media Network." That's the way you spend your media day.

What is the media experience from the point of view of the individual target customer?

Aperture™.

A related concept is Aperture™.

What is the best time to reach that person for your product?

It includes places and habit patterns – when and why they read, watch TV, or listen to radio.

For example, is the media for information, entertainment, or background?

It also includes things you might not think of as media, like the package itself.

Thinking like this can help pizza companies decide to advertise just before halftime on a football game.

Thinking like this can help you add in-store advertising to complement your TV schedule.

Helpful Hint.

A good way to get to know your target is to look at their media.

For example, if you have a business trade ad, look through the trade journals where your ad will appear.

Where can you be reached? And when? To be effective, your message has to be at the right place and at the right time. Then, if it's the right message, you've got a shot.

#10: Media Evolution

This exercise may be enjoyable and mind-expanding, or you may hate me for it. (Either way, you can send an e-mail with compliments or complaints.)

The idea is to take a piece of traditional media and evolve it into a piece of new media.

To begin, you'll have to collect the materials listed in the sidebar.

OK – here goes.

1. The Brand – Build a Digital Strategy.

Indicate in a few sentences, the major focus of marketing activities for the brand you've chosen in digital space.

2. Out-of-Home – from Billboard to Banner Ad.

Take your chosen outdoor board and design a banner ad – you can use limited animation, or a more complex interactive format.

Draw a rough of your evolved banner.

If it's more complex, just describe in a sentence (i.e. when you click on a straw the drink level lowers with a loud straw sucking sound).

3. Brochure to Website.

How would you convert this brochure to a website?

Rough out a home page and menu. Indicate on the menu what other sub-pages you'd use. If one would be particularly "sticky" how would you drive traffic to that page and what would happen?

4. From Direct Response to Direct to Your e-Mail.

Turn the direct response package into an e-mail appeal.

How would you deliver various aspects of the package?

COLLECT THE FOLLOWING:

- **An article** about a traditional brand or business that has been around for at least fifty years. *Advertising Age*, *Brand Week*, *Business Week*, and your old friend the Internet have profiles of these companies. For example, Walgreen's.
- **An outdoor board**. Go to the website of the Outdoor Advertising Association of America (www.oaaa.org) and select an award-winning outdoor board you like. You should be able to download a jpeg.
- **Pick up a brochure** at a restaurant, bank, travel agency, or off a card table at the student union.
- **Some direct mail.** Sometime during the week your mailbox, or a friend's mailbox, will receive some direct mail – grab a piece of direct mail that's trying to sell you something.
- **An ad from a current magazine**, like *People* or *Better Homes and Gardens* – one with a lot of ads – select an ad and tear it out of the magazine.
- **A radio spot**. Check out the Mercury Awards (award-winning radio ads – they're on a site sponsored by the Radio Advertising Bureau – www.rab.com). You should be able to download an mp3 – write down – either in general or word-for-word – the radio spot.
- **A TV commercial**. Grab a TV spot off of YouTube or AdForum.

5. Print Ads Go Online.

How would you make the print ad work as a relatively small online display ad?

For now, use a square or large rectangle format – not a banner.

What parts of the message do you have to reduce or eliminate to make this effective online design and communication?

Describe what happens if and when you click on the ad.

6. Radio Response.

Reviewing the radio script, what interactive components might you add?

Assuming that you would see a relatively small amount of online information on your screen as the ad runs, what information would be useful? Anything else?

7. From Video to Viral.

What would you do to the current ad to make the video just a bit more outrageous and encourage viral visits?

How would you encourage additional versions of user-generated versions of this idea?

Could you turn this video idea into a larger digital presence? If so, how?

GOSSAGE ON MCLUHAN.

"Imagine a series of clear plastic domes, one within another.

You can only see them from the outside; from the inside they are invisible.

You become aware of an environment – one of these domes that surrounds you – only when you get outside of it.

At that point, you can see it. But you can't see the one which is now about you."

Gossage's point (and McLuhan's) is that our media environment is a constantly expanding awareness – and each contains our previous environment.

Furthermore…

"In each instance, you will notice that the old environment becomes content for the newer one, never the other way around. McLuhan notes that this seems to work out even in décor. Victorian furniture fits into a modern room, but a modern piece looks simply awful in a Victorian room."

Therefore…

As you think about our evolving media, realize that the content is the previous evolutionary stage.

Today, the computer-driven digital media environment carries all that has gone before… old radio shows, news, TV, encyclopedias, and, of course, your latest video masterpiece, which are kind of home movies evolved through technology.

The MarCom* Matrix

✻ In this book, we call it MarCom – it's kind of a West Coast term – short for marketing communications.

MILKING OPPORTUNITIES.
The "Got Milk" campaign by Goodby, Silverstein shows how you can grow a simple ad concept into a wide-ranging multi-media campaign.

Visit their www.gotmilk.com site and see things ranging from the mock rock videos for "White Gold" to healthy advice.

There's a bit of PR in their "newsroom" and you can even see their classic advertising online.

OUR CONCEPTUAL MODEL.
The MarCom Matrix. Six major forms of MarCom: Advertising • Public Relations & Publicity • Sales Promotion • Direct Marketing • Event Marketing • New Media (including the Internet).

They all revolve around the "Idea."

What's the Idea?

It could be the idea of the brand, a current ad campaign, or an event.

Put this in the back of your mind as you read the rest of the chapter.

Then, at the end of this chapter, we'll have an initial exercise where you try to develop an idea that works with every part of The MarCom Matrix.

ONCE UPON A TIME, when a manufacturer had a dollar for marketing, it was spent on advertising.

Today, there are a lot of interesting things that can be done with a marketing dollar.

All of these things add up to one big thing called "marketing communications" – MarCom for short.

Today, we need to think about delivering messages across the whole spectrum.

Advertising is no longer the only thing.

Today's copywriters need to be familiar with all the MarCom disciplines. You should know their strengths. You should know the basic tactics.

Here's a simple conceptual model:

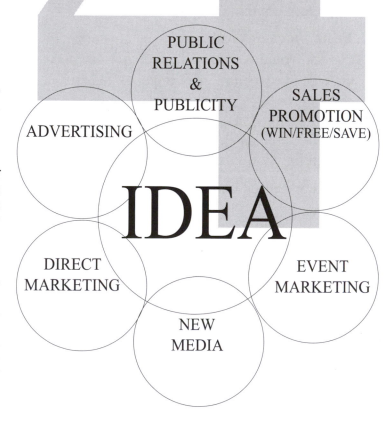

The Basics

Basically, MarCom is strategic communication in support of marketing objectives – communication with a task to accomplish.

Each of the MarCom disciplines has different strengths and weaknesses.

For example, advertising provides total message control, but it's expensive and lacks the credibility of "third-party endorsement." You get more credibility from media messages generated by public relations.

Remember, successful examples can be very successful. And, be aware that ordinary and unsuccessful examples are usually in the majority.

Here's a chart listing strengths and weaknesses.

Of course, unique combinations of messages and delivery channels have the potential to be uniquely effective.

MARCOM IN ACTION.
Here are a few brands who do it well.

Nike mixes sports sponsorship, PR, and web-based media extensions, like nikeplus.com, in addition to their cutting-edge advertising.

Starbucks' main media platform is their store. They extend into music, PR, cause marketing, and, when they perceive special opportunities, traditional advertising.

Apple. CEO Steve Jobs has provided consistent PR, coordinated with product intros. Not surprisingly, they have a solid web platform – what you'd expect from a computer company.

With major growth opportunities (Apple's share is still small), and desirable new products, their well-designed advertising is consistently effective.

Burger King. The humorous and ironic work by CP+B consistently leverages web-based extensions – such as mockumentaries for "Whopper Virgins" and the classic Subservient Chicken.

(*Continued on next page.*)

Strengths & Weaknesses:
Five Forms of Marketing Communications.

Factor	Advertising	Public Relations	Direct Response	Sales Promotion	Personal Selling
Timing	moderate/long	long	short	short	immediate
Control of Message Delivery	total	little	moderate	moderate	little
Control of Message Content	total	minimal	high	high	moderate
Ability to Target	high	low	very high	moderate	moderate
Type of Contact	non-personal	non-personal/ personal	personal/ non-personal	non-personal	personal
Typical Appeals	emotional/rational	image/news	rational/personal	rational	rational
Adds Perceived Value	high	high	moderate	low	low
Credibility	low	high	low	moderate	moderate
Closes Sale	low	low	moderate	high	very high
Trade Acceptability	high	low	moderate	very high	N.A.
Expense	high	low	high	moderate	high
Accountability	low	very low	very high	very high	high
Profit Contribution	moderate	low	moderate	high	moderate

Target, a broad-based retailer, promotes their low-cost offerings with high-style messaging that adds quality perceptions to their offerings.

Get the Message?
Geico takes a simple value proposition and keeps offering it in fresh new ways.

Here, we are reminded of the money we could have saved.

RIGHT PRODUCT, RIGHT TIME...
responds well with appealing advertising. Like the iPod.

Now let's take a short walk through all the ways MarCom works. We're giving you a short introduction to all the MarCom disciplines.

You'll get the sense of each very quickly. But getting good at each will take a bit of work.

One more thing. You're already kind of familiar with them – because you've been a consumer of MarCom for as long as you can remember.

Advertising

You're most familiar with advertising.

Communicating to consumers with an ad message is still usually the biggest part of marketing budgets.

Historically, advertising has been the leading MarCom discipline. But with all the changes going on, that is evolving, too.

Nonetheless, if you have the right product at the right time, advertising can still be a powerful force in the marketplace – even for a product that's been around for 100 years – like orange juice. OK, that's it, for now.

Since we'll spend most of the book focusing on improving your ad-based thinking and writing skills, let's use this chapter to give you a quick intro to the other major MarCom areas.

Sales Promotion
IT'S ABOUT THE BEHAVIOR.
Simply put, promotion strategy is about the behavior you want to "incent."

To incent = to provide an incentive. Or, as my friend and sales promotion adviser Larry Minsky puts it, "what's the bribe?"

Think. What do you want people to do?

Try it for the first time? Buy an extra large size? Use more?

First, you need to determine the behavior. That strategic insight will help you shape your tactic.

One of Colleen Fahey's favorite promotional items involved a dinosaur head squeezer for Heinz Ketchup. Kids would use more because of the fun squeezer head.

You can have a lot of fun thinking up ways to get at that behavior – but you have to begin with that simple concept in mind.

To help you get started, we've posted an article on Sales Promotion by Colleen called *Double your Chances of Finding a Job. Start Your Promotion Portfolio Today*! (You'll find it posted at adbuzz.com/resources/fahey_double.html.)

Sales Promotion is an important part of Mar-Com and, if you're good at it, there are lots of jobs available – even in a tough economy – maybe particularly in a tough economy.

Because, if you're a brand that wants to stimulate buying behavior, hiring people who can do that makes a lot of sense.

INCENTIVES DRIVE BEHAVIOR.
To get the behavior, the incentive is the driver.

For example, one way I can get your attention is to offer you something. A bribe. A free sample. A chance to win a prize. A rebate. A toy in your Happy Meal.

How about that refrigerator magnet with the phone number of a local pizza place?

That's a promotional product with the intent of stimulating phone dialing behavior.

If you provided an incentive to a sales person, do you think that might affect their behavior?

You bet. That's a trade promotion. You might incent the store manager to put up your display, or

AND THEY SAID WE COULDN'T GIVE IT AWAY.

Sales Promotion *uses an incentive to stimulate sales. With the right incentive, you can usually get people to try something once. After that, the product better deliver.*

BIULD YOUR BRAND.
An annual sales promotion event can become part of a brand's heritage – like the Pillsbury Bake-Off.

DON'T FORGET THE TRADE.
The people that run the stores are usually a key part of your promotional program.

AEROSPACE JORDAN MPR PLAN:
Here's Nike's MPR program for the pre-miere of their second Michael Jordan & Bugs Bunny spot on the Super Bowl:

1/7 – Mailing of Letter and Stills
These confirm that Michael is back with Bugs.
Special targeting of major marketing writers, *USA Today* and *Ad Age*.

1/8 – Telephone Interviews with Scott Bedbury, Nike's Director of Advertising.

1/13 – PR Newswire Release
This goes to sportswriters with a new element – Marvin the Martian is the Scream Team coach. Art from the TV spot is included. Entertainment writers are added to the target group.

1/18–FedEx Video News Release #1
- The Nike/Jordan VNR goes out with selected scenes from the commercial. (It isn't finished yet!) Plus…
- Copies of the first Hare Jordan spot.
- **"B-roll interviews"** with Jordan and other Nike-contracted athletes, like Charles Barkley.

1/27–Satellite Release of Second VNR
This VNR includes the completed commercial (finally!), allowing news media to "scoop" the Super Bowl!

With this approach, it is possible that TV sports and entertainment media will pick up the story and play the spot free before it runs on the Super Bowl. That's right, free exposure!
It's treated like news.
This is exactly what happens on both sports and entertainment news features.

1/31 – Super Bowl Sunday!
As you can see, Nike kicked-off their campaign long before the kick-off!

you might provide an incentive to the sales force to recommend your product.

For some products, they might spend more on sales and trade promotion than on advertising.

It's a big part of the MarCom Matrix.

Marketing Public Relations (MPR)

IT'S THE MEDIA.

Next, we'll cover public relations and publicity. Everyone loves good press. It has "third-person credibility," and it's free. Sort of.

Now, we're talking about Public Relations that supports marketing – MPR.

There are other parts of public relations that support other corporate objectives (CPR = Corporate Public Relations), like keeping in touch with stockholders and the financial press.

Here, it's not about what your client wants to say, it's about what's interesting to the media.

Sometimes that involves being unusual, and sometimes it involves making trouble (something that makes some clients nervous). But if you want to get the media's interest, looking like an ad or talking like an ad won't get it done.

You have to be news.

"THE HIDDEN WEAPON."

Successful MPR programs can be key to successful marketing.

National Soup Month? Campbell's pulled it off and stirred up a 36% sales increase.

A feature article in *Gourmet Magazine* titled "The Phenomenal Food Processor" was critical in launching the sales success of Cuisinart.

Ever see a movie called *E.T.*? Product placement of Reese's Pieces increased sales 65% the first month after the movie came out.

Herb Baum, former marketing head of Campbell's Soup, had this to say: *"The hidden weapon is PR... PR is probably more effective in changing consumer attitudes about products today than advertising.*

It is easier for consumers to believe a message if it's coming from an independent third party *than if you're shouting it in an ad."*

THE HARRIS GRID.

Tom Harris, who invented the term Marketing Public Relations has an interesting little grid that helps you focus on what is interesting to the media. It's in the sidebar. Tom's point is some things are interesting to the media and some things aren't.

Did you see the new iMac on the cover of *Time?* Ever read a movie review? How about a review of software in a computer magazine? Or an article about a company in a business magazine?

That's "Marketing Public Relations," (MPR) and it's more important than ever.

THE POWER OF THE THIRD PARTY.

Notice how persuasive testimonials can be?

Or how when a friend recommends something it's going to mean more to you than an ad.

We look at the non-advertising part of our lives with a different mindset.

Of course, every ad will say good things about the brand being advertised, but we look at things like movie reviews, product reviews, articles, and the news quite a bit differently.

We tend to believe a movie review more than an ad. And if an ad uses quotes from movie reviews

		MEDIA INTEREST	
C O N S U M E R I N T E R E S T	H i g h	**High News**	**Low News**
		Computers **(A)** Cars Entertainment	Beer **(C)** Soft Drinks Athletic Shoes
	L o w	Soup **(B)** Cereal Aspirin	Cigarettes **(D)** Car Mufflers Cookies

THE HARRIS GRID.
Certain business categories are more "newsworthy" than others.

With that in mind, Tom Harris created this interesting model for developing your MPR strategy.

The Harris Grid categorizes by Media News Value and Consumer Interest.

"At 60 miles an hour the loudest noise in this new Rolls-Royce comes from the electric clock"

THIRD PARTY CREDIBILITY...
gave extra strength to Ogilvy's headline in this famous Rolls Royce ad.

The line was from a review in a British car magazine.

PR WRITING STYLE.

Remember, writing a press release is different from writing ad copy.

Here are some of the basics:

• **Write it like a news story.** You want it to be newsworthy. It should feel like news. Who. What. When. Where. Why.

• **Start with a strong lead.** Then, use an inverted pyramid form, emphasizing the most important stuff first.

• **Easy on the stylish stuff.** You want the reporters and editors to be the stylish writers – help supply them with good material – but don't compete.

• **Be accurate.** You need to be a good and trustworthy news source. Spell all names correctly. Get the facts straight and the quotes exact.

• **Be specific.** News is about facts. Use examples. Name names, give dates, times, addresses. Provide meaningful, hard information.

• **Do not editorialize.** Try to let the facts speak for themselves. Try to quote others for conclusions.

• **Vary paragraph and sentence lengths.** Be readable, not mechanical.

• **Be clear.** Remember, the language of the news reporter (your initial target audience) is simple, direct, and clear. Yours should be, too.

HOOKS AND LEADS.

How do you "earn" newsworthiness? For a start, you'd better do it with your first sentence.

The "hook," or the lead, is the opening thought of a press release. It's the "headline."

PR firms spend a lot of time doing creative thinking on what is the most interesting angle for their press release.

It is a key strategic decision.

The right lead generates interest, the wrong one doesn't.

(i.e., "third party endorsements") they have more credibility with us. Don't they?

Remember that wonderful headline in Ogilvy's Rolls Royce ad?

It was from a review in a British car magazine.

Done well, MPR can result in press coverage that is worth millions in media exposure (what it would cost if you had to buy it) and the additional value of third party credibility.

IT HAS TO BE "NEWSWORTHY."

Like good advertising, good Marketing PR is also "receiver-driven" communication – with one critical difference. That communication has to be *newsworthy*.

Think about it. If you pay for the ad, you can put pretty much anything you want into that ad.

But when someone else is deciding what to feature in their media – whether it's a national computer magazine or a local radio talk show – they usually have a lot to choose from.

These media "gatekeepers" judge what will be most interesting to readers, listeners, and viewers.

It has to seem newsworthy to them.

Sure, *Advertising Age* and *AdWeek* may carry news about your just-breaking ad campaign, but for regular news channels, it's not news. Unless, like Nike, you can figure out how to make it news.

GREAT ADS. GREAT PR.

Some ad people are also good publicists. The legendary Howard Gossage and Hall of Fame Art Director George Lois are two examples.

Let's spend a minute on George Lois. (We'll talk about Howard Gossage in a bit.)

He not only knew how to generate noise with advertising, he was actively and effectively involved in many political campaigns – needing to work hand-in-hand with PR.

He was a key player in such PR-driven causes as the effort on behalf of Rubin "Hurricane" Carter.

Lois instinctively looked for ways to use PR to increase the impact of his ads – and he was often very successful.

Today, Crispin Porter + Bogusky (CP+B) demonstrates a solid understanding of the power of publicity. It's even part of their planning.

Button for Fund-Raiser.
Designed by George Lois.

Direct Marketing

IT'S THE LIST AND IT'S THE OFFER. Now let's take a peek in your mailboxes – the one where you live and the one on your computer.

That's where marketers direct messages at you for credit cards and travel bargains for Spring Break. That's Direct Marketing.

WHO/WHAT/HOW.
These are the three critical issues:

- **WHO** is the most important thing.
- **WHAT** is the next most important thing.
- **HOW** is the third most important thing you need to think about.

Let's take them one by one:

"The List" – the most important thing is WHO you are talking to.

The first truth of direct marketing is "you're as good as your list." You will have the best results with the best prospects.

Direct marketing is expensive on a per-person basis. With postage, a good mailing could cost $1 a person – or more.

So… one of the first big jobs is making sure we're talking to the right people.

WHAT'S THE BIG IDEA?
How to Win with
Outrageous Ideas that Sell
by George Lois

Words from the master. George Lois knows how to create logos, advertising, advertising agencies, publicity, and controversy.

Each chapter in this readable book highlights one of George's slightly outrageous (and usually very successful) Selling Ideas – like Mick Jagger saying, *"I Want My MTV!"*

The book is out of print, but you should be able to find a copy.

ANATOMY OF A DIRECT MAILING.

Here's a mailing we got from Bose, a smart direct marketer.

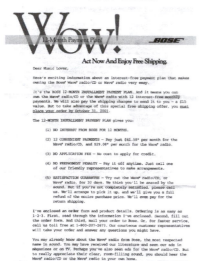

1. The Envelope.

The objective of your envelope is to get your mailing opened for the right reason.

This one asks the question "Why Go Another Day Without Great Sound? Presenting the Bose 12-Month Payment Plan." There's a tasty photo of the Bose CD/Radio. Nice paper, too.

2. The "Wow!" Letter.

Open the envelope, and there's a nice letter – typed on both sides.

The "exciting information" is about an easy way to own the Bose radio.

The appeals are things like "Act Now and Enjoy Free Shipping."

They add up other "savings" like "No Interest" and "No Prepayment Penalty." But wait, there's more…

(Continued on next page.)

Often, some of the best lists are people who are already customers.

When someone is already a customer, you know even more.

The right list is critical in getting your effort off to a solid start.

If you don't do that, everything else is pretty much wasted. Right?

"The Offer" – the next most important thing is "WHAT is the incentive?"

Sometimes the inherent appeal of the product itself is enough.

For example, the Bose Radio.

It looks nice, it sounds nice, and they just sent you a message with your name on it.

But Bose knows they have to do more.

For example, they'll let you try it FREE. And, they'll make it easy for you to purchase by offering easy payments.

See what they're doing? They're reducing or eliminating barriers. Their offer – easy payments and no interest PLUS the Free Home Trial – is designed to overcome those barriers.

"The Message" – Finally, be concerned with HOW you communicate all this.

Getting the message right is also critical. *But remember,* if you're not talking to the right prospects, and if you don't have the right incentive, your good writing will not be as effective.

That said, let's look at what makes good direct. What makes it work?

LESSONS OF THE PIONEERS.

Here's what John Caples (remember him?) has to say.

Now remember, Caples learned many of his lessons when postage was 3¢. People had more time, got less mail, and probably paid more attention to ads.

So you won't get the kind of responses Caples got over 50 years ago, but the basics are pretty much the same. Here are some of his thoughts…

"Times change. People don't. Words like 'free' and 'new' are as potent as ever. Ads that appeal to a reader's self-interest still work.

People may disagree about what self-improvement is important, but we all want to improve ourselves.

Ads that offer news still work.

The subjects that are news change, but the human curiosity to know what's new doesn't. These appeals worked 50 years ago. They work today."

THE IMPORTANCE OF THE BEST OFFER. When a baby joins a family, a new mother is usually made an offer by the company that makes Gerber Baby Food – Send us your name and address, and we'll send you coupons good for *Seven Free Jars* of Gerber Baby Food.

Gerber figured out this was the optimum offer.

Fewer jars would get less response (Would you go to all that trouble for just one or two little jars?). With more than seven jars, the incremental cost wouldn't be worth the incremental response.

That's a simple example of the best offer.

Yet working out the optimum results through test mailings and measuring results can be difficult and time consuming.

BOSE ANATOMY (CONT.)
3. Inserts.

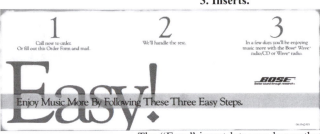

The "Easy" insert lets you know that getting the Bose into your home (their objective) is easy as 1, 2, and 3.

When you open it, you'll find an easy-to-fill-out form – and an 800#.

There's more… to give it a lift…

4. The "Lift" Note.

In case you haven't heard everything, here's a simple but classy brochure.

On the outside, a testimonial. On the inside, some clear, classy "reason why" that tells us "we will enjoy music more."

(Continued on next page.)

119

BOSE ANATOMY (CONT.)

That's the consumer benefit: enjoying music more. Patented technology is the reason why. There are more testimonials and reviews.

5. The Closer.

On the back of the brochure is "The Closer." An "Absolutely No Risk Involved Guarantee." And an envelope.

6. The BRE.

"BRE" stands for Business Reply Envelope. Bose makes it easy for you to pay the way you want to pay. Even though they know a high percentage will use the 800#, they play as many percentages as possible to *maximize return.*

A Quick Review.

Let's think about this mailing again.

Obviously, Bose has been doing this for a while (in direct, respect survival)

What is their current objective?

They know if they can get the Bose into your home, your satisfaction with the product and the hassle of returning it will make their program a success.

Direct marketers work very hard to find out exactly what works best. Then they stick to it.

ON TO E-MAIL.

It's different, but the same.

Lower cost and faster results are big differences. So are spam, "phishing," and other questionable (and criminal) behaviors by certain elements.

Nonetheless, it's an important new way to do direct marketing.

And it's probably no surprise that this is where the direct marketing industry headed – with lots of jobs for people who can do it right.

The basics? Still the same.

Right people. Right offer. Right message.

The lessons learned in old-fashioned direct can help you be successful in that new world waiting in your computer.

The Internet has become the new direct medium.

From e-mail-based direct mail to doing business on websites, the Net is viewed, in many ways, as a whole new platform for direct marketing.

OTHER FORMS OF DIRECT.

Here are some other categories of direct. Some, like DRTV, are pretty big.

DRTV (Direct Response Television). This covers all those infomercials you see, as well as shorter TV spots.

If the purpose of the spot is to get you to respond – either by calling an 800# or going to a website – you're seeing direct marketing at work.

And, of course, there's the telephone.

Telemarketing.

Inbound telemarketing is where the customer (you) responds to an 800# and calls.

Outbound telemarketing is where someone calls you – usually at dinner. Sorry.

Radio. Though almost 50% of all radio commercials feature some sort of response mechanism (an 800# or store address), for a variety of reasons, radio is not currently regarded as a very good response medium. But, for certain "hot" products with good margins, it does work.

Then again, as radio goes online, interaction can kick in, and we think that's going to change things big time. You'll be able to buy and download the song you're listening to. And advertising may be able to make responding easier with a "click here" setting on the site. As a result, radio could become a lot more effective. Stay tuned.

CRM, LTV, AND DATABASE MARKETING. Finally, you really need to understand three more key concepts. We'll be brief.

• **CRM (Customer Relationship Management**): Don't stop with the initial response. You need to understand how to make the most of that relationship from beginning to end.

• **LTV (Lifetime Value):** This is also important. You need to understand the true long-term value of a customer. Not just that first sale, but the lifetime of the relationship.

• **Database Marketing:** This involves understanding how to use data and databases to get at the best prospects for your marketing.

Moving around the MarCom Matrix, we now direct you to…

Soloflex. The Original. They built their business with infomercials. Call Now!

Philips Electronics used the long form of an infomercial to explain their new television technology.

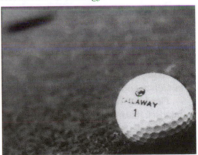
Callaway Golf sold expensive golf balls on outlets like The Golf Channel.

CRM – THE PAYOFF.
"Your payoff comes with repeat business. And whether or not a customer sends in a repeat order depends on the product.
If it delivers what the ad promised, there's a feeling of good value."

Bob Stone

121

NASCAR is just one of the new event-driven marketing programs. It offers entertainment combined with huge sponsorship opportunities. It's a growing area of marketing communications with exciting opportunities for creative messaging.

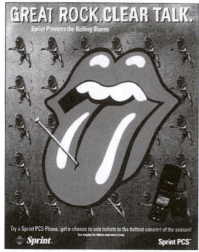

It's an event. It's a promotion. It's advertising. It's publicity. Strong ideas can play anywhere on The Matrix.

Bud World, anyone?

**WHAT'S YOUR
INTERNET STRATEGY?**

Today, every company needs to have an Internet strategy in addition to an advertising and public relations strategy.

As this new media channel matures, you will see a growing range of effective applications that will add up to billions.

Event Marketing

OK, now how about watching a sporting event?

Or maybe you'd like to go to a concert or a festival? Or a NASCAR race?

Marketers are also involved with these events.

In fact, it's an area of explosive opportunity.

The events are often marketers themselves – marketers working with other marketers.

On top of that, the athletes and musicians that make these events special may also be involved in some aspect of marketing communications related to these events.

And there are more kinds of events and involvement than you may realize.

Here are a few.

SPONSORSHIPS.

MPR may organize and supervise or be involved to maximize media publicity.

This covers everything from supporting concert tours, to leveraging local sponsorship of sport teams, to international events like the Olympics and World Cup, to anything having to do with celebrity connections.

One of MPR's important jobs is to maximize the "PR value" of sponsorships.

TRADE SHOWS.

Trade shows may be done by PR or client sales or marketing groups. MPR is involved in the show, regardless, supplying press releases, and connecting with trade media who are also usually in attendance.

For many companies, large and small, these events are critical parts of marketing efforts and well worth a very high "per customer" investment.

CAUSE MARKETING.

Programs like Children's Miracle Network and Campbell's Labels for Education are proven performers in the marketplace.

They demonstrate that doing good can be good business. Working with and coordinating these types of programs, as well as creating the support materials, is another growing part of MarCom.

New Media

Finally, almost every marketer you can think of is trying to build an effective Internet-based program to add effectiveness to their marketing.

There may be other media ideas as well: a custom published magazine, a video, a CD, a DVD – and whatever new combination is created tomorrow.

We'll call all of this all "New Media."

It covers all the new ways marketers are looking to communicate.

It's a new dimension to the media matrix we swim in, shifting from medium to medium – from the TV to your mailbox, to your special interest magazine to that website a friend told you about.

Each represents an opportunity to communicate.

EXPAND YOUR HORIZONS.

The thinking techniques used to create effective ads can also be adapted to develop effective new tactics in new media.

We've seen it demonstrated over and over – as media evolves into new forms, it opens up new ways for marketers to communicate. Time after time, innovators develop profitable new ways.

And, as they attract eyeballs and involvement, advertisers and marketers follow.

GOOD DEEDS. GOOD BUSINESS.
Campbell's Labels for Education builds loyalty with a key group – mothers.

FAULS' FAMOUS, NEVER-QUITE-COMPLETE LIST OF E-TACTICS.

Commercial e-mail – used, in text-only, before Tim Berners-Lee invented the World Wide Web in 1991.

Static Banner Ads – from 1994 (first ad, from AT&T, on hotwired.com).

Rich Media Display Ads – from 1996 (first ad, from HP, let you play a branded game of Pong).

Other Kinds of Online Ads:
- Companion ads
- In-page video ads
- Peel-back ads
- Expanding ads
- Floating, overlay, or "takeover" ads
- Pop-up and pop-under display ads – first used around 1997
- In-text ads (e.g., vibrantmedia.com)
- Online radio ads

PPC (Pay Per Click) Search Ads – from around 1999.

SEO (Search Engine Optimization) – from late '90s.

Paid Inclusion – from late '90s.

Blogging – begun in late 90's, adding advertising in the early 2000's.

Microblogging – with mini-banners ads from 2008.

(Continued on next page.)

Social Media for Marketing – from around 2003.
- Data-targeted ads
- Brand profile pages
- Widgets or apps

Branded Video Content – notable early example, BMW films in 2001.

Video Ads:
- pre-roll
- mid-roll
- post-roll
- overlays
- branded channels on sites like YouTube

Game Marketing:
- in-game ads
- advergames
- ARG (Alternate Reality Games)
- in-game brand placement and integration

Microsites

Sponsorships

Contextual Ad Targeting

Behavioral Ad Targeting

Mobile Marketing – permission-based in the US:
- SMS alerts – short message service text ads, up to 160 characters
- MMS ads – Multi-Media Message Service – adds graphics, video, and sound to mobile messages
- Location based mobile marketing
- Branded apps, e.g., Kraft's iFood

Thanks to Tom Fauls of Boston University.

New Media represents a whole new range of exciting opportunities – one that's expanding with possibility every day. It's McLuhan's "extensions" on steroids.

STRENGTHS AND WEAKNESSES.
But it won't necessarily be easy.

We're certainly all highly aware of the advantages of online messaging.

Cost of entry can be very low. Good news.

If you're a hit, you get forwarded on millions of e-mails – and attract millions of customers with zero spending.

All sorts of things that are expensive in traditional media – color, sound, animation, etc. are relatively inexpensive online. More good news.

But before we get totally dazzled by all that new media wonderfulness, let's also take a look at some of the real problems in the real world.

Some of this is based on a recent study from the 4As and "The Surprising Economics of Digital Marketing" (*Ad Age* 3/18/09).

There are some problems.

First, it's more complicated.

The process of getting an ad into traditional media is pretty straightforward. We all know how to produce it and we've been doing it for years.

It's easy to get people who know how to do an ad. But that new online concept? Not so easy.

And the more cutting edge never-been-done-before you are, the more complex it can get.

Add in customization and more wonderful new ideas and a client request or two, and the complexity keeps rising.

Second, you have to add a new department.

Unlike traditional media, like a television spot, where you go to an experienced production source, online pretty much demands that you do a lot of the work in-house.

Sure, you can go to experts, but if you go down the outsource road, *"pretty soon you've outsourced the whole project."*

Third, it makes you reorganize.

All of this connection planning, creatives thinking about media, and media thinking creatively can wreak havoc with the traditional organization chart. It isn't just adding that new department, which was the second point. New media efforts may start reorganizing everyone else as well.

While you might uncover some hidden talents and organizational strengths, you do it while unraveling what you already do.

Fourth, you probably need to add staff.

These new job functions need new talents.

At the same time agencies are dealing with tremendous cost pressures, this can be additionally disruptive – and expensive for clients as well.

AN EXCITING NEW WORLD.

Nobody said revolutions were going to be easy.

Exciting, yes. Easy, no. But it is most definitely a world that's creating exciting new communication, new capabilities, and new opportunities.

It's a "shiny new toy" and everybody wants some. But client and agency alike may be surprised at the amount of staff time and billable hours these digital projects can soak up.

So, as we work to generate new efficiencies and exciting new programs, let's try to avoid "catching mice with a cheese truck."

That said, there's an exciting new world of new media waiting out there for you.

In the sidebar we've listed just a few of the exciting things we can do in New Media.

IS THIS YOUR SHIRT?

If so, Miss Afflerbach will send you your [ ] label

THIS is a two-color striped button-down shirt designed and tailored by Eagle Shirtmakers and sold everywhere by fine men's stores. Many of them admire our shirts so much they sell them under their own names. High praise indeed, and we should like to reciprocate by advertising their (our) shirts. But it's hard to know just where to start. Obviously we can't say things like "None Genuine Without This Label" when they are all quite genuine, you know. And it would be silly to say "Try An Eagle Shirt Today!" when it is likely you already have a drawerful; even though you didn't know it until just this minute. So all we can suggest is that you send in for your Eagle label. Write Eagle Shirtmakers, Quakertown, Pennsylvania; Attention Miss Afflerbach.

AHEAD OF HIS TIME.

Now we're going to spend a page or two telling you about an advertising legend from 30 years ago – Howard Gossage. The ad man who introduced the world to Marshall McLuhan.

He was interactive before there was interactive. He had a way of looking at things in an "extra-environmental" way. Like his ads for Eagle Shirts that set response records in the *New Yorker*. He then turned those responses into a book – a media extension.

Here, we'll show you what we mean.

Every marketer has to decide the role that New Media will play in their marketing. The Apple Store was part of Apple's commitment to do more business on the Internet. Retailers weren't happy.

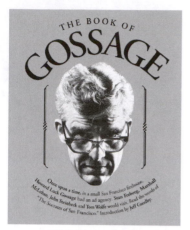

"Nobody reads ads.
They read what interests them."

Howard Luck Gossage

His agency was in an old San Francisco firehouse – no one knew how to start a bigger media fire with fewer ad dollars.

Gossage was also concerned with larger issues – like mass media being taken over by mass marketers – hot dog vendors taking over a football game.

Howard Gossage

HE WAS "MASTER OF THE MATRIX."

Gossage wrote ads – but his ads were more than advertising. His ads launched fads, contests, social movements, books, the Beethoven sweatshirt, and mountains of free publicity.

He introduced the world to the thinking of media guru Marshall McLuhan.

His ads for the Sierra Club helped launch the modern environmental movement.

One Gossage ad almost formed a small Caribbean country – it was debated in the House of Commons.

Basically, Gossage understood how advertising could be made to play a part on a larger media stage – acting as a catalyst for a larger media presence.

When he conceived an ad, he also thought about how it could grow into something larger.

Today, that's part of what many call IMC and what we call The MarCom Matrix.

For example, he grew a small ad campaign for *Scientific American* into "The First International Paper Airplane Competition."

It created a huge PR buzz and was even made into a book! Gossage simply thought of it as a smart way to make the most of small ad budgets.

Gossage Today. This ad by the San Francisco agency Goodby Silverstein + Partners owes a debt to the work of copywriter Howard Gossage and art director Marget Larsen. It's a disarmingly unique and persuasive piece of communication, written literally from a "bird's eye view."

BE THE FIRST ONE ON YOUR BLOCK TO WIN A KANGAROO!

That's how Howard Gossage got you to think about Australia's airline – Qantas.

Most of his ads included a response device. Gossage believed contests, offers, coupons, and surveys were a great way to involve readers and dramatize some important aspect of the product.

This "spread" was two sides of one page in the New Yorker. *You had to flip it back and forth to understand the offer, which was a strange, useless thing that demonstrated various aspects of Eagle's shirtmaking skills. The ad set new records for responses and even inspired a book (yes, a book), called* Dear Miss Afflerbach or The Postman Hardly Ever Rings 11,342 Times.

IN GOSSAGE'S ADS, YOU COULD:
- ❏ Sign up to walk to Seattle.
- ❏ Get recipes for Irish Coffee.
- ❏ Vote for Pride or Profit.
- ❏ Vote for or against the use of billboards.
- ❏ Fill out a stereo survey.
- ❏ Write your Congressman, the President, or the IRS.
- ❏ Get a free Eagle Shirt Label.
- ❏ Order a Beethoven sweatshirt.

Pride or Profit? The copy for the ad on the left started where the previous ad's copy left off. People looked forward to...

Pink Air spoofed advertising years before The Pink Bunny – for Fina Gas.

It had contests (Your Chance To Win 15 Yards Of Pink Asphalt), premiums (pink balloons and pink valve caps), and the world's longest slogan:

[Our Motto] "If you're driving down the road and you see a Fina station, and it's on your side so you don't have to make a U-Turn through traffic and there aren't six cars waiting and you need gas or something, please stop in."

☞**RESPONSE/INVOLVEMENT**✍

Gossage's agency ran as many as seven coupons in one ad (for The Sierra Club).

He believed it was an important way to involve readers. It did!

127

BE THE FIRST HIGHBROW IN YOUR NEIGHBORHOOD TO OWN A BEETHOVEN, BRAHMS, OR BACH SWEATSHIRT

BEETHOVEN BRAHMS J.S BACH

THREE B's
SWEATSHIRT
COUPON

DUBIOUS PREMISES WITH A LOGICAL OUTCOME.

Gossage believed you could create something very interesting by accepting a premise that wasn't very sensible, like selling Rainier Ale on a classical radio station, and then applying intense logic.

The result? The Beethoven sweatshirt.

[Another Public Service Venture By Rainier Ale]

COACH STAHL WANTS YOU TO WALK TO SEATTLE!

Yes, this is your chance to win a free trip to Seattle's Century 21 World's Fair! And the beauty of it is you will be able to enjoy the great out of doors every step of the way 1000 miles from the Opera House in San Francisco to Seattle and the Space Needle. What finer way to measure man than by what he will still be able to fill his lungs with fresh air amidst the marvels of the 21st Century?

However, man does not live by breath alone.

A JOURNALISTIC APPROACH.

The advertising responds to itself, generating its own story.

Above, Coach Stahl (wearing a Beethoven sweatshirt) kicks off the "Walk to Seattle" campaign.

Ad #2, on the right, is the response to the first ad – announcing the winners of the recruitment campaign.

THE GOSSAGE TOUCH.

One of my favorite Gossage campaigns began when the Media Rep for a classical FM station begged Howard for some business. Howard had a heart as well as a brain.

He thought, how do I combine one my clients, say Rainier Ale, with a classical FM station.

Howard invents the classical sweatshirt, featuring Bach, Brahms, and Beethoven. It becomes a pop fad nationwide.

THEN COACH STAHL SHOWS UP.

He was a retired gym teacher and he wanted a sponsor for a "Hike to Seattle." Most people would kick someone like this out of their office.

Not Gossage.

The first ad recruited a "team" to take the hike.

The next ad showed the team and set them off, and after that, PR took over. Everywhere they hiked, it was news.

Gossage notes, *"The newspaper, television, and radio coverage was enormous. Front page stories with pictures – sometimes five-column pictures – and absolutely no reluctance to mention the client's name.*

"I have a notion that this last may have stemmed from the fact that we didn't mention the product's name in the news releases except as an address to show the origin of the handout."

There was no third ad.

There didn't have to be – Coach Stahl hiking up the West Coast, right through Rainier's best markets, did the job for him.

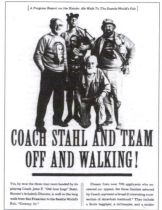

[A Progress Report on the Rainier Ale Walk To The Seattle World's Fair]

COACH STAHL AND TEAM OFF AND WALKING!

Yes, by now the three man team headed by its playing Coach John F. "Old Iron Legs" Stahl, Rainier's Athletic Director, is well on the long walk from San Francisco to the Seattle World's Fair, "Century 21."

Chosen from over 700 applicants who answered our appeal, the three finalists selected by Coach represent a broad if interesting cross-section of American manhood." They include a Scots bagpiper, a millionaire, and a soldier

Matrix Evolution

New media has had an impact on the entire MarCom Matrix.

Public Relations. The Internet is now both a publicity generator and a channel for distributing PR materials.

Press kits are now prepared digitally, Press Releases are sent as e-mails, and speaking engagements become "Webinars."

While barriers to entry for the larger media venues remain high, now it's easy to achieve a PR presence on the World Wide Web.

Sales Promotion. Digital media and interactivity

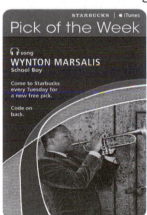

can increase value and reduce costs of promotional programs with on-line redemption, efficient delivery of high-value incentives, and low-cost database accumulation.

Direct Marketing. Low-cost database accumulation is just the beginning.

Interactivity turns virtually every communication into a Direct Response opportunity.

Event Marketing. From pre-event publicity to post-event videos, digital media adds value at every stage of the process.

Look at the sidebar examples.

THE POWER OF CONNECTION.
Remember, the MarCom disciplines often work well together.

And the new connections from New Media give you even more possibilities.

Figure out all the ways that you can make the Matrix help your idea to connect.

And once you do… keep thinking.

You may find that extra dimension of connection that makes it work even better.

EVENT MARKETING EXAMPLES.
- **Online registration** through a dedicated site – or microsite – offers an easy-to-customize opening platform.
- **Custom services** – like event photographs – can be delivered at minimal cost (take the photo, give them a number, they can download the image and print it themselves), and tickets, custom items, and concert recordings can all be handled easily.
- **Interactive kiosks** can add more entertainment value along with additional data capture.

129

#11: Build Your

NEED HELP PICKING A BRAND?

Pick your favorite pizza, software you like, or an upcoming campus event.

Go to the store. Buy something off the shelf – barbecue sauce, a lesser-known beverage (not Coke or Pepsi), or even think about the store itself.

Remember, when you're out there working, you usually won't have much choice about what you work on – so don't worry about it.

Just pick something.

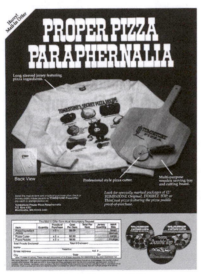

HOW MANY P'S?

How many P's do you want on your pizza?

How will you differentiate?

How will you compete?

Remember, strategy is about choice. So, what do you want on your pizza?

Above, Tombstone tries to get you to buy their frozen pizza with a high-value promotional offer.

OK, let's give our brains a little workout in the various MarCom disciplines.

#1: SALES PROMOTION: TRY/KEEP/RETRY. Remember, your strategy is the behavior you want to motivate. Your tactic motivates that behavior.

Sample Client: Mama's Pizza Parlor. It could be any pizza place, restaurant, or retailer – even a professional services business like a dentist.

Your prices are competitive, your product is fine, and you have lots of new competition.

If you're on campus, you might want to use your favorite pizza place as the sample client.

Assignment: Design messages and offers for each of these three behaviors.

A. **Trial:** Get people to try Mama's Pizza Parlor.

B. **Retention:** Get current customers to keep coming back to Mama's Pizza Parlor (and maybe bring their friends).

C. **Re-Trial:** Get former customers to return.

Assume you have a list of former customers and you can pull out those who have not been back in six months. (Be smart about this. If you're on a campus, realize that many former customers graduated.)

PR Bonus: Create a Customer Newsletter. Do it for your pizza place – or do it for yourself. Make it feel like news.

MarCom Muscles

#2: PUBLIC RELATIONS.
Travel. Pick a State. Travel accounts use a lot of PR – pick a state and do the following:

A. **Develop a Theme** – button & bumper sticker.

B. **Get a Calendar of Events** – think how to turn one into a big tourist draw, or start a new one.

C. **"Third-Party Endorsements."** Make a list of the people who can "endorse" your state: locals, celebrities, those with a unique connection…

#3: DIRECT MARKETING.
Create Your Own Database. Do a Mailing.

You've probably already got one.

It's in your address book or PDA – or maybe it's already in a computer file. Better yet.

You really ought to do this one.

A. **Clean Up Your Database.** Check the entries, add updates. Double-check a few that are in doubt.

B. **Design Your Mailing.** It could be:
   - **A Holiday Card.** Design a card for an upcoming holiday. It could be a big one. Or not.
   - **A Family Announcement.** A new puppy, an award, photo of the family. Whatever.
   - **Your Own Newsletter.** Design a masthead. Write about how you're doing, scan in a photo or two, add a few fun facts, a family update, and perhaps some commentary. Proof it. Print it.

A BASIC OFFER CHECKLIST:

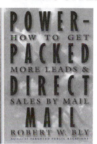

Here's a partial list of offers from Robert W. Bly's excellent book – *Power-Packed Direct Mail.*
- Free Brochure
- Free Booklet
- Free Catalog
- Free Newsletter
- Invitation to Attend a Free Seminar
- Free Trial
- Free Use of a Product
- Free Product Sample
- Free Gift Certificate
- Free Consultation
- Free Estimate
- Free CD or DVD
- Free Gift (for providing names of friends who might be interested in offer)
- Free Special Report
- Free Sample Issue
- Send No Money Now – we will bill you
- Money-back Guarantee
- Enter Our Contest and Win
- Enter Our Sweepstakes and Win
- Enter Our Drawing and Win
- Discount for New Customers
- Surprise Gift
- Order Now – we won't bill you until…
- Order X Amount. Get Y Amount Free
- Free Membership
- Send No Money – pay in easy installments. (Note: this was Bose's offer)

October 2001 landsend.com

LANDS'END

THE BEST-SELLING
REVERSIBLE
DOWN JACKET
IS BACK!
Reg. $89
Sale $68.

REMEMBER LAST WINTER?
GET READY **NOW** AT

OUTERWEAR HEADQUARTERS!

THE CRAFT OF CATALOGUE WRITING.

Direct marketers like Lands' End know how to make money from sending you a catalog of their goods.

Each square inch has to earn its way – either by generating income for the item or by keeping your interest (some super-deluxe items featured in catalogs are there for entertainment value – though even those +$2,000 items do sell).

A Rule of Thumb.

How much do you need to make on an item to make catalog sales worthwhile?

There's a "rule of thumb" in direct that says cost-of-goods should be about one-third to build a good business.

That means if you offer it in a catalog for $33, your basic cost should be no more than $11.

You should also remember that direct marketers generate significant savings by not having the expense of a store or salespeople – so, if they're efficient, you still get a pretty good deal.

Your Assignment.

Pick up some catalogs and study them.

Hey, you might even find something you like. And if you buy it, you'll get to experience a little "CRM" as they work to maximize your "LTV."

See, now you can speak direct.

- **A Fund-Raising Letter.** Maybe you're already involved in something that deserves support. A walk-a-thon, an upcoming charity event. A fund-raising effort. Well, don't just sit there, write a letter asking for funds. And don't be shy about it.

C. **Add a Response Mechanism.**
It may be as simple as listing your phone number and address, or there might be something more you can do – particularly if you're doing the fund-raising version of this assignment.

D. **Get the Envelope or the E-mail Right.**
If it's real mail, get the right size envelope. Print labels, or figure out how to print *on* the envelopes. (If you do that, try to add some additional copy to the envelope.)

Get cool stamps (nice-looking commemoratives). Or, if you've got a lot of them (100 or more), find out how to get a quantity mailing rate. (You'll be smarter knowing what's involved.)

If it's e-mail, use a program that maintains hyperlinks, good type, and graphics, and has a measurable response mechanism.

E. **Do Your Mailing.** Stuff. Seal. Stamp. Send.

F. **See What Happens.** You'll hear from people you haven't heard from in a while.

If you decide to do a real letter, you may be quite surprised – so will the people who get it.

You'll probably get a phone call or two.

And, certainly, you'll get e-mail responses if you give people a reason. Congratulations, you've just done a direct marketing campaign.

#4. SPONSORSHIP.

Your local restaurant account is now a sponsor of a small local team (minor league baseball, a college team, etc.).

A. Create a billboard and bumper sticker

B. Write a "sponsor of" program ad

C. Think up a Free Give-Away for one game

D. Design a T-shirt – one you think someone would actually wear

E. Make a flyer – a special ticket offer for your customers.

Each of these MarCom tactics should promote both your restaurant and the team.

#5. EVENT MARKETING:

A local Jazz Fest has just hired you. They have two well-known groups coming in. The rest of the bands are local. The organizers have no time and no money. Here's what you have to do:

A. Name the Fest – assume it's where you are. Give it an umbrella name.

B. Design a Poster – leave room for sponsors (Note: for your poster art, you can grab promo and label art for any two music groups you select.)

C. Divide and Conquer – Create, name, and promote four event opportunities within your Jazz fest.

Friday, Opening night: _____

It features one of your two big acts.

Saturday, 12–2: _____

Food vendors and a picnic atmosphere.

Two local groups will be featured.

Saturday, 3–6: _____

Three local groups will be featured.

Saturday night, 7–10: _____

Local act opens for the other star act.

DO YOUR OWN PR.

Here are some things that you might want to do to help give yourself a bit of "Good PR:"

- Get a good business card designed
- Get a great-looking fax cover sheet
- Produce a good résumé, with an interesting bio attached
- Draft #1 of a capabilities brochure
- Start thinking about the "publics" you'll be needing to influence
- Get involved with a cause
- Learn more about PR and MPR

EXAMPLE: DOMINO'S PIZZA.
It's easy and it's fun. Let's say our idea is to combine Domino's Pizza and the game of dominoes. Here's what you'd write:

• **Advertising**. An ad with the headline "The Domino Theory." History of Domino's pizza, history of game. Ads would have coupon offer and some sort of game involvement.

• **Sales Promotion** (Win/Free/Save). Give domino pieces with every purchase. Find some way to build continuity – add "Lucky Domino" for extra value/prizes.

• **Public Relations.** Do giant toppling domino designs, have contests, film the event for a news release.

• **Direct Marking.** Send free domino and coupon to every customer in your database – or every student on campus.

• **Event Marketing.** Sponsor a big Domino Tournament, have demonstrations at student centers.

• **New Media.** Build a website with a downloadable domino game and an online tournament, offer software.

And don't forget a downloadable discount coupon.

Got it? Now you do one.

Psst. There's a worksheet on page 447, and a pdf you can download on adbuzz. com – in the café.

If you get into it, here are a few more things to do:
• Write a Press Release announcing the fest – open with a good "hook."
• Write an e-mail invitation to a kick-off Press Event – how will you encourage attendance at the press event?
• Design a promotion to sell/reserve copies of a recording of the event – list what other things you could offer on the Web site.

#6. THE MARCOM MATRIX.

You may or may not think you have a good idea about all the MarCom options there are.

Actually, you do. And you're going to prove it to yourself in this exercise.

First, pick a brand: _____.

Then, in the center circle, indicate a simple core selling idea for that brand.

Now add a related idea for the different types of MarCom, such as:
• An advertising theme
• An event idea
• A direct marketing tactic
• A PR/publicity idea
• A sales promotion idea
• A new media idea

Go ahead. You can do this.

Draw a big version of the MarCom Matrix and fill in the circles.

Then, see if you can connect them.

For example, generate a database at the event (or online). Turn your advertising theme into a sales promotion. Figure out a way to deliver PR impact online. And so on.

Conceptual Tool Box

WE BET YOU'RE FIGURING OUT that this book about copywriting is actually about thinking.

Figuring out what to say is often the hardest part. Once you've done that, it's easier to say it well.

That said, this next section will introduce you to a number of tools for figuring it out.

It's sort of "your brain as Swiss Army knife."

BRAIN-TRAINING FOR BEGINNERS. Imaginative thinking, ideation, idea creation, conceptualization, those are some of the words we use for the fascinating, exciting, frustrating, and slightly messy business of thinking things up.

When we're done (we hope) you'll end up with the abilities to think up advertising concepts (or, you may call them communication concepts – since they may or may not include advertising).

What's a concept?

Our good friend Deborah Morrison at the University of Oregon defines it this way. *"Concept is the marriage of ideas and strategy.*

"It's the result of broad ideation ability combined with strategic business discipline."

For this next section, we're going to focus on stretching and exercising your idea muscles. We might even teach them a few useful tricks.

Then, we'll deal with strategy in Part Three.

OK, here goes…

How to Have an Idea

ACTUALLY, THIS WHOLE BOOK IS ABOUT "CREATIVITY."

This chapter will introduce you to a few basic techniques and principles.

When you think about it, this entire book is about helping you develop your mental flexibility and capabilities.

So you can solve marketing problems effectively – and creatively.

It's Not Creative Unless It Sells.

NOT NECESSARILY TRUE.

This was once a popular ad agency slogan. Catchy, but incorrect.

An ad may be quite creative but not sell, and it may not be the ad's fault.

The product, or some other aspect of marketing, like pricing or distribution, or another product that's better, may be the reason. Not the advertising.

Could you sell an Oldsmobile?

An ad may delight both agency and client for its cleverness but miss the mark with the customer.

Creative, but not effective.

Finally, an ordinary and unimaginative ad may be quite effective if the message is strong and the product and value are above average.

So, even if the ad isn't very "creative," it may sell very well.

"WHAT IS CREATIVITY?" Every day, in speeches, seminars, meeting rooms, classrooms, and Creative Directors' offices, someone asks this question.

Answering it has become a minor industry in itself.

It will continue to provide steady work for the chronically overqualified.

We're interested in how the mind associates and combines what we already know in fresh new ways.

It's called "having an idea," or "ideation." A key part of your job will be to work with ideas that help your client's business.

The business of advertising is about having ideas. So let's talk about it.

Here's what Arthur Koestler said in his book *The Act of Creation: "All great innovations consist of sudden shifts of attention and emphasis onto some previously neglected aspect of experience... They uncover what has always been there (yet) they are revolutionary."*

Leo Burnett said, *"Creativity is the art of establishing new and meaningful relationships between previously unrelated things... which somehow present the product in a fresh, new light."*

And James Webb Young, a well-known copywriter of his time, said simply, *"An idea is nothing more or less than a new combination of old elements."*

The process appears to have six critical stages:

1. PREPARATION.

Collecting input. "Doing your homework."

During the preparation stage, information enters the left side (verbal/storage/memory) of the brain.

The more information and background you have, the more potential connections you can make.

Pasteur noted, *"Fortune favors the prepared mind." "Luck is a matter of preparation meeting opportunity."*

2. FRUSTRATION.

However, unless the answer is obvious, the initial result is often frustration – particularly if the answer is not achieved through simple logic.

The left side of your brain doesn't quite know what to do with all this information. You're frustrated.

Emphasis shifts to the other side of the brain.

Some good news here. The more you work at having ideas, the better you get.

3. INCUBATION.

Now the right side of your brain goes to work with the information – consciously or subconsciously turning that information into new combinations.

You may actually want to sleep on it.

Mull it over. It's a natural process.

Another way of incubating is to discuss it with others. The kind of association your mind does by itself is similar to what happens when a number of brains "kick it around."

In many ways, groups and creative teams duplicate the incubation function.

4. ILLUMINATION.

AHA! The light bulb goes on!

Two previously unrelated elements connect.

Congratulations, you've just had an idea.

Don't always expect a blinding flash of light.

As Leo said, *"The secret of all effective originality in advertising is not the creation of new and tricky words and pictures, but putting familiar words and pictures into new relationships."*

James Webb Young. *JWT Copywriter. He developed a successful direct-mail business in his spare time. He wrote* A Technique for Producing Ideas. *It's only 61 pages long. Read it if you can find it.*

**LEARN TO BE #2
ON A GOOD IDEA.**

True story. The client and agency were in an idea session for a new TV spot.

Nike had just signed Bo Jackson, an outstanding athlete who was both a star NFL running back and a Major League Baseball player.

At one end of the table, they were having fun naming famous "Bo's."

Bo Derek, Beau Brummel, Little Bo Peep, etc. Someone said, "Bo Diddley."

The CD's ears perked up – Jim Riswold recognized an idea that could work.

By next morning, it was written.

The "Bo Knows" series was some of the best of the early Nike advertising.

This is how it often works. Though it wasn't the CD's idea, he knew what to do with it! Often, your biggest contribution can be helping to turn someone else's idea into a terrific piece of work.

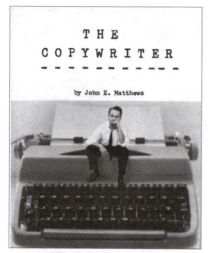

THE COPYWRITER

by John E. Matthews

WHAT TO DO UNTIL
THE IDEA COMES.

(From *The Copywriter* by John Matthews.)
The first trick is simply the mechanical process by which you write.

Do you use a typewriter, a ballpoint, a stubby black pencil, a tape recorder? [Note: This piece was written before computers, but the advice is good – don't just stare at the screen – Ed.]

Whichever you use, try switching to something else whenever the blank moment comes up. Perhaps you'll discover that there's a strange and wonderful two-way communication between your brain and the writing mechanics.

Sometimes if you start talking instead of typing, the brain will get back in working order. (It's kind of like kicking a flat tire. It may not inflate the stupid thing, but it makes you feel you're 'taking action.')

Another category that works is called 'brain jiggling.' This covers anything that goes bumpety-bump-bump – from driving down a country road to taking a train.

All kinds of locomotion belong to this group – even jogging around the block. I admit that many pedestrians on Michigan Avenue (or Madison Avenue, for that matter) may think it odd to see an apparently civilized person jogging up the street.

(Continued on next page.)

5. EVALUATION.

Now, you have to decide, "*is your idea a good idea?*"

This is a major problem for many talented creative people – they have lots of ideas, but can't tell their good ones from their bad ones.

Try to bring back the critical/analytical left side for an opinion. Hopefully, a useful opinion.

Evaluating ideas is also one of the critical roles of the Creative Director.

The difference between having ideas and knowing which are the good ones is equal parts evaluation and imagination. Learn to be critical of your own work in a positive way.

It's also useful to learn to recognize the good ideas others might have – sometimes you can help make them better.

Evaluation might also involve additional ideation to shore up the weak spots of the initial idea or to take your idea one more step – by using it as part of a new combination.

6. ELABORATION.

Working it out.

Copy and layout.

This is the other hard part.

Having ideas, even good ones, is often pretty easy. Making them work is work.

And *that's* how to have an idea.

A "TEAM CREATIVITY" EXAMPLE.

Years ago, I ran into Gary Bayer, who'd been CD on the very successful "Weekends Are Made for Michelob" campaign. I asked him about it.

"*Well,*" he said. "*We had a bunch of ideas up on the wall. One person had written 'Michelob is special,' and another had written 'Weekends are special.'*"

That's how it happened. Good creative teams can create a left-brain/right-brain idea pressure cooker.

FIVE ADDITIONAL POINTS ABOUT THE IDEATION PROCESS:

1. If Illumination doesn't come right away, you might not have done enough Preparation.

If your preparation is not complete, you may still be missing that critical element of insight.

Every successful copywriter talks a lot about becoming immersed in the product and in the prospect. This is *key* to the preparation stage.

Prepare thoroughly and then allow your intuitive process to sort it out. (Remember, incubation may take some time as well.)

A few thoughts while you tough it out.

Einstein said, *"The supreme task of the physicist is to arrive at those universal elementary laws from which the cosmos can be built by pure deduction. There is no logical path to these laws; only intuition resting on experience can reach them."*

Or as jazz pianist Thelonius Monk once said…
"Sometimes I play things I never heard myself."
You can do it. Be prepared.

2. Selling an idea can be harder than having one.

A new idea can be threatening.

Koestler says this about the shock of new ideas:
"They compel us to re-value our values."

Others have *not* gone through your ideation process.

Sometimes the best approach is walk your audience through the process you went through – step by step – from preparation to frustration to illumination.

And then evaluation and elaboration.

Give them time to get comfortable with a new thought. (Like cheap underwear, the mind, once stretched, never reverts to its original shape.)

On the other hand, your idea might not be accepted because it's *too obvious!*

Just as a maze can be solved by going backward, the creative act is sometimes diminished in retrospect.

THE COPYWRITER (CONT.)

But we are not out to impress such pedestrian observers; the main thing is to get your brain working again.

[Note: Written before jogging – Ed.]

Another brain-jolter calls for walking down the street and entering the first shop you spot that you have no business in. Or have never been in for any reason.

There's one school which contends that a couple of afternoon hours in a good movie will work wonders in regenerating creative cells.

I've always considered this 'cinema-system' most unimaginative; something which could be construed by laymen as merely the lazy Copywriter's excuse to goof-off an afternoon.

Much more ingenious and inspiring (and filling) is the system I have discovered of reactivating the brain via the stomach.

This system is extremely practical; it can be applied during your lunch hour.

It involves changing your luncheon habits drastically.

You dine at the Imperial House? Try a lunch counter, a veritable creative wonderland!

Usually have a social lunch?

Make one anti-social.

I don't claim to know what makes this system work so well. But work it does. And it can save hours of waiting for a cold typewriter to thaw.

This is still pretty useful advice for breaking the idea logjam.

About *The Copywriter*:

When we called John Matthews to ask for permission to use this piece, we asked him if he had any remaining copies of this old favorite. (It was written in 1963. I read it as a student.)

John called back a few weeks later to say he'd found the last few copies in his garage and he was sending them to us.

So… if you want to add this classic to your collection, you can now order *The Copywriter* from The Copy Workshop. While Supplies Last.

WHY ADVERTISING NEEDS NEW IDEAS.

Marketers constantly search for advantage – a new selling idea can create "enormous elasticity" in the effectiveness of media dollars.

A breakthrough selling approach can be as many as *10 times more effective* than a predictable selling message – even when the strategy is the same!

Thus, the constant search for new selling approaches by advertisers and agencies alike.

Advertising is a risky business.

There is risk in shifting to a new approach and risk in sticking with an old one.

The marketplace changes with each message, competitive advantages are met with competitive responses.

Unique approaches breed imitators. The battle is constant.

The wars of the marketplace demand fresh ammunition – new Selling Ideas.

The challenge of the marketplace is constantly changing – that's part of the adventure of advertising.

Leo Burnett reminds us, *"There's no such thing as a permanent advertising success."*

DO IDEAS WEAR OUT?

Sure they do. But, more often than not, clients and agencies tire of their advertising long before consumers.

Remember, you've seen your work hundreds of times more than the average reader or viewer.

Much of Leo Burnett's success was keeping ideas fresh over the long haul.

ASK THE RIGHT QUESTION.

Creativity often comes from asking the right question. Here's one:

What might be substituted, combined, adapted, magnified, or put to other uses?

The path that was once unclear is now there for all to see. "Aha" becomes "of course."

Leo Burnett had this to say about new ideas… *"Great copy and great ideas are deceptively simple."*

Trout and Ries agree. *"The best positioning ideas are so simple that most people overlook them."*

In that case, dramatize your concept's *simplicity*. (People don't have to know how clever you are.)

In every case, emphasize to the client or the people you work with how this idea relates to *their* needs and solves *their* problems.

Help *your* idea become *their* idea.

3. Your idea isn't always the right idea.

Try to be objective. Many bright creative people are victimized by their inability to know their good ideas from their bad ones. They confuse *their* idea with the *right* idea.

This is compounded by a competitive reluctance to like other people's ideas.

Learning to tell good ideas from bad ideas can be tough. And, since it's a bit like predicting the future, you'll never be perfect at it.

As a start, try to learn to like the best idea… no matter whose idea it is. Also, it's more credible when you speak up for someone else's idea.

Evaluation is another important part of this process. Get other opinions.

Try to become objective about your ideas. (It ain't easy.) Learn to keep going. Stay open to new insights and new ideas. What seemed like the destination may be only a stop along the way.

It may be a piece of a larger puzzle.

4. Just because you've got a good idea, that doesn't mean you know what to do with it.

Elaborate. Once you get that idea, even a great one, you have to work to make it work.

And you probably need help.

Working together on ideas is one of the joys of this business.

Learn to get others to help you make your idea work better and work harder. In fact, one other characteristic of successful ideas is a lot of people worked together to make it work. Bill Backer talks about "idea families."

There are many ways to elaborate.

The root word is "labor." Once you get an idea, your job hasn't ended, it's just begun.

5. Oops! Maybe you already had the idea.

With many advertising and marketing projects, a lot of thinking has been before.

The brand may have some heritage. Some smart people may have already given this some thought.

There's good news and bad news. The bad news is that if it's already been thought of, people may discount it. So even though the idea was never tried, it may already be viewed as a "failure."

The good news is one of the best ways to do your preparation is take a look at all that's gone before.

True story. When I first joined FCB, producer Phil Hagenah said, "*Let me play you something.*"

He took me to his office and played a demo of "The Ah Song," composed for Pizza Hut by jingle writer Gary Klaff, based on a Bernie Washington idea – but it had never been used.

It was wonderful. (Thanks Phil, Gary, and Bernie.)

Well, I remembered that wonderful piece of music. About a year later, the agency was fired. Yow!

It was one of the critical elements in a campaign that both saved the account for the agency *and* helped turn Pizza Hut's business around. Wow!

If Phil hadn't played me that music, I'm not sure what would have happened. Hmm…

You know, it doesn't hurt to be lucky.

IDEA CHANNELS, IDEA FAMILIES, AND "THE POWER WHO CAN SAY YES."

These are some of the concepts that populate Bill Backer's *The Care and Feeding of Ideas.*

It's a fresh and practical approach to one of our most important jobs.

Published by Times Books

A NEW COMBINATION OF OLD ELEMENTS.

Garbage bag + Jack-o'-Lantern.

Turning lawn and leaf bags into pumpkins pumps up sales in the fall for plastic bag companies.

It was a simple idea.

Don't you wish you'd thought of it!

Alex Osborn. The "O" in BBD&O. Inventor of "BrainStorming." Author of Applied Imagination. *Cool guy.*

BRAINSTORM GUIDELINES:

1. Suspend Judgement. No negative comments. No critics. Evaluation and criticism is postponed during session.

2. "Free Wheel." The participants have to let go of traditional inhibitions.

Wild ideas are encouraged. It's easier to tone down an idea than think one up.

3. Quantity not Quality. The objective is to generate the most ideas you can think of.

4. Cross-Fertilize. Participants are permitted and encouraged to work off of other people's ideas.

Authorship is not a concern.

Ideas are tossed around in the group and new versions are developed.

TO: _____

YOU ARE INVITED TO ATTEND A BRAINSTORM MEETING ON (DATE) AT (PLACE) AT (TIME). THE PROBLEM/TOPIC IS

_____

Looking forward to seeing you.
JOHN DOE (Phone #)

Notify participants of the meeting and topic in advance – it enables them to start thinking about the topic. Include useful background materials.

Team Creativity

BrainStorming & "The Brain Wall"

THE SECOND SECTION OF THIS CHAPTER is about having ideas with others. "BrainStorming" is a technique that was developed in the 1930s by Alex Osborn of Batten, Barton, Durstine & Osborn.

It's a method of generating a lot of ideas in a short amount of time.

"The Brain Wall" is a variation I use (as do many others – under a variety of names), and it's covered in the upcoming sidebar.

For a brainstorming session, you'll need a group, a group leader, large sheets of paper, and a room with lots of space. In general, let people know the topic ahead of time – to prepare.

Here's how BrainStorming works:

THE SIX STAGES OF BRAINSTORMING.

1. The Problem.

The group leader states the problem. For example, *"Today, we're going to talk about new ways to sell hamburgers. The hamburger business is suffering from no news and increasing concerns about eating red meat. Plus, there are too many burger places."*

The problem to be addressed is discussed, initial questions are answered, and the problem is discussed by the group in more detail.

2. "How to..."

Now, we step away from the problem and re-state it in a "How to" format. The problem is...

"How to end the Ho-Hum Hamburger."

"How to establish the Tradition of the Hamburger."

"How to put more fun on a bun." And so on.

They are written on large sheets of paper, in large letters, and displayed around the room.

This stimulates more thoughts.

This opens participants' minds to the possibilities, and is usually upbeat and stimulating.

All statements from this point on are written down and displayed prominently.

3. "How Many Ways..."

The group selects the first statement to be Brain-Stormed. The selected statement is written down in a "How many ways…" format. *"How Many Ways Can We End the Ho-Hum Hamburger?"* Etc.

Solutions are called out and written down.

As ideas dry up on the first restatement, you may move to another.

The ideas are numbered, reinforced, and built on as you move into the session.

Now, take a step back. Pause and leave the Basic Restatement up on the wall.

It's time to get the group ready to "storm."

4. The Warmup – "Other Uses for…"

There should now be a short session to "step away from the problem." About five minutes.

Participants throw out ideas like "Other uses for…" a paper clip, an ash tray, whatever.

The idea's to get the mental muscles warmed up and create a positive, freewheeling atmosphere.

For naturally "creative" people, this stage can sometimes be eliminated, as they'll be "chomping at the bit."

The Brain Wall.

For major advertising projects, here's a technique I like to use. I call it "The Brain Wall."

It's not a formal technique, like Brain-Storming or Synectics, just a general approach to creative problem-solving within an agency creative group.

Others use this technique – under many different names. Here's all you need:

1. People. Art, copy, even account executives and people from the Research Department (or your student agency team).

2. Flexible Leadership. Don't force your will on the group (at least at first).

"Go with the flow" as you look for the strongest lines of development.

3. Paper (not too big) and Markers (lots). Get everything possible on paper. And get as many possible pieces of paper on the wall. Index cards can work. 3x5" or 5x7". Post-Its are OK, too.

4. A Room with a Cork Wall or a Big Piece of Fome-Core. It could be your office or a conference room. You should be able to leave the stuff up on the wall.

A good-sized piece of Fome-Core can work – it's light yet big and it can be set aside if it's in the way.

5. Pins and Thumbtacks (tape, too).

6. Multiple Meetings. People need time between meetings to think and work.

Here's how it works…

Meeting #1.

The assignment is presented.

"Just got the account."

"We need to show the client some new product ideas."

"If we don't come up with something new, we're going to lose the account!"

Note the use of the word "we."

This begins to build a group approach to the problem.

The problem is discussed.

Perhaps the AE or research person gives some background. Relevant material is shown or handed out.

(Continued on next page.)

A business summary and competitive ads can also be helpful.

A good set of handouts for the first meeting gives it substance – but... not just piles of data.

If the time is right, you might kick it around in a pleasant, casual, and optimistic way. Set the tone.

And set a time for the next meeting.

Meeting #2.

Everybody gets together and you go around the room. Thoughts and impressions are stated, shared, and put up on the wall as Headline Ideas.

Some may be rough layouts or key frames. Or scrap. Or samples.

Put 'em up.

At first, they will be placed randomly.

As the meeting develops, ideas and approaches will begin to "cluster."

Move them around and start to organize: Benefit Ideas. Target Consumer Ideas. Graphic Ideas. Theme Ideas. And so on.

You might want to add some "Title" heads for each cluster.

You'll see the thinking begin to pattern. Strengths and lines of development will emerge.

Often, certain people will show up with a similar approach – they may actually have the same idea.

Terrific. It helps defuse the authorship issue, and you can start to form creative teams.

After all the ideas are up, ask for new thoughts or variations.

People should work off of each other to stimulate new lines of thinking.

Put 'em up.

Now, take a deep breath and head into the second part of the meeting (a short break here is fine).

Now, ask for reaction to others' ideas.

At first, compliments only.

Strengths are reinforced.

People are asked to refrain from "selling" their ideas. (That's for the next meeting.)

(Continued on next page)

But even with people eager to begin, an additional shift in perspective can be helpful.

Then, the group leader turns to the basic restatement and the "Storm" begins.

5. BrainStorm!

The Leader reads the restatement and calls for ideas. Write them down as quickly as possible and put them up on the wall.

Displaying ideas stimulates additional ideas.

Laughter and noise should be part of it as ideas are continually written down.

As it slows, take a short time out – a silent minute. Stretch. Let people look at the ideas that are displayed around the room.

The flow of ideas should start up again.

Then, select another restatement.

And do it again.

Ideas are continually generated, written down, and built on. The leader is also allowed to contribute ideas as well (but don't get in the way of other participants). The idea is to keep the storm going.

In a good session, one feels like one is riding a surging mental wave.

Traditionally, the leader then ends the session with a technique called "The Wildest Idea."

6. The Wildest Idea.

The group takes the wildest idea and tries to turn it into something useful.

This tends to brighten up the session again, and a few more ideas are usually generated.

Usually, it will become obvious when the session has run its course. One-and-a-half to two hours is good for a first session – a morning or afternoon is usually plenty.

Don't make them marathons!

Everyone is thanked and given positive feedback. Now it's time for that next step – evaluation.

"AFTER THE BRAINSTORM."

Evaluation is a critical, logical left-brain process.

The search is for *quality* in the *quantity.*

And naturally, the next steps are up to you.

The BrainStorming technique has been quite helpful over the years in generating fresh, new perspectives and new ideas. It has also generated new variations on the technique.

SYNECTICS™ & "STORYBOARDING."

"Synectics" is a copyrighted technique developed by W. J. J. Gordon and George Prince.

It's a more focused version of BrainStorming, concerned with practical problem solving.

Specific exercises, such as analogy metaphor and discontinuous stories, are used to stimulate fresh, rich beginning connections.

It is practiced by Synectics, Inc., and licensed users around the world – casual, nonlicensed versions of Synectics' techniques are commonly used in "idea sessions," or BrainStorms.

A related technique is "StoryBoarding," which relies on visual display. It's not like a TV storyboard – it's more of a visual outline. It looks like this...

TOPIC:

SUBJECT:	SUBJECT:	SUBJECT:	SUBJECT:	SUBJECT:
DETAILS:	DETAILS:	DETAILS:	DETAILS:	DETAILS:

BRAIN WALL (CONT.)

For now, they can only be positive about *someone else's* idea.

Leadership at this point can be tricky, particularly if the group has never worked this way before.

There can be initial discomfort.

But if you promote a positive attitude toward everyone's contribution, you can solve the problem *and* strengthen your group.

Don't expect the problem to be solved at this meeting – but the beginnings of an answer may appear.

You're creating an "Input Soup" and accelerating the ideation process.

Keep an upbeat attitude. It's the beginning of the journey. Don't expect the problem to be solved right away.

Next Steps.

Compliment the group. "A lot of good ideas here." Etc. Indicate ideas you think are particularly interesting.

Give out some assignments ("pull this together... expand that idea," etc.), but keep it flexible.

If possible, leave the ideas up on the wall. Save them for the next meeting.

Meeting #3.

This is the watershed meeting.

Unless the problem is complex or wide-ranging, it's the meeting where you "pull it together."

Generally, you'll see some developed approaches, theme lines, a few new ideas, and some ad roughs.

Major lines of thinking will start to become clear.

Here's how to handle it. Take down the old cards and put them in a pile(s).

Let people present.

First, the new work is put up on the wall. Then the best of the old – with your comments.

Now, people can sell their ideas and promote their point of view.

Enthusiasm is encouraged.

When everything has been presented, take a deep breath and say, *"Wow"* (or words to that effect).

(Continued on next page.)

145

BRAIN WALL (CONT.)

Look around at all the good work. Talk about what you like, and why.

Gently ignore ideas that, in your judgement, aren't working.

Give people permission to work on those ideas further, if convictions are deeply held – but it's time to start thinning the garden.

Focus on the strongest approaches.

Hopefully, it will become obvious.

Now, start to organize things into a Presentation. You can kick it around in a pleasant, casual, and optimistic way, or turn it into a real high pressure type of team effort.

Outline the order of presentation for your next "work session" with account executives or clients (or both), and proceed to develop a final presentation in whatever way is typical for your agency or group.

The Brain Wall can be a fun way to build a strong campaign – and a better, stronger group.

A HELPFUL THOUGHT.

Remember, in most cases, there will be only one winning idea. (Though often two or three ideas might go into the next round of research.)

Here's a positive way of discussing a negative subject. Share your disappointment ahead of time that there's going to be a lot of good work and probably more than one good answer – but only one "winner."

Many contributions will not be "bad" ideas, just good ideas that didn't make it.

Happens all the time.

Try to make everyone feel better about the inevitable and positive about their contributions.

There are other business uses for these techniques – as part of annual marketing meetings and to help people in structured jobs stretch their mental muscles.

Companies are finding it's very productive for groups of people to be creative and have good ideas.

Under proper circumstances, it can be an effective way of dealing with business problems.

If you're interested in learning more, there are books with techniques and guidelines as well as the training programs available (see Reading List).

Do these techniques work?

Certainly they don't work every time, and they probably don't work for everybody.

But they've worked for me. Particularly the Brain Wall version, which is more focused.

In a wide variety of circumstances, I've seen this technique identify the key issues of a difficult advertising problem and solve that problem with a variety of approaches.

I've seen relationships revitalized, new talent identified, and sad to say, those in the group not pulling their weight exposed for all to see.

This approach should only be used when the problem is big enough to allow for the presentation of a number of alternative solutions.

Inviting too many people to work on a small problem can be demeaning.

But on the right project, it can help develop an upbeat team spirit within a creative group.

Not only will people enjoy working together more – they'll get better with each new problem.

And in this business, the more problems you solve, the better you get.

Learn to solve problems – it's problems that keep us all in the business. Hey, if we didn't have 'em, there'd be nothing to do.

A TRUE STORY.
I remember my freshman year at JWT.

Sears had just assigned us a new battery.

"*I was thinking*," said Tom Hall, "*a battery doesn't wear out… it* dies."

Marion Dawson looked up from strumming his baritone ukulele. "*Let's call it The DieHard.*"

And they did.*

Advertising is a team sport. The better we learn to work together, the better we'll do.

Together.

A TEAM SPORT.
Art and copy work together.

Creative teams, account management, media, research, and clients all play their key role in creating work that works.

An engineering team developed a better battery for Sears. Sears went to their agency at the time – JWT/Chicago –and the agency named the product and designed the graphics for the product.

And it was a hit.

Mind Mapping

A mind map is a diagram, usually of words, used to represent words, ideas, tasks, or other items linked to and arranged around a central key word or idea. While they have many functions, for our purposes they are one more tool to help generate new ideas and solve problems.

The elements of a given mind map are arranged intuitively, starting with the core word, concept, or brand. Then you make natural connections, going outward in whatever direction seems to suite you.

This approach is generally described as *Radiant Thinking*.

*

Years later, I found out that Marion had been kicking ideas around a bit earlier, strumming his ukulele, with Howard Rieger, a very talented art director, who also developed the original DieHard graphics. Howard insists he had the idea first – and the uke's not talkin'!

MIND MAPPING DEFINED.

Here's a definition from *The Mind Map Book* by Tony Buzan, a British pop psychologist who did much to popularize the concept.

"The Mind Map is an expression of Radiant Thinking and is therefore a natural function of the human mind. It is a powerful graphic technique which provides a universal key to unlocking the potential of the brain."

Four Essential Characteristics:

1. The subject of attention is crystallized in a central image.
2. The main themes of the subject radiate from the central image as branches
3. Branches comprise a key image or key word printed on an associated line. Topics of lesser importance are also represented as branches attached to higher level branches.
4. The branches form a connected nodal structure.

Simply put, you start with a key word or concept and, using a natural associative function which we all have operating inside our heads, we put down on paper whatever comes to mind.

We build out in branches or links and end up developing a "connected nodal structure" of thoughts, images, and related ideas.

It's kind of one person brainstorming.

BAM!

That stands for Branching Association Machine – an acronym for something our brains do naturally.

This approach helps us break out of lists and hierarchical note-taking, which often limits thinking.

Mind mapping literally lets your mind wander – and explore some fairly interesting territory.

It's natural and automatic.

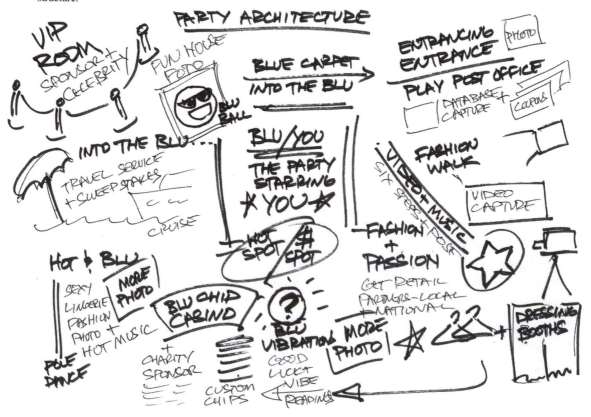

HOW TO DO IT.

It's pretty simple, actually, just write down the core concept and start.

As you develop branches and nodes, you'll see that some start their own mind map with the newly generated concept at the center.

Some people use this approach quite a bit. I use it to help me get a grip on complex projects.

These days, I think about targets, channels, and environments. That drove me to the "Hip History" poster idea on this page – for a screening of a World War One documentary at a Kansas City Museum.

On the other page, "Party Architecture" for a *Magazine BLU* launch party for "social singles."

Give it a try. By the way, the original scribbles were a whole lot messier.

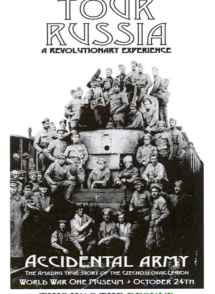

THIS WAS THE RESULT.

"Hip History" was the clue that made it all come together.

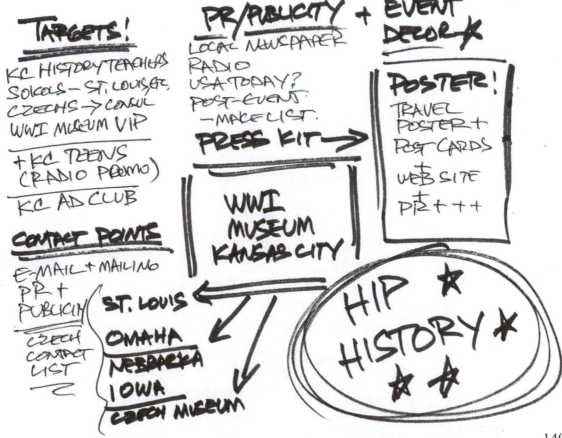

#12: Idea Exercises:

Having an Idea:

Briefly, let's review the stages of "ideation."

You're going to be doing this a lot – so better get used to it.

A. PREPARATION.

List the types of source material you can assemble for preparation on a product assignment.
Don't forget product-related experiences.

B. FRUSTRATION.

Think about times you've experienced frustration. How did you feel? How was it resolved.

C. INCUBATION.

Think about ways you can incubate alone.
Now think about who you'd want to work with in a group – to cook-up/incubate some ideas.

D. ILLUMINATION.

Describe two times you've experienced illumination. Short paragraphs.
What did it feel like?

E. EVALUATION.

How would you evaluate an idea?
How do you know if you're right or wrong?

F. ELABORATION.

What work do you have to do to put your idea in presentable form? Are you just going to "talk it," or can you prepare some sort of visualization of your idea?
What else can you do to make that idea work?

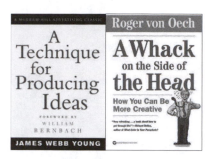

READING LIST:
Some books on how to have an idea:

A Whack on the Side of the Head
How You Can Be More Creative
Roger Von Oech.
This is a best-seller with lots of useful tips for unlocking your creativity.
You might also look for a "Whack Pack."

The Act of Creation
Arthur Koestler/Pan Picador

The Care and Feeding of Ideas
Bill Backer/Times Books

A Technique for Producing Ideas
James Webb Young/Crain Books

DeBono's Thinking Course
Edward de Bono/Facts on File

The Office:
A Facility Based On Change
(Available through
Herman Miller Furniture)

Applied Information
Alex F. Osborn
Charles Scribner & Sons, 1957

Your Creative Powers
Alex F. Osborn
Charles Scribner & Sons, 1948

BrainStorming:

ORGANIZE a BrainStorming session.

- Pick an assignment:
  - New Product, Fund-Raising Project, a Party, or something else.
- Get everyone together in a room with all the tools that you need.
- Follow the steps and **BrainStorm!**
- Implement the best idea, if practical.

Brain Wall:

GOT A BIG PROJECT? Start a Brain Wall.

Find a room. Find a wall. Or get a big piece of Fome-Core. Then, fill 'er up!

Mind Mapping:

MAKE SOME MIND MAPS.

They can be for class projects or something else, like writing a birthday poem or thinking about what you might like to do this weekend.

Helpful hint – plenty of paper and a few different colors of writing implements.

12 TIPS TO GET STARTED.

Some practical advice from John Caples. (from his wonderful book, *How to Make Your Advertising Make Money.*)

1. Don't wait for inspiration.
2. Start with something easy.
3. Write as if talking to a companion.
4. Write a letter to a friend.
5. Forget the "Do's" and "Don'ts."
6. Describe the product.
7. Make a list of benefits.
8. Write what interests you most.
9. Get inspiration from others.
10. Copy successful copy.
11. Start by writing headlines.
12. Write fast and edit later.

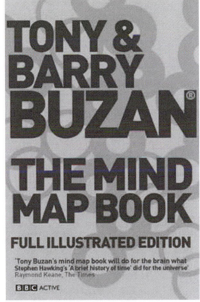

TONY & BARRY BUZAN®
THE MIND MAP BOOK
FULL ILLUSTRATED EDITION

'Tony Buzan's mind map book will do for the brain what Stephen Hawking's 'A brief history of time' did for the universe'
Raymond Keane, The Times

BBC ACTIVE

READING LIST (CONT.)

The Mind Map Book
Tony & Barry Buzan
BBC Active, 2006

Synectics
J. J. Gordon Williams
Harper & Rowe, 1961

Creative Thinking and Brainstorming
S. Geoffrey Rawlinson
John Wiley & Sons, 1981

Some books listed in the previous chapter also deal with ideation.

Conceptual Models

IF WE DO IT RIGHT, you'll be referring back to this chapter repeatedly.

We're going to cover a number of conceptual models that can be very useful in thinking about the kind of business and communication problems you'll have to solve.

It's kind of a Swiss Army Knife for your brain.

Some tools will help you have ideas.

Others will help you think about how to use those ideas.

Others will help you evaluate the relative strength of various ideas.

Others may help you see new ways to use the ideas you have.

And still others can be very useful in presenting those ideas.

Which is which? Up to you.

But, along the way, we think you'll find most of these conceptual models to be reasonably useful. They are:

- **M.O.S.T. – Mission, Objective, Strategy, Tactics**
- **The FCB Grid & "Exploding the Dot."**
- **The Learn/Feel/Do Circle**
- **The Four A's & the Four R's**
- **The Four P's & the Four C's**
- **Laddering**
- **Positioning & Marketing Warfare**

OK, here goes.

WHICH TOOL TO USE?

That's up to you and "that ultimate non-linear thinking tool – the human brain."

FREE POWERPOINT.

Your professor may use it in class. But, if you don't have a professor handy, you can download it yourself.

Go to www.adbuzz.com and click on Café.

There you'll find a number of teaching tools (sorry, no test answers), and you can download what you want.

The PowerPoint that covers material in this section is called "Conceptual Models: for Solving Marketing Problems and Creating Advertising Solutions" (the file is 2Concept.ppt).

152

M.O.S.T.

Businesses and people operate at four different levels – though they may not be aware of it.

Those four levels are:

- **Mission:** the overall purpose of the business, organism, or social movement.
- **Objective:** Primary goal to be accomplished in fulfilling the mission. If there are too many objectives on your list, this may be a problem. Things seem to work best with just a few clear objectives – one big one is good.

  Churchill observed during World War Two, *"Victory is my objective. War is my strategy."*
- **Strategy:** This is how you're going to do it. Very often, a strategy is an hypothesis, a best guess as to the best way to do it. It takes a lot of thinking. In fact, thinking about strategy will be the next part of this book. For now, we're just going to teach you the conceptual tools that help you get there.
- **Tactics:** These are the individual actions, compatible with your Strategy, that help you reach your Objective. This, in turn, helps you accomplish your Mission.

See how it works? OK, let's go over it again. We'll use Apple Macintosh from the '90s as an example. (This was before the iPod and "Mac vs. PC" campaign. Though, these statements could be easily applied to Apple's later iMac launch.)

M.O.S.T. = Mission, Objective, Strategy, Tactics

Some definitions and examples:

Mission – Principles by which a company is run.

Example: Apple Computer's stated mission is *"Our goal is to put Macintosh computers in the hands of as many people as possible."*

THE OBJECTIVE…

of most advertising is to sell the products or services offered.

Advertising that does not accomplish that objective is a waste of money.

"Half my advertising is wasted – but I don't know which half." *

John J. Wanamaker

*

Actually, the original quote was by Lord Leverhume, who founded Lever Brothers. Wanamaker was quoting him.

And, clever as they are, these "Going Out of Business" ads remind us that creating a business that works and advertising that works is a tough job.

EXAMPLE: THE COPY WORKSHOP

Even a small textbook publisher can have Mission, Objective, Strategy, and Tactics.

Our Mission: To help young men and women prepare for an industry undergoing revolutionary change.

Does this help you understand what we're about? It helps us do the same.

Objective: Become a significant source of top-quality instructional materials in advertising and marketing communications.

OK, that makes sense. As things evolve, we might be looking at things other than books. For the moment, books will be our focus.

Strategy: "Best Practices in a reader-friendly format"

That's the kind of book we need to do to meet our objective, containing the best contemporary business practices in the field, presented in a way that will be easy to read.

Tactic: These are specific actions that help us meet our Objective, according to our Strategy.

One of those tactics is this book.

FROM TACTIC TO MISSION.

As it happens, we kind of figured things out backward.

We wrote a book. It was successful. Suddenly, we had to figure out what we were doing, what we should be doing, and how to go about it.

So we kind of backed our way into it. We figured out what made our book successful. We got to know the marketplace. Gradually, it emerged.

This reinforces a point that we'll make more than once.

Plans and strategies don't always develop in a logical "top-down" order, where wise people have all the answers early on.

Sometimes you just kind of figure it out as you go along. Sometimes successful tactics give you hints about what your successful strategy should be.

And sometimes when you have a spare minute, you force yourself to think about higher goals – which isn't a bad thing.

A mission helps a company maintain focus in a complicated business environment.

Objective – A specific task to be accomplished.

An Objective Statement for a Marketing Strategy might be: *To double unit sales of low-end computers next quarter.*

An Objective Statement for an Advertising Strategy might be: *To convince decision-makers (parents and small business owners) that our entry-level computers offer the added-value of the Macintosh operating system.*

Defining Objectives is key to developing good Strategies.

Strategy – How you will meet an Objective. There may be alternate strategies to choose from – even when objectives are clear. And different parts of the business (advertising, PR, sales promotion, in-store retail) may have somewhat different – but compatible – strategies.

Example: *Our strategy will be to:*
   a. *increase advertising*
   b. *offer price-off incentives*
   c. *provide easier financing*
   d. *lower the retail price*
   e. *some or all of the above*

The chosen (or "recommended") strategy is the best hypothesis as to how to meet the objective.

Tactics – These are specific planned actions that execute the Strategy.

Ads, sales materials – the whole range of marketing communications tools are *tactics*. So is a sales call. So is an incentive program that gives the sales person a bonus for every computer sold.

Example: *Advertising that features Mac Classics starting at $999.*

The FCB Grid & "Exploding the Dot"

Now we're going to look at some conceptual models based on everyone having "two brains," a logical side and an emotional one.

Let's think about this for a minute.

YOUR BRAIN HAS TWO SIDES* – left and right.

The left side of your brain is connected to the right side of your body. And vice versa.**

Basically, the left side is logical and verbal, rational and conservative. It does not take risks.

The right side is different.

It is intuitive, visual, liberal, and imaginative.

The left side reads.

The right side feels.

A well-organized Ogilvy-style reason why communicates to the left side of the brain.

Bill Bernbach's ads surprise the right side.

The right side listens to music. (But not always.)

The left side does math. (But not geometry.)

And, while both sides work together, it's important to consider how you will be communicating – emotionally or rationally.

Image or reason why.

Visually or verbally. Or both.

To rephrase a famous observation, "two brains are better than one." That's particularly true when both of them are yours.

So, we understand intuitively that we're both emotional and rational. How can that make us smarter?

Here's how.

YOUR "LEFT BRAIN"
Logical
Verbal
Math
Words
Facts
Memory
Asks "Why?"
Conservative

YOUR "RIGHT BRAIN"
Associative
Visual
Geometry
Music
Playful
Asks "What If?"
Imaginative

---

*

The two major modes of human brain hemisphere function were first described by psychobiologist Roger W. Sperry.

His groundbreaking research was honored with a Nobel Prize.

**

The connection between the two sides of the human brain is called the *corpus callosum*. It literally lets the right hand know what the left hand is doing.

And… women usually have a much larger *corpus callosum* than men.

That's right, on average, women have many more connections between left and right brain hemispheres!

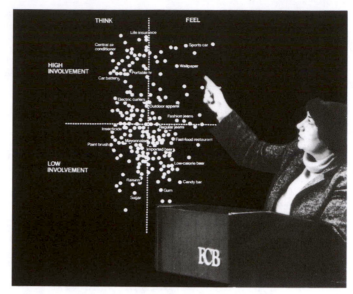

*Dona Vitale explains **The FCB Grid**. From the FCB annual report.*

THINKING	FEELING
THINK **HIGH** **INVOLVEMENT**	**FEEL** **HIGH** **INVOLVEMENT**
THINK **LOW** **INVOLVEMENT**	**FEEL** **LOW** **INVOLVEMENT**

THE FCB PLANNING GRID.

The horizontal dimension goes from the rational to the emotional.

Thinking to **Feeling**.

And vice versa.

The vertical dimension is **interest** level – it goes from **low interest** to **high interest.**

Or vice versa.

Below, some early examples, based on development work done by the FCB research department.

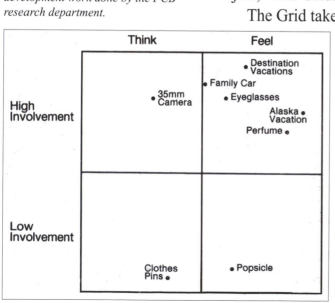

The FCB Grid

THE RESEARCH DEPARTMENT at Foote Cone and Belding developed something called the **Vaughn Grid** (Richard Vaughn was Research Director in FCB's L.A. office).

It's been called The FCB Grid for Advertising Planning, The FCB Planning Grid, or sometimes just, "The Grid."

The Grid takes this emotional vs. rational difference, plus a number of other advertising theories – economic, social, psychological, and responsive –and organizes the whole thing into a "playing field."

It's a pretty useful tool.

How do you use it?

HOW DO YOU USE IT?

You use The Grid as a helpful technique and mental exercise for determining your advertising approach.

It helps you relate the type of product you're selling to the mind of your target consumer.

Because we're each a different type of consumer, depending on what we're buying. Consider ...

WHERE IS YOUR PRODUCT ON THE GRID?

Let's think about some different types of products and how they match up with the different quadrants:

Thinking/High Involvement: like a 35mm camera, a costly piece of office equipment, or perhaps the best terms for a student loan?

Thinking/Low Involvement: like clothes pins, a floor cleaner, or motor oil?

Feeling/High Involvement: like perfume, fashion, motorcycles, or cosmetics?

Feeling/Low Involvement: like a Popsicle, candy bar, or a soft drink?

Get the idea?

IT CAN BE BOTH.

As the Saab ad at the end of this chapter demonstrates, selling messages can contain elements of *both* thinking and feeling.

You may decide to sell your product in a rational way when others are selling theirs emotionally.

The key is to make a rational, strategic, or tactical decision – even if, ultimately, the logical conclusion is to be emotional.

There may be alternative hypotheses as to the proper placement of your product on The Grid.

This, in itself, can lead to interesting discussion and, hopefully, a better decision.

INTO THE GRID.
A three-step process for using The Grid:

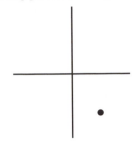

1. WHERE THE PRODUCT FITS.
First, place the product category in what you believe is the proper place on The Grid.

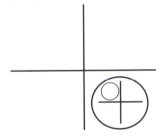

2. WHERE THE BRAND FITS.
Next, decide where your brand fits within the product category.

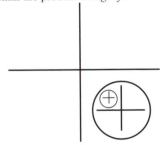

3. WHERE THE BRAND ATTRIBUTE FITS.
Finally, decide where the distinguishing product attribute of your brand fits.

So, for example, you could have a relatively emotional brand in a rational category. And vice versa.

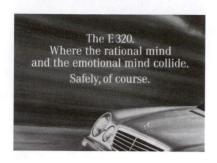

**READING LIST: TWO BOOKS ARE
BETTER THAN ONE.
MAKE THAT THREE.**

Every day, there are more and more books examining aspects of left-brain and right-brain thinking.

There is a fascinating technique for teaching you to draw *upside down!* It generates right brain/visual connections in left brain/verbal people.

Writing the Natural Way by Gabrielle Lusser Rico helps you hook into associative areas of the right brain and unlock your writing creativity.

A Whack on the Side of the Head by Roger Von Oech, a Silicon Valley creativity consultant, is a lot of fun.

Whole Brain Thinking: Working from Both Sides of the Brain to Achieve Peak Job Performance, is a business book based on Roger Sperry's Nobel Prize winning research on split-brain theory, by Jacquelyn Wonder and Priscilla Donovan.

Read a few of them. You'll be a more effective and creative thinker.

And, you'll have more fun.

Maybe twice as much.

Thinking or feeling. High involvement or low. All have their place. In the heart. And mind.

"Exploding the Dot."

Many advertising techniques involve developing mental flexibility. Learning one way of thinking about things. Then learning another.

Mike Koelker was a visionary creative for FCB on the West Coast. His Levi's work was some of the most important work in the 70s and 80s. He observed how almost all ad messages had some elements of both logic and emotion, *"We are all realizing that the viewing public wants a lot of facts, plus emotional values. The product can be the most rational in appearance, but there always are emotional factors that overlay the decision to purchase."*

With that in mind, here's an approach that's *almost* the exact reverse of the FCB Planning Grid. It was developed while working with The Grid. After you determine where you want to place your dot/product on the Grid, "explode" it!

Turn your focus inside out and look at the forces pushing out in different directions. Sort of like this:

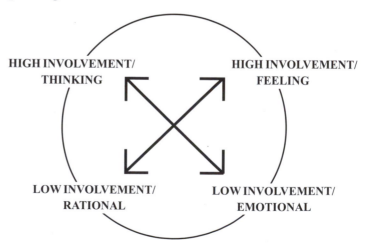

HIGH INVOLVEMENT/
THINKING

HIGH INVOLVEMENT/
FEELING

LOW INVOLVEMENT/
RATIONAL

LOW INVOLVEMENT/
EMOTIONAL

Often, these forces can be expressed as little "quotes" about the feeling or thinking involved.

Here's an example for Old El Paso, a leading brand of Mexican food.

In this case, The Grid can be a useful tool for opening up new ways of thinking about a product or product category.

"EXPLODING THE DOT."
Example: Old El Paso
Mexican Food.

HIGH INVOLVEMENT/ FEELING
Initial decision – High Risk –
Fear of embarrassment
Success – Creative Satisfaction.
A creative way to enjoy a meal.

HIGH INVOLVEMENT/THINKING
Initial decision – High Risk– "What do I do?"
Meal Planning – New Recipes, Procedures.
A good way to serve good nutrition.

LOW INVOLVEMENT/RATIONAL
Success – Low Risk/No Risk
Good, Easy, Economical.
America's Favorite Brand of Mexican Food.
An economical way to serve good food.

LOW INVOLVEMENT/ EMOTIONAL
Fun & Flavor.
A fun, exciting meal.
"¡Ole!"

EXAMPLE: ARCHWAY
"THE GOOD FOOD COOKIE."
We'll use this example a number of times.

Here, we want to make the point that one idea can have different synergistic aspects within The Grid.

While the cookie category tends to be "lower right," Archway, a leading baker of oatmeal cookies, developed a "Good Food" position in the early '80s – this was a relatively "high think" position.

It matched up with other marketplace trends – increased concern about ingredients and good news about oat bran.

They also "exploded" their dot a bit with a range of tactics – all based on the same strategy:

High Think: Mini-brochures containing nutritional information.

Low Think: A promotional display program featuring a low price.

High Feel: "Be a Good Cookie" tie-in with Children's Miracle Network.

Low Feel: Slogans like "Did You Have Your Oatmeal Today?"

159

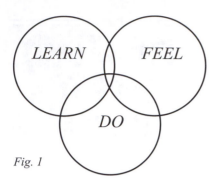

Fig. 1

THE LEARN/FEEL/DO CIRCLE

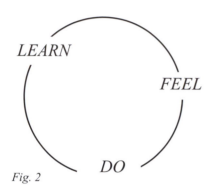

Fig. 2

DO/LEARN/FEEL.

Remember, you can go in any direction.

For example, what is the process by which your customer gets involved with your product?

For a new snack food, you may try a free sample first (do), then, as you eat it, you find out how it tastes (learn).

Finally, there will be some sort of feel dimension–taste, sensate feelings (crunch/texture), satisfaction, and how this snack compares to others.

This process can continue.

The more you do, the more you learn, and the more you feel. Get it?

Learn/Feel/Do Circle

THIS CONCEPTUAL MODEL addresses the ways we interact with products and services.

It can be very helpful in developing ways to involve people and products.

First, we'll learn about it.

Then, we'll tell you what to do with it.

How you feel about it will be pretty much up to you.

You can picture it either as three overlapping circles (Fig. 1), or as one circle (Fig. 2)

THREE WAYS WE RELATE.
The L/F/D Circle reminds us that we relate to products in more than one way.

Learn. We read about a product in an ad, look at the label, or learn about it as we experience it.

Feel. We may have feelings about the product or product category. Some of this is based on our experience, some on personal preference, and some on who knows what.

Do. We buy a product, use it, and experience it. Perhaps we get a free sample at a street fair.

Generally, these three circles are shown as one circle, which we call The Learn/Feel/Do Circle (Fig. 2).

It's a sequence that can be very helpful in how we think about the role of advertising.

TWO SIMPLE RULES.
Whichever way you draw it, our little circle has two simple rules.

1. You may enter at any point on the circle.

Your initial experience with a product may be learning, feeling, or doing (see sidebar).

2. You may go in either direction.

The sequence of experience can go in either direction – any way you wish. Think about it…

Think about the way people involve themselves with your product and with your advertising.

For example, a high involvement/thinking type of product may encourage you to try to "teach" people with a long copy ad – Learn/Feel/Do.

For an inexpensive snack food, perhaps you should encourage sampling – Do/Learn/Feel.

Different approaches may find you entering at different parts of the circle – even with the same strategy.

Think about how your target customer will relate to the product and the advertising.

Think of the point of entry and the sequence.

And realize that experience in the real world does not always duplicate the sequence you imagine.

You might find it helpful to think about all of this in the context of The MarCom Matrix.

The Learn/Feel/Do Circle is an excellent conceptual tool for thinking about the dynamic you wish to create for your brand.

Don't Make this Mistake.

It can also help you get out of a rut that almost every writer falls into.

As we prepare for a project, we're usually in the "learn" mode.

And why not?

But, all too often, we stay there and then try to teach people why our product is better.

Sometimes that can be a good way – but it's certainly not the only way.

The Learn/Feel/Do Circle reminds us that we can relate to a product in different ways. Think about it.

What do you want them to learn?

What do you want them to feel?

What do you want them to do?

And in what sequence?

FEEL/DO/LEARN.

For a new perfume, the advertising might create feeling first.

Based on the imagery, you think it might be a nice perfume (feel).

So you try it at the perfume counter (do), and you find out whether you like it or not (learn).

MY FAVORITE COOL THING ABOUT THE LEARN/FEEL/DO CIRCLE.

Hold this thought.

You can work your way around the circle and still be working with the same strategy.

It gives you a number of entry points to build your message.

Enter with some sort of interesting Learn bit of message. Or enter with an emotional play. Feel.

Same strategy. Dramatically different approach. Cool. You can go from Learn to Feel. Or vice versa.

Finally, as we add other MarCom approaches into our messaging, don't forget the power of *Do* – whether it's an offer, an event with a sample, or some other invitation to participate.

TRUE STORY.

We'd been on the same campaign for two years. It was a "Brand Names for Less" approach with nice testimonials.

But, frankly, the work was wearing out. Nice, but enough already.

However, the strategy was still right. What to do?

First, I presented the client with the Learn/Feel/Do Circle and indicated that we were doing Learn. So, let's go to Feel.

We did a music/fashion approach. It was the same message, Brand Names for Less, but now we emphasized the positive emotions associated with getting these great clothes for a great price.

Same strategy. Dramatically different approach.

Thanks to the Learn/Feel/Do Circle.

161

ATTENTION!

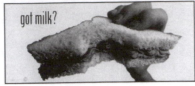

got milk?

On Empty?

**

"AIDA"

This is the more common acronym for the process: Attention, Interest, Desire, and Action

However, in our view, "Interest" and "Desire" overstate the case for many product categories.

"Awareness" and "Attitude" seem more accurate. And easier to remember.

The 4A's & 4R's

SINCE I FIRST entered the advertising business, my point of view has evolved rather dramatically. I began, with the commonly accepted advertising model, AIDA (Attention, Interest, Desire, Action). Then I changed into what I thought was a more memorable acronym – 4A's (Attention, Awareness, Attitude, Action). Let's start there.

THE FOUR A'S OF ADVERTISING.
The traditional view is advertising works through four levels: Attention, Awareness, Attitude, Action.**
Let's take them one by one…

Attention.
First, advertising has to get *attention*.
Breaking through to get that attention is also one of the toughest jobs. And due to media fragmentation and the increase in the number of messages, getting that attention gets tougher every year.

You're not only competing with a lot of other messages done by other skilled ad people, but people are very good at tuning out what doesn't interest them.

The thing to remember is that the ad doesn't necessarily have to jump out at you.

It's even better when people *jump in* to the ad.

That's the real breakthrough – when people break into your message.

When people notice your ad, to some extent, they remember it. And a certain percentage of these people will buy your product.

Generally, this will be a greater percentage than those who don't know your name or notice your ad.

Overcoming all the barriers to communication and getting attention is advertising's first job.

Awareness.

Second, advertising must build *awareness*.

You want the product that you're advertising to move from merely being noticed to being remembered.

You want your brand to occupy a space in the conscious or subconscious mind or memory.

This is usually a cumulative process, and building awareness is a constant goal of virtually all advertising.

It takes time, and as NW Ayer said over 100 years ago, "*Keeping Everlastingly At It Brings Success.*" That often means sticking with it.

At this second level, your brand is beginning to have an ongoing existence *inside* people – or, as Trout and Ries say, "inside the mind of the consumer."

If they simply remember you, a greater percentage will be disposed to buy your product.

If they remember the right thing about you, it will be an even greater percentage.

As David Ogilvy said, "*Every advertisement is a long-term investment in the image of the brand.*"

Attitude.

Third, advertising works on *attitude* – the feeling people have toward your product.

Attitude is more active than awareness.

Here, people can usually say how they feel – positive, negative, or neutral.

To state the obvious, you want to build a positive attitude toward your product.

However, some ads work to build up negative attitudes toward the competition, or the problem.

Political advertising is a good example.

But it's more than just advertising. An attitude is usually an accumulation of experiences:

AIDED & UNAIDED AWARENESS.
One of the basic research techniques used to measure advertising's effectiveness is to measure awareness.

In its simplest form, you ask people what ads or products they remember.

As in, "Do you remember any beer commercials?" or "What brands of beer do you remember?"

The percentage of people who remember your brand or advertising is called awareness or "unaided awareness."

If your brand or commercial is not mentioned, the person is then asked, "Do you remember such and such a beer commercial, or such and such brand of beer?"

If the answer is "Oh, yeah," or something to that effect, this percentage is "aided awareness."

A 50+ SHARE.
Most brands are happy with a 30 share – that's 30% of the market.

In politics, you need over a 50 share.

That's why you'll find some of the smartest, toughest, and hardest-working communication people in the world of politics.

You'll see advertising, direct, and event marketing working together to get your attention, build awareness, shift your attitudes (positive for their candidate and negative against the opposition), and finally, on Election Day… Action!

The J. Peterman Company

Owner's Manual No. 35b

Spring 1995

p. 37

p. 102

p. 86

p. 10

p. 104

p. 42

The Peterman Catalog. *Very successful for a number of years with its inviting copy and unique items. Then, either due to the wrong product mix, too much expansion, or people just getting tired of it (how many Australian bush jackets with a boomerang pocket does anyone need), it folded. But, if you can find an old Peterman catalog, you'll see some of the best catalog writing ever.*

If You're Pregnant, You Should Fill This Out.

Then send it or bring it with you for a 10% discount on your next purchase.
At Baby It's You, we have maternity wear that's actually fashionable. So you can look good. Even after your form's been filled out.

baby, it's you
MATERNITY WEAR

Name
Address
Zip
Telephone _____ Due Date _____

Open 11-3 weekdays, Saturdays, or by appointment.
Call 528-BABY. 1188 Bishop Street, Suite 2911.
Offer good through August 31, 1989.

- An ad
- A product experience
- Imagery of the product name or package
- Product display at the point of purchase
- "Word of mouth" (A powerful force)
- All of the above (The MarCom Matrix)

In most cases, advertising has a major responsibility for building positive attitudes about the brand.

This process is often referred to as "building brand equity." When well executed, it often has a specific strategic focus – e.g., improve reputation for quality or "the hot new golf brand."

Action.

Finally, there is *action*!

The person buys the product, downloads a brochure, or votes for his Congressman's opponent.

Sometimes you can move someone all the way to action in only one ad.

Direct Mail catalogs do this all the time.

The interactive potential of the Internet makes this a constant possibility.

Retail advertising has this focus. Retailers measure ad effectiveness by store traffic and sales.

But with all advertisers, even those concerned with short-term sales, or even survival, the cumulative power of advertising is also a long-term process. It builds with each ad.

For virtually every advertiser, advertising should be part of a long-term process… even when it's designed for short-term results.

Once more, that process is: gain *attention,* build *awareness,* shift *attitudes,* and motivate *action.*

That's the Four A's of Advertising.

Ask for the Order. Look for ways to activate *the consumer and involve her (or him) in your ads. Invite them into your store – give them a reason to make the trip or to try your product for the first time.*

THE FOUR R'S – AN EVOLUTION.
My point of view has evolved.

Today, I practice what I call the "Four R's." These are: Reaction, Relevance, Response, Relationship.

Again, let's take them one by one.

Reaction.

People react – even if that reaction is no reaction. I have a new appreciation for today's consumer's ability to navigate the media environment and select what they choose to react to.

When you watch TV, page through a magazine, or go into a store, you notice pretty much everything – even if you don't think you do. Here's what happens next...

Relevance.

People (including you) select what is interesting to them. We're all pretty good at it.

So the real challenge is figuring out what people find important to them and to serve it up in interesting ways. As Gossage said, *"People read what interests them. Sometimes it's an ad."*

Response.

In a world of "overchoice" it's a tough job.

Most people already have too many demands on their time and discretionary dollars. It takes more than ever to make it worth their while to respond.

What are you doing to encourage response? Can you make it easier? Can you make it more appealing?

That's one reason more marketers are using incentives to improve response rates.

It's more than "asking for the order." Ask yourself, "What would it take to get you to respond?" Or maybe, "How can I make responding more fun or rewarding?"

Reaction. *"This car has room for 324 people. (And trillions of germs.)" This message has a chance of getting a reaction for Keri Anti-Bacterial Hand Lotion in a crowded subway car.*

Relevance. *This visual, this topic, and this product are relevant to the target – the mother of a baby.*

Relationship. *Business is built on long-term relationships with your customers. Effective advertising isn't the end of your job – it's the beginning.*

Reaction. Relevance. Response. Relationship. Often, you can do them all at once. Here's a particularly interesting bit of communication – the media vehicle actually gives you a Free Ride. Nice.

NIKE+
CRM + LTV

The Nike+ site goes after long-term brand involvement directly, by involving Nike in your running every step of the way.

A Nike+ unit slips into the shoe and, working with other software, you can track your running progress – training goals – competitions with other runners, and, in general, a measurement of the mileage you log as a runner.

This is an excellent use for technology to generate involvement in this key fitness activity for Nike.

Relationship.

Don't think of that response as the last step.

Traditionally, once that purchase was made, many advertisers thought their job was over. That's not true.

Some of the most avid readers of automobile advertising are those who just bought the car.

Retaining current customers is important for virtually every brand that wants to stay in business.

Think of that purchase as the first step toward a long-term relationship.

After all, the most valuable person a brand has is a current customer – that's who's paying the bills.

CRM & LTV

This is key to direct marketing concepts such as CRM (customer relationship marketing) and LTV, which stands for "lifetime value."

LTV is the total amount of what a customer is worth to a brand over the lifetime of that relationship.

Just think, what's your LTV with your favorite pizza place? Or the place you buy books and magazines. How about coffee?

Even with something fairly low cost, like the daily newspaper, your LTV is pretty substantial.

And how are you working to maintain and grow that relationship. Long-term, that's where you'll prosper. And that's why that fourth R needs to be a part of your thinking.

Your message should be the first step in a growing relationship between the brand and those who use it.

On the left, an example of how Nike uses new media to build a connection with runners. And, my guess is, let them know when it's time to get new shoes.

The 4P's & 4C's

I HAD BEEN WORKING in business and marketing for many years before I wandered into the basics of marketing. As you build your mental tool box, you should probably have these basic principles.

The Four P's are the basics of marketing.

The Four C's are an update (thanks to Bob Lauterborn) that address some of the changes in today's marketplace.

Here goes.

PRODUCT/PRICE/PLACE/PROMOTION. Those are the basics – most marketing strategy addresses these four concerns.

One or another may be emphasized – for example, Walmart emphasizes Price – but, in some ways, all four are usually addressed.

Product.

This one seems kind of obvious. Though you might want to remember that the "product" might also be a service – like a trip to Florida on an airline – or a combination of products and services – like a meal at a restaurant.

In general, to be successful, a product needs to have what we call "functional superiority," fulfilling its function in a way that at least a segment of the market judges as superior, whether for value, taste, or some other dimension of performance.

As Bill Bernbach observed years ago, *"Nothing will kill a bad product faster than good advertising."*

Price.

Henry Ford's success with the Model T was not merely a triumph of manufacturing technology, he was able to lower the car's price to a point where it was affordable for a large number of Americans.

SERVICE AS PRODUCT.
Travelers Insurance has symbolized their service – insurance protection – with the visual of a red umbrella.

Here, they take an environmental approach with their now familiar brand icon.

DRIVEN BY PRICE.
Ford's mass manufacturing provided a low-priced car for a large market. But, after a while, people wanted style and individual variety.

PLACE = DISTRIBUTION.
Think. How many ways are there to get coffee into a cup? Each option can represent a big marketing decision.

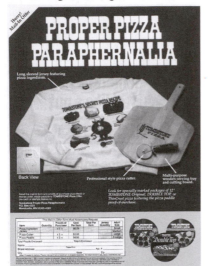

WE REPEAT... HOW MANY P'S?
How many P's do you want on your pizza? Here, advertising and promotion work together.

ALL OF THIS = PROMOTION.
When marketers talk, they mean all of these things.

To state the obvious, the price needs to cover all the costs involved with manufacture and promotion of an item with a bit left over.

This, as you can imagine, is easier said than done – particularly in today's competitive marketplace.

Place.

This is the distribution "P." Place was selected as the word to give us a nice 4P acronym.

Distribution can be a major strategic component, whether it is local retail, where the three most important things are, "location, location, and location" or the state-of-the-art distribution infrastructure of a company like Walmart that squeezes extra cost efficiency from their highly integrated warehouse/information technology operation. The Internet, a ubiquitous information network, has had a huge impact on many businesses – allowing even small operators to tap into widespread distribution with information distribution networks like Amazon, CraigsList, eBay, and the World Wide Web itself.

Promotion.

These are all the activities we generate to market our product – it's our MarCom Matrix.

It includes advertising, sales promotion, marketing public relations (MPR), direct marketing, sales, event marketing, and anything else we can think up that will help us move our merchandise.

Advertising is listed under this P, along with the other MarCom disciplines.

This is the territory covered by our MarCom Matrix.

THE FOUR C'S.
The world changes. As we mentioned, the Media Revolution has, to some extent, put the consumer in the driver's seat. Henry Ford said you could have a Model T *"in any color so long as its black."* Today, your color options are pretty much infinite.

With that in mind, Professor Robert Lauterborn took a look at the classic Four P's and offers us a slightly different perspective – one a little more in keeping with the way the marketplace is today.

While they're not as widespread in usage as the classic Four P's (so don't expect your marketing prof to know what they are), we think they provide a more relevant framework for what's going on in today's marketplace.

The Four C's are: Consumer, Cost, Convenience, Communication. Here we go again.

Consumer.

Consumer replaces Product.

Today's marketplace is driven by the consumer, not the manufacturer or retailer.

Today, an outside-in consumer-focused perspective is necessary to build products the way consumers want.

Successful mass marketers need to look at the world from the consumer's point of view, and use that information in the design and manufacture of their products and services.

Cost.

Cost replaces Price.

Today, consumers have a lot of options and strategies. They can shop with coupons, or choose lower-cost retailers.

Peter Drucker, a well-known business writer, recommended that manufacturers needed to pay closer attention to the price consumers would pay.

So that instead of cost-based pricing, where companies added up their costs to come up with the price, they should aim for "price-based costing."

That is, determining the price the consumer would pay, and use that as a target for the manufacturing division.

CONSPICUOUS CONSUMERS.
Products can be defined by who consumes them. Here, Campbell's adds strength to their product's reputation with big NFL players.

CHANGE OF HABIT.
McDonald's adds equipment and product quality to compete with Starbucks – at a lower cost.

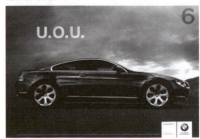

WHAT'S IT WORTH?
Expensive products need to make a total connection with those that can afford them. This ad tells a wealthy person, "you're worth it."

STEP BY STEP.
In a "time-poor" world, new ways to save time can be the basis for a new business. Zappos demonstrates that even shoes can be sold online.

COMMUNICATING WITH CORPORATE CULTURE.
People, place, and product combine to deliver Starbucks' message. Above, average employee benefits translate to an above-average experience.

The whole store is a communication vehicle.

Convenience.

Convenience replaces Place.

Today, retailers and manufacturers must make their products and services easily available. And, again, the new world of information technology is changing things that nobody thought would change.

Buying shoes on the Internet? Web-retailer Zappo's is proving that this can be a big business.

In a world of "Click here," marketers have to work harder and harder to make it easier and easier.

Communication.

Communication replaces Promotion.

Now we have to think about all the ways we connect with the consumer – not just how the ads look. Certainly, advertising may still be the most visible (and expensive) part of the communication mix, but other contact points may be just as important.

For example, IMC guru Tom Duncan notes that often the lowest-paid employees have the most frequent contacts with customers and prospects.

Today, we need to assess how we're communicating top to bottom.

It's a crowded and complicated marketplace – today's marketing communication has to understand that complexity and overcome it with focused and effective communication.

DEEP BREATH…
OK, a lot to think about.

Don't feel bad if you can't quite get it all stored in what is becoming a very crowded brain – but, as the years go by, you'll find that all of these concepts can be surprisingly useful.

As you work through this chapter, you might want to skip ahead to some of the exercises, to help your head find room for these different ways of thinking.

Laddering.

THIS IS ANOTHER USEFUL WAY of looking at various aspects of your business.

You'll find that a lot of discussion will focus on what factor to emphasize. Sequencing these factors is called "laddering."

Here are generally agreed upon definitions – listed "bottom to top:"

Attribute (Product Attribute). Characteristic of product, usually inherent or natural – *Applesauce comes in wide-mouth glass jars.*

Product Feature. This is usually based on some manufactured or designed aspect – *Applesauce spoons smoothly out of the wide-mouth jar.*

Product Benefit. A benefit to the consumer, usually based on a Product Feature or Attribute – *Applesauce is easy to serve.*

Consumer Benefit (Customer Benefit). A benefit usually based on how the Product Benefit delivers a positive result to the consumer – *I save time, and my children get extra nutrition (which tastes good – so they'll eat it).*

Values. The human dimension reinforced by the benefit – *I'm a good mother because I serve Applesauce.*

Laddering is the process of moving through this sequence. The general method is to ask people *why* the Feature (or Benefit) is important. The answer generally moves you up the "ladder."

WHERE ON THE LADDER?

A continuing issue is where to focus.

Generally, the "lower" on the ladder you are, the more product-specific your message and the more you are differentiating your product.

PRODUCT FEATURE.
This new iPod Shuffle has a feature that talks to you.

PRODUCT BENEFIT.
This iPod will hold 1,000 songs and fit in your pocket.

CONSUMER BENEFIT & VALUE.
The dancing silhouette communicates the benefit to the consumer – music you love that you can take with you. The overall graphic approach communicates – in an iconic way – that it's part of contemporary pop culture.

It says that you are part of that culture with an iPod.

WHERE ON THE LADDER?

You need to develop your skills at identifying how messages are constructed.

A good start is to identify where on the ladder they decided to build the message.

And, remember, we're all good at doing the translating – we can figure out what the Consumer Benefit is of an Attribute, and we can also usually figure out what Features and Product Benefits went into building the Consumer Benefit.

The key is often finding the best way to dramatize.

Here are two examples.

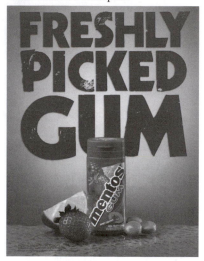

PRODUCT BENEFIT

This ad looks great in color.

The appetizing fruit flavors are dramatized and reinforced by the strong simple headline.

If we like fruit-flavored gum, we will be attracted and tempted to try the product.

(Continued on next page.)

The higher up you are, the more you deal with what's important in the consumer's life – and the more generic your benefit.

All we can say is look for the strongest line of development.

SOME ADDITIONAL THOUGHTS.

The "lower" levels tend to be about the product and the "higher" levels about consumers, with the highest level being something we call "Values."

Values are about internal needs and self-image.

Every product we use relates in some way to values that are important to us.

The part of us that nurtures.

The part of us that wants to succeed.

The part of us that wants to have a good time.

Values can be important – but remember, they're not exclusively about your product.

Most nutritious food products reinforce nurturing maternal values and most fashion and personal care products are about a positive self-image.

Think. How does the benefit *within* the product manifest itself *within* the consumer? And what aspect of the sequence is "ownable?"

NO RULES.

Some will try to turn this useful tool into a ruler.

They will decide that the higher you go on the ladder the better. Well, not necessarily.

As we just noted, many Values are pretty much generic across the category.

Often, the same thing goes for Consumer Benefits.

Some studies showed that Product Benefits, which were more often based on some specific and unique manufactured aspect of the brand had more distinctiveness.

My best advice is to approach it with an open mind.

One afternoon, I was doing a laddering exercise with a local cable group.

The client was a local sports bar. I was pretty sure that we'd end up in some sort of Product Promotion/Product Benefit territory – Game Day Special, or maybe something with baseball pitchers and pitchers of beer. But they threw me a curve.

The group's best effort ended up in Values territory. They talked about their desired target and the recommended theme was "Where Winners Come to Play." Not bad.

I learned a lesson myself. Don't decide too early – you have to climb up and down the ladder to find your best line of development.

ATTRIBUTES, BENEFITS, & "INHERENT DRAMA."
Inherent drama. Leo Burnett (and others) solve this by using unique visualizations for generic benefits or inherent attributes (e.g., the Maytag Repairman for washing machine durability or the Pillsbury Doughboy that pops out of the package). Then, the benefit becomes, to some degree, ownable for your brand.

And, along the way, the brand develops Values.

MORE THAN ONE PLACE ON THE LADDER?
Sure. Unique combinations can be powerful.

Examine the whole ladder – from Attributes to Features to Product Benefits to Consumer Benefits to Values – and look for unique strengths.

Find out what is most meaningful.

You may discover your Objective is communicating that unique dimension – or combination.

Or… maybe you keep looking.

The nice thing about the ladder – it helps make all this stuff easy to find and easy to understand.

WHERE ON THE LADDER (CONT.)

CONSUMER BENEFIT.
A can of SlimFast blasting through two fat donuts tells consumers this diet product will stop cravings for four hours.

A nice approach to nutritional maintenance – a rational sell served up with visual and emotional power.

I like this ad for two more reasons.

First, they tell you how to use it – once every four hours.

Simple, but they get into the "Do" mode.

Second, it encourages repeat usage.

Sure, that's part of all these diet maintenance/meal substitute products, but they do a nice fresh job of getting you into the "use regularly for best results" mode.

AND ONE MORE THING.
Not only can you use these conceptual tools to think things up, *you can use them to present!*

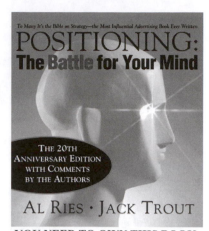

YOU NEED TO OWN THIS BOOK.
Voted the #1 all-time book on advertising and marketing in an *Advertising Age* poll of industry professionals.

"CHERCHEZ LE CRENEAUX."
"Look for the hole" in the prospect's mind.

It's one of the best strategies in the field of marketing.

Creneaus don't have to be exciting or dramatic or even have much of a consumer benefit to be effective.

Rolex was the first expensive watch.

Orville Redenbacher was the first expensive popcorn.

Michelob was the first expensive domestic beer.

Where is the consumer benefit in being more expensive?

Well, as L'Oreal would say, "I'm worth it."

Each of these brands were the first to fill those "holes" in the prospect's mind.

All were successful.

Like a good running back – find the hole and run for daylight.

(From *Positioning: The Battle for Your Mind*. 20th Anniversary Edition)

Positioning Re-Visited.

We covered *Positioning* in Chapter One and, since *Positioning* is regarded as possibly the best advertising book ever, it's probably a good idea to cover it again – particularly since it's one of the most useful conceptual models.

In general, whatever other conceptual models you use in generating your idea for the brand, there will be an ongoing concern with the question "What's our Position?"

INSIDE THE MIND OF THE CONSUMER. The first thing to remember is that, even though you're probably sitting in an office or meeting room, that isn't where positioning happens.

Positioning happens inside the mind of the consumer. It doesn't matter what you say in the meeting about your brand, it matters what the consumer thinks about your brand.

So don't be fooled by well-intentioned, well-articulated statements like, "Our position is the leading ink-jet printer in the under $200 category." There may be some useful thoughts in that sentence, but, until the consumer decides there is a meaningful category called "ink-jet printers under $200" it's not useful in terms of positioning.

You need to discover what is meaningful to the consumer in terms of printers: dependability, print-quality, reasonable cost (including the cost of replacement cartridges), and so on. Then, once you know what is inside the consumer's mind, you can start to go to work.

Want to put something new in the consumer's mind? Hey, it can be done, but don't think that saying it loud and often in the meeting will be enough to carry the day.

And, as we are all too well aware, the consumer usually has a lot of other stuff on his or her mind. The better we know what's there, the better we can develop and execute simple, strong positioning.

This also leads us to the not surprising observation that positionings are pretty simple.

That said, let's take a look at the four basics.

1. THE BEST POSITION

While the broad stroke leaders in major categories are clear in everyone's mind, you should also remember that "Best" positions also exist at the local level and within fairly narrow categories.

For example, some fairly large categories – like pizza restaurants – often have local leaders. The fact that Pizza Hut churns out more pizzas on a weekend nationwide doesn't tend to be meaningful to a half-dozen teenagers on a Friday night.

Likewise, technical categories, like desktop publishing, may have very different "bests" than machine tools and CAD-CAM engineering – even though both use powerful computers.

Some categories, like video games, may have great volatility. Others, like laundry detergents and peanut butter preference may have roots all the way back to the brand that your mother bought at the grocery store.

2. THE AGAINST POSITION

This one is tough duty. But, in some categories, you might not have much choice.

For example, the leader brand may be setting the perceptual standard – Hershey's has been a leading US brand in chocolate. It tastes much different than British chocolate, which has different leadership brands – like Cadbury's.

And it is quite common that the leader brand has a dominant share – that's where all the business

#1 IS WHERE YOU FIND IT.
Here, Colgate leverages performance with "dental professionals."

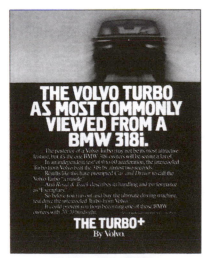

VOLVO VS. BMW.
With an overall "safety" position, Volvo positions this model against "the Ultimate Driving Machine."

175

BALL PARK PLAYS HARDBALL.

As this book was going to press, Sara Lee Corp filed a lawsuit against Kraft Foods' Oscar Mayer, saying the hot dog maker misled consumers in their advertising by claiming its hot dogs are superior to Sara Lee's Ball Park brand.

The lawsuit focuses on an ad by Oscar Mayer that compares the taste of their beef hot dogs to Sara Lee's Ball Park brand beef hot dogs.

"It is both false and misleading to consumers," Sara Lee said in a statement. They say the ad is false and misleading because in large type it implies one Oscar Mayer dog bested the taste of all Ball Park dogs. But the footnote, "in very small type," says that Oscar Mayer compared its hot dogs to "the leading beef franks" of its main rivals. A spokesperson for Kraft and Oscar Mayer said simply, "We stand by our reputation for accurate advertising."

Two other factors to consider, Oscar Mayer had recently re-formulated their beef hot dogs and the Ball Park brand had been showing growth

It's Not Subtle.

The Against Position isn't subtle.

In one way or another, sometimes by direct comparison, you're taking on the competition directly. Don't be surprised if the competition reacts.

One Big "Against" Category.

Of course, there's one category where advertisers can say almost whatever they want against the competition… and they pretty much get away with it.

What category is that you ask?

Politics!

is – so if you want to grow your brand, you have to take it from that leader brand which, more often than not, also occupies the "best" position.

You have to strap it on and go to war. (In this section, we'll also cover a related book by Trout and Ries – *Marketing Warfare.*)

One core question is do you go against the leader in a direct obvious way – such as the famous Avis/Hertz warfare of the '60s and '70s.

Or, are you a bit more indirect? Energizer advertised durability against a leader brand called DuraCell – but didn't name names.

They did, however, successfully co-opt the DuraCell advertising format, which featured long-lasting battery-powered toys.

Seven-Up's well-known and successful "Un-Cola" campaign was rooted in the mind of the consumer. In the mind of the consumer, soft drink meant cola. For Seven-Up to even be considered as a soft drink, they had to enter that competitive set.

Burger King tried some direct comparison with McDonald's and, while it did not seem that McDonald's responded in advertising, they did respond with brutal levels of price promotion (and even a lawsuit) – something you often find in American business, where big marketing rivals hammer each other with deep discounts to see who says "ouch" first. It happens.

You may still find that the ugly realities of your market position demand that you go against the biggest brand in your category.

If so, you might also want to read *Marketing Warfare*, which we'll talk about in a page or two.

3. NICHE POSITIONING

If you do it right, this can be a clean stylish road to marketplace success.

You need to identify an important characteristic in the category and make your position and that characteristic one and the same.

Volvo and safety is a classic example.

My own background included a bit of time working in the detergent category for the fine folks at Leo Burnett and Procter and Gamble.

Tide owned the primary characteristic – cleaning – but there were other attributes that were meaningful. Back in my day, we positioned Cheer – re-branded as All-Temperature Cheer with the variety of colors and fabrics that were part of contemporary wardrobes. It grew the brand to #2 in the category.

Today, the position for Cheer has evolved to color brightness, an evolution that made sense for a variety of reasons.

Every category has a different set of meaningful characteristics, and not every one is strong enough to maintain a profitable market position.

But, if you do it right, you end up with a distinctive brand position, distinctive messaging, and a solid business.

4. THE NEW CATEGORY

If you can do it right, a #1 position awaits.

Sometimes, you just re-configure an existing category. That way, Memphis becomes, "The #1 Distributor in the Mid-South." Conveniently eliminating Atlanta, Memphis grabs a #1.

More often, it comes from a genuinely new category – PDAs, digital cameras, energy drinks.

Then, more often than not, if you are successful, the category grows and all of the other position variations, such as "Niche" and "Against" emerge. And then, one day, someone changes the game enough that you have another New Category.

NO VEGETARIANS NEED APPLY.
A steakhouse needs to connect with people who eat steaks – serious meat eaters.
These ads connect with this mind set.

**NEW CATEGORIES.
NEW BEHAVIORS.**
"Breakfast on the run" is a new category for people who are increasingly time poor. Other factors, like longer commutes and late-night TV, can impact breakfast.

**POSITIONING BY
PRODUCT DIFFERENCE.**

Every other cookie company had chocolate chip cookies. Archway had the #1 oatmeal cookie. That was the basis for this successful positioning.

**POSITIONED BY USER.
POSITIONED BY PROBLEM.**

The "Absolutely Positively" campaign from FedEx is an excellent example.

Though shipping had been around for years, FedEx was basically a New Category. All by itself, that was not meaningful enough in the consumer's mind.

By positioning themselves with *the right user* – business people who had to get it done – and by identifying exactly *the right problem* – a critical package that had to get there – they built a winning combination.

And a winning position.

178

Combinations

THE FOUR BASIC TYPES OF POSITIONS can have many combinations and variations. The following work was done by Roman Hiebing in *The Successful Marketing Plan,* one of the better marketing books available.

These are quite useful. Just remember some positions can be accurately described by more than one of them.

1. BY PRODUCT DIFFERENCE.
Generally, all positions work to establish some sort of brand differentiation within the category.

The difference between your product and the competition can be the basis for your position.

2. BY KEY ATTRIBUTE/BENEFIT.
There should be some sort of consumer benefit either stated or implied in your position.

For example, "The Quicker Picker Upper" positions Bounty as it communicates a clearly stated attribute/product benefit.

Other more general attributes, such as quality, may have an implied benefit.

Many successful brands have been built by pre-empting the key attribute or benefit generic to the category. Leo Burnett does this often.

3. BY USERS OF YOUR PRODUCT.
Virginia Slims is an excellent example – particularly during its introductory period, when they were able to connect with emerging issues.

Many brands are built by heavy users – those who use a great deal of the product.

One aspect of product usage is a surprisingly accurate pattern known as **The 80/20 Rule.** That is, 80% of your business comes from 20% of your customers. For example, 20% of beer drinkers drink 80% of the beer.

Many brands are built with heavy usage and loyalty from a relatively small group of people.

4. BY TYPE OF USAGE.

Michelob was successful with "Weekends Are Made for Michelob." They weren't quite as successful with "The Night Belongs to Michelob." (Some of this was due to a changing beer market.)

Types of positionings can be combined. Years earlier, Shaefer Beer combined Type of Usage with a Heavy-User position – *"Shaefer is the one beer to have when you're having more than one."*

5. POSITIONING AGAINST A CATEGORY.

Light beer can be positioned against regular beer; discount clothing stores are often positioned against department stores.

6. AGAINST A SPECIFIC COMPETITOR(S).

You can go against the overall leader, as Avis did, or against a specific competitor.

Truck marketers often play this game.

Ford goes against Chevy and vice versa.

Meanwhile, various small Japanese-made pickup trucks position against each other.

7. POSITIONING BY ASSOCIATION.

This is generally associated with image advertising. It can also be used to reinforce other attributes, such as a firm's heritage in the community being used to reinforce their caring and service – or even their old-fashioned recipes.

8. POSITION BY PROBLEM.

This is similar to positioning by benefit, only the problem is dramatized more than the solution.

Successful products fulfill needs – that need is often a problem that needs solving.

For example, calcium products that combat the effects of osteoporosis in women.

FedEx positioned itself against the problem with "absolutely positively…"

"BUCKET HEADS."
Church's Fried Chicken went after KFC users by calling them "bucket heads."
  Funny? Yes.
  Effective? What do you think?

Association with Celebrity. The right celebrity can reinforce your position.

"WHERE'S THE BEEF?"
Wendy's went after people standing in line at McDonald's by reminding them in a humorous way that there was a bigger beef patty on a Wendy's burger.
  Funny? Yes.
  Effective? Very.

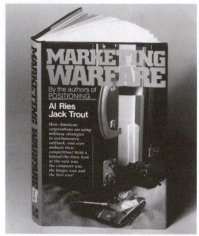

Ronald McDonald House Charities®

Help us help.

CHICAGOLAND &
NORTHWEST INDIANA

KEEPING THE HIGH GROUND.
Activities like Ronald McDonald House also help a leading brand maintain its position.

Marketing Warfare

A few years after writing *Positioning*, Trout and Ries wrote another very interesting and useful book called *Marketing Warfare*.

Positioning was about message overload and the difficulty of finding a place "in the mind of the consumer."

Marketing Warfare dealt with "zero-sum marketing." That is, categories had become so crowded that, if you were going to win a sale, it meant that someone else would lose a sale.

No longer would buoyant growth make everyone look smart. (As they say, "a rising tide lifts all boats.") In days when growing affluence meant families were buying a second car, auto manufacturers had a relatively easy time of it.

With those markets saturated and growing manufacturing capacity, it's a different world for marketers in virtually every category.

With that in mind, they took a look at the principles of a military strategist named Von Clausewitz, and they served up a variation of positioning that considered these tougher realities of a more crowded marketplace.

DEFENSE.

Von Clausewitz says that if you're #1, you play defense and protect your position. You have the advantage of "the high ground," a leadership position.

If you attack, attack your own weakness.

OFFENSE.

If you have no choice, you attack the leader.

This is the "Against" position.

If you do attack, find the dimension where you have superiority and attack narrowly along that line.

FLANKING.

This is their version of Niche positioning.

Here, the key is to find some open territory and establish yourself there.

In my experience, an example would be Popeyes Fried Chicken, a spicy New Orleans-based formula that went into the fried chicken category and found open territory called "spicy fried chicken."

By the time they were well-established, it was too late for competitors, like KFC, to move them from their turf.

GUERRILLA.

OK, this one is a bit different – and has nothing to do with The New Category.

It describes a marketplace behavior that occurs when you are surrounded by bigger players with deeper pockets.

One classic example was the promotional planning by a small cookie company. Cookies are a business where off-shelf and end-aisle displays can really have an impact on sales.

You couldn't just pick the time you'd like to promote, because the best times were taken by big cookie companies like Nabisco.

So, what you had to do was figure out when Nabisco was not promoting, and schedule your promotions for those times. That way, you had a better chance of getting those end-aisle displays into the stores.

This is just a cursory view. If you find you're interested in some of this marketing thinking, *Marketing Warfare* and *Positioning* are highly recommended.

YES, THAT'S ELLEN.
While working as a comic in New Orleans, she showed up at the commercial shoot.

PROMOTE THE PROMOTION.
A guerilla marketer has to look for "windows of opportunity." In the cookie business, a key is getting off-shelf display.

181

#13: Conceptual Workout

THINKING   FEELING

THINK **HIGH** **INVOLVEMENT**	**FEEL** **HIGH** **INVOLVEMENT**
THINK **LOW** **INVOLVEMENT**	**FEEL** **LOW** **INVOLVEMENT**

1. M.O.S.T.

Currently, Apple has a campaign that competes directly with the PC.

We're sure you're familiar with it.

What do you think their Mission, Objective, Strategy, and Tactics are today?

2. FCB GRID.

A. Right to Left. Take a right brain (emotional) ad. Make it a left brain (rational) ad.

B. Left to Right. Pick a left brain (rational) ad. Do the opposite. Make it a right brain (emotional) ad.

C. Draw The Grid.
Make a list of 10 different products.
Place them on The FCB Planning Grid.

D. Both Sides. The Saab ad below appeals to both. Pick another product with *both* rational and emotional appeals.

Write an ad that appeals to both. (It can be a spread.)

3. EXPLODE THE DOT.

Take the product from #2D and show the various forces at work in all four sections of The Grid.

Repeat the process with a second product.

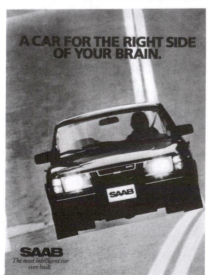

4. LEARN/FEEL/DO CIRCLE.

A. Select a product.

What is there to Learn about it?

What Feelings might be associated with using it?

What do we Do? There may be a number of actions.

B. Now, think of a message approach that uses each as an entry point.

Don't worry that you're not doing a polished script. Just rough it out.

5. 4A's/4R's.

A. In two columns – with plenty of space – write the 4A's and then the 4R's.

B. Pick a product or service – indicate what aspects of a program match up with each of these A's and R's. Again, don't worry about not having much of a message or strategy, the idea is to become more familiar with this kind of thinking.

6. 4P's/4C's.

A. Write them down and try to remember them.

B. That's it. This will come in handy if and when you find yourself in a marketing class. Remember the concepts, particularly if you find yourself doing heavy lifting in the area of marketing strategy.

THE LEARN/FEEL/DO CIRCLE

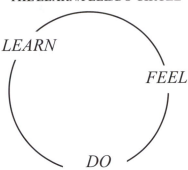

LEARN

FEEL

DO

What Will You Do to Generate…

Attention _____

_____

Awareness _____

_____

Attitude _____

_____

Action _____

_____

Reaction _____

_____

Relevance _____

_____

Response _____

_____

Relationship _____

_____

P _____

P _____

P _____

P _____

C _____

C _____

C _____

C _____

Extra-Enviror

HOWARD GOSSAGE ON EXTRA-ENVIRONMENTAL THINKING.

You have noticed, I am sure, that talented immigrants to our shores do very well indeed and in a remarkably short time. I think it is mostly because they are extra-environmentals. They see things that we don't and are not stuck with our load of "experience" experience.

The big advantage the extra-environmental has is that he has no rules to hamper him doing things the environmental not only wouldn't think of doing, but also wouldn't be caught dead doing, even if he could. However, once they are done and accepted within the environmental power structure, then he will do them, and do them, and do them.

The best art, the best ads... and the people who do them, will tend to be extra-environmental.

From "Environment and Creativity" in *The Book of Gossage.*

THIS CHAPTER IS ABOUT intuitive and non-linear thought processes. The conceptual model might be from Plato or maybe Howard Gossage.

The idea is this. We live in a world of constantly expanding awareness.

So, if you had Plato and the cave in philosophy 101, that's kind of it. Howard Gossage talks about how we are in a constant sequence of discovery – with newer wider-ranging intellectual environments encompassing our previous level of awareness.

The fish is swimming in water. Step back. The water is inside an aquarium. The fish is used to the invisible boundaries and, furthermore, conditioned by that environment, rising to the surface when the top is opened. Food comes from above. Magic.

This seems to work whether we are expanding our awareness of the universe in general, or expanding our awareness of just fertilizer and herbicides for an agricultural client.

One interesting thing about communicating on a wide range of topics is your awareness grows with every assignment. That expanding awareness provides a new context that, rather often, results in something useful for the next job.

But the key is an extra-environmental perspective.

Many account planners are Brits and Scots. They speak English, but have a foreigner's perspective on our behavior. Artists often have that external view. They're a step removed. That extra perspective provides insights you don't get inside the invisible box of culture.

TRUE STORY.

George Washington Hill, head of American Tobacco, is wondering how to get more women to smoke Lucky Strike cigarettes.

He's thinking about this when his limo drives by two women. One, fairly slim, is smoking a cigarette and the other, more heavy-set, is eating candy.

Hmmm…

He's on his way to Albert Lasker's agency, Lord and Thomas. They come up with "Reach For a Lucky Instead of a Sweet." Cigarettes become a diet aid.

Growing sexual equality in lung disease is an unhappy result, but the conceptual point is useful.

An expansion of perception can often result in a useful new selling perspective.

Let's see how we can make use of that kind of thinking today.

A NON-LINEAR LIST.

We're going to look at a few ways to kind of "sneak up" on the answer to a problem.

Cumulatively, they seem to be things you ought to have in your mental tool box..

Here they are, in no particular order:

- Zen Copywriting.
- Reduction/Relevance/Resonance
- Inside/Outside
- Velcro & "Vibe"
- The Personal Truth
- Nine-Wheel Logic.

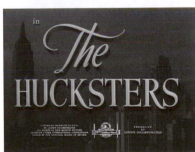

LATE NIGHT HISTORY LESSON.
Keep an eye out for an old movie called *The Hucksters*. The Sidney Greenstreet character is based on George Washington Hill. The Adolph Monjou character is loosely based on Emerson Foote, one of the founders of Foote Cone & Belding, the successor agency to Lord and Thomas (Lasker sold his agency to his three office managers).

Oh yeah, and it stars Clark Gable and Deborah Kerr. Not bad.

Zen Copywriting

IN ZEN ARCHERY,
the archer and the act become one.
The copywriter's job
is much the same.

Imagine
the destination
before you begin
the journey.

Your job is to take
information
and images
and ideas
and make them
what they were
meant to be.

You must
organize them,
imagine them,
write them,
and
sell them.
As your journey progresses,
your destination will be seen more clearly.
As your skills develop, your arrows
will fly closer to the invisible
target's center.
That's your job.
Imagine
the future.
Make it
come
true
.

Q: How many Zen Masters does it take to change a light bulb?

A: Two.
One to change the light bulb.
One to not change the light bulb.

Two key aspects of Zen are:
- accommodating contradictory thoughts, and
- being in touch with the moment.

Both are important in advertising.

SOME KEY CONTRADICTIONS.

We take small products that play a minor role in people's lives and work to make them important.

We must embrace contradiction in many ways.

For example, this is a business where you must really take it seriously to be successful.

Yet, take it too seriously, and it makes you crazy.

A NOW MESSAGE FROM NOW.

You must embrace the moment.

Good advertising seems to have intuitively good timing. It seems to know the right moment – a knowing without knowing.

Some of this may be rooted in Bernbach's belief that good advertising was a bit "sociological."

Some of it is the simple fact that if your goal, your target, is people living their lives right now, well why shouldn't your message be in harmony with that simple reality?

It is often hard to explain.

But we tend to know it when we see it.

And feel it.

PRESENTATION ZEN.
10 rules for making good design

I thought I'd have a moment in the Now.

So I Googled "Zen Ten" and found this gem (I also found a band with that name).

Here are ten pieces of good advice for many things graphic.

The basics are from a book called *Design Elements: A Graphic Style Manual* by Timothy Samara.

(1) Communicate – don't decorate.
(2) Speak with a visual voice.
(3) Use two typeface families maximum. OK, maybe three.
(4) Pick colors on purpose.
(5) If you can do it with less, then do.
(6) Negative space is magical – create it, don't just fill it up!
(7) Treat the type as image, as though it's just as important.
(8) Be universal; remember that it's not about you.
(9) Be decisive. Do it on purpose – or don't do it at all.
(10) Symmetry is the ultimate evil. Some clarification here. Symmetry isn't evil, in fact it can be quite beautiful, and calming, (or serious, etc.). But symmetry can also be rather dull and predictable. Asymmetrical designs are more dynamic generally and can allow for a bit more freedom of expression.

The Zen aesthetic is all about asymmetry as well.

[From Garr Reynolds blog on presentation design. A nice find.]

#14:Ad Haiku

ZEN READING LIST:
Want to know more about Zen?

Don't get carried away, but I believe that a general understanding of Zen can help in doing your job.

The Way of Zen
Alan Watts
Vintage Books

Zen in the Art of Archery
E. Herrigel
Pantheon

Zen and the Art of Motorcycle Maintenance: An Inquiry into Values
Robert M. Pirsig

Shogun.
James Clavell
(The book is better than the movie.)

PAPER NAPKIN HAIKU.
This can be a lot of fun with the right group of people — at a restaurant, or wherever.

Someone starts a haiku on a napkin (or a piece of note paper) and writes the first five syllables.

The next person writes the next line – seven syllables.

And a third person does the third line – five syllables.

Try it.

Let's do some *haiku.*
It's Japanese poetry
of only three lines.

First five syllables
then in the middle seven
followed by five more.

It's five seven five
a rhythm made from phrasing
that doesn't need rhyme.

How do you haiku?
Feel the thought within the thing.
Put it on paper.

You can haiku, too
Just start at the beginning
let the writing flow.

Try These:

1. TRADITIONAL HAIKU.
   Based on an object or scene in nature.

2. DO A HAIKU.
   About a tool or kitchen appliance.

3. HOW TO HAIKU.
   Do a haiku about how to do something.

4. MOVIE REVIEW HAIKU.
   Do a haiku about a movie or TV show.

5. ADVERTISING HAIKU.
   Do a haiku about a brand name product.

Reduction & Relevance

First, a key way of thinking and a key way of evaluating. Most mass marketing communication works with "reductionist" thinking.

That is, reduce the messaging to the most important benefit in the category and then repeat that claim for widespread awareness – The Quicker-Picker-Upper – 15 Minutes Could Save You 15% – The Pause That Refreshes – it keeps going and going…

This works best when that claim is relevant to the target market – that's the evaluation standard you have to make.

First, is it as simple as you can make it?

Then, is that simple statement/claim relevant to the people you're trying to reach?

Reduction and relevance are particularly useful for mass marketed packaged goods – and may apply to other businesses – like car insurance.

So, the segment of the car insurance category concerned simply with cost will be susceptible to the claim "Fifteen minutes could save you 15%."

The wide variety of commercials for GEICO all end up delivering one simple message. We like the recently added device to "visualize the benefit." Now you can see the money you save.

However, the savings claim is still single-minded.

Paper towels are about picking up spills – batteries are about lasting.

So it can make a lot of sense to get your product/benefit message down to one simple statement and then keep banging away.

However, and this is worth repeating – the claim has to be relevant.

SIMPLE + STRONG.
Dog ownership has strong emotional connections. Here, Pedigree connects with strong, simple visuals that show their love of dogs.

"The Quicker Picker Upper"
Same thing. Over and over. Even Bounty's website is <u>quickerpickerupper.com</u>.

Visualize the Benefit.

_A_ IS FOR ADVERTISING.

When it works, it's more than the ads.

It's the beginning of a relationship.

It's something that happens _to_ a person, whether reader, viewer, listener, or someone not paying much attention. It's not just the ad, it's _the response_ to the ad.

It's not what happens in the ad, it's what happens _inside the person._

That's how advertising works. Advertising that does not do that merely "talks to itself."

It may be handsome. The client may love it.

Hey, you might even win an award.

But it probably won't work very well.

As my psychology professor said (Yes, Professor Gilchrist, I was paying attention), you have to get "_inside the other person's skin._"

Once you start to see the world from that perspective, it becomes easier to think about how to create advertising that works.

THE DAISY COMMERCIAL.

A little girl is counting daisy petals. The track cross-fades into a missile countdown. We see a nuclear mushroom cloud. A calm voice tells us that in times like these we need Lyndon Johnson as president.

The power of the commercial wasn't in what was said, the power was in the internal processing of what was said.

What was said was that it was a dangerous world and you might want Lyndon Johnson to be president.

The response of viewers was, "Holy Smoke! Barry Goldwater (the other candidate, who'd advocated using nuclear weapons) might Drop The Big One!"

Johnson won in a landslide.

If it is not meaningful, it doesn't matter how clever it is and how often you say it. If it is relevant, then it may have surprising power.

I remember talking to an executive familiar with disposable diapers – dominated by Pampers and Huggies.

He had an interesting observation that made me realize how powerful reductionist thinking can be.

"_When you get down to it,_" he observed, "_the attitude of mothers toward their baby is very much wrapped up in the brand names._"

Both values are, of course, relevant to mothers.

Resonance

Now let's go one level deeper – it's more than relevance, it's a value that resonates _inside_ the person you're talking to.

Great advertising happens _inside_ people.

As a writer and producer, Tony Schwartz has been responsible for some of the most powerful and effective ads ever made – the "Daisy" commercial helped create a landslide victory for Lyndon Johnson.

He has also made important contributions to the way we think about communicating.

When you achieve _resonance,_ your external message connects with internal values and feelings. "_Resonance takes place when the stimuli put into our communication evoke_ meaning _in a listener or viewer… the meaning of our communication is what a listener or viewer gets_ out _of his experience with the communicator's stimuli._"

For example, think how you react when someone says, "_Don't worry about the money_"? You immediately worry. Right?

That's the point. We need to understand how our messages work inside the other person's skin.

Not what we say – how people respond to what we say. How we connect with what is already inside their minds.

Schwartz says *"It concentrates on evoking responses from people by attuning the message to their prior experience."*

And JWT says, *"It's not what you put in the advertising that counts – it's what people get out of it."*

The Personal Truth

A related concept, that we think is very useful, comes from Dan Wieden of Wieden + Kennedy. He wants his agency to discover the "personal truth" in the products they advertise.

How do they relate to the individual customer's feelings and experience?

Nike products cover a wide range of activities – each has a different reason for being in people's lives.

Nike advertising tries to match the personal values attached to those activities.

For example, their advertising to women is dramatically different from that aimed at competitive tennis players or older runners.

Basketball, football, and golf are different still – even though it's all Nike.

Thinking like this helps Nike's advertising "ring true." Even their celebrity advertising is crafted to allow you to empathize with the individual.

It's not just about Nike – it's about *you*.

RESONANCE IN RADIO.

Here's a spot Tony Schwartz designed to recruit new sales people for Bamberger's Department Stores.

Before writing the commercial, some of Bamberger's best employees were interviewed, asked why they chose Bamberger's as a place to work, and what they liked about their job.

They were also asked what radio stations they listened to.

Here's part of the spot.

ANNCR: Well, what are you doing with yourself now that the kids are all grown up and gone?

Wouldn't it be fun to go out and meet new people, maybe even start working again? You've got a lot to contribute.

And an extra paycheck could go a long way.

You know, there's a new department store opening in September at the Lehigh Valley Mall. Bamberger's.

And they really do need people like you. People who like to shop and who like to help other people shop.

And Bamberger's will have so many different work schedules – mornings, afternoons, evenings, full time, part time, weekdays, Saturdays – and they'll have employee discounts and nice benefits, too.

You know, Bamberger's really appreciates people like you, people who care and try.

So you probably won't stay at your starting salary very long...

Guess what? *Exactly the right kind of people showed up at Bamberger's – looking for jobs!*

VELCRO.

As Dan Wieden observed, the Nike theme, "Just Do It" accumulates meaning.

Even though it's all about sport and achievement, different sports and different individuals have different values.

Nike's consistency comes from its "in touch" tone of voice. Nike hooks into this variety of feelings and connects them and collects them into one big cultural hairball.

ADDING INGREDIENTS.

Sometimes you want a single-minded sales message, and sometimes you need to reach different targets.

Best of all, sometimes a lot of different things add up to one big thing.

"Just Do It" is a theme that gathers strength as each commercial adds its own "truth" to the Nike image.

Velcro & "Vibe"

Then again, we're not one-dimensional.

Not only that, but, quite often, our interface with a product has more than one dimension.

This was driven home to me when I worked with the smart folks at Apple computer.

Maybe batteries are only about durability, but a Macintosh from Apple Computer is about a whole lot of things.

Reductionist thinking is still useful, but now you have more complexity. To different target groups – artists and teachers, for example – the key benefit of using a Mac may be entirely different.

Moreover, we're going to be spending serious money. We want to process more than one message. And, after all, it's for a product with more dimensions than a paper towel, so it's not unreasonable that there would be more to say and think about.

"VELCRO."

So, instead of a single-minded "hook," you might want to think about what Canadian marketing thinker John Della Costa terms "Velcro." (By the way, the copyright lawyers would like to remind us that Velcro is also a brand of fasteners.)

Different Groups. Different Approaches. *This "Design Your Own Shoelaces" promotion took a* Foot Loose *(ever see the opening credits?) approach for a whole range of their casual footwear.*

Here's a little chart from the Canadian Advertising Institute that offers some perspective:

Hook	Velcro
Single benefit	Multiple benefits
Single-minded	Many-sided
Repeat consistently	Consistently surprise
Fixed for the long-term	Flexible for the short-term
Differentiates vs. competitor	Engages the customer
Presents a positioning	Surrounds with inducements
Focuses on transaction	Builds toward relationship
Simple for memorability	Complex for involvement

As you work your way through the marketing problems that emerge in the course of a career, you'll come to understand the difference.

For the most part, we're asked to write single-minded hooks that solve short-term problems.

But, sometimes, we get involved in a long-term relationship between a brand and its customers – and when we do, we might need to realize that we might need a new kind of thinking.

"VIBE"

As long as we're down to "V" in the alphabet, let's talk about cultural intuition, all the subtle things that we pick up from the world around us – almost without noticing it.

Women with a fashion sense pick that up. I've walked past an Army Supply store with Lorelei, my favorite fashionista, and she'd point at something and say, "six months." Sure enough, six months later it's in fashion.

Music, fads, fashion, art, all the things happening in culture are part of the vibe, "buzz," whatever you want to call it.

THE COOLHUNT.

How do we find out what's cool?

Some people just know. And some people hunt for the people who just know.

In this thought-provoking article, Malcolm Gladwell tracks down Dee Dee Gordon, a "coolhunter." She finds out what the cool kids think – because their styles and values will become, in many cases, the styles and values of the culture.

Coolhunting is like account planning for the fashion industry.

It's not a coherent philosophy, but a collection of spontaneous observations from people who have their antennae tuned to styles and trends that evolve from one moment to the next.

Diffusion Research.

Part of coolhunting research is understanding how ideas spread.

And, as we hope to get our commercial ideas into the cultural conversation, it helps to see if we can tune our antennae to the various cultures we want to be a part of – teen culture, business culture, soccer mom culture…

So read the article, rub it all over yourself and remember, you are a part of that changing edge of pop culture. You might not be the coolest of the cool, but you're a part of it.

See what you can do with that.

Tune those antennae.

To read the complete coolhunt article, go to www.malcolmgladwell.com

A version of this article also appears in Malcolm's first book, *The Tipping Point*.

Malcolm Gladwell is, in theory, a science writer for the *New Yorker* and, somewhere along the way, his articles end up being blended into books like *Blink* and *The Outliers*.

They're worth a read.

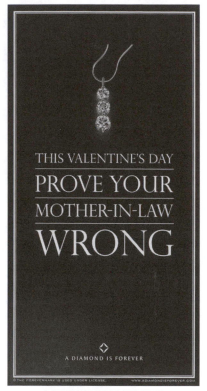

A DIFFERENT ANGLE.

Think of how this ad connects.

Instead of typical man/wife emotional relationships, they speak to a different connection – one that is also true – the mother-in-law.

Now, this headline may or may not speak to the actual relationship, but it connects. Think about the response…

"Hmmm. I buy my wife an expensive gift… I get major cred with her mother and the whole family. Hmmm…"

As a result, this traditional advertiser opens a fresh new way into consideration.

Some pick up on it more than others.

What we have to do is learn to be aware and in touch with all of that.

This is particularly valuable when you're young.

My musical tastes are now pretty locked in, but way back when, I could tell you what was what.

Now it's your turn. Your tastes are forming, you like hearing new things, and you're in touch with a wide range of what's happening now.

Want a trip down memory lane? Hey, I'm your guy. But if you want to be putting out messages that are "in the now," we need the contemporary vibe that your young ears bring to the party.

Inside & Outside

When working on a problem, I try to get inside.

Into the product.

Into the problem.

Into the target consumer.

Into the relationship between people and product.

Yet, the answer, or part of it, may also be *outside* – at the cutting edge of art, fashion, or music. Or a unique combination of concept and circumstance.

But, to get outside, I think sometimes you must go so far in that you come out the other end.

Just like in some parts of New Jersey.

Once you go inside a problem deeply enough, you can almost feel yourself standing outside.

A good copywriter should be able to go both ways and have both kinds of thoughts – all at once.

That's why you must continually broaden your outside perspective at the same time you journey inside the products you advertise and try to get *inside* the minds of the people you talk to.

Nine-Wheel Logic

You're standing by the railroad tracks with a small child and a steam locomotive goes chugging by. (This is the way they tell the story at P&G.)

The child asks, "Why does that train go so fast?"

You can't really explain how a locomotive works to a small child – who isn't paying much attention. So you say, "Look at all the wheels."

That's a good answer. One thing – the wheels – symbolizes something else – the power of the locomotive. See what we're getting at?

You can't explain the new detergent formula in the time allowed, and even if you could, who would listen. And who cares? So you put "green power crystals" in an otherwise colorless detergent formula and now you can communicate quickly and clearly. Everyone "gets it."

That's Nine-Wheel Logic at work.

One of the more popular contemporary examples is that work for Altoids. "So strong they come in a metal box."

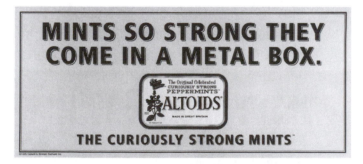

When we examine that statement, it's kind of ridiculous – part of its charm. Plus, it actually does a pretty good job of reinforcing the fact that Altoids have a rather strong flavor.

Got it?

"FIVE THOUSAND ACRES OF HOLLYHOCKS."

These are some observations by Howard Gossage on the creation of advertising – and, perhaps, some larger truths about life.

"*What it amounts to is this:*" says Gossage, "*if you start off with a ridiculous assumption but develop it henceforth with fastidious logic, you don't have to dream up things, they simply evolve as you go along.*

"*Let us suppose that a farmer has five thousand acres which he has plowed and harrowed and fertilized and it is all ready for seeding.*

"*Well the seed arrives. However, through some awful mistake they sent him hollyhock seeds instead of corn. Then, due to a series of circumstances, they are sown and we now have to deal with the consequences – five thousand acres of hollyhocks.*"

At this point, you have to take it seriously, though "*with a certain amount of bafflement as to what to do next.*"

Gossage's advice, "*retain a logical mind throughout and don't attempt to improve on nature.*"

Many advertising problems are like this. Let's say you're working on Burger King, with a solid young adult customer base and a fairly hip image. Now let's say the client comes in and tells you that you need to advertise a Kid's Meal that features Sponge Bob.

Do you screw up this hip image by doing kids' advertising – where you're way outspent by McDonald's? Or do you somehow reconcile Sponge Bob and "The King" and Sir Mix-a-Lot, while hoping the result will get Burger King regulars to bring in little brothers, nieces, and nephews. Square booty, it is.

Five thousand acres of hollyhocks in action.

#15: Stretching Exercises

Tony Schwartz is a copywriter turned media consultant who puts McLuhan into a practical context.

A brief discussion of his "Resonance Theory" appears at the end of Chapter Three. You might want to read…

The Responsive Chord
Tony Schwartz/Doubleday

Media: The Second God
Tony Schwartz/Random House

You never forget your first Girl.

ST. PAULI BREWERY, BREMEN

ST. PAULI GIRL

BEER

Imported from Germany

ADS TO REMEMBER.
The quick little emotional vibration off the double meaning in the St. Pauli Girl ad creates resonance.

At least, that's what happened to me. For you, it could be entirely different.

Pick some ads that resonate with you. Study how they work on you and how and why you respond.

"The mind is like a parachute. It only functions when it's open."

Let's take a minute or two to review some of these thinking approaches.

On your next assignment, give them a workout.

I'll grab a topic – music – and, for a brand, you can pick your current favorite band.

1. **Reduction.**
   The Rolling Stones managed to get a memorable graphic in place. What can you generate for your favorite band? Do they already have something? Can you reduce it further?

2. **Relevance.**
   What is it about this band that is relevant to the listening audience? Is it dancing? Concerts? What kinds of activities go on while listening to the music? How do groups of fans connect?

3. **Resonance.**
   Now let's get even more personal. How did this band get inside your head? And, do they have a place that's a bit more special than other groups – probably. So what is it about that connection that you can leverage. Let's assume that even those who like a different band, might have some of those same strong internal feelings. Can you put it in a headline or a radio commercial?

4. **The Personal Truth.**
   What's your "personal truth?"
   A. Make a list titled "Things I Like."
   B. Make a list titled "Ads I Like."

C. Now, think a bit. What truths are there in advertising that persuade you? Not just things you want to own, but attitudes and images that touch you.

D. Write down truths that are true for you. (Learning what it takes to persuade ourselves is the first step in learning to persuade others.)

4. **Velcro.**

   How can you make the idea of your favorite band more sticky? What are the brand contact points? (website, concert tour, CD, _____, _____, and _____.) Make a list of tactics. Then, make a list of experiential moments and possible feelings. Remember, we often "flip" into doing the opposite – this is the opposite of "reduction."

5. **Vibe.**

   What's going on culturally that you can connect with? Go on your own "cool hunt." What are the cool kids doing? How can you be a more important part of the cultural vibe?

6. **Inside/Outside.**

   OK – now go into the band and one of the tunes – really focus – pick your favorite cut – listen to it two or three times – think hard – see if you can come out the other side. Really. Try it.

7. **Nine-Wheel Logic.**

   OK, how can we get one thing to symbolize another – the band. The Rolling Stones had a memorable graphic from one of their covers and – boom – the mouth and tongue thing is now a big part of their brand. What can you think of for the brand that's your favorite band?

SOME ROOM TO THINK:

Paper clips, note cards, Post-Its, note books, folders… Why don't you take a minute to put down your thoughts on these interesting, but slightly fuzzy, topics?

Pick a topic – like music.

Then, take a deep breath and a quiet moment to think about…

Your Personal Truth.

What's going on with you and music? How and when is it really important. What's the road into how you feel?

Velcro.

How does music hang together in your mind? Is there a central thought with everything else attached?

Are there a lot of related thoughts tangled up? What sticks to what?

Vibe.

Trust me. Our feelings about music evolve. All that stuff you like right now will be "retro" soon enough.

Right now, your musical tastes are likely part of the mainstream culture.

In your view, what is the cultural vibe right now?

If you were going to hear your favorite group, who would be there?

Where would it be?

Inside/Outside

Do the exercise. Put on some of your favorite music.

Let your mind drift into the topic.

Make notes as you listen to the notes.

Nine-Wheel Logic.

What can you think of that symbolizes the music or the musical group?

Remember, it's something that symbolizes something else.

A brand contact point.

"In business as on the battlefield,
the object of strategy is to bring about the
conditions most favorable to one's own side.
In strategic thinking, one first seeks a clear
understanding of the particular character
of each element of a situation, and then makes
the fullest possible use of human brainpower
to restructure the elements
in the most advantageous way.
Phenomena and events in the real world
do not always fit a linear model.
Hence, the most reliable means of dissecting a
situation into its constituent parts and then re-
assembling them in the desired pattern
is not a step-by-step methodology
such as systems analysis.
*Rather, it is that **ultimate nonlinear***
***thinking tool,** the human brain.*
No matter how difficult or unprecedented
the problem, a breakthrough to
the best possible solution
can come only from a combination of rational
analysis based on the real nature of things,
and imaginative reintegration
of all the different items into a new pattern,
*using **nonlinear brain power.**"*

—Kenichi Ohmae
From *The Mind of the Strategist*

The Strategy.

ARE YOU FEELING SMARTER?

We hope so.

Do you have some new ways of thinking about things? We hope so.

We've given you a range of tools to help you develop intellectual flexibility and see the range of possibility.

Now we're going to go a little bit the opposite way – we're going to focus on strategy.

As David Ogilvy noted, "*Strategy is about choice.*"

And as Kenichi Ohmae notes in one of our favorite quotes (on the opposite page), we need to use that "*nonlinear thinking tool – the human brain.*"

We need to use those thinking tools to work through the possibilities and focus on the prob-abilities.

We need to go from all the different ways to do it to "the best way to do it."

Some of it will be based on facts, and some will be on informed judgment. Some of it will be based on educated guesses – though we're going to add a bit to your education.

However we do it, here's where we put it all together – and develop the Strategy.

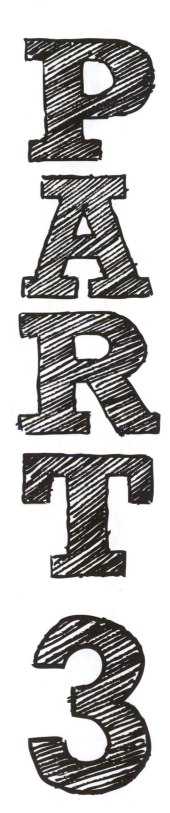

PART 3

Strategy

"Advertising is salesmanship in print."
John Kennedy. Copywriter.

The quote is dated. The reality remains.
Salesmanship.
Your communication has to *sell*.
It must persuade. Influence. Motivate.

Understanding the customer helped build a whole new market for cigarettes.
Note the continued use of the preemptive "It's Toasted" theme line.

IT MIGHT BE MORE ACCURATE to describe what we're working on as Selling Strategy, since, for the most part, the purpose of the strategies you develop will be to sell the products or services offered. Maybe not always, but pretty much always.

Sometimes that means taking the direct route – one of those "buy this product for this specific benefit" propositions such as those used by Claude Hopkins and Rosser Reeves.

Other times, it is less direct, sort of a "we share the same values and that makes us the brand of shoes you want on your feet." Like Nike.

We call it strategy, and we often treat it like a science, but the hidden power is often the artistry of persuasion and salesmanship.

The Basics

Styles may change, but the basics will stay the same.

Good salesmanship will always be a combination of artistry and common sense, hard work and easy answers, smart thinking and dumb luck. Most of all, it comes from thinking about the person you need to persuade.

This is the general process –

You'll develop a Strategy. Copywriting is strategic writing. It's designed to accomplish something.

From that Strategy, you'll generate a Selling Idea or a concept. Copywriting is persuasive writing.

Finally, you'll do it with Style.

You'll communicate in a way that connects with the people you're talking to. Whether it's a distracted teenager with a cheeseburger habit or a canola farmer concerned with soil moisture.

Strategy: Many Types

First, let's talk about Strategy. And the first thing we should say about that is this… *there are many types of Strategies.*

MARKETING STRATEGIES.

Many companies have a large, complex document called a Marketing Strategy.

This covers a wide range of things related to selling products, such as pricing, distribution, and other factors of the marketplace.

There are also Promotional Strategies, which focus on promotional tasks, and Public Relations Strategies, which focus on communication goals for publicity and unpaid media.

There are even Packaging Strategies.

In this book, we will focus primarily on developing and executing an *Advertising* Strategy, or a *Communication* Strategy.

ADVERTISING STRATEGIES.

Advertising works with a shorter document. It may be called an Advertising Strategy, a Communication Strategy, or Creative Platform – or something else.

It is part of the larger Marketing Strategy.

An Advertising Strategy generally indicates what the advertising should communicate and to whom it will be addressed.

From this point on, when we say "strategy," we mean advertising or communication strategy. But remember, you may be in a meeting where that's not what they mean at all.

THE BASICS: VOCABULARY.
There's a good bit of overlap in these sidebars, but it's important enough that you read the same thing two or three times in the hope that you'll remember it once.

Mission, Objective, Strategy, Tactics
Mission – Principles by which a company is run.

An example, in the '90s, Apple's stated mission was: *"Our goal is to put Macintosh computers in the hands of as many people as possible."*

In this case, their Mission Statement was also an Objective Statement.

Objective – Specific task to be accomplished.

P&G believes objectives should be: Specific, Measurable, Achievable, and Compatible. Their acronym is "SMAC."

Defining Objectives is key to good Strategies. An Objective Statement for Apple marketing might be: *To double unit sales of low-end computers next quarter.*

Strategy – How you meet the Objective.

There are many types of strategies: advertising strategies, communication strategies, marketing strategies, promotional strategies, and design strategies, to name a few.

There are often alternate strategies available even when the objective is clear.

You may have an advertising strategy, a promotional strategy, and other sub-strategies for key niche markets and new product introductions. To some extent, they should all be compatible.

Example: *Our strategy will be to:*
   a.) increase advertising,
   b.) offer price-off incentives,
   c.) provide easier financing,
   d.) lower the retail price,
   e.) some or all of the above.

The chosen strategy tends to be the best hypothesis as to how to meet the objective. Sometimes this is based on experience, sometimes not.

When something is "on-strategy" it conforms to the hypothesis. When it is "off-strategy" it may fail to meet the objective or it may represent an alternate hypothesis.

(Continued on next page.)

Tactics – Specific planned actions that execute the Strategy. Ads, sales materials, promotional programs – the whole range of marketing communications tools are tactics. So is a sales call.

Example: *Advertising materials featuring Mac Classics starting at $999.*

Strong strategies beget strong tactics. A mediocre execution of a correct strategy is better than an excellent execution of an incorrect strategy. In theory.

Key Fact (*Y&R Creative Work Plan*) – Based on analysis of all pertinent facts, the key piece of information that defines the business problem.

Problem – In this context, the specific issue that marketing communications must overcome to meet our objective.

Much of Strategy development is aimed at overcoming Problems.

The *Y&R Creative Work Plan* looks for "The Problem the Advertising Must Solve."

Example: *People perceive Macintosh as too expensive.*

Mandatories – Legal requirements or other aspects of corporate policy.

Example: *Macintosh is a registered trademark of Apple Computer, Inc.*

**Important Terms with
More than One Definition:**

Event Marketing. 1. A marketing discipline that specializes in events and sponsorships. 2. Marketing an event. 3. Treating advertising or promotional programs as events.

Position. 1. Place product resides in mind of consumer (Trout & Ries, *Positioning. The Battle for the Mind*). 2. Relative position (or place) in market.

Positioning. 1. Process of determining the correct position. 2. Process of achieving that position in the marketplace.

Re-Positioning. 1. Changing current position in market or mind of consumer. 2. Changing the advertising.

(Continued on next page.)

COMMUNICATION STRATEGIES.
Similar to advertising strategies, they will usually be a starting point for a variety of IMC strategies. In general, there is a movement from narrow advertising strategies to broader communication strategies.

For PR, there may be thinking as to what is the "angle" most appealing to media.

For Sales Promotion, there will be consideration as to the behavior desired, and then the offer/incentive/bribe necessary to make it happen.

Direct Marketing will work to narrow down the list, so that efforts are most effectively aimed at the best potential prospect, and then, in a perfect world, they will test their way from hypothesis to measurable results.

A good Communication Strategy will provide the basics of benefit and target while providing a clear platform for the various IMC disciplines.

MEDIA/MESSAGE/CHANNEL STRATEGIES.
Once, the Media Strategy was relegated to the back end of the agency presentation.

But, with the increasing proliferation of media channels, the growth of Media Agencies, and the overall cost of saying things, whatever media you use, there has been an evolution to strategies that focus on *where* and *when* you say it.

We covered this in our Evolution chapter, where we talked about the rise of Connection Planning.

CP+B, as mentioned, has a job that they call Creative Content Distribution.

Marketing disciplines like Event Marketing and Sports Marketing also have a major when and where component.

And, while we may be focusing on the *what* of message strategy, keep in mind that your strategic breakthrough may come from this direction.

Often, message content in various categories is pretty basic, no matter how much nuance we add. Good taste. Good value. Good style. Good goods.

You may find that the delivery channel can make things interesting all over again.

For example, take a look at how CP+B took an ad in a men's magazine for a beer (there were probably a lot of beer ads in that issue) and, by serving up their "phony cover" idea – to make women think you weren't just another guy reading another guy-zine – they "cut through the clutter" and, in some ways, gained ownership of the magazine with the coolest ad in the book. Not bad.

Improved Molson Back Cover

Inside Molson Back Cover

OBJECTIVE, STRATEGY, TACTICS.

Even though you can "back into" a strategy, or "back out" a strategy, or build a "bottom-up" strategy from an effective tactic, you still need to end up with something that hangs together front to back.

It's pretty much impossible to develop a final strategy until you know where you want to go.

Discovering the Objective is your real first step.

Before you can have a Strategy, you must have an Objective. Developing a Strategy begins with clearly defining what you want to accomplish.

Target Talk.

Target (Target Audience, Target Consumer, Target Customer, Prospect) – Person most likely to buy or influence purchase. Usually the person at whom the marketing communication is aimed.

Demographics – Specific quantitative facts about the target: age, income, etc.

Psychographics – Qualitative information about the target, sometimes based on quantitative information, sometimes based on smaller qualitative studies, sometimes based on considered judgement. Life Style, attitudes, etc.

Usage – Information based on use of product, product category, or competitive products.

Support Statements.

Strategies often have a Support or "Reason-Why" section, indicating the reason the product delivers the benefit. They range from the specific to the tangential.

Support – Facts or information that support the claim or benefit stated in the Objective section of the Strategy.

Reason Why – Specific reason the product delivers a benefit or proves a claim.

Permission to Believe – a piece of information, factual or otherwise, that allows a person to believe the delivered benefit or advertised claim.

"Nine-Wheel Logic" – Type of Support which seems to prove a point, even though it doesn't (covered in Chapter 6).

Tone or Brand Character Statements.

Advertising strategies often have Tone, Brand Character, or Tone & Manner Statements designed to describe and define qualitative aspects of the brand or the advertising.

Brand Character – This is a statement about core values of the brand itself.

Examples: *Macintosh is friendly and easy-to-use.*

Tone (Tone & Manner) – This is generally a statement about the kind of advertising that will appeal to a certain Target in a certain product category.

LADDERING VOCABULARY.

Let's review the "laddering" vocabulary one more time.

Much Strategic discussion focuses on the Benefit that a Product offers the Target. Sequencing these factors is called Laddering.

Here are generally agreed upon factors listed bottom to top:

Attribute (Product Attribute) – Characteristic of Product, usually inherent or natural. *Applesauce comes in wide-mouth glass jars.*

Product Feature (Feature) – Aspect of Product, usually based on some manufactured or designed aspect. *Applesauce spoons smoothly out of the jar.*

Product Benefit – A benefit to the consumer, usually based on a Product Feature or Attribute. *Applesauce is easy to serve.*

Customer Benefit (Consumer Benefit) – A benefit to the consumer, usually based on how the Product Benefit delivers a positive result to the consumer. *I save time and my children get extra nutrition (which they enjoy), because I serve Applesauce.*

Values – The human dimension reinforced by the Benefit. *I'm a good mother because I serve Applesauce.*

Laddering is the process of moving through this sequence.

The general method is to ask people why is that Feature (or Benefit, etc.) important, and the answer generally moves you to the next level of the ladder.

A continuing issue is where to stop on the ladder. After all, every food product reinforces nurturing values, every business product allows us to "be our best."

Generally, the farther down the ladder you are, the more product specific your message. The higher up the ladder, the more you are dealing with the consumer's life and the less you are dealing with and differentiating your specific product.

This is a major area of strategic choice.

Which to choose? It depends.

The Objective is a statement of the task that must be done and, sometimes, the Problem to be solved (i.e., "The Problem the Advertising Must Solve").

The ad you write is an execution of your Strategy – it is a "tactic."

It's what you do after you go through the process: determine an Objective, develop a Strategy, think of a Selling Idea, and, finally, execute the tactic – the ad.

Through it all, remember, advertising is communication written with a consciousness of the *receiver.*

Writers may write for themselves.

Copywriters write with others in mind.

It's *receiver-driven* communication.

STRATEGICALLY POSITIONED VOCABULARY.

Before we move forward, let's get our vocabulary straight – so we're all using the same words. Then let's try to figure out what we have to do first.

So, if you haven't been reading the sidebars, go back a few pages as we cover the commonly accepted definitions of important words and concepts.

Got it?

OK, by now you should be starting to have a fairly clear idea of what we're talking about.

Now let's work our way through the first step – discovering the objective.

PRODUCT FEATURE.
Apple advertises a distinct product feature. They leave it to the consumer to translate the Product Feature – thin – to the Consumer Benefits – lightness and portability.

The world's thinnest notebook.

 MacBook Air

Discovering the Objective

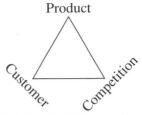

THE STRATEGIC TRIAD.

Your Objective is in there somewhere.

Product. Customer. Competition.

Your Strategy will address all three.

It will tell us why customers will choose your product in preference to that of the competition.

This often involves solving a Problem – but before you can solve a problem, you have to figure out what it is.

WHERE are you going? Developing Strategy begins here – determining the job you have to do.

Sometimes that Objective is clear.

But often, your first job is to figure it out.

Here are some ways to help you get started.

1. THINK ABOUT THE CUSTOMER. The better you know the person you're talking to, the better you'll understand what you must accomplish. Remember Hopkins: *"The advertising man studies the consumer. He tries to place himself in the position of the buyer."*

Try to envision the Target Consumer.

Try to become that person.

What is his or her state of mind?

Perhaps total ignorance. If that's the case, *awareness* may be your Objective.

Building awareness is an implicit part of almost every ad Objective.

But consumers aren't ignorant.

More likely, they already have some thoughts about your brand, about the product category, and, probably, about the competition.

You have to get at those thoughts.

• **Demographic information** can help, but you must use it as a tool to imagine the real live person.

• **Psychographic information** can help. VALS (Values and LifeStyles), can provide valuable insights and help you get

This copywriter understood the consumer problem. *A dramatic but thoughtful ad, with empathy and insight into the difficulty of maintaining and losing weight and the fact that many "diet" products don't taste very good. A* Product Benefit *(taste)* that leads to a Consumer Benefit *(weight loss).*

ANNOUNCING THE TASTE YOU USED TO CHEAT FOR.

Bald, rubbery, hard-boiled eggs. Endless vistas of cottage cheese. The relentless boredom of carrots and celery.

Conventional diet food is enough to drive you off a diet.

Happily, Weight Watchers 19 New Frozen Meals are good enough to drive

you on.

Like this Chicken Oriental in a snappy soy-spiked ginger sauce with crunchy Chinese vegetables.

Lean, juicy beefsteak smothered in a thick, brown gravy.

Lasagna dripping with spicy tomato sauce.

Yes, even Sausage Pizza. Now you can have them.

Even if you're on a diet.

So if you're really serious about dropping those extra pounds, our exciting new taste can help.

After all, how can you go off your diet, if the taste you want is on it?

WEIGHT WATCHERS 19 NEW FROZEN MEALS. TRY IT. YOU'LL DIET.

OUR OBJECTIVE IS TO INCREASE SALES.

Seems clear. But, actually, the road to increased sales may be anything but.

Here are three classic examples:

Change of Place.

Baked anything with baking soda lately?

Me neither. In fact, we're not sure anyone has baked a single thing with baking soda in the last decade. But, Arm & Hammer baking soda is doing just fine.

A marketing consulting firm noted that, among the useful uses of baking soda – it was an effective refrigerator deodorant. The baking soda absorbed odors.

It turned baking soda from an unused box in the back of the cabinet, to a regular part of household hygiene.

Change of Dose.

Alka-Seltzer, a combination aspirin/antacid in an effervescent tablet, was used by those who had too much to eat and drink.

Sales went down as habits changed and alternatives were introduced.

Then, in the '60s, Alka-Seltzer hired a hot new agency – Jack Tinker & Partners.

Meeting with the client in Elkhart, Indiana, a young copywriter, Mary Wells, asked, "*If you had two would it hurt you?*"

The answer? "*No.*" Two wouldn't work better, but it wouldn't be worse.

Suddenly, ads featured two tablets – instead of one.

Sales stopped going down – not because of more usage occasions – that kept declining – but because the average dose went from one tablet to two.

"Plop. Plop. Fizz. Fizz" came later, but from the moment ads showed two tablets, the sales curve had extra fizz.

Change of Habit.

With medical information that a daily aspirin was a sensible health measure, my use of aspirin went from the occasional headache to a daily pill pop – along with a multi-vitamin and something called resveretrol (you can look it up).

That means I went from about a dozen aspirin a year to 365 a year – a 3000% increase.

to know your customers. VALS offers a way of looking at and getting to know people who may not be a lot like you.

• **Focus groups** can help. You can listen to real people talk about their real lives and how the products you want to sell them fit into their lives.

• **Usage information** can help. This is information that helps you understand how the product fits into people's lives.

Sometimes it can be as simple as talking to people who've purchased the product.

In general, good customers and "heavy users" can be a valuable source of good ideas.

However you do it, you need to get to know the people you'll be writing to and selling to.

2. THINK ABOUT THE PRODUCT.

Describe the product and what it does.

For example, let's say you're working on…

• Toothpaste plus mouthwash.

• A convenient diet product.

• A radial tire.

We've just listed Product Features (sometimes called Features or Attributes).

They are, quite simply, features of the product.

Now, how do these features become benefits for the person you'll be talking to? Like this…

• Cleaner breath.

• An easy way to lose weight.

• A safer ride.

Just think of the benefits that these features deliver. These are Product Benefits – benefits *of* the product to the consumer.

If the Product Benefit is meaningful, you'll probably want to communicate it to your Target.

Factors That Influence Purchase Behavior.

What's most important to customers?

206

It's dry!
But so shiny it looks wet.

Mr. Clean's lemon fresh formula never leaves dull streaks when it dries, even when you don't rinse. Mr. Clean cleans your whole house right down to the shine.

Mr. Clean. The man behind the shine.

One big job will be determining "Factors That Influence Purchase Behavior."

Simply put, why do people buy this type of product?

You may find a generic benefit which encompasses the whole category – like durability for batteries.

Or you may find a category, like shampoo, where there are a number of factors ranging from hair manageability to price to dandruff control.

Advertise Your Advantage.

Historically, products that advertise their advantages do well… when the advantage is worth advertising.

Communicating the Product Benefit to the Target Audience may be your Objective (remember laddering?).

Or perhaps that is only a step on the ladder leading to a benefit *within* the consumer –

• Fresher breath could translate to greater personal attractiveness and better relationships.

• A smaller dress size could mean greater personal attractiveness and better relationships.

• A safer ride makes you feel more confident that you are doing all you can to protect your family.

These are "Consumer Benefits."

They are benefits that the consumer receives when they use your product. Communicating the Consumer Benefit may be your Objective. It often is.

FACTORS THAT MOTIVATE PURCHASE BEHAVIOR.

Sometimes it's a Product Benefit.

Here's one from P&G for Mr. Clean.

Note the *visualizing* of the benefit.

This ad also performs a second function – building Mr. Clean's powerful but friendly *image*.

GIVE A TOY
A CHILD
FOR
CHRISTMAS.

KAY·BEE
STOREWIDE CHRISTMAS SALE

CONSUMER BENEFIT.

Again, note the *visualizing* of the benefit.

This ad uses a headline device I call "The Double."

It turns a common phrase inside out and gives it new meaning.

The visualization has great appeal for the target – parents. A very nice ad.

FREE
Oscar Mayer
Wienermobile
Toy Bank

WITH 11 PROOFS-OF-PURCHASE PLUS SHIPPING AND HANDLING

when you buy America's favorite Hot Dogs and Bologna.

WHAT'S THE BENEFIT?

Your child gets a cute toy and you have warm feelings toward the brand.

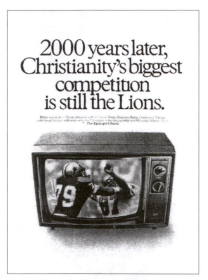

Everyone has competition...

...and it's survival of the fittest.

USPS VS. FEDEX.
Before they started cooperating, FedEx and the US Post Office ran very competitive ads for their services.

Now they both compete with UPS.

3. THINK ABOUT THE COMPETITION.
The competition is also important.

Most marketing plans and strategies consider what they call "source of business."

If you win, who loses?

Sometimes new usage will be the source of overall business. For example, as soft drink consumption grew, people drank less water. Then, as bottled water consumption grew, people drank less tap water.

Even if you don't compete directly in your advertising, you should consider what other similar products are already *inside* the consumer's mind as well as what habit patterns are already out there.

Think about what's going on in the marketplace.

Category Insight. On the way to developing insight into your brand, you may want to develop insight into the category overall.

This is the first step in positioning.

POSITIONS…

To start this part of the process, think about what goes on *inside* the consumer's mind when he or she thinks about the product category.

Where is your product on the product ladder?

Where are you on the Positioning Grid? In a perfect world, where do you want your product to be?

Ask those questions. Do some positioning.

Establishing a distinct position for your brand versus the competition may be the Objective. If it is…

1. Don't underestimate the expense and effort it might take to achieve that position.
2. Realize establishing that position may not generate increased sales (e.g., "diet beer").
To be successful, Trout and Ries maintain,
"Your position must be:
  1. A unique position
  2. With broad appeal."

208

…AND PROPOSITIONS.

Rosser Reeves addresses the competition in his USP (Unique Selling Proposition).

"The proposition must be one that the competition either cannot or does not offer.

It must be unique – either a uniqueness of the brand or a claim not otherwise made in that particular field of advertising."

Person… product… and competition.

THE SWEET SPOT & THE STRATEGIC TRIAD.

"Consumer Insight" is one factor that can help you unify these elements. One type of Consumer Insight concept is called *"The Sweet Spot."* You want to hit it. But first you have to find it.

Finding it is the result of insights into the consumer, the consumer's feelings and attitudes about the product category, and feelings and attitudes toward your specific brand.

Consumer Insight + Brand Insight = Sweet Spot.

These same three factors – customer, product, and competition – are the general basis of many types of business strategy development.

Together, they are often referred to as the "Strategic Triangle" or "Strategic Triad."

Your Objective is most likely involved with some combination of these same three factors: customer, product, and competition.

But, in advertising strategy, there is a fourth dimension which you must consider.

Now you must think about… *the Problem!*

4. THINK ABOUT THE PROBLEM.

Ask yourself a very simple question…

"What's The Problem?" What's the *real* problem?

Is it the product (Yikes!), the image, lack of awareness, the sales force, the ad budget, or simply unrealistic expectations?

CONSUMER INSIGHT & ACCOUNT PLANNING.

From advertising's earliest days, insight into the consumer has been key.

However, as marketing and advertising became more specialized, clients and agencies became more and more removed from their customers and "understanding the consumer" became more and more difficult.

During the '70s, British agencies addressed this problem with a new agency function called "Account Planning."

Simply put, the account planner "becomes" the customer.

Through interviews, "ethnology," and other forms of insight generation, the planner brings the Target Consumer into the agency.

The account planner helps you find the *"Sweet Spot"* and helps you hit it.

The best planners are able to represent the target group in a way that inspires fresh, new insights.

Jay Chiat, of Chiat/Day, imported the Account Planning system and gives it credit for much of his agency's success.

Today, some sort of account planning or consumer insight function is common at many US agencies.

Readings in Account Planning, Edited by Hart Weichselbaum. [From The Copy Workshop.]
Hitting The Sweet Spot, by Lisa Fortini-Campbell, Ph.D. – the first US book on Account Planning. [From The Copy Workshop.]

IF AN EAR THERMOMETER SOUNDS PECULIAR, IMAGINE THE REACTION TO THE FIRST RECTAL THERMOMETER.

Until now, parents never had much choice. And kids had even less.

If there was a temperature to be taken, the standard rectal thermometer was the way to take it. An uncomfortable, messy, risky way. But the only accurate way.

That is, until we introduced the Thermoscan® Instant Thermometer. It takes an accurate temperature at the ear in one second. The same way many doctors' offices and hospitals do, millions of times each year.

Just position it and press a button. You'll get an easy-to-read temperature. With no struggle. No fear of injury. And no unhappy kid.

The first name in fast temperatures
THERMOSCAN
INSTANT THERMOMETER

INTERESTING PROBLEMS CAN MAKE INTERESTING ADS.

Above, the message is dramatized with humor and a powerful visual.

Below, a dramatic contrast in words create impact.

Each ad qualifies its target charmingly and disarmingly. And each appeals to the instincts of a certain type of person.

Insight into the problem and insight into the target.

Sometimes it's the ads and, almost always, the ads are the easiest thing to change.

But there are often a few other factors squirming around in the stew. Peel the onion.

Put yourself in your client's shoes, your customer's mind, and the account exec's briefcase.

Turn the situation upside down and inside out.

And vice versa. Let it incubate.

You might even ask a few more questions.

Why? Because there is *danger* here!

Don't Solve The Wrong Problem!

It is not uncommon to have large numbers of bright, well-informed people focused on the wrong problem.

It's not uncommon to find situations where people passed the real problem and solution a long time ago.

Trout & Ries noted, *"The best positioning ideas are so simple that most people overlook them."*

And Leo Burnett observed, *"Great copy and great ideas are deceptively simple."*

Simple, but not easy.

THE PROBLEM THE ADVERTISING MUST SOLVE.

In their *Creative Work Plan*, Y&R focuses on *"The Problem the Advertising Must Solve."*

In virtually every agency planning system, some part of the document addresses this issue in one way or another. Think about it. What's the Problem?

Jay Chiat notes, *"The creative process is really a very structured thing that has to do with problem-solving."*

George Lois says, *"You should be able to distill a marketing problem – which precedes the advertising solution – into one simple sentence."*

What Problem can the *advertising* solve?

There are a lot of problems out there, but what problem should advertising address?

The right answer to this question can give your whole advertising program a clear focus.

The Problem may be contained within the Strategic Triad, but it often has a life of its own.

Getting a handle on that slippery little thing called the problem is often key to getting your Objective right – so you don't just have *a* strategy, but *the* Strategy.

Sometimes, you'll find the Problem has already been identified. Only people don't realize it.

I suggest a little historical research: old memos, old ads, people who used to work on the business.

There are discarded ideas and valuable insights scattered about just about everywhere.

Some are good ideas orphaned by circumstance. Some are *terrific!*

If you can make one of them get up and walk, your reputation may be enhanced by the miraculous nature of your deed and the gratitude of those whose ideas you have saved.

Give credit to the original authors of the idea!

This can be a tricky area. Some will be appreciative. Others will not. Do it anyway.

By making a point of giving credit, you will at least protect yourself from being branded as a thief.

Meanwhile, remember that your obligation is to see to it that the product gets *the best ideas available.*

PROBLEM/CONSUMER BENEFIT.
"Morning Breath" was an engaging way for Scope to tell a simple story that contained a combination of strategic elements: the consumer problem and the product solution.

Plus a Competitive Claim.
Some Scope commercials also positioned the brand *against* the leading competitor (Listerine) by mentioning "Medicine Breath."

VISUALIZE THE PROBLEM.
In this case, a bad haircut.

A good use of humor. While it sort of makes fun of models and fashion, it allows any of us who've had a bad haircut to smile without being embarrassed, and to consider getting a better haircut at Sassoon's.

And because they connected with us, we accept their implied claim that their haircuts are better.

THE BUD LIGHT PROBLEM.

Their problem was at the bar, when the customer said, "Gimme a light" – it could mean Miller Lite, the leading light beer (at the time), or any light beer.

How could they communicate in a fresh, memorable, and persuasive way that people should order a Bud Light?

That was the problem.

The answer was the "Bar Call" campaign, originally planned as a few ten-second commercials.

This simple (and humorous) solution became a successful campaign that built the brand (causing Lite problems).

For Bud Light, it was advertising that effectively solved the Problem.

Q. WHAT'S BAND-AID'S STICKY PROBLEM?

Let's say you're at Y&R, working on Band-Aid brand bandages.

What's the problem your advertising should solve?

You already have dominant share in America's medicine cabinet.

Major usage is by mothers of active young children (2-10, the "Owie Age"), who use them to deal with the common cuts and scrapes of childhood.

Awareness is high. Image is positive.

People already have the product.

So, what in the world is "The Problem the Advertising Must Solve?"

Look for the answer on page 214, and the execution at the end of chapter 17, TV Formats.

No matter whose.

Wherever you find it, whoever thought of it, whatever it is, you must know the answer to the question – **"What's the Problem?"**

You have to understand the problem before you can solve the problem.

Once you have an answer, you may proceed.

You now understand The Problem.

Solving the Problem is often the Objective of your advertising. It usually combines key aspects of product, customer, and competition.

A cautionary note – your conclusions may not lend themselves to widespread publicity.

For this reason, it is not uncommon to have both stated and unstated Objectives.

For example, the *stated* Objective might be, *"To give the sales force a rallying cry."*

The *unstated* Objective might be, *"Now that we've got the product fixed, let's get the sales force to try and get it back into the stores again."*

Or, worse yet, you may have to reconvince turned-off customers who have already been burned once, while dealing with a client who refuses to acknowledge the problem. Now *that's* a Problem.

If you're still not sure of your Objective… go back to where you started…

THINK ABOUT THE **CUSTOMER.**
THINK ABOUT THE **PRODUCT.**
THINK ABOUT THE **COMPETITION.**
THINK ABOUT THE **PROBLEM.**
now…

5. COMBINE THEM.

That's right, think of everything. All at once.

Sometimes the answer is simple and obvious, and sometimes not. Look for patterns of reinforcement.

Use your *"nonlinear thinking tool."*

Pattern Recognition.

"Pattern recognition" is the ability to see something based on incomplete information.

It's the way some people recognize new and emerging trends *before* the hard data is in.

Sometimes it's called intuition. Basically, it's coming to a conclusion based on a few clues.

Advertising thinking is often like that.

Pattern recognition can be key to identifying new marketing and advertising opportunities.

It may be a trend in art or fashion, or a changing lifestyle. It may be rooted in old-fashioned values or it may be a new-fashioned product.

It may be one person in a focus group, one customer, or a salesperson out in the field.

The challenge is to recognize it.

Feel the forces at work. Think of it like a chess board, or as a playing field…

Positioning opportunities that have been left open by the competition. Problems unsolved.

Benefits undramatized. Needs unmet.

Targets to hit in a way that connects.

Look for ways to turn negatives into positives.

Your Objective will be at a conjunction of forces.

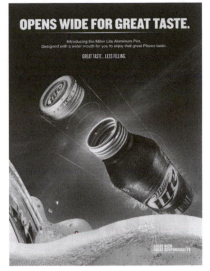

PROBLEMS CHANGE –
THE LITE BEER PROBLEM.

Today, Miller Lite is working to reinforce taste and quality. 30 years ago it was different.

Previously, light beers failed.

Why? That was the Problem.

"Diet Beer." A sissy drink.

Lite solved The "Diet Beer" Problem.

They moved to a unique Consumer Benefit (less filling – i.e., *you could drink more*) in a way that appealed to the target.

They talked person-to-person to the Target Consumer – a beer drinker who likes sports – with a humorous campaign featuring retired athletes.

It established Miller Lite as the #2 beer brand.

THE LITE EXAMPLE.

It's worth mentioning again. The product became a success only after numerous expensive failures.

Finally, the Lite agency turned a consumer negative, "diet beer," into a benefit, "you can drink more."

After the fact, it seems simple. Once you recognize the pattern.

A QUICK CHECKLIST:

Things to do to discover your Objective:

1. Think about the Customer.

A. Consumer Information. Customer profiles, demographics, product usage studies, sales data.

B. VALS. Values and LifeStyles.

C. Focus Groups.

D. Talk to consumers one-on-one.

2. Think about the Product.

A. Use the Product.

B. List Product Features and Product Benefits.

C. List **Consumer Benefits** and **Values.**

D. Do some **Laddering.**

3. Think about the Competition.

A. Do a "Store Check." Look at the competition in the marketplace. Compare package, price, in-store promotions, and performance.

B. Clip Competitive Print Ads. Make a clip file. If possible, tape a few competitive TV commercials.

C. Look for Articles. Read "the trades."

D. Talk to Customers. Find out why they like your competition. Find out the competition's weaknesses.

4. Think about the Problem.

Here are some common problems:

A. Low Awareness. Consumers unaware of product. (If it's a good product, a good problem to have.)

B. Old Product Didn't Perform. Or outperformed by competitive product. (If current product doesn't perform, try removing self from Problem.)

C. Pricing Problem. (Hard to solve with ads alone.)

D. Distribution Problem. Consider trade as target.

E. "Political" Problem. Obvious answer not recognized, irrational bias, office politics, etc.

F. Budget Problem. Not enough money to do job, unrealistic expectations, too many things to do, etc.

G. Advertising Problem. Previous ads did not "work." (Find out why before you write new ads.)

The Objective…

when discovered, will be simple and *synergistic*.

While The Objective of a marketing plan may be a specific numerical sales goal, the objective for an advertising strategy should be a clear and simple communications goal.

It should be clear and simple, even if the process might not have been simple at all.

Your Objective should be a simple statement of something that can be done relatively soon that will create a *dynamic system* that will help your brand achieve its goal.

Meeting The Objective will create or reinforce forces that will move your business forward.

Because once you know where you're going, you can start to figure out how to get there.

For example:

• Solve the "Diet Beer" Problem.

• Solve the "Gimme a light" Problem.

• Get women to use more Band-Aids.

Whatever your Objective, it should be clear, it should be simple, and you must have one before you can take the next step.

STRATEGY.

How you get there.

The path you must travel…

A. HOW TO GET MOTHERS TO USE MORE BAND-AIDS.

Y&R discovered an important opportunity – after the Band-Aid was initially applied, a scab formed and the old Band-Aid (which was now a bit dirty) was taken off and the scab protected the cut.

However, re-applying a Band-Aid to protect the scab promoted better healing. The cut was not re-opened and the scab was not knocked off (or picked off by the child). On average, cuts healed faster when a Band-Aid was used for this purpose.

The Problem became: Mothers do not realize that they can promote better healing by re-applying a Band-Aid to protect the scab.

Advertising which focused on this point promoted increased usage, which resulted in increased sales.

214

The Strategy Selection Grid

This is a useful tool when you are in the very early stages of strategy development.

It helps you look at possible alternatives related to the three primary strategic variables:

- Target Group Selection (Customer)
- Product Class Definition (Competitive Set)
- Message Emphasis (Product)

Then, to help with the evaluation of alternatives…

- Rationale

This grid allows you to lay out the alternatives in an easy-to-understand way. It can also help you become familiar with the basic elements of strategic development.

SELDOM USED IN AD AGENCIES. During a fairly lengthy agency career, with a lot of strategy development, we never used anything like this – for a very simple reason.

In the agency environment, client marketing organizations are usually pretty clear about Target Group Selection and Product Class Definition. Perhaps there would be some fine-tuning in the Target Group area, but, again, by the time the brand shows up at the agency, the basics are pretty well worked out.

Situations Where the Grid Is Helpful.

In new ventures, whether a new brand, a new store, or a special event on campus, this grid can be very clarifying.

Helpful Hint: You don't have to generate alternatives in every category. Product class or target group may be fairly clear.

Strategy Selection Grid:

Product Class Definition				
Target Group Selection				
Message Element Selection				
Rationale – based on information and/or judgement				

THE BEETHOVEN SWEATSHIRT.

Remember Gossage and "5000 acres of hollyhocks"?

Here, Gossage had to find a connection between classical music and Rainier Ale.

In addition to this ad, there were commercials on the classical music station.

Sometimes accepting one somewhat unusual fact – and then being very logical based on an illogical premise – can have a pretty interesting result.

As an exercise, you might try to take some fairly distant idea – say a violin and the back seat of a car – and figure out how to connect them.

Now a violinist (or maybe two) demonstrates that there is enough room to play in the back seat of the car – demonstrating roominess in an entertaining and memorable way.

SOME HELPFUL HINTS ON USING "THE GRID." As mentioned, this is not used much in agencies, since "Product Class Definition" and "Target Group Selection" are already pretty well worked out.

But you may very well find yourself dealing with these issues when you're dealing with new businesses, high-tech start-ups, or clients without a clue.

A few things to think about.

- **More Than One Strategy.** Remember, a strategy is an hypothesis – a best guess. You may very well have more than one.

  At the same time, your business may have more than one operational strategy.

  For example, some restaurants also operate a catering service. Others do take-out and delivery. Seems simple, but the communication strategies for these "products" are a bit different.

- **"What if" exercises.** Sometimes, taking a counter-intuitive point of view, i.e. "let's sell hockey tickets to women" or "let's sell Rainier Ale to people who listen to classical music" can have interesting results. For Rainier Ale, the Beethoven sweatshirt – also available in Bach and Brahms.

- **"Drilling Down."** When you have a complex, multi-faceted problem, the Grid can help you identify all the different aspects on a grid-like playing field and start to make some decisions. Some things will start to connect. For example, a connection between Product Class and Target Group. Then, the preferred Message Element often emerges.

Bonus: There's a bit more in PowerPoint on our AdBuzz website. We have a collection of these materials in the section labeled CAFÉ.

"Strategy is about choice."

— David Ogilvy

Many things are true.

Products and services can have many aspects.

The people you are talking to have even more complexity. They have a lot on their minds.

They have hopes and aspirations, and daily worries. Try to find the clear and simple path to what is interesting to them.

Let's go from Ogilvy's simple statement to Ken-ichi Ohmae's slightly more complex thought.

"No matter how difficult
or unprecedented the problem,
a breakthrough to the best possible solution
can come only from
a combination of rational analysis
based on the real nature of things
and imaginative reintegration
of all the different items into a new pattern,
using nonlinear brainpower."

THE VOLVO SAFETY STRATEGY.
Here's why Volvo chose to concentrate on safety in its products and its ads.

VOLVO "Margit" :30
ANNCR: (VO) *She was a physical therapist working with car accident victims in a hospital in Sweden 40 years ago. Yet Margit Engellau continues to save lives the world over. The reason? She instilled her horror of accidents in her husband... who happened to run a car company called Volvo.*
You may never have heard of Margit Engellau, but maybe you've seen the monument they've built her.
Historical facts reinforce the safety component of Volvo's brand character. The result is strong appeal to a key target – women.

Briefs.

"GOT MILK" & DEPRIVATION.

When Goodby Silverstein was assigned the task of halting the decline of milk consumptions, they reviewed the work done by others, which had not worked.

Over and over, the ads communicated the "milk is good for you" message.

It was true. It was, seemingly, meaningful to the audience.

And it had not worked. Repeatedly.

Jon Steel, who was Head of Planning at the time, notes, "…*belief – even if that belief is passionately held… is no sure indicator of behavior.*"

In planning, one often has to deal with the seeming contradiction of what people say and what people do.

The messaging – reminding people of how terrible it was to run out of milk when consuming the not necessarily "good for you" companion foods of chocolate chip cookies, brownies, and peanut butter and jelly sandwiches, hit a nerve. This was their life and it worked.

It was based on the way people really used milk – not the way they were taught to talk about it.

As you will see, one of the functions of planning is to remove those layers of "what we say" and gain insight into the reality of "what we do."

(Excerpts from *Perfect Pitch* by Jon Steel)

got milk?

*unpaid product placement

THIS IS A BRIEF INTRODUCTION to Creative Briefs. Briefly, they are documents that "brief" the Creative Department.

Their purpose is to provide you with the kind of information you need to do the job – in addition to the "non-linear thinking machine" you already carry between your ears.

THE ROLE OF THE ACCOUNT PLANNER. In a perfect world, a highly competent account planner will be in charge of putting the brief together and will have spent considerable time distilling all the information, collecting incredibly useful insights into the category and the target customer, and then laying it out in a fascinating and inspirational presentation.

In a perfect world, this would be a perfect definition: *"The planner's ongoing function is to accumulate, originate, and synthesize data pertinent to the advertising's target audience; to independently pre-test, post-test and monitor – as an ongoing account assignment – both the advertising itself and the dynamics at work in its marketplace."*

WORDS FROM THE HART.

That would be Hart Weichselbaum, former head of account planning for The Richards Group and Executive Editor of another book we publish, *Readings in Account Planning* (available at a 20% discount on www.adbuzz.com).*

In fact, here's an edited excerpt from the book…

218

Writing Creative Briefs.

IN MOST AGENCIES, the defining role of the account planner is leading the development of the creative brief. It's often the most tangible output of the planner's work.

Good planners learn to write good briefs.

Usually no more than a page or two, it's the end result of a larger process that includes strategic business analysis, brand and target audience understanding, refinement and debate with the client and other agency players, and planning and conducting the meeting in which the brief is presented to creatives. The brief has to engage the team responsible for creating the ads and inspire them to do great work.

ANY KIND OF STRATEGIC COMMUNICATION.
Creative briefs can be written for any kind of strategic communication – not just for traditional TV, radio, magazine, billboard, and newspaper ads, but also for direct mail, banner ads, viral ads, mobile ads, sales promotion programs, brand names, logos, and websites.

The length and amount of detail in the brief will vary, but the basic principles remain the same.

A brief for an infomercial may have a lot of factual information and supporting material, while one for a billboard had better be quite short.*

WHY DO WE HAVE BRIEFS?
Simply put, briefs increase the probability that we will get the ads right. We increase our chances of success by:
  • thinking through who the target is and why the message is important to them,

Dr. Weichselbaum is president of The Planning Practice, an ad and brand planning consultancy based in Chicago. He was head of planning at The Richards Group for 13 years, has been an adjunct faculty member at DePaul University's Kellstadt Graduate School of Business, and was a founding member of the organization that became the Account Planning Committee of the 4A's. He is executive editor of *Readings in Account Planning*.

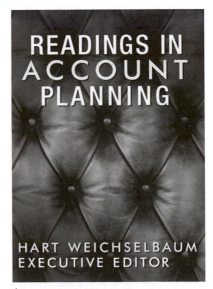

*At The Richards Group, a brief longer than one page required special dispensation from Stan Richards himself.

THREE BRIEF BRIEFS.

Asking the right questions is key to getting the right answers.

Here's how three smart agencies ask those questions:

JWT (Point of View).

What is really going on?
Whose time are we after?
What are they interested in?
What is the brand going to do?
What do we know that might help?
Thought starters.

Wieden + Kennedy London.

Background
Audience
Creative challenge
Practicalities Inspiration/Stimulus

The Richards Group.

Why are we advertising?
Who are we talking to?
What do they currently think?
What would we like them to think?
What is the single most persuasive idea we can convey?
Why should they believe it?
Are there any creative guidelines?

The Planners at Wieden + Kennedy helped Nike understand how to communicate to women. For men (and boys), hero athletes are meaningful. For women, it's personal.

- making sure the message addresses the communication objectives, and
- considering alternative directions and debating them with the other members of the team.

Not only do we increase our chances of getting the ads right, but the process increases our chances of getting it right *the first time*. Good briefs save everybody's time.

WANTED: GOOD SHEPHERDS.

Planners are more like shepherds guiding gently and tending patiently, rather than some sort of master strategist managing with the all-knowing brief.

In fact, first briefs are often just the first step.

Briefs are neither written in stone nor chalk.

The brief often evolves in the course of creative development. Creatives sometimes come up with new and compelling ideas, and sometimes the strategy implicit in their work will cause us to change the brief.

On the other hand, if the team agreed to a brief ahead of time, there shouldn't be a change without a good reason. Any new solution has to fit the evidence that led to the brief in the first place.

AN AD TO CREATIVES.

Think of the brief as an ad to creatives.

When you think about it, good briefs and good ads have many things in common. Here's some good advice for both.

Be brief. At its most basic level, the creative brief tells the creative team what to do.

It functions as a work order that specifies the objective, target, and main message of the communication – all the essential information they need to do their job.

Because the amount of information you could put in a brief is potentially very large, often the toughest decisions are about what to leave out.

Like a good ad, good briefs get their point across in a concise and compelling way.

A common mistake in brief writing is giving the creative team too much information. Unnecessary or distracting information makes their job more difficult. This is sometimes called understanding the importance of what's important.

Avoid jargon. Good ads speak in the language of their audience. So do good briefs. Since the target audience for the brief is your creative team, it makes sense to write it in language they can understand.

Marketing is full of jargon that marketers hide behind. Sometimes the planner's task is to take the client's brief, trim out the unnecessary information, and translate the jargon into everyday English.

Inspire your audience. The brief is your chance to provide creatives with your best, most original thinking.

If the brief is fresh and insightful, you improve the chances that the ads will be, too.

Here is where much brief writing falls short. It doesn't go that extra step of expressing the idea in a compelling way.

There's a big difference between an unfocused proposition like "Corona is a great tasting beer from Mexico" and something more specific and

A DIVISION OF LABOR.

Although the planner is usually the one to put the words on paper, he or she doesn't write the creative brief alone.

In practice, the planner manages the process of getting input from other members of the agency team (and the client) and distilling their thinking. The planner plays this central role because he or she is the one who understands consumer behavior, follows consumer trends, has studied the latest market research, understands the competitive context, has talked to the product manager, and most important, has the greatest experience in performing this essential task.

The planner chooses from among all the things that might be said and picks the ones that he or she believes will be most effective, while the creative team chooses how to say it. It's a division of labor that allows specialists to do what they do best. In writing the brief, the planner provides the bridge between strategic thinking and the creative work.

A CONTRACT WITH CREATIVES.

The brief is a kind of contract between the creative team and the people who develop the strategy.

While the brief should guide and stimulate the process, it also has to be flexible enough to allow the creative team to express their creativity.

Then, when the ads are being evaluated, the judgment should be about whether the objectives have been met, the audience has been addressed, and the key thought communicated, not the exact way those things were accomplished.

By the way, if the planner doesn't make those decisions, the creative team will make them. They will create something whether they get specific direction or not. While they probably won't bother to write down their brief, their ads will nonetheless have an imagined target, main idea, tone of voice, etc.

provocative like "Unlike the posturing, self-conscious brown-bottled beers it competes with, Corona is relaxed and unpretentious."

Which do you think would inspire better ads?

The brief on the left inspired the ad above.

FOUR BASIC QUESTIONS.

1. What Are We Trying to Accomplish?

The goal is to convey communication objectives as specifically and straightforwardly as possible.

Ads do more than raise awareness or get people to buy. Often, the real objective of advertising may be something like creating a new occasion for use, or justifying a higher price, or boosting the morale of the people who serve customers, or just getting people talking about the brand.

Starbuck's holiday advertising had a primary goal of evoking warm feelings in its audience – with the hope those feelings would transfer into sales of gift cards for family and friends. They did.

The ultimate goal of communications may be to increase sales, but that may be far too distant a goal to be useful in a brief. More important, it doesn't help creatives.

The real question is: *How* will sales be increased?

By getting customers to buy more often? By attracting new customers? By changing perceptions? Or by getting regular customers to purchase a gift card?

If you are at a loss about finding a sufficiently specific objective, check out the 4A's book called *One Hundred Reasons to Advertise*. Even though it's a bit dated, it's a handy reference for thinking about all the things ads can do.

One more thing: Clients are sometimes wildly optimistic about what communications can achieve. Ads can accomplish wonderful things, but in most business situations they don't make the sale alone.

By being honest about what the ads will achieve, you can save yourself some trouble down the road.

For example, the goal of the Motel 6 advertising, a very successful radio campaign, was to make guests feel comfortable about staying in a low-priced chain motel. Many worried they'd be perceived as too poor or too cheap to stay anywhere else. So the advertising had to create another reason for staying there, one that transcended merely saving money.

2. Who Are We Talking To?

This part of the brief tells creatives what they need to know about the target audience in order to write ads to them.

The question is sometimes posed as "What do we know about the target audience that can help us?" or "What is the consumer insight that will drive the work?"

The demographic definition of the target audience is only a starting point. "Adults 18-64" really doesn't help the creative team much in their search for a solution.

MOTEL 6 CREATIVE BRIEF.

Warning: People don't like ads. People don't trust ads. People don't remember ads. How do we make sure this one will be different?

Why Are We Advertising?
To make people feel good about their decision to stay at Motel 6.

Who Are We Talking To?
Medium-income (HHI between $30,000 and $50,000) business and leisure travelers who pay for their own accommodations.

They intend to spend only a short amount of time in their motel room (either crashing for the night or planning to be out for the entire day).

They either don't have a lot of money to spend on a room, or they feel virtuous in saving money.

What Do They Currently Think?
"I feel embarrassed about staying at Motel 6 because it's the lowest price."

What Would We Like Them to Think?
"Staying at Motel 6 is the smart thing to do."

What Is the Single Most Persuasive Idea We Can Convey?
Motel 6 is the smart choice.

Why Should They Believe It?
At Motel 6 you get all you really need: a clean, comfortable room at the lowest price of any national chain.

You won't get any of those unnecessary features that cost you a fortune, like french-milled soap, chocolates on your pillow, or fancy drapes.

Are There Any Creative Guidelines?
Continue folksy down-to-earth style and tone of the current campaign.
(Source: The Richards Group)

When you're sleeping, we look just like those big fancy hotels.
Motel 6

MORE ON MOTEL 6.

Motel 6 knew a lot about the segments of travelers it appealed to: young couples on a budget, retirees seeing the country, per diem business travelers – their demographics, travel habits, likes, and dislikes. But the most important thing about them was that they all needed reassurance they would still get a clean, comfortable room even though they were spending less.

SOME TIPS ON THE PROCESS.

Briefs don't occur in a vacuum. Although the planner leads the team, strategy development is usually a collaborative enterprise. Here are some tips for increasing the odds of success.

- **Make sure you have the facts.**
  Although the amount of information will vary, the brief should be based on the best information available. It's amazing how often a client has an untested hunch that bears no relationship to the target's reality. Nor is the agency team immune to personal prejudice or wishful thinking. Fortunately, the planner is often in the position to recommend additional research to settle differences.

- **If you can, write multiple briefs.**
  Multiple briefs often clarify. If there's time, it's usually a good idea to write briefs organized around several propositions. Planners and account service people can compete to produce the best one. "Dueling briefs" create useful debate on the strengths and weaknesses of different approaches. The end result? Better briefs.

- **Involve others.**
  Brief writing is a team sport. Involve your client – he or she has a lot of experience with the product or service. Involve creatives – they are the best writers and are, well, creative. After all, only they can tell you whether the brief makes sense to them and provides a starting point for an interesting creative execution.

(Continued on Page 226.)

This is the place to tell the team how and where consumers use the product, how it relates to their life goals or their lifestyle, how it relates to their psychology or culture, why they stop or start using it, how they use advertising in the category – anything that will help the creative team envision who they are writing to and give them a way into consumers' lives.

Another feature of the description is that it must link in some way to the proposition presented in the next section. *There are many interesting things about any target audience, but only a few offer an insight that will be useful to creatives.*

3. The Single Most Persuasive Idea We Can Convey.

This section contains the focal point for the communication. Sometimes it's called the Main Thought or the Proposition.

This is the idea we want the target to accept, and it's usually the single most motivating and differentiating thing we can say about the brand.

Ideas can come from anywhere, though often they are grounded in our knowledge of what the brand's strengths are, what's really motivating to people, and some aspect of what the product or service is or does.

If the communication is to be single-minded (and for most short-form advertising, that's the only kind that has a prayer of being noticed and remembered), it has to be focused.

Let's say the ad needs to generate interest in a new mobile phone. Should it focus on the phone's quality, reliability, famous brand name, low price, or one or more of its new and unique features?

Or, maybe the most important message isn't about the product at all. Perhaps it's some practical customer benefit like keeping track of your kids or succeeding in business or being able to leave your camera or your PDA at home. Or maybe the thing to emphasize is an emotional benefit like being the first to have it or being cooler than your classmates or having a phone to capture embarrassing moments so you can tease your friends. Or, in the case of T-Mobile, the larger value of connectedness and the resulting theme "Life's for Sharing."

Choosing among these alternatives depends on good product knowledge, recognition of the brand's strengths and weaknesses, and a deep understanding of the target's needs and motivations.

Not only is there a lot of work in choosing the one most important thing to say, but there is also the challenge in saying it in a provocative way.

Try to state the proposition as imaginatively and succinctly as possible.

The agency for Motel 6 could have chosen a prosaic proposition like "Really low prices." Instead they chose "A smart choice because you don't pay for what you don't need." And then they added a human dimension with "We'll leave the light on for you." A good proposition points the way to a solution and has in it the seeds of good creative executions.

4. Why Should They Believe It?

Sometimes a proposition requires factual support to change attitudes or behavior.

Sometimes it's the way the proposition is stated or the attitude it projects that supports the main idea.

One thing is certain: the amount of support must be appropriate for the media you are planning to use.

If it's a 30-second TV spot, one support point is often enough (and some think one is too many).

CELL PHONE VALUES:

As Hart Weichselbaum indicates, a good brief inspires creatives.

We don't have the brief in our hand, but looking at the result, it seems that a brief that focused on the value of sharing – something that may be generic to every phone call – helped inspire T-Mobile to creative executions that generated some ownership of that value.

Here, at Liverpool Street Station, 350 dancers, dressed in ordinary commuter clothes, perform routines to the music coming from the public address system. The dance as well as the reactions of commuters, including their using cell phones to capture the moment were caught by hidden cameras.

The result was a three-minute guerrilla style ad, which is part of T-Mobile's "Life's for Sharing" campaign. It aired less than 48 hours after being shot during an entire ad break on British TV, and then went viral on YouTube.

The campaign is clearly "value-driven." As Lysa Hardy, head of brand and communications at T-Mobile, noted, *"Dance brings to life the fact that there are often unexpected, wonderful, exciting things that happen that you want to be able to share with your friends and family."*

Clearly, people wanted to share this moment. Over ten million have viewed it on YouTube so far.

There was also digital outdoor and print, online, cinema, and radio advertising. The online presence includes a "making of" video that contributes to the overall buzz.

The campaign was created by Saatchi & Saatchi London.

- **Plan the briefing.**

  A meeting that communicates the brief to creatives is far more effective than slipping it under the door. The briefing is an opportunity to provide additional information and make the brief come alive. It's an opportunity for supplemental materials – music, images, ads, and other artifacts of the consumer – anything to bring the brief to life.

- **Stay humble.**

  Remember, the brief is merely a means to an end. Briefs are only as good as the ads that come out of them. As one ad sage remarked, "*You don't have a great brief until you have a great ad.*"

AN EVIL PLOT TO DESTROY THE WORLD. ENJOY.

People who enjoy television also know that it rots your brain.

Hey, everybody knows that. So it stands to reason that CP+B would leverage this little bit of "social tension" and "consumer insight" into memorable and persuasive advertising.

To see the commercials in full, go to www.hulu.com/hulu-tv-ads

Thus, briefs for outdoor tend to be short; those for infomercials or websites are much longer.

As Mike Hall says, "*all kinds of things can make advertising persuasive.*" Offering a functional benefit or unique selling proposition, communicating brand values that resonate, identifying the right call to action, or simply making the brand stand out from the crowd.

Sometimes the ad's attitude or tone of voice can make it more persuasive. If the planner has a point of view about tone of voice, it should go here.

Should the ad be authoritative, humorous, factual, emotional, spiritual?

What will work best with this audience?

WHERE BRIEFS ARE HEADED.

Life was simpler in the days before agencies had such a broad arsenal of new media to choose from.

Because marketing is being asked to do more things in more ways, many of the old formulations – including the questions asked in the creative brief – are changing in response to changing times.

Crispin Porter & Bogusky is an agency that has had some rather spectacular success recently – in a world where advertising success is no easy task.

Their unique ads for Burger King, beautifully designed work for the Mini, clever "Man Laws" for Miller Beer, the "Truth" anti-smoking campaign, and the strangely weird, but effective television for Hulu seemed to hit the right note in a cynical world.

CP+B is also a perfect example of an agency that has created a brief that reflects both the new roles advertising has been asked to take and the agency's unique approach to creative communication.

Their brief addresses each of the four basic questions discussed above; but in a way that evolves and elaborates their meaning.

First, let's look at how these questions are similar, yet different, from what we've been discussing. My comments are in italics.

The CP+B Creative Brief.

- **At-a-Glance.** What is the most relevant and differentiating idea that will surprise consumers or challenge their current thinking or relationship with the brand?

  In an over-communicated world, it's important to boil the issues down to something quick and simple. The CP+B brief instructs us to reduce our complicated idea to its essence.

- **Tension.** What is the psychological, social, categorical, or cultural tension associated with this idea?

  CP+B believes that engaging stories (and engaging communications in general) are based on tension between opposing forces. Is the brand an upstart in an established category? Can the brand be a "good guy" to a competitor's "bad guy," or vice versa? Tension creates emotion, drama, and suspense. Often it begs for resolution, causing people to act.

- **Question.** What is the question we need to answer to complete this assignment?

  The communications problem can often be solved by identifying – and then answering – a key question. Charles Kettering said, "A problem well-stated is half-solved."

WHAT WORKS FOR YOU?

Just as an ad reflects the personality of an advertiser, your Creative Strategy, Brief, or Blueprint can say something about you and your company.

Your approach to Strategy is a big part of how you do your job.

You'll "own" your Strategy even more when you have a Strategy format that you can call your own.

SOCIAL TENSION?
So where do you find Social Tension in a Whopper?

One answer is the inter-generational conflict between Whopper and Whopper Jr.

In one spot, Junior is ready to run away from home.

At a peak dramatic moment he says, "I wish I'd never been broiled."

Funny stuff.

Note how seeking out that tension provides you with the basis for dramatic conflict and contemporary humor.

In a business that traditionally avoids conflict, CP+B has found an interesting way to be… interesting.

TALK VALUE.
Whether it's Brooke Shields doing a phony mock-umentary on couples having babies so they can buy a family-size VW, or schlock-value ads about "Whopper Virgins," CP+B looks for some way to enter the cultural dialogue.

ENTERING THE CULTURAL CONVERSATION.
Know who wrote and designed this book? Alex Bogusky and Chuck Porter. They look for ways to engage the culture.

Sometimes it's an ad. Sometimes not.

**GO VISIT
ACCOUNTPLANNING.NET**
This British site provides a marvelous guide through the craft, as practiced in the UK.

It includes such gems as the original guide to account planning written by Stephen King (no, not the one who writes horror books). He was Marketing Director at JWT/London and it introduces you to some of the seminal thinking of the profession

- **Talk Value.** What about the brand could help us to start a dialogue between the brand and our target, among our target and/or within popular culture in general? It could be the little rationalizations that people use to support their emotional decision.

   As much as any other US agency, CP+B has found ways to multiply the impact of their work – and extend their clients' communications budgets – by getting people to talk about it. Their 2004 viral campaign "Subservient Chicken" for Burger King generated 20 million hits as it was passed around the world.

In many ways, the CP+B brief points the way to where briefs are heading.

1. Rather than describing merely the business context, it places the communication problem in a larger social and cultural context.
2. It acknowledges that people are consuming media in new ways and that what people tell each other about the ad may have more impact than the ad itself.
3. It reflects a unique model of how advertising works by advising creatives to exploit the inherent tension in the brand's situation.
4. It uses language that is "media neutral." It makes no assumptions about what media channels will be needed to solve the problem.

As communications problems and media options become more complex, there will be an increasing need to strategize, prioritize, and distill into a document that helps the creative team get it right.

In brief, we'll always need some kind of brief.

Here are a few more you might want to look at.

Sample Brief

Here is a standard Brief format:

1. What is the Opportunity and/or Problem the advertising must address?

This section features a brief summary of why you are advertising.

You need to take consumer point of view, not "sales are down," but "consumers are choosing cheaper alternatives."

2. What do we want people to do as a result of the advertising?

Try to make this as specific as possible.

It may be a shift in attitude or belief. Or it may be a marketplace behavior.

3. Who are we talking to?

Try to develop a rich description of the target group.

Indicate beliefs and feelings about the category.

Avoid demographic information only.

Add personality and lifestyle dimensions.

4. What's the Key Response we want?

Focus in. What *single* thing do we want people to feel or notice or believe as a result of the advertising?

5. What information/attributes might help produce this response?

It could be a key product attribute, or user need the brand fulfills, etc. Avoid a laundry list.

6. What aspect of Brand Personality should the advertising express?

Here, there should be some sort of agreed-upon Brand Character Statement.

7. Are there media or budget considerations?

Even in a "media neutral" environment, there are probably cues and clues about the target's media behavior that can be useful.

8. This could be helpful...

Finally, provide any additional information that might affect the creative direction.

READ ALL ABOUT IT.

These books by John Steel, who ran account planning at Goodby Silverstein, the "Got Milk" agency, offer excellent insights into how planners can help in the development of effective advertising.

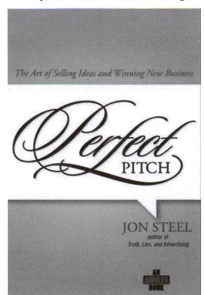

WHAT'S A BACKGROUNDER?

Before you can write a Strategy, you often need a lot of background – information about the brand.

A Backgrounder is usually some form of questionnaire designed to collect and organize that information so the Strategy can be developed.

IF YOU'D LIKE TO KNOW MORE ABOUT YOUR CUSTOMERS...

Just ask. Here's a handy start at a good questionnaire.

Don't be reluctant to do a few one-on-one interviews.

A lot of people think they're better than focus groups. Not to mention quicker and cheaper.

So, get out your clipboard and go talk to a few customers.

CUSTOMER QUESTIONNAIRE

How long have you shopped at_____?

When did you first discover _____?

What was your first impression?

Why do you keep coming back?

What would you say to a friend who had never tried _____?

What similar places do you shop, and why do you like these places?

Backgrounders

When a planner isn't around, a "Backgrounder" can help organize information in one place.

Here's an example of a Backgrounder for a local or regional business. It can be used by a local media company such as a newspaper, a local TV station, or a local cable company. You can write one to suit your needs.

---

1. Name and Location.
For a local advertiser, one of the most important communication tasks is your Name and Address (maybe your phone number, too).
Name:
Location(s):

Addresses and/or Location Identifiers (Intersections, etc.):

Phone Number:
Do you have any unique graphics, such as logo or signage?
(Attach copies. Indicate source of "master" graphics.)
Do you have any existing slogans or advertising themes?
(Attach examples of print ads, flyers, brochures, and/or scripts.)

2. Products and Services.
Tell us about what you make and sell and/or what services you provide. Don't just make a list – let us know some of the things that make your company special – because those are some of the things you'll want to tell potential customers or clients.

Do you have any existing materials that describe your products or services? (Attach brochures, menus, catalogs, etc.)

3. Your Customers.
Tell us about your customers.
Chances are your new customers will be a lot like the customers you have now. They'll live in the same area and have many of the same characteristics.
Let us know what you think is special about you and your company.

Do you have any letters or customers' comments?
(Attach examples – not originals!)
By the way, don't forget that good advertising can also reinforce current customers' attitudes as well as bring in new customers. That means, with a good commercial, you should see your current customers more often, as well as new customers.
If you'd like to know more about your customers, just ask them.

Client _____ Project _____

What's the Problem?

I. Marketing Background:

1. Current Marketplace Reality
- What's the current market situation?
- What are our problems/threats?
- What is making the competition successful?
- What's made us successful/unsuccessful to date?

2. Major Objectives & Measurements
- What do we want to achieve?
- What would indicate success?
- How might we measure that success?
- How might we measure the contribution of different communication elements?

3. Product Attributes, Features & Benefits.
- Attributes
- Features
- Benefits

4. Consumer Benefits & Values
- Consumer Benefits
- Values

II. Audience Background

5. Who is the target?
- Who is the primary audience?
- What do we know about them?
- What are the primary needs we will be meeting?
- How should we talk to them/not talk to them? (TONE)
- Are there any secondary audiences (including dealers and trade)?
- What is important to the secondary audience?

6. Situation - Before the Message
- What does our audience think/feel about us?
- Are there any barriers/obstacles to overcome?
- What do they think/feel about the competition/category?

APPLE WORK PLAN & BACKGROUNDER.

Here is a set we developed for Apple a number of years ago.

You might notice there is room for a secondary audience.

Apple had a number of secondary audiences, developers, a retail channel, and the media - so plans were not simply consumer-driven communication.

Even for consumer products this can be helpful, as it reminds you that you have a trade channel and, sometimes, a sales force.

There may also be internal audiences.

(Note: This is the final section of a Strategy Seminar that's available as a pdf in CAFE at adbuzz.com.)

7. Desired Result - After the Message
- What will they think/feel about us after the communication?
- What do we want them to do after the communication?

8. Reasons Why:
- Why will they change their mind?
- What are some of the real reasons?

III. Tactical Background:

9. How:
- How can we best reach the audience?
- What's the suggested medium?

10. When:
- What's the window of opportunity?
- Is there a deadline or key 'drop dead' dates?

11. Quantity (If materials):
- How many will we need to proceed?
- Are all the materials needed at once?

12. Longevity:
- How long will the program last?
- How long should the supply of materials last?

13. Mandatories:

IV Integrated Communications:

14. Integration:
- How will this project work with other elements of this program?
- How will this program work with other programs?

Approvals: Who must approve the Work Plan? _____
When? _____

#16: Build Your Own.

1. WRITE A FORMAT THAT WORKS FOR YOU.

Feel free to borrow from any part of this section and use any combination of elements.

Your format may be a single form or a two-part process (e.g., Backgrounder & Brief).

2. GIVE YOUR FORMAT A NAME.

Have that name reflect the "Brand Personality" you wish to project.

Again, you may borrow from elements already presented in this section.

3. FILL OUT YOUR BRIEF.

Take a product you know something about and see if your format works.

4. DO A LITTLE "HYPOTHESIS TESTING."

Now, see how your format works for a few other products you're familiar with.

Feeling ambitious? Write some ads based on your Strategy Format.

5. DON'T FORGET THE MARCOM MATRIX.

Often, we're working in a company that just handles one aspect of The MarCom Matrix.

Having a MarCom idea outside of your discipline can be a problem.

That said, as far as this book is concerned, you should think of, suggest, and work on any discipline that makes sense.

As for strategy formats, I've found it best to have a core Communication Strategy and then list Tactics in the various MarCom disciplines.

SECOND THOUGHTS.

Don't forget secondary audiences and secondary benefits.

In many businesses there is a second audience that's very important.

For food marketers – the grocery trade.

For computers, it's dealers and "opinion leaders," which includes the media.

For office equipment, it's secretaries and "decision-makers."

At a fast food place it's often "the crew."

Many complex products, like computers and office equipment, may have additional benefits or features that appeal to those making the final purchase decision.

For example, if both copiers are reliable, which has the best service?

Or the best price?

Or the best lease?

Or…?

THE JUMP START.

When Scott Bish and I were at a sales promotion firm, we had to implement some sort of system to deal with a "loose cannon" situation. People would come in with jobs that contained a chaotic collection of hopes, dreams, fears, and requirements. Plus a rush due date.

We put together a simple form we called "The Jump Start."

It acknowledged that we had to get moving, and asked for the information in such a way that we could turn the job around as fast as possible.

Since it was sales promotion, the first thing we asked was what?

Right, "what's the behavior?"

Did we want velocity off the shelf, or did we need to get a display into the liquor store?

If that was the case, the "Dealer Loader" might be as important as the offer.

Know what a Dealer loader is? It's the thing the retailer gets for putting up your display.

Example: We do a "Fishing for Value?" display with a nice fishing rod on it. Then, when it's time to take down the display, guess who gets the fishing rod?

THE ART OF STRATEGY.

In strategic development, market facts of varying accuracy and relevance are linked with hypotheses of varying validity in a long complex sequence.

In the process, many business people forget that a strategy is a hypothesis.

It's a theory, a blueprint, a road map.

It's a "best guess."

It's an art, not a science.

And, as you can see by this "strategic" advertiser, sometimes strategies don't keep working.

*"Our best work
has always begun with
a marketing solution,
not a creative solution.
The ads flowed
from the Strategy,
not the Strategy
from the ads."*

Jay Chiat

*"As far back as the late '50s at Doyle Dane Bernbach, where instinct and talent fueled their breakthrough creative work, 'positioning' and 'strategy' were regarded, almost unconsciously, as the first **implicit** steps of the creative process."*

George Lois

Formats

NOW THAT WE'VE BEEN briefed, how do we get there?

That's strategy. It's a subject taught at great length and expense in business schools across the nation.

Seminars abound. Sober businessmen endorse its healthful benefits. We'll leave that to finer minds than ours. What we'll provide are some useful formats and some helpful advice on how to use them.

STRATEGY AND THE WEATHER.
Sometimes, strategy is like the weather – everyone talks about it, but less is done than most will admit.

And, as we discussed, there's often more than one strategy hanging around. Finally, sometimes it's not like the weather at all – because everywhere you go, it often seems to be pretty much the same. Brand names for less. Better than the rest.

Best value. Quality and service. Blah blah blah.

Today, many businesses seem to have pretty much the same strategy. That's easy to understand. The forces at work and the people who work there are also pretty much the same.

Just keep in mind that victory in the marketplace tends to go to those who best accomplish *relevant differentiation*.

A BIT OF HISTORY.
Once upon a time, some companies had MBAs and marketing departments and some didn't.

Strategies and smart marketing offered important differentiation.

Once upon a time, manufacturers were able to maintain a competitive difference with patents or production secrets.

234

There were fewer products, but they seemed more different. Remember Hopkins? When he was writing, baked beans in a can were a big deal. That was then.

Today, all companies have MBAs. Most marketers march to the same strategic drum. Suppliers can manufacture and deliver what we can't.

Canned beans. Beer. Toothpaste. You name it.

Sometimes it seems the only thing they can't copy is the brand name, which, incidentally is one reason brands have greater value.

That's why marketing communication is so important for brand differentiation. And that's why a successful copywriter has to know strategy.

COMPLEX. BUT SIMPLE.

Strategic development can be complex.

Yet, its essence is simple.

Simply put, an Advertising Strategy answers the question, "*How do you sell the thing?*"

A successful copywriter is a successful salesperson.

And, to survive in the complex world of an advertising agency, you *must* become involved in developing, understanding, and *selling* strategy.

Strategies are instinctive to good salesmen.

"That suit looks good on you."

"You're going to love this restaurant..."

"An offer you can't refuse."

P&G defines it this way...

"Advertising Strategy is that portion of a brand's marketing strategy which deals with advertising copy.

"It is a statement which identifies the basis upon which we expect consumers to purchase our product in preference to competition."

A successful strategy must have the potential to persuade. Remember Bernbach:

TACTICS, STRATEGIES & OBJECTIVES.

Strategists ask, "What should I do?"

Tacticians ask, "What *can* I do?"

The strategist is concerned with consistency and payout over the long haul.

The tactician is concerned with effectiveness and short-term results.

Sometimes available tactics can determine what strategies and objectives are possible.

Marketing Warfare and *Bottom-Up Marketing* by Trout and Ries are good sources for examining this process.

Sometimes, tactics can help you discover the best strategy. Hal Riney opines, *"I don't know what the Strategy should be till I do the creative."*

Here is Kenichi Ohmae's graphic description of strategic thinking.

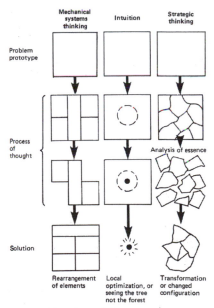

Figure 1-1 Three kinds of thinking process.

Strategic Thinking Is...

"Dissecting a situation into its constituent parts and then... imaginative reintegration of all the different items into a new pattern using nonlinear brain power."

From The Mind of The Strategist *by Kenichi Ohmae. (A great book!)*

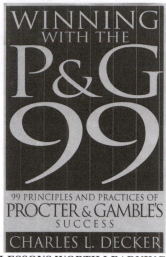

WINNING WITH THE P&G 99

99 PRINCIPLES AND PRACTICES OF
PROCTER & GAMBLE'S SUCCESS
CHARLES L. DECKER

LESSONS WORTH LEARNING.

You may not like all their advertising, but if you owned their stock, you would love what they do. Consistent growth. Ethical behavior. Intelligent decisions. And, when they do make the occasional mistake, they fix it.

Here are a few lessons from this book:
• Trust the consumer.
• Keep listening.
• Strategic thinking is a way of life.
They're tough.
But they're smart.

"I'm a !#@¡?! strategist!"*

Helmut Krone

That's how Helmut Krone, the DDB Art Director, described himself to us.

He is.

He's one heck of a strategist.

And it's one of the main reasons his ads worked so well.

It's more than fine design.

It's strategy.

A Strategy is
• **Simple**
• **Clear in intent**
• **Contains no executional elements**

*"Advertising is fundamentally **persuasion.**"*

Your strategy must be able to generate movement in the marketplace. It must *sell*.

THE P&G COPY STRATEGY MEMO.

On the following page is a copy of a memo which outlines the basic thinking on Copy Strategy that is taught to trainees at P&G and to people who work for their many ad agencies.

Those who leave P&G for other jobs take these lessons with them, as do agency people who work on their business.

This memo has become a standard industry view on the topic of Copy Strategy.

MORE ON P&G.

A good friend, a former P&G executive, summed it up as *"The triumph of the topical sentence."* He's not far off – the objective of a good P&G memo is clear as a bell from sentence one.

You can get a feel for it from the memo on the opposite page and from the *99 Principles and Practices* book mentioned in the sidebar.

Want a few more?

We've got a bit of space left on the page, how about these?

• Find the consumer insight.
• Show what you say, say what you show.
• The memo is a template for strategic thinking.
  • Use an interesting visual.
  • Put the benefit in the visual.

See what's going on? This is a company that puts a lot of emphasis on how well it talks to, and listens to, the consumer.

We can all do that.

236

Copy Strategy.

A copy strategy is a document which identifies the basis upon which we expect consumers to purchase our brand in preference to competition. It is the part of the marketing strategy which deals with advertising copy.

The fundamental content of a copy strategy emerges directly from the product, and the basic consumer need which the product was designed to fulfill.

A copy strategy should state clearly the basic benefit which the brand promises and which constitutes the principal basis for purchase.

While not mandatory, the strategy may also include:

- A statement of the product characteristic which makes this basic benefit possible.

- A statement of the character we want to build for the brand over time.

PURPOSE OF A COPY STRATEGY.

Copy strategy provides guidance and direction for a brand's advertising. It should be a long-term document, not subject to judgment changes.

The copy strategy provides guidance and direction for the agency's creative people. It prescribes the limits within which an agency is to exercise its creative imagination, while being flexible enough to allow latitude for fresh and varied executions.

The copy strategy provides a common basis upon which to evaluate and discuss merits of an advertising submission in terms of intent and idea content.

A clear copy strategy can save a great deal of creative time and energy, because it identifies those basic decisions which we do not intend to review and rethink each time we look at a new piece of advertising.

CHARACTERISTICS OF A GOOD COPY STRATEGY.

Here are some things which characterize a good strategy statement:

- It's clear.

The basis upon which the consumer is being asked to buy our brand in preference to others should be quite clear to everyone involved.

- It's simple.

Key here is that the number of ideas in the strategy be kept to a minimum.

- It's devoid of executional considerations.

The copy strategy identifies what benefits we are to present to consumers, avoiding executional issues which deal with how these benefits are to be presented.

-It's inherently competitive.

The copy strategy should provide the answer to the question "Why should I buy this product rather than some other?"

237

SOME COMMENTS ON CONVENTIONAL WISDOM ABOUT STRATEGIES.

It is generally believed that…

1. Strong strategies = strong tactics.
This is probably true.

But what if your strategy is *not* getting you strong, motivating communications that are meaningful to the consumer?

• Perhaps the people creating the tactics aren't good enough.

• Or, perhaps, the strategy itself is not inherently persuasive.

If a strategy is strong, you *should* be looking at a wide variety of persuasive communications based on that strategy.

If you're not, it's not unreasonable to conclude that you should be taking another look at the strategy as well as the people who are executing it.

2. A mediocre execution of a correct strategy is better than an excellent execution of an incorrect strategy.

Sure, but, again, there are limits to what is generally accepted to be true.

For example, a commercial that makes fun of your Target Customer probably won't work very well – no matter how on-strategy it might be.

Concurrently, some alternate strategies may be just as persuasive (i.e., "as correct") as the recommended strategy.

In this case, all bets are off.

How to Write a Strategy

THE PURPOSE of this section is to show you a basic format for writing an Advertising Strategy.

We can't tell you how to write the *right* strategy, but we can tell you how to write one that:

1. makes sense
2. is written in a format that will be clear to everyone who reads it.

Writing strategies takes practice.

The more you do it, the better you'll get.

Just being aware of strategies that worked (and failed) in the past can be a big help.

It also helps to work with good people – developing a Strategy is usually *a team effort:* research, account management, clients, creatives, even consumers (in the form of focus groups or account planners) can be a part of that team.

As a mental process, it involves logical analysis, intuitive thinking, high-minded hypothesizing, and tough-minded negotiation.

And even though it's often complicated and frustrating, developing a strategy can be tremendously exciting and satisfying – as you work with others to shape the future of a business.

Let's get started.

On-Strategy or Off-Target?
Here's a clever visual. It tells its target (people who eat Kentucky Fried Chicken) that they're "Bucket Heads" and they should switch to a different fried chicken. It's on-strategy, but how persuasive do you think it is?

THERE ARE NUMEROUS FORMATS for writing an Advertising Strategy.

We'll cover others at the end of this chapter, and your instructor may want you to use a different format. Don't worry.

As you will discover, they have common characteristics.

The one we'll start with is a simple format that was used for years by clients and agencies such as P&G and Leo Burnett. It has three parts:

1. AN OBJECTIVE STATEMENT.

The Objective is stated *within* this first section of the Strategy. It identifies the brand's Target Customer and states the Objective, which is usually (but not always) communicating a meaningful Benefit.

2. A SUPPORT STATEMENT.

This indicates the support you will use to "prove" your benefit. It may be a "reason why" for that benefit, or it may be something else.

3. A STATEMENT OF TONE OR "BRAND CHARACTER."

This may describe the desired "selling attitude" of the advertising or the long-term values of the brand.

It looks like this.

**Advertising will [verb]
[Target Customer] that [Product/Brand]
is/will/provides
[Statement of Benefit].
Support will be [Support/Reason Why].
Tone will be
["Selling Attitude" Adjectives].**

– or –

**[Brand] is
[Description of "Brand Character."]**

Advertising strategy is that portion of a brand's marketing strategy which deals with advertising copy. It is a statement which identifies the basis upon which we expect consumers to purchase our product in preference to competition.

P&G says a strategy "customarily contains the following information."

1. A statement of the basic benefit which the product promises and which constitutes the principal basis for purchase of the brand.

2. A statement of the product characteristic which makes it possible for the product to deliver this basic benefit.

3. A statement of the character we strive to build for the product.

STRATEGY FORMATS.

This section contains a number of commonly used advertising strategy formats in addition to this one.

You'll find them at the end of this chapter. They are:

- The Y&R Creative Work Plan
- GE Focus System
- Leo Burnett Strategy Worksheet
- DDB ROI System
- Creative Action Plan
- Creative Briefs
- Blueprints and Backgrounders

Finally, there's an IMC Strategy Discussion. We'll talk about how to develop strategies for The MarCom Matrix.

1. Objective Statement

OUR ADVERTISING OBJECTIVE STATEMENT starts simply: **"Advertising will…"**

Obviously, it will *do* something. We need a verb.

"Convince," "persuade," and "communicate" are the verbs most commonly used.

"Remind" has also been used. For example, "Put a Jell-O out tonight" was a Reminder Strategy.

We prefer "convince." It demonstrates confidence and reminds us that we are talking about *persuasion,* something that will occur inside the consumer's mind.

PART ONE. TARGET CUSTOMER.
Next, the Strategy defines who we're talking to… the Target Customer. Hopefully, this will be more than a simple statement of demographics.

"Women 18 to 45" may be correct, but "mothers" or "traditional homemakers" may be closer to a real description of your target.

"Usage" is another good way to describe your target.

It's often helpful to include some phrase describing the type of person you're targeting.

Remember, you're talking to a *person,* a real person. Describe that person.

Your description may be qualitative (taste-oriented, price-conscious, etc.) or quantitative (18-45, A&B Counties, etc.). Or both.

It may be broad, it may be narrow, but try to give your target a *dimension.* Look for important characteristics that your Target Customers have in common.

Even broadly based products have targets that can be described with insight.

Y&R places great emphasis on this – they call it "Prospect Definition." They believe it's critical to

The Objective of Energizer's Pink Bunny advertising was to establish leadership in the generic category benefit of durability by out-executing the competitive brand – DuraCell.

STEP BY STEP: ARCHWAY "GOOD FOOD COOKIE" ADVERTISING STRATEGY.

Background: In the early '80s, Archway Cookies, a small national brand, was caught up in "The Cookie Wars."

Large marketers, such as Frito-Lay and P&G, entered the cookie category while Nabisco and Keebler defended their positions aggressively.

Archway moved to a strategy based on a niche position.

While other cookie companies competed with chocolate chip and other chocolate varieties, Archway developed a strategy based on the brand's strength in *oatmeal-based* cookies.

"FOR YEARS I HID MY INTELLIGENCE SO GUYS WOULD LIKE ME. THEN I NOTICED THE ONLY GUYS WHO LIKED ME WERE STUPID."

Insight into your target is critical for developing effective communication. Here, a magazine uses that insight to communicate to their target customers –advertising executives.

understand what's important to consumers.

They believe prospects should be defined in terms of: product usage, demographics, and psychographics (lifestyles, attitudes, etc.).

Often, simple descriptions of the target are backed with additional in-depth information.

For example, your strategy may refer simply to *"men who drink premium beer."* This will be backed with additional information – such as attitudes toward sports, women, and their job.

Broadly defined targets may have important subgroups described in support material.

Here are some typical examples:

Women who wash confidently in all temperatures.
Working mothers.
Fashion-conscious women, 18-35.
Young adults concerned about nutrition.
Adults who wear eyeglasses.

Now, add the name of your product.

That should be easy.

So far, your strategy reads

"Advertising will [convince] [Target Customer] that [Product] is/will/provides…

Now it gets tough.

ARCHWAY COOKIES OBJECTIVE STATEMENT.
Part One. Target Customer.
Advertising will convince adults who eat cookies…

Though much cookie consumption is by children, Archway is basically an adult product.

This was supported by a wide range of market research as well as focus groups that addressed this specific issue.

A key question – were adults naturally "migrating" to the brand, or was Archway an "old" brand with an eroding customer base.

Research focused on this key issue. The answer – adults naturally "discovered" Archway Cookies as they looked for something "more homemade" and less sweet.

Additional barriers were discovered to increased consumption by children, such as cost per cookie.

Information about Archway purchasing habits, which skewed older and female, was used to assist in media selection.

A decision was made to advertise both to older consumers, who were the most loyal Archway customers, and to younger adults who were migrating into Archway's market.

*P&G believes
objectives should be:*
Specific.
Measurable.
Achievable.
Compatible.
They call it "SMAC."

**ARCHWAY COOKIES
OBJECTIVE STATEMENT.**
Part Two. Benefit.
*...that Archway Oatmeal
Cookies are uniquely
nutritious and delicious.*

Strategy is about choice.

Archway's major strategic decision was to focus mainly on their popular oatmeal cookies.

Rather than advertise the whole line, the decision was made to focus on oatmeal-based varieties (over 30% of sales).

The benefit was actually based on an Attribute – oatmeal.

Oatmeal naturally has good nutritional characteristics and, even more important, a wholesome, positive image with our target consumers.

The decision was made not to overstate "healthy" aspects, but rather to depend on the inherent "good nutrition" of oatmeal – this was a unique claim in the category.

Taste was added to the benefit claim to remind everyone that we were talking about cookies, but was a secondary part of the benefit statement since it was generic – cookies taste good.

PART TWO. BENEFIT STATEMENT.

So, what is the Objective? The Advertising Objective.

What is the movement within the consumer's attitude or awareness which, if accomplished, will result in meeting your Marketing Objective (usually selling more product) and turning a Target *Consumer* into a Target *Customer*?

Sometimes, in the case of products with a clear dimension of difference, it's communicating product *superiority* in a persuasive fashion.

It might be a general (or generic) superiority or it may be superiority with a specific dimension of product performance.

Very often, your objective will be communicating some form of superiority, uniqueness, or differentiation in a convincing way. This dimension of superiority should be meaningful in terms of purchase behavior.

The movement may be psychological – such as "confidence" or "satisfaction."

It might be tangible – "feels soft" or "tastes terrific!"

Your product might be:

• Easier – Convenience Strategy
• Cheaper – Economy Strategy
• Better quality for the price – Value Strategy

Your product might be a service, or a combination of product and service, which adds other dimensions.

Sometimes it's rational, sometimes it's emotional – every time it's important.

A key consideration is that it be *meaningful* – again, a *"factor that influences purchase behavior."*

Many well-supported strategies have failed because, when you got right down to it, the difference was not meaningful to the consumer – or not worth it.

Either it wasn't important enough, or it wasn't worth the extra price (products that do more often cost more).

Ask this question – What is it we want the person to believe or feel about our product or service?

And, will that be enough to move them toward a purchase decision? Here's an example for Cascade:

**"Advertising will convince
automatic dishwasher owners
that Cascade provides
virtually spotless end results."**

This is a clear statement of what they want their advertising to communicate.

In this case, their Objective is communicating the benefit of "virtually spotless end results."

The movement in the consumer's mind is increasing conviction that Cascade delivers in this dimension of product performance.

The word "virtually" clearly communicates that neither the advertising nor Cascade can promise or deliver *completely* spotless results.

If you have a clear idea of the movement in the consumer's mind you wish to achieve, you understand the Objective.

In the case of products without dramatic differences or with multiple benefits, this might not be as clear. (A common strategic problem.)

Once you've developed your Objective or Benefit Statement, your strategy reads

**"Advertising will [convince]
[Target Customer] that [Product]
is/will /provides
[Objective/Benefit]."**

You've just finished the first section of the Strategy.

A simple statement that sets out the mission to be accomplished by your advertising.

But saying it isn't enough. You need help.

"Support will be…"

DISCOVER THE BENEFIT.

In general, you will want to discover the benefit a consumer derives from the product.

You may wish to ask yourself these questions:

1. Is it a Product Benefit?
i.e., "spotless end results"

2. Or is it a Consumer Benefit?
i.e., "I'm a good homemaker."

3. Or is it both?
i.e., *"cleans down to the shine and isn't that a nice reflection on you?"*

A statement of the basic benefit which the product promises consumers and which constitutes the principal basis for purchase of that brand.

243

2. Support Statement

support (så pôrt´)
5. *To show or tend to show to be true; help prove, vindicate, or corroborate [evidence to **support** a claim].*

Webster's New World Dictionary

ARCHWAY COOKIES SUPPORT STATEMENT.

Support was based on the inherent nutritional characteristics of oatmeal cookies with additional emphasis on other emerging health concerns – such as palm oil.

A low-calorie claim was added later. ("Ounce-for-ounce lower in calories than most other cookies in your store.")

Archway's other varieties were used as further support for Archway uniqueness.

Support will be:
Archway Cookies are made with nutritious oatmeal,
Archway Oatmeal Cookies are naturally low in sodium and fat – they contain No Palm Oil.
Archway has many unique varieties.

Longer ads, like :60 radio spots, and package copy went deeper into the Support section.

Shorter ads, like in-store posters, concentrated on the first points.

THE SECOND SECTION OF THE STRATEGY begins **"Support will be…"**

Generally, Support is the *reason* you can provide the benefit mentioned in the Objective Statement.

For example...

"Virtually spotless end results will be attributed to the sheeting action produced by the Cascade formula."

The Objective is communicating the benefit, which is the reason for buying Cascade.

Support is the *reason* you provide the benefit.

Sometimes this is clear and simple – Cascade's "sheeting action" is a reason why.

And sometimes it isn't simple at all.

Many ambitious strategies have failed due to an unrealistic attitude toward this critical issue, promising more than they could deliver.

Others failed to prove what they promised to skeptical consumers or priced themselves higher than people were willing to pay.

The Strategy may have sounded great in the meeting but could not be made into effective advertising.

LINKAGE.

Finally, Support and Objective are *linked*.

What can you deliver as Support for your benefit? The link may be logical – Cascade's sheeting action.

Or, linkage may be an effort of imagination and determination – like Marlboro becoming linked to the imagery of Marlboro Country.

One important concern is establishing *linkage* throughout the strategy – you must *link* an Objective that can be accomplished with Support that can be delivered.

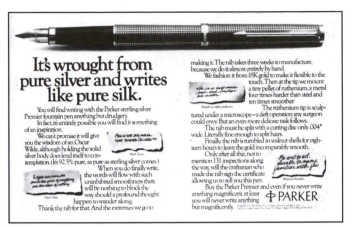

Whether your Support is a product-based fact or pure imagination and attitude, these two parts of your Strategy must be well-connected.

Here are some of the common issues related to developing Support.

PRODUCT BENEFIT VS. CONSUMER BENEFIT. One of the most common debates in advertising strategy development revolves around this issue.

When the strategy features a Consumer Benefit (you're a good mother), the support is often a Product Benefit ('cause you serve your children tasty and nutritious…)

The discussion goes something like this…

Is the Objective communicating a Consumer Benefit (or Value) with the Product Benefit as the Support ("You're a Good Mother because you serve Yum Nut Peanut Butter to your kids.")?

Or, should we communicate the Product Benefit with a reason why as the Support ("Yum Nut tastes better because it's made with more nuts.")?

Strategically, this is a good question. And a good case can often be made for both sides of the argument.

Remember P&G's theme for Jif Peanut Butter?

It's "Choosy Mothers Choose Jif." Then, they gave some sort of "more peanuts" reason why as support.

CAN YOU COMMUNICATE IT ALL?

Can you communicate consumer and product benefits and reason why?

Sure you can.

But you may need a longer format – like this magazine ad for Parker Pen.

**Product Benefit as Support
for Consumer Benefit.**

Great manufacturing is the reason why. Great writing is the benefit.

**LOW PRICES = SUPPORT
FOR BETTER LIVING.**

Take a look at the logic in this relatively new Walmart theme – from the Martin Agency.

Sure, you knew Walmart had low prices – you've known it for years.

But they translate that fact into strategic support for a larger Consumer Benefit – better living overall.

This takes a somewhat dull and prosaic piece of information and elevates into a larger and more interesting proposition.

This is very smart.

LOOKING FOR SUPPORT?

Often, while discovering the Objective, material for Support has been generated in the process:

* Product Facts
* Product Benefits
* Consumer Needs
* Consumer Benefits
* Competitive Advantages
* Positioning Opportunities
* Whatever It Takes to Solve the Problem

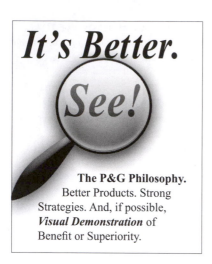

It's Better. See!

The P&G Philosophy.
Better Products. Strong Strategies. And, if possible, *Visual Demonstration* of Benefit or Superiority.

"The key to successful marketing is superior product performance.

If the consumer does not perceive any real benefits in the brand, then no amount of ingenious advertising and selling can save the brand."

**Ed Harness
Former P&G Chairman**

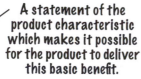

A statement of the product characteristic which makes it possible for the product to deliver this basic benefit.

A "Reason Why" Support Statement.

Consumer Benefits are generally regarded as strategically superior – yet, in one survey done by Y&R, TV commercials that focused on product Attributes or benefits were judged more effective and distinctive.

The only thing certain is that this will continue to be the subject of strategic discussion.

FEATURES AND ATTRIBUTES.
Product Benefits may also be called Features.

We usually think of a Feature as a reason why for a benefit. (Are you following this? Let it settle in, feel how they're all connected on the ladder.)

Finally, an Attribute is just sort of a generic quality of the product – peanut butter is made from peanuts. Though this doesn't mean you can't leverage that fact into some meaningful communication.

Peanut butter is made from peanuts. Certain types of candy bars contain peanuts. People who buy these products like peanuts.

So you might find a way of dramatizing this attribute, and it could be a key part of your strategy.

TYPES OF SUPPORT.
Here are some different types of support statement:
Reason Why.

This type of support is often a product fact, such as Cascade's sheeting action. Classic package goods strategies try to provide a logical reason why.

As P&G would say, *"A statement of the product characteristic which makes it possible for the product to deliver this basic benefit."*

P&G brands are based on superior product performance supported by an extraordinary commitment to marketing superior products.

This is not always possible.

Many products compete in areas where there is no specific "reason why." Or, where the reason why is either not motivating or "ownable."

For example, in the floor wax and floor cleaner category, it's hard to really own clean shiny floors. If this is the case, you have to look for another type of linkage.

Combinations.

Sometimes a *combination* of facts can support a single and specific benefit.

> **"Support is that Special K is
> low in calories and sugar,
> high in protein."**

These two characteristics combined help support Special K's "healthy weight loss" benefit.

It's common to link two Product Benefits to create a Consumer Benefit or a larger Product Benefit. Here are three examples:

A. The Value equation links quality and price.

$$Price/Quality = Value$$

B. Liquid laundry detergents combine special cleaning properties (removal of stains or collar soil) with general cleaning effectiveness.

C. Convenience plus good taste is a common combination for many prepared foods. Yet, the benefit is relatively single-minded ("It's easy to serve a great tasting meal.")

Permission to Believe and Nine-Wheel Logic.

Here, the logic is trickier. 9-Lives cat food tasting good enough for finicky Morris the Cat lets you believe the products perform as advertised.

You're caught up in the story, and Morris reminds you of your cat. That's why you give the advertiser "permission" to make the claim.

It's the Keebler Elves, as well as all the stories about cereal for kids.

That's Nine-Wheel Logic at work.

Image.

Here, Support is almost ephemeral. At the same time, the linkage may be quite powerful.

Combined Support *(low fat and high taste) lets Subway deliver the Consumer Benefit of weight reduction.*

ATTRIBUTE + INHERENT DRAMA. The result is uncommonly interesting, considering all they're saying is that their shortbread cookies have fruit. See how the "inherent drama" adds interest and story value to what would otherwise be a very ordinary statement.

MORRIS CODE.

Is that all I am to you, a "Reason Why"? Or am I "Permission to Believe"?

It's hard to know sometimes.

Morris likes to think of himself as "Inherent Drama."

IMAGERY AT WORK.

Marlboro's ownership of the West is now so complete that even small pieces can communicate the entire range of imagery. Here, a graphic variation for a flanker brand.

THE KEEBLER ELVES.

They're cute and entertaining, and we give them our "permission."

UNIQUE VISUALIZATION OF GENERIC BENEFIT.

There's nothing that special about the durability benefit, but the unique visual property of the Energizer Bunny helped Energizer gain ownership of the position.

Objective and Support are often linked by imagination, artistry, and ad budgets.

The linkage between Marlboro and the imagery of Marlboro Country is an act of will supported by heavy media expenditures. The heritage of the name is of English nobility – it's not Western at all.

The "lifestyle" imagery of many campaigns, seeks to place the product in a certain type of environment with certain types of people.

Fashion advertising does not try to persuade you by talking about the fabric or their unique stitching process, but by projecting a look (visual support) and an attitude. And maybe someone famous.

Some aspects of image may be based on a brand's long-term heritage. And that heritage may contain its own "permission to believe."

Years ago, I saw the very first Keebler Cookie commercials presented. I said, *"Are they kidding?"* Years later, you sort of nod your head and accept it.

We don't really believe Keebler Cookies are made by elves in hollow trees, but we give them permission, and as we do it, we buy into the image of the brand.

The result of those feelings and attitudes on the part of consumers can be substantial. It can be as strong and powerful as a logical "reason why."

GENERIC BENEFIT. UNIQUE SUPPORT. In theory, the more unique and distinctive your Support, the more it will be Support for your Product. The benefit may be generic, but with unique Support (a unique proposition, visual support, or other inherent drama) it can be a unique construct.

Or, as The Pink Bunny demonstrates, perhaps it is the uniqueness of your advertising that does it.

As Rosser Reeves' USP clearly states, your Support should be "unique."

"The proposition must be one that the competition either cannot or does not offer.

*It must be **unique** – either a uniqueness of the brand or a claim not otherwise made in that particular field of advertising."*

That's the theory. In reality, many successful brands manage to reinforce their leadership and dominate by staking claim to a generic benefit supported by a generic attribute – one common to the category.

Many dominant brands have established strong positions with generic benefits.

This is the modern version of Claude Hopkins' preemption, Rosser Reeves' USP, and Leo Burnett's inherent drama.

A key issue in developing a winning strategy is what benefit position you can establish and how you can support it.

LINKING LOGIC AND EMOTION.
Remember The FCB Grid? In many cases, there is both emotional and logical support for your brand.

Like the radio commercials for Motel 6. They combine the emotional aspect of being a "smart shopper" and "frugal American" with the facts of Motel 6's low prices.

They can even turn a lack of Features (no mint on your pillow) into a Benefit.

This link of logic and emotion can happen anywhere in a strategy and in the development process.

The emotional benefit of your family's safety, which the tires cannot guarantee, can have the logical support of the construction of the tires.

And the proof of the tire's quality? The high price!

A little radial tire logic, I guess.

Bleach as Reason Why for Whiteness. *A strong brand like Tide can often have good results with a fairly generic claim. A smaller brand like Gain will not get the same punch – even if the ad is quite nice.*

Target Customer as Support. *This is a common Positioning Strategy. Do you see the linkage here?*

A strong benefit delivered with a sweet yet powerful visual. See how the various aspects of tire purchase are linked?

249

*Humorous Commercials featuring
retired professional athletes did some
very serious business for Lite Beer. The
"argument" between "Tastes Great"
and "Less Filling" provided just enough
drama to last thirty seconds.*

*The theme was "Everything You Always
Wanted in a Beer. And less."*

LOOK FOR MORE LINKAGE.

To strengthen your Strategy further, it is often helpful to establish *additional linkage* between the Benefit and the Target.

For example, "Less Filling" was a benefit that appealed to Lite Beer's Target – the heavy beer drinker. So did the visual support – ex-jocks who enjoyed it.

Like a good ad, a solid Strategy *resonates.*

All of the elements work together to build the sale.

DOES IT ADD UP TO A PROPOSITION?

Here are some further considerations:

Is Support Single-Minded?

A laundry list of attributes is not Support. Support in a Strategy should reinforce a single-minded path to the Objective.

Multiple Benefit Strategies (i.e., "Tastes better/Costs less") must be clearly superior to those that focus on a single benefit.

However, by *linking* two pieces of Support, it is sometimes possible to achieve a single-minded benefit. (Remember the Subway ad a few pages ago?)

Is Your Support Clear?

When you read the Strategy, do you understand *why* a person should buy this product?

Does it make sense? Does it seem important?

And finally… **Does It Feel Like You Can Sell the Product with It?**

After all, sooner or later, you've got to write an ad. Will your Support support you?

This may seem like an obvious question, but the "presold" nature of the people writing strategies often makes them more eager to be persuaded than the consumers to whom they'll be advertising.

If your Support is supportable, write it down.

(If it isn't, keep working.)

Now your strategy will read:

Advertising will [convince] [Target Customer] that [Product] is/will/provides [Objective/Benefit].

Support will be [Support].

That's what you say.

Tone is how you say it.

"THE GOLD STANDARD STRATEGY." The product strategies for Taster's Choice Coffee, Merit Cigarettes, and DiGiorno's Pizza are really the same strategy. Different products. Same strategy.

Each takes a "gold standard" (ground roast coffee, full-flavor cigarettes, and delivery pizza) and compares it to the product.

Then, they provide a "permission to believe" bit of support: freeze-dried coffee, "enriched flavor," and rising crust to support the claim.

(Thanks to Dave Moeller, who helped develop all three strategies.)

REASON WHY SUPPORT. Product performance as Support for a Consumer Benefit. "No Cavities!"

ARCHWAY COOKIES OBJECTIVE & SUPPORT.

Most often, communicating a benefit will be your Objective.

In the Archway strategy, oatmeal implied a nutrition benefit that was unique to the cookie category. Note the ways in which the first two statements are *linked.*

Advertising will convince adults who eat cookies that Archway Oatmeal Cookies are uniquely delicious and nutritious.
Support will be:
Archway Cookies are made with nutritious oatmeal.
Archway Cookies are naturally low in sodium and fat – they contain no Palm Oil.
Archway has many unique varieties.

Even *unique* is used as linkage. Unique varieties can be Support for unique taste (uniquely delicious).

This is not an accident. When opportunities arose related to their popular Ginger Snaps, the strategy could accommodate it.

Ultimate. *"The Ultimate Driving Machine" was basically a Product Benefit supported by the design and "road feel" of BMWs.*

3. The Tone or Brand Character Statement

THE RIGHT TONE.
THE RIGHT BRAND CHARACTER.
This award-winning advertising has the right tone for its target – men who fish. It also strengthens the Brand Character.

Whether you use a Tone or Brand Character Statement, your ads should do both jobs well.

TRADITIONAL PRODUCT,
NEW SENSIBILITY.
The smart marketers at Hellmann's saw an opportunity to build the brand with its "real" heritage.

Simple, but resonant.

YOUR STRATEGY MAY ALSO HAVE a third part – a Tone or Brand Character Statement.

Over the years, there has been a movement away from "Tone" or "Tone and Manner" Statements, which describe the character of the advertising, toward statements which describe the character of the brand – *"long-term brand values."*

This is particularly true with clients such as P&G, who view Advertising Strategies as long-term documents which, ideally, should last a number of years.

Over that period of time, P&G believes that while the *tone* of the advertising may vary, the *values* represented by the brand should remain constant.

WHEN TO USE A TONE STATEMENT. There are many cases where a Tone Statement can be a very helpful addition to the Strategy.

Many clients are not P&G, and if the advertising isn't "working," your Advertising Strategy may be in a more or less constant state of revision.

In these cases, Tone Statements can be very helpful as you work to get the strategy right.

Tone Statements can be a place for additional insights into the Target or as a description of the best advertising style for the product category.

In situations where you are trying to reposition a brand, reach consumers in a new way, go after a new target, or deal with a "rejector base" (former customers who no longer purchase your brand), "long-term brand values" may actually be a hindrance and a Tone Statement more helpful.

WHEN TO USE A BRAND CHARACTER STATEMENT.

Currently, Brand Character Statements are preferred by major marketers and agencies.

As virtually every company has placed increased emphasis on the long-term value of their brands, a statement which addresses the issue of "what is our brand's equity?" is increasingly important.

For flanker brands, there may be a Brand Character Statement based on some variation of values of the "mother" brand. Or, more likely, a single Brand Character Statement will be the standard for all.

When your brand advertises to diverse groups, a Brand Character Statement can help focus on values that endure across groups.

By the way, when writing a Brand Character Statement, be patient – developing one that everyone can agree on may take a little time.

Even though a number of people may *feel* the same way about a brand, they may express it differently.

Brand Character Statements can be tough to write, and Tone Statements are relatively easy.

In summary…

Tone Statements are short-term and about the Advertising.

Brand Character Statements are long-term and about the Brand.

You should learn to write both.
We'll start with the Tone Statement.

MORE ON TONE VS. BRAND CHARACTER…

I like Tone Statements for the same reason P&G *does not* like them – they are "about the advertising."

After all, this is an Advertising Strategy we're writing.

Tone Statements can offer an important opportunity for people to talk about how they think the advertising should "feel" just as you're getting ready to create it.

This can be important input during creative development and a helpful reference frame when the advertising is presented.

That's why, as a practical matter, Tone Statements can be very helpful.

MASTER OF ALL THINGS HARDWARIAN

BRAND CHARACTER PERSONIFIED.
This ad for TrueValue Hardware gives a slightly heroic dimension to the True Value employee.

Not only does this make their employees feel appreciated, it's an important way to communicate. It adds Brand Character to nuts, bolts, garden supplies, and duct tape.

When dealing with brand values, try to translate those adjectives into something – or someone – tangible.

This also has applications in other areas, such as public relations.

We don't want stories about coffee beans, we want stories about Howard Schultz, the founder, or about a Starbuck's barista.

We're people.

People connect with people.

253

> *"Finding out what to say is the beginning of the advertising process. How you say it makes people look and listen. And, if you're not successful at that, you've wasted all the work, intelligence, and skill that went into discovering what you should say."*
>
> **Bill Bernbach**

DEVELOPING THE ARCHWAY TONE STATEMENT.

The Tone Statement was used to define the way Archway Cookies should be advertised. They were not vitamins or a nutritional supplement – they were cookies, a dessert and snack item eaten for enjoyment.

Within that context, Archway wanted to identify with good nutritional habits.

Here's how it worked out…

ARCHWAY COOKIES TONE STATEMENT.

Tone will combine the importance of good nutrition with the fun of cookies.

A major internal concern was that we didn't forget that cookies taste good and are fun – that's why people buy them.

In this regard, the Archway Tone Statement related to their Objective Statement.

It also clearly signalled that commercials should have entertainment value – not just nutritional value.

The Tone Statement.

The Tone Statement can begin simply,

"Tone will be…"

Tone is the *how* of the Strategy. It is the key to the type of advertising you will create. A key strategic question in developing the Tone Statement…

"How will you relate to your target?"

The Tone of your Strategy will be the first step in determining the style of your advertising.

More from Bernbach:

"Great execution becomes content.

It brings what you have to say to the eyes and ears of your audience believably and persuasively."

For a period of time, DDB strategies contained what they termed a "Tone and Manner" Statement.

The right Tone will help put you on the right track to great execution.

Stating the desired Tone will be based on your knowledge of your product, how to talk to your target, and the competitive environment.

Sound familiar? It's the Strategic Triad – only this time it's about feeling and attitude.

The Tone Statement functions as a right-brain/emotional description of your Strategy.

Here are two examples:

Tone will convey the spicy fun of Popeyes' New Orleans heritage.
(Popeyes Famous Fried Chicken, '81-83)

Tone will be compatible with today's competitive fast-food environment.
(Popeyes Famous Fried Chicken, '85-'87)

The change in the tone statement was a result of a change in the competitive environment (other spicy chicken products).

In retrospect, Popeyes may have overreacted – but it's hard to know that when it's happening and your biggest competitor is coming at you.

A good Tone Statement is a guide for how to talk to your target.

The words in your Tone Statement should be *meaningful* to your target and helpful to the people creating and judging the advertising.

In addition, it's not uncommon to revise that Tone section as you find out more about how to talk to your target. Often, the facts of an Advertising Strategy are right before the feelings are.

And sometimes the "feel" of the marketplace can change, while everything else – like your product, your benefits, and your support – remain the same. (That's what happened to Popeyes.)

While not executional, the Tone Statement helps guide the execution in the proper direction, and it indicates the type of communication which, on judgment, the target will respond to.

Once you've completed your Tone Statement, your Strategy is written.

It reads…

"Advertising will [convince] [Target Customer] that [Product] is/will [Objective].

Support will be [Support].

Tone will be ["Selling Attitude" Adjectives]."

And that's how a complete Advertising Strategy looks when you use a Tone Statement.

Now let's talk about the alternative…

A SPICY TONE.
Funky rock and roll, hot colors, and upbeat testimonials from people you'd like to party with – they all add up to a tone that reinforced Popeyes spicy taste and position.

SOME EXAMPLES OF TONE STATEMENTS:

Tone will reflect the fun of the pizza-eating experience.

Tone will be fashion-conscious and "state of the art."

Tone will be intrusive and bring excitement to a major improvement in a low-interest category.

This Brand Is a Character. *What do you think the Tone Statement might have been for Slim Jim? Here, where the brand has been personified, Brand Character Statements become even more important.*

A statement of the character we strive to build for the product.

The Brand Character Statement

Clients such as P&G and agencies like Y&R do not believe in Tone Statements.

Y&R says, *"As usually written they are meaningless. If the rest of the Strategy is clear, they are unnecessary."*

At Y&R, they address this issue with something they call the Prospect Definition, which treats the target in depth. (We'll cover the Y&R Creative Work Plan in an Addendum which follows.)

At P&G, they've evolved to what they call Brand Character Statements, which describe the enduring values of their brands – these values are viewed as an important part of a brand's equity in the marketplace.

Here are some Brand Character Statements for a few familiar brands:

Crest is the dedicated leader in improving dental health for the family.

Coast is a product that is exhilarating to use.

Pampers – pre-eminent reputation as the leader in baby care… a warm and affectionate attitude toward babies.

Camay – the soap of beautiful women.

These statements describe the "enduring values," "long-term values," or "core values" of the brands.

Little Characters for Some Brand Character. *Kids eat a lot of Oscar Mayer products, and little kids are a big part of the Oscar Mayer brand character.*

ARCHWAY COOKIES BRAND CHARACTER.

"The Good Food Cookie."
This positioning line was also their Brand Character Statement.

In developing a Brand Character Statement, review all the relevant aspects of the brand history: packaging, graphics, target customer values – everything you can think of.

Then, distill it to its essence.

Try to describe the brand as you would a person – look for the adjectives and phrases that best personify the brand. What does your brand stand for?

Within all this information you should find the elements you need.

Brand Character Statements can begin, *"The Character of the Brand will be seen to be"* or in whatever way seems appropriate.

As you can see by the previous statements, they may simply start, **[Product] is…**

Remember, this is a long-term document.

Don't worry if it takes a while.

And don't worry if you have to revise it a few times till you finally get it right.

And (instead of a Tone Statement), this is the third element of your Advertising Strategy.

Now your strategy reads...

**"Advertising will [convince]
[Target Customer] that [Product]
is/will [Objective].**

Support will be [Support].

**[Product] is
["Brand Character" Statement]."**

And that's an Advertising Strategy with a Brand Character Statement.

Now let's try writing a few.

STRATEGY READING LIST:
Some of the better books in this field.

The Marketing Imagination
Theodore Levitt/MacMillan

**Positioning &
Marketing Warfare**
Trout & Reis/McGraw Hill

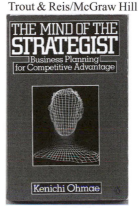

**The Mind of The Strategist:
Business Planning for
Competitive Advantage**
Kenichi Ohmae
Penguin Business Library
(My personal favorite)

**The Y&R
Traveling Creative Workshop**
Hanley Norins/Prentice-Hall
(now out-of-print)

**The Making of
Effective Advertising**
Patti & Moriarty
Prentice Hall

**Planning for R.O.I.:
Effective Advertising Strategy**
Wells, William D/DDB Needham
Prentice-Hall

Planning for R.O.I. Workbook
Prentice-Hall

Also recommended:

Passion for Excellence
Peters & Austin/Harper & Row

Small Is Beautiful
E.F. Schumacher/Harper & Row

Further Up the Organization
Robert Townsend/Alfred A. Knopf

NEW PRODUCTS.
"A new product is a strategy brought to life."

This is good exercise for thinking up new strategies.

New products are usually developed with a specific Target Customer in mind offering a unique benefit – usually with a product-based reason why.

Its reason for being is usually a need in the marketplace. Let's try a few.

Here are some helpful hints:

• Find a problem that needs solving. Invent a product that solves it.
• Think of current trends and growing needs.
• Your best ideas may come from a familiar area.
• Your new "product" could also be a new service. Or a combination of product and service – like lawn care.
• A **good name** is most often one that *communicates the benefit.*

For the moment, you can ignore:

• Technology limitations
• Price considerations
• Size of the market (many new product ideas are developed for small and/or emerging markets)

By the way, in the real world, *80% of new products fail!*

So good luck.

#17: New Product

1. INVENT A NEW PRODUCT.
• What is it?
• Who is your Target Customer?
• What is The Benefit?
• Is it a Product Benefit or a Consumer Benefit?
• What is Support for your Benefit?
• What problem does your product solve?
• What should the Tone be?
• What about Brand Character?
• What is the *name?* (It should describe your product in an appealing way.)
• Does this suggest any advertising themes?

2. WRITE YOUR STRATEGY.

Product Description: _____

_____

Brand Name: _____

Advertising will _____

_____ **that**

_____ **is/will/provides**

_____.

Support will be _____

_____.

Tone will be _____

_____.

Brand Character is _____

_____.

For fun, write an "on-strategy" advertising theme

_____.

Here's a New Product Based on an Old Product! Tom Brancky at Starkist realized that tuna could be convenience food. The result – a Tuna Salad Lunch Kit. Instant understanding by consumers and instant sales accelerated by engaging coupon ads like this, which combined established brand heritage with a brand new idea – that was already familiar!

Strategy Worksheet:

PRODUCT: _____

PRODUCT DESCRIPTION: _____
_____
_____

TARGET CUSTOMER: _____
_____
_____

PRODUCT BENEFIT(S): _____
_____
_____

CONSUMER BENEFIT(S): _____
_____
_____

SUPPORT: _____
_____
_____

TONE OF ADVERTISING: _____
_____

BRAND CHARACTER: _____
_____

ADVERTISING THEME IDEAS:
_____
_____
_____

MISC: _____
_____

ALTERNATE STRATEGIES.

As the Strategy Selection Grid (p. 215) indicates, there are three major determinants for alternate Strategies:

- **Competition (Source of Business)**
- **Target Customer**
- **Message Selection (Benefit)**

Here are some examples:

Competition.

Stove Top Stuffing could have competed with all side dishes, but Stove Top decided to focus on the most popular side dish, which was the major "source of business," potatoes.

"Instead of potatoes" clearly defined the competition as it communicated the change-of-pace benefit.

Instead of Potatoes

Target Customer.

Many years ago, P&G advertised their Jif Peanut Butter to kids.

After all, most peanut butter was consumed by kids, and they influenced similar purchases – like cereal.

However, P&G found this purchase was made by *mothers.* The result?

"Choosy Mothers Choose Jif."

Message Selection.

Attributes, Features, Product Benefits, Consumer Benefits, Values – a single product offers many choices.

In most cases, this will be the major area of focus for alternate strategies.

#18: Best Bets

PICK AN EXISTING PRODUCT.

1. MAKE A LIST.
- Target options
- Benefit options
- Support options
- Tone options
- Brand Character options

2. WRITE YOUR "BEST BET" STRATEGY.

Advertising will _____
_____ **that**
_____ **is/will/provides**
_____.

Support will be _____
_____.

Tone will be _____.

Brand Character is _____.

Advertising Theme:
_____
_____

3. WRITE A "NEXT BEST BET" STRATEGY.

Advertising will _____
_____ **that**
_____ **is/will/provides**
_____.

Support will be _____
_____.

Tone will be _____.

Brand Character is _____.

Advertising Theme: _____.

#19: Business Building Ideas

GOOD IDEAS BUILD BUSINESS. Whether it's putting a box of Arm & Hammer Baking Soda in your refrigerator or making some Rice Krispies Treats.

YOUR ASSIGNMENT:

Have an idea that builds a company's business. Then, write an ad about it. It might be:

- A new use for the product
- A new target for the product
- Something else

There are two requirements:

- Your idea should be for an existing product or service.
- Your idea should be one that generates "plus" business.

It's a simple assignment, but it's one that will help teach you to think about advertising problems in an important way – because everyone is looking for ideas that build business.

Having trouble picking a product?

Grab something close at hand.

Or have someone pick it for you.

Remember, in the real world, you have little control over assignments.

But here's a hint.

Products with the strongest benefit and the greatest competitive advantage usually generate the strongest strategies.

To sell more jeans this year, push the right buttons.

DUAL TARGETS AND SECONDARY BENEFITS.

Programs can often have more than one target. For example, many products have to communicate to the trade as well as the consumer.

After all, if it's not in the store, it doesn't matter how good the ad is.

And, a single product may have different customers who buy it for dramatically different reasons – an example, Apple Computers.

If you have dramatically different target groups, you may have to integrate more than one Strategy into the advertising process.

Remember, secondary targets can be of primary importance.

Here, Lee Jeans talks to the trade.

And it's a good fit.

NEW...THE TASTE OF RICE KRISPIES TREATS IN A CEREAL.

FROM SECONDARY USAGE TO NEW PRODUCT.

Kellogg's discovered consumer familiarity with the Rice Krispies Treats recipe created a ready market for both a ready-to-eat cereal and a popular snack.

Notice how the ad also addresses a potential problem – people might think of it as dessert, not breakfast.

That's why secondary copy works to reassure mothers with a chart indicating "Less sugar than most kids' cereals."

CONVENIENCE STRATEGIES.

Convenience has become more important for "time-poor" consumers.

Convenience strategies generally focus on some factor of product usage or performance and the related benefit.

Faster, easier, less mess, etc.

Support may be simple and single-minded (new formula), or more complex (new package with competitive performance results).

Pick a convenient product and write a strategy for it. You may also need a bit of "quality reassurance." But the communication should be simple.

After all, it's all about being easy.

SUPERIORITY STRATEGIES.

These focus on a dimension in which your product is better than something else.

It may be a competitor, your own previous product, or no product at all!

Support is often a reason why.

Take a product that you think is better (it might be more expensive) and write a strategy that proves it.

IMAGE STRATEGIES.

They're tough to write because the focus and benefit are less tangible.

The focus may be *attributes* (independent magazine for independent women), or *associative* (like a pop star and soda pop).

Try to be *assumptive,* or *preemptive.* (Be of a brand that acts like a leader without having to prove it.)

Sometimes, as in the case of much fashion advertising, it's pure *attitude.*

#20: Multiple Strategies

1. CONVENIENCE STRATEGY.

Product: _____

Advertising will _____
_____ that
_____ is/will/provides_____
_____.

Support will be _____
_____.

Tone will be _____.

2. SUPERIORITY STRATEGY.

Product: _____

Advertising will _____
_____ that
_____ is/will/provides
_____.

Support will be _____
_____.

Tone will be _____.

3. IMAGE STRATEGY.

Product: _____

Advertising will _____
_____ that
_____ is/will/provides
_____.

Support will be _____
_____.

Tone will be _____.

4. SERVICE STRATEGY.

(Bank, law firm, babysitter, shop by phone, etc.)

Service: _____

Advertising will _____.

_____ **that**

_____ **is/will/provides** _____

_____•

Support will be _____

_____•

Tone will be _____•

5. THEME LINE: based on your strategy, write at least one theme line for each of your products.

Convenience Product:_____

_____

_____

_____

Superiority Product:_____

_____

_____

_____

Image Product:_____

_____

_____

_____

Service/Name:_____

_____

_____

_____

Service "Products:"_____

_____

_____

_____

SERVICE STRATEGIES.

Services are a combination of *tangibles* and *intangibles*.

For example, a restaurant has both the tangibles of food and price and the intangibles of service and ambiance.

An airline sells you a seat. But the intangibles of efficiency, comfort, and feelings of safety are more important.

The ticket price is a tangible, but what about the convenience of the schedule?

Financial services offer a difficult combination. Most benefits (like "make you rich") cannot be claimed with certainty.

Financial services are both high-interest (it's your money, so you're interested) and dull (numbers that are hard to understand, plus legal restrictions). Simple communication can be difficult.

Features like "friendly service" are hard to guarantee. Service, as Theodore Levitt points out in *The Marketing Imagination,* is *"generally only recognized in its absence."* People notice bad service. They take good service for granted.

Your service may emphasize tangibles or intangibles. Or both.

Making Services Tangible. *Here, a bank offers a specific product with a specific benefit.*

In this short section, we'll briefly cover other strategy documents.

Blueprints & Work Plans

THERE'S NO SINGLE "RIGHT" WAY to write an Advertising Strategy – though you will find most Strategy systems have a lot in common.

Let's look at a number of popular formats:

Y&R Creative Work Plan

This classic system begins with four elements:

1. **A Statement of the Key Fact...**
   based on an analysis of all pertinent facts.

2. **A Definition of the Problem...**
   which the advertising must solve in light of this Key Fact. This is *"The Problem the Advertising Must Solve."* This should be a *consumer* problem and stated from the consumer point of view.

3. **The Advertising Objective.**
   This stems from the Problem.
   All of this information helps you develop...

4. **The Creative Strategy.**
   In the Y&R system, the Strategy is
   "designed to achieve the objective, which will solve the problem that the key fact has defined."
   The Key Fact and the Problem are related.
   For example, research might show that people think your product has an inferior taste, even if they haven't tried it. *The Problem the Advertising Must Solve* then becomes...
   "Our brand has a poor taste reputation."
   This would then relate to the Objective –
   "To overcome our poor taste reputation with consumers."

WRITING THE WORK PLAN.

At Y&R, writing the Work Plan is the job of the Creative Director.

This may be one of the reasons for their exceptional record of unique, on-target work.

The Work Plan must be written before creative work begins. Its prime purpose is *"to set creative people free... in the right direction."*

THE YOUNG&RUBICAM
TRAVELING CREATIVE WORKSHOP

For the first time–in one place–the creative strategies and practices that have made Young & Rubicam the most consistently creative and successful large ad agency in the world!

HANLEY NORINS

The Young & Rubicam Traveling Creative Workshop
by Hanley Norins (Prentice-Hall)
A comprehensive presentation of the first great agency strategy system.
Find a copy if you can.

264

Y&R Creative Strategy

The Strategy must include:

A. Prospect Definition.

This defines prospects in terms of:
- Product usage
- Demographics
- Psychographics

Sometimes, facts are not available. If that is the case, use an "educated guess."

B. Principal Competition.

The Principal Competition Statement gives *"a clear idea of the arena in which your product will do battle."*

In the case of a new or unique product, use a "reason for being."

C. Promise/Consumer Benefit.*

The best argument your brand can offer.
The Promise Statement has four guidelines:

1. The Promise should be phrased in terms of *"what the product will do for the consumer."*

2. The Promise should be as *competitive* as possible.

3. The Promise should *motivate* prospects in the direction that will accomplish your Objective.

4. The Promise should *not* be written in actual advertising terms.

D. Reason Why.

A statement that *supports* the Promise. Each statement must be "sharp, clear, and specific."

* In some versions of the Work Plan, this is known as the "Promise," in others, it is termed the "Consumer Benefit."

WORK PLAN AT WORK.

Here's an example – a Creative Work Plan for Sanka.

1. KEY FACT.

29% of coffee-drinking households say they are concerned about caffeine, but resist trying Sanka Brand.

2. CONSUMER PROBLEM THE ADVERTISING MUST SOLVE.

Prospects don't think Sanka Brand would taste as good as caffeinated coffee, and they also resist its somewhat medicinal image.

3. ADVERTISING OBJECTIVE.

Convince prospects that *Sanka does indeed taste as good as caffeinated coffee* and has the added benefit of being caffeine free.

4. CREATIVE STRATEGY.

A. Prospect Definition:

Our prime prospects are mildly concerned about caffeine but haven't switched to decaffeinated coffee. They are probably somewhat more hyper than the average coffee drinker, more health aware, and perhaps even self-conscious about giving in to a decaffeinated coffee.

B. Principal Competition:

The regular coffee prospects are currently drinking. Secondarily, any other decaffeinated coffee they may consider switching to.

C. Promise/Consumer Benefit:

You will be surprised how good Sanka tastes, and it has the advantage of being caffeine free.

D. Reason Why:

In blind taste tests, Sanka brand decaffeinated coffee is at parity and sometimes superior to competitive caffeinated coffees.

GE Focus System

GENERAL ELECTRIC is a client that produces numerous communications in-house.

Their Advertising and Sales Promotion Operations (once a 400-person, full-service, in-house agency) developed a simple three-step process that helped them do effective work consistently across their 15 offices in the US, Europe, and Asia.

One big advantage of this system is that it can be implemented quickly. At GE, you could be writing consumer information on light bulbs one day and technical ads for atomic power plants the next.

Here's how the system works.

1. ANALYZE THE RECEIVER.

First, you must know the receiver.

Singular, not plural.

You must know this audience as a person, with needs and wants beyond your product.

2. STRATEGIZE THE PROPOSITION.

"The Proposition relates what we know about the product to what we've learned about the receiver."

The Proposition is a strategic statement, not a headline. But, if you just set the proposition in type and ran it with a picture of the product, *"you'd have something useful."*

GE believes the Unique Buying Proposition (*not* the old Rosser Reeves Unique Selling Position) relates to a Key Fact (Y&R) and a position (Trout & Ries) in the way they are perceived by the receiver.

3. DRAMATIZE THE PROPOSITION.

With the proposition as the basis, the challenge becomes *"break the boredom barrier."*

Find a way to communicate the Proposition in a dramatic way.   ©1976 General Electric Company

---

GE FOCUS SYSTEM.

1. Analyze the Receiver.
2. Strategize the Proposition.
3. Dramatize the Proposition.

GE used the word "Receiver" in the FOCUS Creative Approach because we wanted writers and art directors to think of the advertising they were creating as a gift to the reader or viewer.

When it's someone's birthday who's close to you, you search for days or weeks for the perfect gift. How do you know when you've found that perfect gift? Because you know that person so intimately that you can see him or her opening the box and going, "Wow!"

FOCUS teaches that you should know the Receiver – the person whose behavior you're trying to affect – so well that you could buy a gift for him or her. In your mind's eye as you're creating an ad you should be able to envision the Receiver turning the page or opening the envelope or sitting back down in the chair in front of the TV and saying, "Wow!"

Someone once said that all advertising is response advertising. That's the response FOCUS helped us to strive for every single time we created an ad: "Wow!"

The person should then tear out the page or grab a piece of paper and write a note to him- or herself to do something, whatever the behavioral objective of the ad was – and all good FOCUS ads had a behavioral objective.

As David Ogilvy said, *"We sell... or else."* FOCUS helped us sell a lot more GE products and services.

— Robert Lauterborn

THREE KINDS OF THINKING.

This classic system calls for three different kinds of thinking:

Thinking about the receiver involves *analytic* thinking (and empathy).

Thinking about the Proposition requires *strategic* thinking.

Finally, dramatization demands *creative* thinking.

Leo Burnett Strategy Worksheet

**THIS FORMAT
BREAKS THE MOLD.**

Many successful Burnett campaigns do not fit traditional strategy formats.

This format was developed to accommodate unique components in their campaigns based on Leo's concept of inherent drama, which is stated here as "key drama."

This unique visual property allows Burnett's campaigns to capture generic benefits with unique executions.

This worksheet allows you to include these unique properties as well as more traditional approaches.

CONVINCE	THAT	BECAUSE
Target Audience – Current Belief re: Brand/Category	Desired Belief (Benefit)	Focus of Sale or Proposition (Key Drama)
	SUPPORT	
	Reasons Why	

Key Drama can be deceptively simple. For example, Tony the Tiger for Kellogg's is basic in its core concept. Originally, a range of characters, usually animals, was developed for the various cereal brands. Why a tiger? Well, they figured the sugar in Sugar Frosted Flakes gave you energy and a tiger was energetic, so…

Then they added the simple but memorable selling line, "They're G-r-r-r-r-eat!"

267

A matrix is provided for examining alternative promises.

There is a heavy focus on demonstrations – both *literal* and *dramatic* (an example of a dramatic demonstration is the Bud Light "Bar Call").

When demonstrations are found or developed, they are added to the strategy document.

In addition to product facts and demonstrations, this section allows for what DDB/Needham terms *"external support."*

This includes sales promotion, PR, and direct response.

An example of external support would be pictures of well-known sports figures on the Wheaties package.

THE ROI PROCESS.

DDB/Needham believes that the process is most productive when agency and client work through it together.

For this purpose, a workbook is also provided.

Planning for R.O.I. and *Planning for ROI Workbook* are published by Prentice Hall (ISBN 0-13-679466-1 and ISBN 0-13-679473-4), though not generally available.

The "R.O.I." System

ROI stands for "Return on Investment."

At DDB/Needham, it also means that *"great advertising is distinguished by three fundamental qualities: Relevance, Originality, and Impact."*

Their ROI Strategy System is similar to the Y&R Work Plan, but there are important exceptions – particularly in the inclusion of certain tactical elements (demonstrations) and a media section.

The system is built on five questions:

1. What is the purpose of the advertising?

The ROI process focuses on the specific desired behavior and source of business.

2. To whom will the advertising be addressed?

The target section should have both demographic and psychographic information.
DDB/Needham looks for "aiming points," which allow you to think specifically and personally about your target. An example would be "Cereal eaters who are interested in sports" for Wheaties.

3. What competitive benefit will be promised, and how will that promise be supported?

This is a traditional benefit/reason why section.

4. What personality will distinguish the brand?

This may be treated simply or in great detail.

5. When, where, and under what circumstances will the target be most receptive to the message? What media will deliver that message to the target at the lowest possible cost?

ROI integrates media planning into the process. A key part of this is the concept of "aperture," the time that *"a customer is most likely to notice, be receptive to, and react favorably to, an advertising message..."*

Communication Work Plan

Client/Project _____

SUMMARY: *Briefly summarize your definition of the problem and the solution.*

Problem the Communication Must Solve

Primary Audience

Desired Behavior of Primary Audience

Main Message

    Support/Reason Why (if any)

    Secondary Benefits/Support (if any)

Secondary Audience (if any)

Message for Secondary Audience

Recommended Tactics

Mandatories

Agreements/Approvals:

_____

_____

SOME BACKGROUND ON THE WORK PLAN.

This is the Communication Work Plan developed for Apple.

It was a two-part system – A Backgrounder and a Work Plan.

The Backgrounder helped collect the necessary information and put it into a manageable form.

The Backgrounder is on pages 230–31.

Then, that information was distilled into this Communication Work Plan.

Hopefully, there was a bit of insight. (The people at Apple were pretty bright, and usually brought plenty of insight with them.)

You will note that this Plan also has Secondary Support, Secondary Audiences, and Secondary Messages.

Often, the product offerings had some fairly dense technical features – this helped organize and prioritize.

The technical stuff, which was necessary, was usually assigned to the Secondary Support section and the key Feature/Benefit was the Main Message.

In addition, Apple had a number of secondary audiences: media, particularly high-tech media people, such as product reviewers, purchasing agents in both business and education, retail operators, and User Groups. Their integrated programs often featured tactics aimed at these secondary audiences. Sometimes the message was a bit different.

Most of the work done at Apple was for the retail channel and for introductory events, such as MacExpo and other computer shows – so Tactics might include T-shirts, mouse pads, and other materials.

The advertising was handled by the agency – usually Chiat/Day, but, for a while, BBDO.

As part of the overall coordination, Chris Wall, then at BBDO (now at Ogilvy on IBM) wrote a wonderful piece on the Apple Tone of Voice.

We've featured that as a Bonus Section at the end of this book. Used with the author's permission. Thanks, Chris.

WHY "PRODUCT" AND "YOU."

Here are some good reasons supporting the BBDO point of view:

"Product" image alone is limited because:

• Many product edges (advantages) are short lived, and quickly met by competition;

• Many product edges, as perceived by advertisers, are not important to consumers;

• Many product claims address category issues, but not underlying consumer problems;

• Performance claims often provide little added value;

• Finally, differentiating claims can sometimes have the opposite effect – and lead to perceived parity. This is particularly true when imagery and experience do not match.

The "You" image is critical, because:

• It takes positioning beyond logic into the realm of emotion;

• It adds value to performance claims;

• It can build product relevance and personality;

• It puts product truths and benefits into a meaningful framework for the consumer.

The "You" image takes the consumer beyond fact, and into feeling.

It can build brand loyalty and help provide competitive insulation.

BBDO

THE BBDO SYSTEM is, in many ways, a more complex and complete version of GE's Focus System (GE is a BBDO client). It goes like this:

1. Know Your Prime Prospect

2. Know Your Prime Prospect's Problem

3. Know Your Product

4. Break the Boredom Barrier

See how the sequence works when a variety of research techniques are applied.

Note how BBDO uses the word "image." By this they mean images in the advertising. As the quote on the left indicates, they believe "*it's all images.*"

1. KNOW YOUR PRIME PROSPECT. BBDO research works to understand the market *from the consumer's point of view,* using a tool they call a "Market Structure Audit."

For example, in the gum market, they discovered that gums compete on flavor (i.e., cinnamon vs. cinnamon). So Big Red competes with Dentyne. Period.

Once the competition is defined, BBDO focuses on what they call *the prime prospect: Who* currently consumes competing products?

It's important to view prime prospects not just as demographic statistics, but as human beings – consider how they live and what they do with their time.

BBDO uses research tools such as Lifestyle Indicators and Photo Sort for insight into user dynamics and imagery.

They believe understanding "You" in terms of *attitudes* versus *lifestyles* is key to the differentiation of selling messages. Understanding attitudes can provide deeper insights into the consumer and lead to true differentiation.

2. KNOW YOUR PRIME PROSPECT'S PROBLEM.

BBDO believes the best way to get a purchase decision in your favor is to solve a problem for the prospect. They use a "Problem Detection System" to develop insight into these problems.

For example, when asked what they want in dog food, consumers most often responded with "nutrition" or "good taste." No surprise there.

But when asked what problems they have had with dog foods, consumers complained about their dog's bad breath and the food's odor or mess.

You can see from this example that this could lead strategically to some radically different approaches.

3. KNOW YOUR PRODUCT.

The "Product" position is developed by the client and agency with research input, such as the Market Structure Audit and Problem Detection Study.

Like all marketers, they isolate key performance characteristics, but rather than offering category benefits, they focus on solving consumer problems – approaching the product from a "Problem" standpoint, as opposed to a "benefit-attribute" standpoint.

It's not problem/solution. For example, Dodge's "product problem" for their prime prospects is "too many cars look alike and are boring."

4. BREAK THE BOREDOM BARRIER.

See how the Dodge campaigns of "Different" and "Grab Life By the Horns" combine a "Product" (Performance) image with a "You" (User) image while solving the "boring cars" problem.

If you can pinpoint a problem that is frequent and preemptable, you have some grist for the development of a not-so-obvious strategy.

For BBDO all execution is strategic. The result of their approach is "Imagery That Works."

BBDO POSITIONING.

BBDO combines these elements:

Brand Equity.

Brand Equity trade-off analysis helps determine which are the most important "Product" imagery problems vs. the competition and which are the most important "You" imagery problems.

"Product" + "You" Positioning.

With this information, they develop the "Product" image and the "You" image that will position the product.

SOME EXAMPLES:

Pepsi Cola. The "Product" stance is Leadership. The "You" attitude is Contemporary ("Hot," "In").

The resultant combination has been an evolving campaign, beginning with "The Pepsi Generation," continuing through "Pepsi. The Choice of a New Generation," "Generation Next," and, most recently "Joy of Cola."

Though they have evolved through variations on this basic product stance, the core position has stayed the same.

Gillette Dry Idea Antiperspirant. The "Product" stance is that it "goes on dry, stays dry." But this did not differentiate this superior performing product until the "You" attitude was added: Control, Aspiration.

The resulting theme was, "Never Let Them See You Sweat," with a campaign featuring young entertainers.

General Electric. The "Product" stance is "contemporary products of good quality.

The "You" attitude is Contemporary ("Hot," "In") and Quality ("The best I can afford").

The campaign uniting these elements is "We Bring Good Things to Life."

Information for this section was excerpted from *The Making of Effective Advertising* by Charles Patti & Sandra E. Moriarty ©1990 Prentice-Hall.

THE GAME BEHIND THE GAME.
You need to develop a new habit.

From now on, when you look at ads in a magazine, or watch ads on TV, try to figure out what the underlying strategy was.

What was the objective? Who was the target?

What were they trying to do with the communication?

Too often, media is like a ventriloquist act – we pay attention to the dummy, instead of the one that's pulling the strings.

X-Ray Glasses.
You need to put on some X-Ray glasses and learn to look past the dazzle and see what's going on behind the ad. What's making it work?

Those are some of the lessons you need to start learning.

A Few New Habits.
These will benefit your career.

Give them a try.

#1. Ask about the business. Think I mentioned this earlier. Worth repeating.

Show the client you care about their business – not your advertising.

#2. Work on businesses that work – even if some of them ain't all that glamorous.

Learn what makes companies successful in a complicated world. That's part of learning to be part of that success.

#3. Make at least one business magazine part of your reading list. *Wired*, for a start, then see how you can handle *Business Week*, *Fortune*, and the Marketplace section of the *Wall Street Journal*.

See how the world looks when you get the story behind the story.

You may thank me.

Ready? Fire! Aim…

Your strategy is an hypothesis.

Getting it right is a process.

Sure, sometimes we get it right the first time.

But sometimes the answer isn't obvious.

For example, taking away milk to sell milk is not linear logic – but the result was much more powerful than "milk is good for you."

BREAKING THROUGH.
An underlying objective for every strategy is to somehow make your message break through a blizzard of messages.

How do we have a snowflake's chance?

The key is to get on the receiver's side of the message. Real "breakthrough" is when people "break in" to our messages.

The same people can be very different depending on whether they're buying toilet paper, chewing gum, a digital camera, or a gift for a grandchild.

People aren't all that simple. So, it's easy to see why we don't always get it right the first time.

GETTING SMARTER.
As our campaigns build, and people react, they offer us an opportunity to get smarter.

If GEICO had started with the Gecko, it would have seemed stupid – and "off-strategy."

But, as the strategy dug in, and consumers became used to a wide variety of executions wrapped around the same message – well, why not?

Strategy needs to be a living document that responds to the world around us.

Strategies get better as we get smarter.

The MarCom Matrix...

HERE'S HOW TO ADJUST your strategy statement.

Go from this...   ...to this.

**Advertising will [convince]
[Target Customer] that
[Product]
is/will [Objective/Benefit].
Support will be [Support].
[Product] is
[Brand Character Statement].**

**[Target Customer] –
[Product]
[Benefit].
[Support].**

[Brand Character Statement].

TARGET CUSTOMER, PRODUCT, BENEFIT, SUPPORT, & BRAND CHARACTER.

These are still the building blocks for all of your MarCom strategies, though the emphasis may vary.

Once you've determined these core strategic elements, developing the individual substrategies can be relatively straightforward.

Then, you can move to the real challenge – determining the best tactics.

MARCOM MATRIX: STRATEGIC CONCERNS.

Marketing Public Relations.

Publics. (PR word for target)

Channels. Best media opportunities for the brand? Strategic message?

Creating Media Interest. Remember, when you're not paying for the media space, you really have to be interesting.

Sales Promotion.

Incentive (Appeal, Cost, Payout). It's easy to "give it away," you need to offer an incentive that will pay out.

Secondary Targets (Trade, etc.). Your objective may be to get retail display, so that consumers will be exposed to the brand at the point of sale.

Direct Marketing.

Target Database. You're "as good as your list." The better you know your target, the better you can direct your program.

Offer/Incentive. What's the deal?

The right offer can increase responses dramatically.

Message Emphasis. Saying the right thing also has an impact, though the list and the offer are more important.

Testing & Results Measurement.

This is key. Smart direct marketers keep testing to make sure they are using the optimum combinations of target, offer, and message emphasis.

Event Marketing.

Brand Character. Is it appropriate for the brand?

Target Involvement. Will it connect the brand with the right people?

Coordination with other activities. The event may feature additional PR, advertising, promotional, or even database capture activities.

New Media (Internet).

Business Objective. Is it a site for sales and transactions, consumer involvement, PR "buzz," investor information, or...

This is the *critical* initial decision.

Once that has been determined, an effective program can be developed.

Selling Ideas

FIRST A STRATEGY.

Next, a "Selling Idea" that's based on that strategy.

We discussed "How to Have an Idea." Now let's have an idea that emerges from our strategy.

WORDS TO THE WISE.

As we noted in the strategy section, sometimes it's necessary to get our vocabulary in order.

We're about to enter the next stage. After the strategy is established, our next job is to figure out how to make that strategy work effectively.

If that weren't difficult enough, a blizzard of words often accompanies the task. They all mean somewhat similar or related things. In the name of better mental hygiene, let's clarify.

UNDERSTANDING THE BRAND.

Brand. Basically, it's the result of your product and the brand name of your product in the mind of the consumer.

If you have a brand new brand, you may have a somewhat blank slate – though even words and colors bring a bit of connotation.

If it's a brand name with multiple products, like McDonald's, well, it can be complex.

My advice: "*Think like a designer.*"

Consider all the ways the brand exists in both physical and mental environments.

Remember, it's about what's in the minds of the people you want to connect with.

Brand Character. Usually a statement – often backed by a bit of research or at least strong opinion – that articulates the core values of the brand.

It's a kind of measuring stick you can use as you develop the communications.

IS A TIGER A "BIG IDEA?"
It was for a cereal and a gasoline.
How about a lion or a panther?
Who knows? Nobody.
Hey, "Nobody" may be a Big Idea, too.

FROM "GRRRR!" TO "R-R-R-R!"
"R-R-R-Ruffles have R-R-R-Ridges" is still a memorable Selling Idea.

CONCEPT/IDEA/SELLING IDEA.

Concept. Some people like this word "concept." Our friend Deborah Morrison defines it as, *"the marriage of ideas and strategy."*

If that's what you mean by "concept," you're using a good word.

Creative/creativity. We have mixed emotions. Effective creativity is certainly something we want – but effectiveness is seldom known immediately. So, whether or not something is creative is interesting, but not always on point.

Idea. We like this word. We're in the business of having ideas. But, remember, not every idea is useful for the task at hand.

Big Idea. We don't like this phrase. Not because we disagree with it – lasting ideas that have big impact are most certainly a good thing. But…

Ideas become Big Ideas only in retrospect. That is, *after* they've performed in the marketplace.

In the beginning, it's a guess.

Selling Idea. We like this phrase, though it's a bit prosaic for some – in which case, keep it to yourself.

Just remember that's what we're trying to do.

I like it for another reason.

To some degree, we're all competent to judge a Selling Idea. It's an idea that sells. Duh.

Is a tiger an idea? Tony the Tiger sells Sugar Frosted Flakes by saying, "They're Grrrrreat!"

"Put a Tiger in Your Tank" sold the power of Exxon. It was "associated with business success."

Both emerged from strategies about power and energy.

The fact is, a strong, meaningful selling idea will still power a brand with a relevant difference.

"BRAND JOURNALISM."

Larry Light, who led the thinking behind McDonald's "I'm lovin' it" worldwide campaign offers some useful thinking. For a big brand like McDonald's, he's looking for more of a "Velcro" approach. *"We don't need one big execution of a big idea. We need one big idea that can be used in a multi-dimensional, multi-layered, and multi-faceted way."*

Four Cultural Languages.

McDonald's worldwide uses four cultural languages… sports, fashion, music, and entertainment.

They also look for media platforms to come up with a concept. *"We're asking media to come to us with creative ideas, Just like the (ad) agencies compete, why don't media compete?"*

Broad and Holistic vs. Narrow and Reductionist.

While smaller packaged goods brands may have to stay more simple and focused in their messaging strategies, Light recommends a holistic strategy for dealing with today's new consumer and today's new media environment.

"Each communication provides a different insight into our brand. It all adds up to a McDonald's journalistic brand chronicle."

THIS MAY NOT BE A FAVORITE AD CAMPAIGN.

But it's a memorable one. In a low-interest category (toilet paper), P&G presented their simple "softness" strategy over and over simply by having Mr. Whipple ask "Please don't squeeze the Charmin." How successful was it? After "retiring," the actor was brought back. Many saw it as the return of an old friend.

It's certainly not Luke Sullivan's favorite campaign, but it inspired him to write this excellent book about how to squeeze out better ideas.

CHARACTERISTICS OF SELLING IDEAS. P&G studied this a bit. They made some observations that you might find useful.

The Purpose of a Selling Idea:
 • *To register the brand's strategic objective – memorably – over the competition.*

What Is a Selling Idea?
 • *It's the primary executional ingredient and the main thread of executional continuity.*

Sounds simple. It's something that communicates your brand's advantage, and it's the idea that holds your campaign together. So far, so good.

Three Characteristics of Selling Ideas.

P&G found that successful Selling Ideas seemed to do well against "Three Principle Variables":

1. Substance – This has to do with *meaningfulness* or desirability to the consumer.

2. Credibility – Capable of being believed. However, it's OK if it's a bit of a challenge. (Don't forget what we talked about related to "permission to believe.")

3. Provocativeness – The way the idea is expressed is *"a thought-provoking method of expression."*

How do you judge a Selling Idea?

Here are some questions you might ask:
 • Is it faithful to Strategy?
 • Does it have genuine substance?
 • Is it credible yet challenging?
 • Is it provocative?

Here are some of the conceptual areas where we seem to find effective Selling Ideas:

1. DRAMATIZE THE BENEFIT.

If you have no other type of idea than this one, you can do very well in advertising.

These ideas can be served up as: slogans… dramatic demos… mnemonics… Tony the Tiger saying, *"They're Grrrreat!"* and even Mr. Whipple squeezing the Charmin. (Sorry, Luke.)

They *dramatize* the benefit.

Jared, who lost weight on a Subway diet, dramatized a benefit.

George Lois looks for words that *"bristle with visual possibilities."* Dramatize and visualize.

It is worth saying again. If you have no other type of idea than this one, you can do very well in advertising.

2. A DISTINCTIVE SELLING PERSONALITY.

The Volkswagen campaign did this marvelously well.

Each ad projected a personality consumers could identify with. Unique. Smart. Frugal. And honest about being a little bit ugly.

That little bit of honesty gave their other claims more credibility and made the brand more likeable.

A lot of the brands you like project a personality that you connect with.

The reassuring calm of a Volvo concerned with your safety, or the outrageousness of a Slim Jim – "definitely not part of a balanced breakfast."

Much fashion advertising does this with a visual personality. From good old Levi's to the latest designer jean. They sell style… with style.

Beers also seek to achieve a personality… though many seem to have the *same* personality.

There's a good reason for this. They have the exact same target consumer.

SMILE.
We're dramatizing the benefit – the money you save with GEICO.

Sprint dramatized the Product Benefit of quality sound by literally letting us hear a pin drop over the phone.

Our image.
An old VW visual. This was the visual for an ad that talked about their brand image. Nice change of pace.

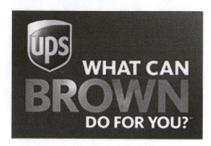

WHAT COLOR IS YOUR BRAND?
With UPS, it's easy to know.

A McSelling Idea. The simple use of "Mc" is able to give McDonald's incredible branding flexibility. Simple but powerful bits of imagery, like "Mc" and their Golden Arches provide McDonald's with their own look and their own language,

Dramatize the Problem. Here, Lubriderm dramatizes the problem of dry skin with a high impact visual – an alligator!

3. A UNIQUE SELLING ENVIRONMENT.

Marlboro moved from the "Marlboro Man" to "Marlboro Country" – an environment. It included cowboys, but it was enlarged to include all the feeling of the American West.

Sunkist Orange Soda became a major soft drink by utilizing an environment with almost universal appeal for its audience: California, the beach, The Beach Boys, and surfing.

Design can create a selling environment.

An ad can be a selling environment all in itself, created by your typeface, the overall sense of design, even a photographic attitude.

Design can send a strong selling message.

Apple, a company with strong design as part of its strategy, does this with product advertising that both complements and dramatizes their products.

Color values can reinforce your Selling Idea.

Is color a Selling Idea? Yes it is.

Leo Burnett knew it instinctively.

Red meat on a red background.

Is it the picture or the frame?

Sometimes the environment is the idea or it may be complementary to the main Selling Idea.

For example, McDonald's selling environment plays a consistent role in most of their advertising.

4. SOMETHING ELSE.

Why not? For example, *Dramatize the Problem*.

"Halitosis," a dramatic way of saying "bad breath," built the Listerine business.

Then it was "morning breath" for Scope.

FedEx dramatized their benefit, delivering a package on time, by giving the Problem unique dimension. Happy people getting happy packages wasn't going to do the job.

Name awareness mnemonics may also be Selling Ideas. Like Ken-L-Ration Kibbles 'n Bits.

Or Rolaids. Or local retailers who sing their phone number over and over and over again.

Subway's $5 Footlong campaign reminds you of two simple, but useful facts about their sandwiches.

A Selling Idea Is an Idea that Sells.

Yet, an abundance of opinion and uncertainty can cloud this simple issue.

Selling Ideas should be strong and simple.

"Great copy and great ideas are deceptively simple," said Leo Burnett, whose agency came up with many "Big Ideas." Or, perhaps more accurately, they grew many ideas into big ideas.

Build your Selling Ideas strong and simple and they may grow up to be big ideas.

IN CONCLUSION.

Your advertising should have a Selling Idea.

That idea, which will emerge from the Strategy, should probably be simple and easy to understand – even though the process of getting there may have been long and hard.

Many ad people labor long and hard searching for a breakthrough so advanced that almost no one can understand it or describe it.

Work hard, but do not be confused.

But in the beginning, your Problems will be:

• First, having an idea that sells.

• Second, selling your Selling Idea.

Now, let's talk about your most important partner – the Art Director.

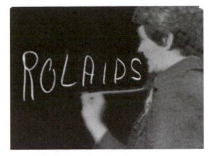

HOW DO YOU SPELL "SELL?"
A simple mantra, "How Do You Spell Relief?", is consistently paid off with the brand name – Rolaids.

Mnemonic Devices. These are memory devices, usually with a rhythmic "hook." In this case, the last part of the name repeated over and over and over, gave the brand an engaging approach that helped them make the most of a small budget.

Q. How many art directors
   does it take to change a light bulb?
A. Does it have to be a light bulb?

Q. How many copywriters
   does it take to change a light bulb?
A. I'm not changing it.

Art Director Appreciation

ADVERTISING IS A TEAM SPORT.
Copywriters and art directors depend on each other. No business relationship is closer.

Except perhaps a trapeze act.

A major factor in how well you succeed in this business will be based on how well you work with an art director.

Earlier, we discussed the left and right sides of the brain. There is a parallel here.

THE ART DIRECTOR IS VISUAL – Right Side.

THE COPYWRITER IS VERBAL – Left Side.

Your contributions reinforce each other.

This was part of Rubicam's revolution and the genius of the DDB approach.

Simply put, the better you team up, the better the two of you will do. Together.

Here are a few hints:

1. DON'T FINISH TOO FAST.
We know it's due yesterday. Try to give it a minute to breathe.

Put thumbnails, roughs, and headline ideas up on the wall. Let it incubate.

2. TALK ABOUT TYPE.
Type is one important way to establish tone of voice.

You're entitled to a vote!

What attitude do you want your words to project?

The typeface can even influence the headline itself. (And vice versa.)

Certain words look better in certain typefaces. Talk about it. Learn about type.

And, talk about readability. If you wrote something worth reading, it should be readable.

Or… maybe you wrote too many words.

Learn to edit. Fewer words. Art directors like that.

3. STORYBOARD OR KEY FRAME?

Chances are, you don't need a storyboard right away.

Learn to present with "key frames."

An office filled with unsold storyboards is a monument to wasted time.

4. BE A FRIEND.

The two of you are literally the parents of your creations. You have responsibilities to each other and the product of your combined talents.

Invest time and energy in that relationship, and it will pay off in the work you do. Together.

5. THE MEETING IS THE MEDIA.

You probably think you do ads for print and TV.

Wrong! ***You do meetings!***

Your medium is not the magazine page or TV screen. It's the meeting room. Sometimes it's your boss's office.

Here's the first thing you need to do…

Visualize the Meeting:

How big is the room? Where is the wall?

Where are the people you'll be presenting your ads to seated? Close? Far? Who are they?

You'll have to make an impact in that space.

Attack the Wall!

Give the meeting a headline. Get the theme up big.

Have a simple right-brain visual to go with all that left-brain verbiage. Remember, if you don't do the meeting right, the work will never run.

Or worse. Another team wins.

GRAPHIC DESIGNERS VS. ART DIRECTORS.

Fine artists and great graphic designers aren't necessarily good advertising art directors.

Fine design may arrange the page with pleasing proportion.

Fine art may express the artist's feelings and touch the heart (and the wallet) of the gallery-goer.

Good advertising art direction motivates action in ordinary people!

It grabs the casual reader and moves him in a desired direction.

It may invite him in, or pop off the page and poke him in the eye.

Whatever the effect, it can't just sit there looking nice. It must be noticed.

The advertising art director uses art and design to accomplish these objectives. They are means to an end.

For the same reason, excellent journalists, novelists, poets, and playwrights aren't necessarily good copywriters.

And vice versa.

REMEMBER HIM?

Paul Rand was one of the great graphic designers – and, as we mentioned in Chapter One, his influence extended to advertising because of his influence with key players at DDB.

As design becomes a more important part of some brand strategies (think of how Apple uses design to gain competitive advantage), you may find it a more and more important part of your own MarCom Matrix.

KRONE ALONE

Helmut Krone was one of the influential ADs at DDB.

This interview was for the *Wall Street Journal*. On the following pages, with Mr. Krone's permission, is another – a classic view of the art of art direction from one of the classics.

In 1950, a 25-year-old designer saw The Art Directors Club annual exhibition dominated by a very new and very small advertising agency. The designer's name: Helmut Krone. The agency: Doyle Dane Bernbach. The rest is history. Here, from a recent conversation, are the singular views of DDB's executive vice president, a creative director, and a member of the Art Directors Hall of Fame, with creative talent so extraordinary the late Bill Bernbach suggested he should be included in this series.

On early ambitions:

I was interested in industrial design and architecture. At 21, I had two interviews scheduled. First, with a designer named Robert Greenwell who was doing freelance ads for a magazine. The second with Raymond Loewy. Greenwell offered me $40 per week. I said, "Gee, that's great." I never interviewed with Loewy. And never looked back. I tell my children, it's not so much what you do but how you do it. Kids today spend half their lives agonizing over their first move, first job. It doesn't matter, it's how you tackle your work. Stop worrying so much and just do *something*.

On advertising:

I was Bauhaus-based. My idol was Paul Rand. Advertising? If you had any respect for design—any self-respect—and you wanted to tell your mother what you were doing, you worked *around* advertising, but *not in it*. So I worked for Greenwell, in pharmaceuticals, in fashion, for publishers—but not for the hard-core advertising agencies. I had to wait for Bernbach to start his agency. I came here in 1954. I was 29, and one of four art directors.

On alternatives:

I have always said there were only two people for whom I could work: Bill Bernbach and myself. Bill did more than start an agency. He made advertising *respectable*, a profession, a high art. We argued a lot. With genuine disagreement but real affection. We could fight like cats and dogs because we *knew* we were both after the *same thing*.

On television and print:

I'm not crazy about *things that move*. I like things that stand still; that you can study, hold in your hand, look at, contemplate. That's what I hate about television commercials. They're happenings. They go by and you don't even remember the details. In a print ad, you can study them. There's a point to caring about details in print. If you can give a photo just an extra ounce of *caring,* just a touch of inspiration, it shows. While I do my share of TV, I'm known as the print maven around here. I really do like it. After all these years, the idea of the *page* continues to fascinate me.

On work:

Beauty and style are qualities I count as secondary. If they are in the work, they come along for the ride. The only quality I really appreciate is *newness,* to see something no one has ever seen before. New comes at 11 o'clock at night, after you've spent all day hunched over the board. I have worked with a couple of geniuses. I spend long hours making up for not being a genius.

On confidence and clients:

I am very insecure. Nothing I do ever turns out exactly right. It's never what I expected. I like to work with clients. I need their judgment. All I know is that what I'm doing is new. The client can tell me if it's right. I hate presentations: agency people filing in with a big portfolio, taking out their acetate-wrapped comprehensives and saying, "Here. Make a decision." I like to have clients work with me. I show them scraps of paper. I pull things out of the wastebasket, tissues off the wall. I say "What do *you* think? Should I keep going?" It's not a matter of giving clients what they want. It's a matter of making sure you're on the same wave length.

On working with writers:

I talk with the writer. We come up with a concept. The writer leaves. But I stay. I want to *top* the concept. I want to lay something on top of the concept that's totally unexpected. Most people go home. For my work begins *after* we've settled on a headline and picture. The next day, the writer will see the ad. It'll have the headline and the picture we discussed. But it won't look or feel the way they thought it would. And that's unnerving to some writers.

On staying ahead:

I try to have some idea of what I want to do even before I know what has to be done. So before I get an assignment, I know what my attack will be, even before I know the product. You can't explain this to a client. They don't understand the process. But I believe you can bend and twist the idea to fit the problem, and come up with something totally new. Does it sound crazy? Bernbach used to say, "First, you make the revolution. Then you figure out why." Thinking ahead isn't unfair to the client. It gives him a head start.

On ads as information:

I think people want *information*. They don't get it from advertising. Say you're buying a tape deck. Well, you're up against it—especially if you read the ads. You know the formula. A double-entendre headline. Nice photo. But *no real meat* in the ad. Because the people who did the ad don't think you *really* want to know. Advertising people argue that it's good to make it simple. But that's not the point. People want to know Advertising ought to give them the information they need.

On the page as a package:

The page ought to be a *package* for the product. It should look like the product, smell like the product and the company. If it's a highly technical product—like the Porsche—that's how the page ought to look and feel. I tried to make the Porsche ads look a little like what you see when you raise the hood of the car. It's a *package* for Porsche. Every company, every product needs its own package.

On ideas and making them work:

Good ideas announce themselves. A bell rings. But that's just the start. To stage an idea at the level where I want to work, to do work that's *out at the edge,* you need to know about the tools. Type, photography, illustration, are tools. You need to know how they work, to know nearly as much about them as the people who specialize. For if you can't use the tools, you can't really make a good idea work.

On drawing pads:

Some people begin by drawing layouts. I can't work that way. I begin by *thinking*. I don't want to be influenced by that first scribble. Scribbles can box you in. Think first. I don't want to design *ads*. That's why I've spent my life fighting logos. Logos say "I'm an ad, so turn the page." I don't just leave out the logo. I give the client something better. And it doesn't look like an ad.

On The Wall Street Journal:

Form follows function. That was the Bauhaus revolution. The Journal is Bauhaus. Its form follows its function: information, organized for the reader, gathered for business reasons. I've said you ought to be able to identify your ads if you hang them upside down, forty feet away. The Journal *is* The Journal; there's no mistaking it. I've also said the graphic image ought to reflect reality. The Journal *looks* like business, and it *is* business. Of course, I read The Journal. Of course, I like to see my ads in The Journal. I have had a lifelong fascination with *the page,* and no publication gives me a bigger page than The Journal. As an art director, I am in the business of *staging* ideas for our clients. The Journal does a magnificent job of *staging* advertising.

The Wall Street Journal.
It works.

6.64.31 *Copyright, Dow Jones & Company, Inc., 1983. All rights reserved.*

HELMUT KRONE TALKS ABOUT THE MAKING OF AN AD

By Sandra Karl
Doyle Dane Bernbach, New York

Q. Is it true that you are a perfectionist?

A. I resent the charge. A perfectionist is someone who finishes the backside of a drawer, which I consider completely unnecessary. I spend a lot of time on the front, but I am definitely not interested in the backside of the drawer.

I feel that there's this imaginary line, and you have to get over that line. As soon as I feel I'm over that line, I quit. I don't go any further. I'll leave a thing without all the ends pulled in as soon as it's over that line.

Q. You mean you have a certain standard, and when you reach it, you stop?

A. Yes, just like everybody else. Now, maybe that line is in a different place for me. It all depends on where you place that line. For example, in engravings or television production, I feel that I'm not a stickler no matter what anyone says. If the page has the effect I was after, I'm not interested in petty little corrections.

Q. How did you come to work on Volkswagen when DDB first got the account?

A. I got on Volkswagen because I was the only one who'd ever heard of the car. I had one of the first Volkswagens in the U. S., probably one of the first 100, long before I ever worked here.

And just to show you how wrong a person can be—and how fallible I am—I was dead set against the Volkswagen campaign as we did it. I felt that the thing to do with this ugly little car was to make it as American as possible. Like, let's get Dinah Shore also. What's that thing she used to sing? "See the U.S.A. in your Chevrolet." I wanted "See the U.S.A. in your Volkswagen." With models around the car and tv extravaganzas.

Q. But it was on Volkswagen that you changed the look of ads. You changed the way the copy looked.

A. Well, first let me say that on Volkswagen I felt so strongly that we were doing the wrong thing—even though I contributed my third to it, certainly—that I finished up three ads, went on vacation to St. Thomas, depressed, came back two weeks later and I was a star.

Q. You say you contributed your third. Not your half?

A. My third, Bill Bernbach's third and Julian Koenig's third.

In his 14 years at Doyle Dane Bernbach, Helmut Krone has, until now, refused interview requests. That hasn't kept him from winning nine New York Art Directors Club medals, dozens of other awards and the title of vp-director of special projects at the agency. After numerous tries by Sandra Karl of the DDB pr office, he agreed to an interview for the agency's house publication. Attired in his newest outfit—cowboy pants, suede shirt and neckerchief—he sat back and talked to Miss Karl about his work, how and why he does it. Here is the interview taken from the October "DDB News."

Q. What was Bill Bernbach's third?

A. Mostly in keeping me from doing the other. Also, the whole concept of speaking simply, clearly and with charm belongs to him. There was nothing new about the Volkswagen idea, the only thing was that we applied it to a car.

Probably eight years before that, Bernbach did an ad for Fairmont strawberries, where he showed a whole strawberry in the middle of a big page—just one life-size strawberry. And the headline was: "It seemed a pity to cut it up." What they were selling were the only whole frozen strawberries on the market, the point being that a strawberry has to be perfect in order to keep it whole.

Volkswagen is not any different from that ad that he did a long time before. The only thing different about it was its application to cars—and that's different enough. I took traditional layout A, which had always existed—two-thirds picture, one-third copy, three blocks with a headline in between. But I changed the picture. The picture was naked looking, not full and lush. The other small change was the copy, which was sans serif rather than serif.

Q. And nobody had ever done that before?

A. Not with that layout, no. It was an editorial look, but with sans serif type.

Q. The look of the copy was very different. The use of "widows" which we spoke of once before.

A. I actually cut those "widows" into the first Volkswagen comps with a razor blade and asked Julian Koenig to write that way. I deliberately kept the blocks from being solid, and when I felt that a sentence could be cut in half, I suggested it just to make another paragraph.

I wanted the copy to look Gertrude Steiny. The layout in that case actually influenced a new copy style, which Bernbach later referred to as "subject, verb, object."

Q. You mean the layout came before the copy style? The copy style came about because of the way it would look on a page?

A. Definitely.

Before then, it was usually the art

283

director's job to get writers to fill out "widows," so that they could have a neat, No. 2-looking gray wash on the page.

As far as layout is concerned—which I consider a lost art—I feel that almost no one is looking around for a brand new page, a new way of putting down the same old elements, a new way of breaking up that 7x10" area.

Q. You're saying that they should be?

A. Yes. but everybody wants to belong to the current club. There's safety in that, I suppose. And they want to show they're smart enough to recognize what's good, what's "in." They think being current, being fashionable is being new. And it's really the opposite of new.

If you get a medal in the Art Directors Club, the chances are that what you did was not an innovation. I'd say that about almost every medal that I've gotten. They were for innovations that were already a year or two old, and, therefore, easy to digest.

If people say to you, "That's up to your usual great standard," then you know you haven't done it.

■ "New" is when you've never seen before what you've just put on a piece of paper. You haven't seen it on before and nobody else in the world has ever seen that thing that you've just put down on a piece of paper. And when a thing is new, all you know about it is that it is brand new. It's not related to anything that you've seen before in your life. And it's very hard to judge the value of it. You distrust it, and everybody distrusts it. And very often, it's somebody else who has to tell you that that thing has merit, because you have no frame of reference, and you can't relate it to anything that you or anybody else has ever done before.

Alexey Brodovitch at the New School was the one who put me on to "new." Students would bring in something to class that they thought was spectacular, but he'd toss it aside and say: "I've seen this once before somewhere." And he wouldn't even discuss it.

Q. What was his reaction when you did something he'd never seen before?

A. I never did anything he'd never seen before while I was in his class. I wasn't ready.

And now that I've done all that talking about "new," let me contradict myself and take a swing at the current trend toward "doing your own thing."

I asked one of our writers recently what was more important: Doing your own thing or making the ad as good as it can be. The answer was: "Doing my own thing." I disagree violently with that. I'd like to propose a new idea for our age: Until you've got a better answer, you copy. I copied Bob Gage for five years. I even copied the leading between his lines of type. And Bob originally copied Paul

Think small.

Avis is only No.2
in rent a cars.
So why go with us?

We try harder.
(When you're not the biggest, you have to.)
We just can't afford dirty ashtrays. Or half-empty gas tanks. Or worn wipers. Or unwashed cars. Or low tires. Or anything less than seat-adjusters that adjust. Heaters that heat. Defrosters that defrost.
Obviously, the thing we try hardest for is just to be nice. To start you out right with a new car, like a lively, super-torque Ford, and a pleasant smile. To know, say, where you get a good pastrami sandwich in Duluth.
Why?
Because we can't afford to take you for granted.
Go with us next time.
The line at our counter is shorter.

Big illustration area, small type in Volkswagen ad was reversed for Avis.

Rand, and Rand first copied a German typographer named Tschichold. The thing to do when you get a requisition is to find an honest answer. Solve the problem. Then, if through the years a personal style begins to emerge, you must be the last to know. You have to be innocent of it.

Q. I'd wanted to ask you about the Avis layout. That was new too, wasn't it?

A. Yes. I remember going home on the train one night with Bob (Gage). Everybody at that time was doing Volkswagen layouts. In fact, the headlines were getting smaller and smaller, and the fashion at the time was to write three meaningful words, so strong in themselves that you could set them in very small type.

We had a discussion about this on the train, and he said: "How much smaller can headlines get before they become invisible?" And I thought about it. I was working on Avis currently and looking for a page style. Now that's very important to me, a page style. I feel that you should be able to tell who's running that ad at a distance of 20 feet.

Q. Just by the page style?

A. Just by the page style. You can tell a Volkswagen ad from a distance of 30 feet, and an Avis ad from a distance of 40 feet.

Anyway, to get back to this headline thing. I started thinking about what he'd said, how absurd it was getting with these headlines getting smaller and smaller. So what I did was I took the Volkswagen style and turned it inside out: The headline became big, and not in the middle, I put it on top. The picture became small, and the copy became large. It was very carefully, methodically done, very coolly arrived at. It was *not* inspired. It was a mathematical solution. I made everything

that was big, small, and everything that was small, big.

Q. Anything else?

A. Why don't you come clean and ask me why I'm so slow.

Q. Okay. Why are you so slow?

A. I have no defense, only a reason. Though a New Yorker, I had a German upbringing. And I'm the recipient of the best of such an upbringing as well as the victim of the worst part of it.

A German son is always wrong until he's proved himself to be right. He is a know-nothing and has everything to prove. It gives you a certain insecurity which is the opposite of "chutzpah." You tend to rework things and believe they're never good enough, because, after all, you're a "know-nothing."

David Ogilvy once said: "An agency ought to be on time, just like a good tailor." But in defense, I'd like to say that I've got the best tailor outside of Rome—and he's always late!

Q. Do you enjoy it, the work?

A. I don't know. I go back and forth. Advertising is stupid. Advertising is great. Advertising is totally unnecessary. Advertising is the most vital art form of our day. It depends on what week it is I think they're both true.

I didn't plan out my existence. "I'm going to do this for two years, this for three years, and then I'll be a vice-president, and so on." I never heard of stock options.

All I did was keep my nose on the board. I worked my ass off. I worked just like my father and mother worked. My father was an orthopedic shoemaker and my mother was a seamstress, and I believe that they were probably the best shoemaker and seamstress in America. I believe that with all my might. And I guess that's how it all happened. They used to work their heads off. And people said they were the best. #

Selling Your Ideas

*"Plan the sale
as you write the ad."*
Leo Burnett

This section was originally called "Sales Power."

I wrote this corny little sequence where everything started with "S" and "P." I figured that would make it seem like a theme.

When I went to update the book, I figured the corny subheads were going to go. But, as I read it again, I said to myself, "*Hey, this ain't bad.*" Years later, it's still good advice.

Meeting technology has changed – now it's Flash, PowerPoint, New Media, and dancing hamsters – but the basic points, "old school" though they might be, are still pretty useful.

Here it is – from way back in the 20th century.

SELL BETTER FIVE WAYS.
We wish all you had to do was take a bow while the world admired.

The world isn't like that.

How well you sell ideas is as important as how good those ideas are. Maybe more so.

So, how *do* you sell ideas?

It's complicated. And, it's simple.

It starts with understanding *the other person's point of view.* And helping them feel confident (and excited) about the possibilities represented by your idea – which, like all ideas, is unproven in the marketplace.

To make it a little easier to remember, we built this little list with "S.P." initials:
- STRATEGIC PRECISION
- SAVVY PSYCHOLOGY
- SLICK PRESENTATION
- STRUCTURAL PERSUASION
- SOLVING THE PROBLEM

Let's go step by step.

"Where is that big black bag going with that little man?"

STRONG STRATEGIES MAKE STRONG SELLING IDEAS.
If they're not coming, it may be you, or… it may be the Strategy.

If that's the case, look at the Strategy, look at the work, and try to figure out what's wrong.

Good luck.

WHAT IF YOUR IDEA ISN'T ON-STRATEGY?

Then you must either have a different idea, or... a different Strategy!

Do not ignore this risky second option. Here's why:

Some strategies look nice on paper and sound nice in the meeting room, but when it comes time to execute them, they don't lead to strong executions.

For example, FedEx could have had a strategy that emphasized the benefit of on-time delivery.

Yet, happy normal people receiving their packages on time may not be powerful persuasion (Emery tried this, with no great success). So FedEx *dramatized the problem!*

Suddenly, the executional stage opens up – memorable comedic dramas and characters develop into a powerful and *resonant* campaign that every businessman can relate to.

Because every businessman has experienced the pressure of the deadline, when it "absolutely positively has to be there overnight."

ACCOUNT PLANNERS = CONSUMER PSYCHOLOGISTS.

Account planning can really help.

A good account planner brings consumer insight into the equation when you need it most.

You can gain early insight into how the consumer feels about the category and how they'll react to the advertising.

Savvy Psychology in action!

1. STRATEGIC PRECISION.

First, your Selling Idea must be on-strategy.

Your idea should be perceived as an expression of The Strategy. So...

Before You Talk about the Idea, You Have to Talk about The Strategy. Consider this rule.

An idea that relates strongly to your Strategy has the potential to be a strong Selling Idea.

Emphasize that strength.

And once you get the idea, and believe in it, that's the first thing you say to sell the idea.

Strong Strategies Make for Strong Selling Ideas.

It's a good idea because it's on-strategy. You'd also better be prepared to tell people why the Strategy is right. Show that you know the Strategy before you start to sell that idea.

Then, as you sell your idea, you're also communicating that you believe in the Strategy.

2. SAVVY PSYCHOLOGY.

As you present to people, think how *they* feel. Not how you feel.

Presenting good ideas is receiver-driven – like good advertising.

In fact, your presentation begins long before you present. Learn to involve others in your Selling Idea.

Everyone wants to get with a winner – including your boss and your client. It might be as simple as communicating that you have a winning idea.

Invite early input from the AE and research.

Look for information that bolsters your case.

Leo said it, *"Plan the sale as you write the ad."*

Look for ways to make your idea better. And look for others who will support your idea.

Someone else may have a valuable addition to your idea – and may also become a valuable ally.

Help your audience focus on the psychology of the target customer.

Try to show how good your Selling Idea is from the target customer's point of view.

Through it all, remember, your idea has to meet *their* needs. Not yours.

Relate your idea to the needs of your audience.

3. SLICK PRESENTATION.

You must become accomplished at presenting.

A good presentation makes people *want* to do the ads. Two team members are vital partners – the account executive and the art director.

They want to win, too.

Rehearse. Discuss.

Often, the AE can make some of the key arguments on behalf of the Selling Idea.

And the art director can make it look good.

A Great Presentation Needs Great Art Direction.

Your other important partner is the art director. He'd better like the idea – and it should show.

How about a big title card with the theme? Maybe a button for the sales force?

Your work should sell itself – *visually*.

Look at it this way. A good presentation should make you *want* to do the ads.

It doesn't have to be tight – but it must be enticing.

Remember, the Meeting Is the Medium!

That means you've got to get good at putting presentations together.

Like copywriting, it's a skilled craft.

4. STRUCTURAL PERSUASION.

You persuade by meeting other people's needs.

They might not do it for you, but they'll certainly do it for themselves.

"Selling is an art of passion. When you're passionate about an idea, it shows."
Tom McElligott

HELPFUL HINTS FOR BETTER PRESENTATIONS.
Psychological and Physical.
Be confident, likeable… and persuasive.
Learn to tell a joke or a story.
Have a few you know.
Learn about body language and get comfortable.

Scripts, Outlines, & Talking Points.
Outline your opening remarks.
Write down your closing arguments.
Rehearse answers to the toughest possible questions. (This is good advice. Asking yourself tough questions – and answering them – makes you better.)
Learn to work from notes. (I use a clipboard.) Talk about:
• Consumer Needs.
• Consumer Benefits.
• Product Benefits.
• The Strategy's Strength.
Overall.
Show that you know your stuff.
Show that you care about the client's business.
Show that you're the one who can solve tomorrow's problem.
And finally…
Practice.
Practice reading copy aloud.
Practice presenting the storyboard.
Practice might not make you perfect, but it will make you a better presenter.

There Are Two Times In Life When You're Totally Alone. Just Before You Die. And Just Before You Make A Speech.

VANDER ZANDEN, INC.
Executive Speechmaking And Storytelling.

HERE ARE SOME OF THE THINGS I GO THROUGH.

I take notes – lots of 'em.

When other people talk, I make notes. It's helpful, and it's clear to everyone that I'm listening.

Just like Leo, I'm planning the meeting as well as the ad.

I usually start with a rough outline of the presentation with titles and subheads for each part of the presentation sequence.

As it's coming together, I try to think about the toughest questions that will be asked and try to have answers ready.

I'm always looking for ways to strengthen the Selling Idea and the presentation using other's suggestions.

It makes the Selling Idea stronger and the selling team larger.

The more people who believe in the Selling Idea, the better the chance it will sell.

So let's talk about what you're going to talk about. Remember Bernbach…

"Persuasion is not a science, but an art."

Art has form. So does persuasion.

Your point of entry is critical.

This is the beginning. Context.

It's *"tell 'em what you're going to tell 'em."*

Whether it's the first sentence in your ad or the opening thought in your presentation, you must be concerned with that vital first step.

Remember, in today's cluttered communications environment you're competing for people's attention – even in a meeting. First impressions are critical.

So, what *do* you say first?

Do you say, "Here's my great idea"? Wrong!

You might start with "Here's the problem."

Or you might set the mood.

Or, you might acknowledge other points of view.

But whatever you do, have an idea of where you're going.

To do this, organization and sequence are essential.

That's why it's *vital* that you develop the habit of structured, organized thinking. So people can follow what you're saying.

Don't forget the importance of pace and the visual part of your presentation.

Remember, you only have one first chance.

5. SOLVE THE PROBLEM.

Clients have needs. And clients have clients.

Chances are, the Big-Shot you're presenting to works for an Even-Bigger-Shot who likes to ask tough questions about the advertising.

Make it easy for your client to answer them.

You must give him answers as to how this Selling Idea and these ads *Solve the Problem.*

Every client has a problem.

If he didn't, he wouldn't need you.

And that's the last helpful hint...

Solve the Client's Problem, and You'll Sell the Selling Idea.

The more your Selling Idea can be seen to solve *their* problem, the better the chance *your* Selling Idea will become *their* Selling Idea.

And that's how to sell ideas.

A FEW MORE THOUGHTS ON "THE PROBLEM THE ADVERTISING MUST SOLVE." It's easy to say that the problem is "we have declining share and a small budget." Probably true.

And it's also probably true that "We need great advertising to overcome our problems." But that's not the point of figuring out what the problem is.

Or, what the problem is that the advertising can solve.

You need to frame it in terms of a consumer problem, not a brand problem or a business problem.

We can't make this point too many times. It's not about you, it's about the person on the other side of this page.

"People Aren't Aware."

Lack of awareness is certainly a problem, one almost every brand has to some degree. But, again, if there isn't a reason for the consumer to be aware, well, what's the point.

We can shoot a gerbil into our logo, as an Internet brand called Outpost did not too long ago, but if there's no consumer need and no consumer action to meet that need, well, again, what's the point?

And that's the point.

As you work to develop Selling Ideas and *sell* Selling Ideas, the best place to be is inside the mind of the consumer.

So you can turn him or her into a customer. Got it?

Remember...
Clients have clients.
Every client has a problem.
Your job is to help their business.

A CONSUMER PROBLEM.
"A Maalox Moment" is a consumer problem. Whether we have those moments or not, we understand what the proposition is.

SELLING IDEA EXERCISES:
This exercise is to help you realize how
hard it is to connect with (and remember)
a motivating idea.

1. **List the most memorable ad campaigns you can remember. How
   many can you list?**

   In your own words, write down
   the Selling Idea.

2. **Name an advertisement (or promotional) message that motivated
   you to act in the last 90 days.**

3. **Can you name two Selling Ideas (or
   slogans) that dramatize a Product
   Benefit?**

   Other products probably offer the
   same benefit.

   How did these make their benefit
   seem unique?

4. **Name two brands that project
   a selling personality or a selling
   attitude that you like.**

   How are they different from others
   in the category?

5. **Name two Selling Ideas used by
   a service.**

   Is there a symbol involved? What
   is it?

   What does it mean? Look up the
   word "semiotics."

6. **Name two Selling Ideas that dramatize a Problem.**

   Other products may solve the same
   problem.

   How did these products build
   distinctiveness?

   WORK BACKWARD!
Learn to become more of a visually
driven writer.

   Rough out visuals first.

   Write words to pictures.

   Try to think about products in a totally
nonverbal way and see what essential
communication imagery you discover.

   Then, write the words.

   See what happens.

#21: Selling Ideas

Take the Strategies and Theme Lines that you
wrote in Assignments #6, #7, and #8.

   Pick your three favorites. If you have no favorites, write some new ones.

1. DEVELOP ONE SELLING IDEA FOR
   EACH PRODUCT AND STRATEGY.
   How do they develop visual drama?
   How do they reinforce name awareness?
   How do they communicate the benefit?

2. PRESENT YOUR SELLING IDEAS AS PRINT
   CONCEPTS, TV KEY FRAMES, OR BOTH.

#22 Visualize!

1. THE ART CENTER EXERCISE.
   Do an ad for Lava Soap
   that communicates with
   only a visual! No headline. No copy.

2. STRATEGY VISUALS.
   Did you do a visual for each of the strategies in
   #21? If not, do it now.

3. VERBALIZE VISUALS.
   Pick three ads you like.
   Verbalize why you like them *visually.*

4. PLAN A MEETING.
   Do a rough chart of the meeting room and
   display space. Outline visual materials you'll
   need.

Tactical Tool Box

FINALLY. Even though you've been writing ads and bits of communication from the first pages of this so-called Workbook, now we're really going to get into it.

You now have – in theory – the tools to think things through.

Now we'll do that – think things through – and then create the message that is the logical outcome of that strategy.

But remember, just saying it in a flat logical way is often not the most effective way to do it.

So that's your next challenge – in all kinds of media forms.

Sharpen those tools.

Here we go.

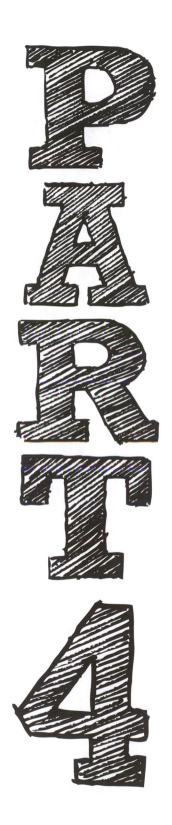

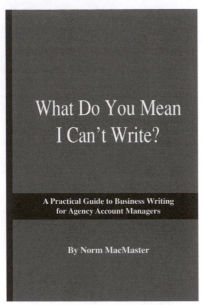

WHAT DO YOU MEAN?

This little book was written to help Account Execs learn the basics: Contact Reports, Recommendations, Media Strategies, a whole range of business documents.

It wouldn't hurt for you to pick up a copy as well.

It's called *What Do You Mean I Can't Write? A Practical Guide to Business Writing for Agency Account Managers*. It was written by Norm MacMaster, a top account exec who trained at Ogilvy and ended up on JWT's Board of Directors.

It offers useful writing advice, such as:

Be clear.

Be simple.

Be short.

Be specific.

Who knows, it might even improve your copywriting.

Business Writing & Copywriting…

THIS NEXT SECTION is about teaching you a certain kind of writing style.

It came out of advertising, but it's also used in many other fields of MarCom – Sales Promotion, Events, New Media, and more.

For some other types of writing, this style is not appropriate. For example, if you write a press release that sounds too much like an ad, the next sound you hear will be your press release hitting the wastebasket.

MEMOS AND RECOMMENDATIONS. Often, you'll be called upon to add your voice to the dialogue of business writing. Cover memos, positioning "think pieces," inspirational essays about the essence of your brand… these and more can be important documents for the business of marketing communication.

Contemporary business writing style is related to contemporary copywriting style, but it's not the same.

You'll need a bit more adherence to the rules of grammar, though sentence fragments are often used, along with bullet points, to list key facts, or support for a recommendation.

DEATH BY POWERPOINT. And speaking of bullet points…

If you don't know PowerPoint (or its better looking cousin, Apple's Keynote), you better learn it.

And you better learn to do good ones.

Because even the best Selling Idea usually needs a solid presentation to get itself sold.

Readin'
Writin'
Rhythm
Re-Writin'

BEFORE WE GO INTO SPECIFIC tactical areas, like headlines, scripts, and body copy, let's talk about some of the habits you'll need to develop for all of them.

This is a way of writing that's a good bit different than what you're used to.

AN EDITORIAL.

In school, most of your writing assignments were exercises in grammar, vocabulary, and reading comprehension – done for the approval of a teacher.

Often, it had to be a certain number of words or pages – so brevity was penalized.

So you were taught to overwrite!

Furthermore, you're probably carrying around the baggage of years of overexposure to overwritten material.

In school, long words are preferred to short ones. Complex concepts win out over simple statements.

The lecturing language of education is preferred to the simple rhythm of conversation.

This verbal inflation has been encouraged by bureaucrats, lawyers, politicians, and academics.

Advertising works in the real world.

Here's what we'll do:
First, we'll cover the Four R's of Copywriting.
Next, basics of modern copywriting style.
Then, we'll have some fun as we work in print, radio, and TV.

The Science of Hopkins. Take this easy test. Compare modern copywriting style to that of Claude Hopkins. Then, send for a Free Offer!

Are you insane yet?

Take this simple test.

DISARMINGLY DIRECT.
Rich Binell's approach is to get "down to the bone."

Starting Dec. 23 the Atlantic Ocean will be 20% smaller.

EL AL

The Art of Bernbach. *Visuals and words combine to create surprising impact. This ad cleverly says El Al is "making the Atlantic 20% smaller." Now this ad might seem a bit subtle, but think about the target – people reading the* New Yorker *and considering a trip to Israel. For this target, the style was right.*

Instead of performing for marginally interested teachers who are, let's face it, paid to read what you write, you must talk to totally uninterested consumers.

You don't have to exercise your vocabulary, demonstrate your intellect, or get a good grade.

Everything just got simple.

Do writing worth reading.

End of editorial.

A FEW NEW HABITS.

Whatever media you'll be working in, you need to talk person to person.

You must develop a short, straightforward writing style – and then it has to be a bit better than that.

The words we use to serve up our ideas have to be a little bit special. At a minimum, they must deserve the attention of people who have other things on their minds.

Because advertising must be more than well-structured information.

It must have enthusiasm and artistry.

Here's a thought from Bill Bernbach:

"There are a lot of great technicians in advertising. And, unfortunately, they talk the best game.

They know all the rules.

They are the scientists of advertising.

But there's one little rub.

Advertising is fundamentally persuasion… and persuasion happens to be not a science, but an art."

Hey, I'm inspired.

How about you?

The New Writing

AS THE WORLD GOT WIRED, a brand new writing style emerged. Post-television copywriting.

Today, we read, hear, and feel our way through a flow of information. We inhale, skim, and absorb.

We take bites, bits, and chunks and change the channel. We turn the page, or tune out till we see or hear something of interest.

We've evolved from readers to "viewers."

Even when we read, we graze as we gaze.

Today, we're all more selective and demanding consumers of information – even if we insist on a diet of tabloid junk food.

More and more, we choose our news.

Channel changer in hand, we zip and zap as we interact with our information.

It's casual and natural.

Contemporary copywriting must connect with these new realities.

Literary traditions based on novels, short stories, essays, and other pre-electronic forms are replaced by those based on news, movies, music, and the cadence of conversation.

Yet, most writing is still taught as a logical, literary, left-brained skill – writers practicing their art for interested readers.

Copywriting is different.

In copywriting, the most important person is not the writer, but *the receiver.*

Got it? Good.

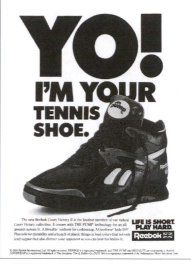

NEW FASHIONS IN FASHION.
They help inspire new fashions in writing. Street fashion? Street language!

TOM MCELLIGOTT'S STYLE.
A terrific copywriter and founder of Fallon McElligott, one trait of Tom's early award-winning print was using old pictures with contemporary copy. Did you know that his father worked for the Episcopal Church? Ads done for Dad!

The best way to unearth a new and interesting advertising campaign is to dig into the interesting facts about the product itself. And the agency which digs deepest usually comes up with the most pay dirt.

YOUNG & RUBICAM, Inc., Advertising

**LOOKING FOR THE
CAPO D'ASTRO BAR.**

(This ad classic is from a newsletter article by Bud Robbins, copywriter.)

Back in the '60s, I was hired by an ad agency to write copy on the Aeolian Piano Company account.

My first assignment was for an ad to be placed in the *New York Times* for one of their grand pianos.

The only background information I received was some previous ads and a few faded close-up shots… and, of course, the due date.

The account executive was slightly put out by my request for additional information, and his response to my suggestion that I sit down with the client was, *"Jesus Christ, are you one of those? Can't you just create something? We're up against a closing date!"*

I acknowledged his perception that I *was* one of those, which got us an immediate audience with the head of our agency.

I volunteered I couldn't even play a piano, let alone write about why anyone would spend $5000 for *this* piano when they could purchase a Baldwin or Steinway for the same amount.

Both allowed the fact they would gladly resign the Aeolian business for either of the others, however, while waiting for that call, suppose we make our deadline.

(Continued on next page.)

Readin'

BEFORE YOU CAN WRITE CLEARLY about a subject, you have to understand it.

As a copywriter, you will find yourself continually becoming an expert on things you know little about – so you can then write about them with authority.

It means assembling information. Digging for facts – the preparation stage of the creative process.

Much of the difficulty of not knowing what to say is rooted in not having anything to say.

This can be a difficult problem for a copywriter, particularly with so-called "parity" products, older products and other advertisers without much news.

It seems like it's all been said before.

Nonetheless, your writing must have *substance*. Interest is maintained with content as well as style. Credibility must be earned. And that takes work. Read all about it. Take notes. Make lists.

Read memos, fact sheets, magazine articles, and anything else you can lay your hands on.

READ PRODUCTS.

Involve yourself with the product. Dig.

As Julian Koenig said, *"Your job is to reveal how good your product is, not how good you are."*

A True Story.

One night, copywriter Dan Nichols dumped a box of cereal on his kitchen table and counted the raisins!

And that's how "Two Scoops of Raisins in a box of Kellogg's Raisin Bran" was born.

SAVE 50¢
"Hey, that's 25¢ a Scoop!"
Kellogg's RAISIN BRAN

You won't find the answer staring into space, getting stoned, feeling alienated, insecure, or above it all.

You must get *into* the product – just like the Capo d'astro bar, they all have a story to tell.

READ PEOPLE.

It's some of the most interesting reading you can do.

The product you're working on is surrounded by people – clients, customers, and competitors.

The have a story to tell, too.

And you never know where you'll find those stories.

One day, I was suddenly working for a retailer of women's clothes – the kind you wore to work.

I asked my sister, guessing she was in the target.

Not only was she in the target, she'd been to that retailer's wardrobe coordination seminar, and after half an hour in her closet, I understood a good part of the story I had to tell.

Some good news.

People like telling you stories about themselves.

They like it when someone is interested in them – even if it's a stranger "working on a project."

Learn to be interested in others, and they will reward you with stories worth telling.

READ PICTURES.

It's all becoming more visual, remember?

Learn to do some visual reading.

Add art shows, magazines, movies, television, and websites to your "reading list."

Can you create your target's visual environment?

Read their magazines. It can be as simple as paging through some of the trade magazines you'll be in.

Go to the dealership. Or the retailer.

Take a look at the world of the people who use your product and pay attention to what you see.

You may come back with that picture that's worth a thousand words.

CAPO D'ASTRO (CONT.)

I persisted and, reluctantly, a tour of the Aeolian factory in upstate New York was arranged. I was assured that "we don't do this with all our clients" and my knowledge as to the value of company time was greatly reinforced.

The tour of the plant lasted two days, and although the care and construction appeared meticulous, $5000 still seemed to be a lot of money.

Just before leaving, I was escorted into the showroom by the national sales manager. In an elegant setting sat their piano alongside the comparably priced Steinway and Baldwin. *"They sure do look alike,"* I commented.

"They sure do. About the only real difference is the shipping weight – ours is heavier."

"Heavier?" I asked. *"What makes ours heavier?"*

"The Capo d'astro bar."

"What's a Capo d'astro bar?"

"Here, I'll show you. Get down on your knees."

(Continued on next page.)

"Encourage your children to read a newspaper every day. You'll be preparing them for the most important role of all...life."

My most important role is being a parent. My children aren't impressed by awards, they just want me to be there for them. That's why I've always loved reading to my kids (they think I make a very scary witch and a great duck). I urge you to read to your children every day – especially newspapers. Reading newspapers will give them the whole story of what's going on around them. And reading will prepare them for the most important role of all...life.

—Meryl Streep, Actress

It all starts with newspapers.
www.newspaperlinks.com

THIS MESSAGE IS BROUGHT TO YOU BY THE NEWSPAPER ASSOCIATION OF AMERICA

HOW TO READ WITH STYLE.

Here's an ad from a campaign Jerry Della Femina did for the newspaper industry. The real message is simple and direct. Newspapers are cool. Cool people read them.

CAPO D'ASTRO (CONT.)

Once under the piano, he pointed to a metallic bar fixed across the harp and bearing down on the highest octaves.

"It takes 50 years before the harp in a piano warps. That's when the Capo d'astro bar goes to work. It prevents that warping."

I left the national sales manager under his piano and dove under the Baldwin to find a Tinkertoy Capo d'astro bar at best. Same with the Steinway.

"You mean the Capo d'astro bar really doesn't go to work for 50 years?" I asked.

"Well, there's got to be some reason why the Met used it," he casually added.

I froze. *"Are you telling me that the Metropolitan Opera House in New York City used this piano?"*

"Sure. And their Capo d'astro bar should be working by now."

Upstate New York looks nothing like the front of the Metropolitan Opera House where I met the legendary Carmen Rise Steven. She was now in charge of moving the Metropolitan Opera House to the Lincoln Center.

Ms. Stevens told me, *"About the only thing the Met is taking with them is their piano."* That quote was the headline of our first ad.

The result created a six-year wait between order and delivery.

My point is this.

No matter what the account, I promise you, the Capo d'astro bar is there.

GOOD ADVICE.

In A *Technique for Producing Ideas,* James Webb Young recommends two types of reading:

1. General Reading.

To expand the range of experience critical in idea producing.

2. Specific Reading.

Related to the products, people, and problems at hand.

OLD ADVICE.

For complex projects, some people recommend the use of note cards.

I think that was before computers.

ORGANIZATION, MAN.

I don't know if you want this next bit of advice.

If you take it, you'll end up with piles of "stuff."

But here goes… since the creation of ideas is based on new combinations of previously expressed ideas, the greater your resources, the greater your chances of achieving the best combination.

My own technique is to accumulate piles of notes, random scribblings, memos, magazine articles, competitive ads, and product literature. Folders help.

I let my subconscious incubate and organize during this period. And I start as soon as possible.

Because even when due dates seem far off, they sort of sneak up on you.

When the pile is a certain size, or the deadline is approaching rapidly, I'm ready to write.

First, I try to organize the material in an orderly, rational way, which gives me a chance to review it again and see if some initial ideas still hold up.

I'll generally use an outline, which I continually revise and update. I think the computer helps, but when you're writing by hand, you tend to write a little less and scribble and scratch out.

I usually write by hand for about two-and-a-half scribbles. During this time, as the details pile up, you continually refocus on what's important.

Then, having dealt with the material to some degree in a right-brained *and* left-brained way (making notes as you go), see where it takes you.

Alternate between looking for more details and then looking at what's most important.

Over time, you'll find yourself working with an ever-growing database, and you'll find that experience will help you get there faster with fewer clues.

You'll also end up with lots of files. Sorry.

It's life on the learning curve.

Writin'

YOUR NEXT STEP is to build a working vocabulary for your product and your brand.

You may or may not have your Selling Idea yet.

Either way, you need to collect the vocabulary you'll be working with:

• Nouns, verbs, and adjectives
• Slang and jargon
• Interesting ideas
• Facts and figures
• And figures of speech

These are the building blocks for your copy blocks.

Much of this material will originate in your notes and the process of reading about your product and working on your Strategy.

In general, you should probably avoid using a thesaurus. You should try to avoid obscure words and look for exactly the right words.

As Mark Twain said, *"It's the difference between lightning and lightning bug.*

Here's what you should look for:

1. FIND YOUR VERB!

Your job is to *move* people.

The first things you should look for are verbs associated with your subject.

Verbs *activate* your writing – they are key to successful persuasion.

Many successful campaigns have been based on active verbal constructions:

"We Try Harder"
"Fly the Friendly Skies"
"Let Your Fingers Do the Walking"
"Got Milk?"

Can you think of a few running right now?

**BUILD A PRODUCT VOCABULARY,
BUILD A BRAND VOCABULARY:**
1. Find Your Verb.
2. Add Adjectives.
3. Pick Up the Pieces.
4. Organize Your Thinking.
5. Dis-Organize Your Thinking
6. Re-Organize Your Thinking.

FIND YOUR VERB!
This verb helped position a new liquid detergent against powdered detergents.

A FRESH NEW VERB...
brings extra energy and a bit of extra excitement to a familiar and not all that exciting product.

ACTIVATE THE BENEFIT.
"Turn up the Volume" adds energy to Agree's conditioning benefit.

AN ABSOLUTELY TRUE STORY.
The original line for FedEx was "When it has to be there overnight."

As TV Director Joe Sedelmeier was casting the commercial, one actor did an absolutely marvelous job saying "Absolutely. Positively."

Joe had the actor keep saying the words over and over. It had Velcro.

It caught the ear and dramatized both the problem and the benefit.

The agency realized this added extra drama and intensity to the need for FedEx, and extra memorability to their theme.

2. ADD ADJECTIVES.
Be selective. Advertising adjectives need to be like Baby Bear's porridge. . . "Just right."

They should clarify, inform, and intensify.

They should resonate with the target.

They should relate to the Strategy.

After adding up all the adjectives that meet your objectives, ask one question.

Is there one adjective strong enough to sustain your campaign? It may be the only one you need.

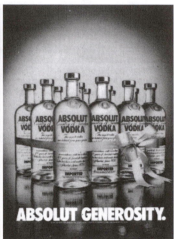

Absolut Success.

Many brand names are based on adjectives – it's a good name awareness device.

Absolut Vodka is an award-winning example.

But be sure you don't jeopardize your brand name.

It makes lawyers absolutely crazy.

300

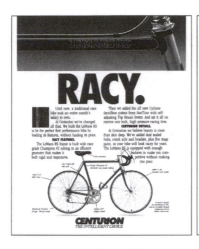

Adjective as Headline.

These handsome ads for Centurion bikes communicate three lines of bikes quickly and charmingly.

The powerful cumulative effect of this tactic is affordable for the brand in a medium like a bike specialty magazine.

Rhythm. Rhythm. Rhythm. See how repetition can build a positive feeling about a brand?

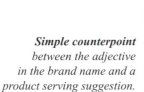
Simple counterpoint between the adjective in the brand name and a product serving suggestion.

Adjective du jour. Sometimes, certain words, just like certain people, become cool. Go figure. Sometimes, it can work. Here's a good example. Or, an extreme example.

SHOULD I MAKE UP WORDS?

Well, it's worked and it's failed.

Volvo tried it with their ReVolvolution campaign. Clearly, they're trying to grow the brand image from the conservative boxy styled "safety" position into one that is more performance-oriented.

It's not clear how much Velcro there is in "ReVolvolution."

Then again, how much controversy is in "Cointreauversial."

What do you think?

STOREHOUSE SMALL SPACE.

These ads rephrase familiar phrases and make easy puns to add extra style.

Note that each phrase ties into a selling feature of the featured products.

THE NATURAL
WAY TO WRITE.

Here's another take on "mind mapping" explored in *Writing the Natural Way* by Gabriele Lusser Rico.

She shows you how to tap into the associative connections in both sides of your brain with a technique called "clustering," a nonlinear brainstorming process that you can do on a sheet of paper. It looks like this...

The phrases above are concepts from her book.

Instead of an outline, you start with "Clusters" of words and concepts that form chains and patterns of meaning.

Highly recommended.

3. PICK UP THE PIECES!

Find unique combinations of words and ideas that relate to your brand, your product category, and Strategy.

Pick 'em up and jot 'em down. Assemble:
- **familiar phrases**
- **cliches and puns**
- **endorsements**
- and **reasons why.**

Build your arsenal.

It's a jungle out there.

The Double. By reversing one aspect of a common cliché, a negative can become a positive in an intense and startling way.
Here, Volkswagen does it.

4. ORGANIZE YOUR THINKING.

Now you're ready to write. Finally.

You have many of the pieces of the puzzle.

Now you have to put them together.

Take a short break. Think.

Utilize the incubation stage of the creative process.

Think about the path you must travel...

Take your time.

Focus past initial concerns… like what headline to write… or when your assignment is due.

Think of the target with your arrow in the center.

Now, describe your destination.

Think of themes.

And variations.

Start writing.

Go ahead.

We'll wait.

Once your thinking's organized, doing more ads is a lot easier.

Another Double Meaning Ad – With a Single-Minded Strategy. *This ad accomplishes its objective as tastefully as possible. The double meaning helps. To some people, this is important information. Their problem might not be your problem. Think target. Try to see the world through their eyes – not yours.*

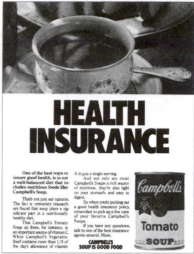

A SLIGHTLY NEW WAY OF THINKING ABOUT SOUP.
For a while, "Soup Is Good Food" revitalized Campbell's business.

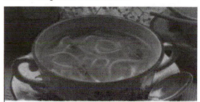

REPHRASE FAMILIAR PHRASES.
The gentle pun, replacing "Care" with "Fare," was a natural extension of Campbell's "Soup Is Good Food" campaign.

DOUBLE FEATURE.
FROM HONDA.

"Are you using the right car for your gasoline?" features a "verbal double" which takes a familiar phrase and turns it around to add double meaning.

The "Folds flat for easy storage" ad features a "visual double" where the double-meaning works off the visual.

Folds flat for easy storage.

AFTERWARDS, IT'S OBVIOUS.

Often, we see breakthrough work and we say, "Well, of course."

But before the awards and the sales results, it's not obvious at all.

5. DISORGANIZE YOUR THINKING.

As you write, you can almost double your output if you challenge yourself.

Is what you wrote right? What if it's the opposite?

Continually challenging your own writing can open up new opportunities and perspectives.

See what happens when you turn things inside out or upside down.

An example: "Got Milk?"

For years, nice ads talked about how good milk was for you. Year after year, the same basic message went out – and people got tired of it.

When the folks at Goodby took a look at the problem they found that the usual positive way of talking about milk was a yawn.

So they looked at it a new way. They asked a group of consumers to do without milk for a week and then come back and talk about it. Bingo!

Suddenly they found an interesting story.

There were some things where *you just had to have milk!* A peanut butter sandwich. Cookies.

Suddenly there was exciting new drama where before there had been only the same old story.

So, as you construct all those great thoughts and sensational sentences, see what happens when you deconstruct all of your good thinking.

Is there new perspective that can make the same old story slightly new again?

Or how about a new attitude? Like an upscale jewelry brand getting just a bit sassier.

New is good.

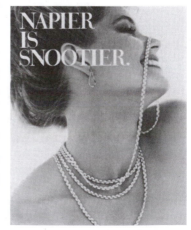

6. REORGANIZE YOUR THINKING.

Hey, if it were easy, anyone could do it.

And they wouldn't need you.

Good writing is based on good thinking.

By this time, a lot has been said. Try to figure out what is really and truly the most important thing.

This isn't easy. Sometimes, every time you turn around, someone has something new to say.

Often, very bright people can tell you the exact opposite of what the previous bright person just said.

Keep reprioritizing. What's most important? In advertising, you cannot say everything, just the most important things.

When in doubt, think target. Hey, even when you're not in doubt, think target. Try to see, read, and think through the consumer's point of view.

And, with that in mind, look again at what you wrote. What was important to you, the person who wrote it, might not be that important to the really important person – the one who's going to read it.

FRESH BUT LOGICAL.
The strategy said that Chevy's competitive advantage was freshness.

Ever heard fresh before?

Well, the challenge was to find a fresh way to say "fresh."

And the good folks at Goodby did it.

Simply. And memorably.

Fresh Mex.

Why Will They Buy Your Product in Preference to the Competition? For the brand, they'll need an emotional connection. For the product, they'll need a reason.

THIS SHOULD HAVE RUN LAST WEEK.

We're looking for a media buyer with at least 1½ years experience in television and print buying. If you're interested in placing ads rather than reading them, call David Cairns at 585-9992.

CHIAT/DAY

For the right person, this may be the most important ad in the magazine.

305

Theme &

HUNGRY? WHY WAIT?

A Simple Question
*can establish what your product
is all about.*

KILLS BUGS DEAD

A Simple Sentence
can do it all.

Built for the Human Race.

A Good Theme
usually makes a good outdoor board.

ALTOIDS
WINTERGREEN
THE CURIOUSLY STRONG MINTS

THE CURIOUSLY STRONG MINTS.
A good theme will usually work with, and
inspire, a variety of visuals.

MOST GREAT ADVERTISING CAMPAIGNS
have a great theme – a strong set of words that can
give your campaign a "War Cry."

An advertising theme, whether it's a campaign
line or a headline, will focus on the one thought
you want your target to remember.

And, for that reason, it should be *memorable.*

It should have that certain something that makes
it stick in the mind. Velcro!

By this time, you've probably written a few
early theme lines and headlines and copy lines.

Sometimes it's hard to know which is which.
Write it all down. . . everything.

Because the more you write, the better the
chance you'll be right. Imagine the destination.

Let the Strategy give your thoughts direction
and the Objective give you focus.

Try to think like the reader, not the writer.

Send your thoughts to the words that describe
the benefit. Or the Problem.

Think. How do you get their attention, and what
do you want them to remember?

Of all the things you've written, which of them
is the right thing?

You may write two dozen theme or headline
ideas (or more), yet you must end up with one.

How do you reach that goal?

How will you know you're right?

First, **it'll make sense.**

Second, **it'll feel right.**

Third, **someone else will like it.**

Fourth, **it will inspire more great ads.**

Let's try some variations on your theme.

Variations

TAKE YOUR THEME as your new starting point. If you have a good Selling Idea, there should be a natural flow of *variations*.

Look for the *structural relationships* that make the communication work.

Write 'em down. You may need 'em later when you present your idea.

Let your thinking flow. Go with it.

Write various variations on your ideas.

Try different possibilities.

See where they lead.

Turn them inside out and upside down.

Play with the ideas. Have fun. Be prolific.

Get it all on paper.

It won't be all good, but at this stage, it's more important to just write it all down.

This is one of the most enjoyable parts of our business. . . enjoy it.

Respect your first idea, but don't fall in love with it right away.

Write Down Everything You Can Think Of!

See what generates additional thoughts.

Write 'em down.

If you have time, sleep on it.

Utilize the right-brain incubation process.

When you're done, sort it out and take a look at what you've written.

When you're through, certain phrases and constructions will emerge.

Some things will work better than others.

And, without seeing a single sentence, I'll tell you the one single trait that will distinguish your best writing… *rhythm.*

"Betcha can't eat just one"

A Provocative Statement.
There are a lot of ways to ask it.

"I got my job through The New York Times."

Secretary at Consulate General

A Simple Statement.
It can be powerful and effective.

The world's greatest zoo is right under your nose.
San Diego Zoo

The world's greatest zoo is right under your nose.
San Diego Zoo

HOW DO YOU KNOW YOU'RE RIGHT?

First, it'll make sense.

Second, it'll feel right.

Third, someone else will like it.

Fourth, it will inspire more great advertising ideas.

GOOD COPY'S GOT RHYTHM.
1. Short, Simple Sentences.
2. Active Verbs and a Positive Attitude.
3. Parallel Construction.
4. Alliteration, Assonance, and Rhyme.
5. Puns, Double Meanings, and
   Word Play.

ONE. TWO. THREE.
Punch. Punch. Punch.
Easy to read and easy to understand.

ONE TWO. ONE TWO.
Feel the rhythm. Short and sweet.
Easy to read. Hard to beat.

In Fredericksburg you can sleep in a bed that's right out of the 18th or 19th century. You'll awaken to a delicious breakfast (go ahead and cheat on your diet—we won't tell). And you can spend the day looking for bargains in the more than 70 antique shops in our renowned historic district. Now wouldn't it be a crime to miss out on all of that?

For more information about our bed & breakfast selections or other get-away packages, call or write the Fredericksburg Visitor Center.

Fredericksburg, Virginia
706 Caroline Street, Box SP3, Fredericksburg, VA 22401. Phone 1-800-67VISIT

ONE MORE TIME.
All good copy's got rhythm.

Rhythm
ALL GOOD COPY'S GOT RHYTHM.

As a copywriter, your writing must *move* people – and much of it depends on the rhythm of your writing.

You should look for:

1. SHORT, SIMPLE SENTENCES.
Good copy gets to the point.

One idea follows another.

It keeps the reader's interest.

Not only does this force your copy to be easy to understand, it creates a tempo. Movement. Cadence.

As Leo said, *"Great advertising writing, either in print or TV, is always deceptively and disarmingly simple. It has the common touch without being or sounding patronizing."*

Winston Churchill said, *"Little words move men."*

Or, as Ed McCabe said, *"Show me something great and I'll show you a bunch of monosyllables."*

'Nuff said.

ED MCCABE'S MACHO STYLE.
Tough as a Volvo.

Hard-hitting and to the point.

Ed said, *"You Can't Eat Atmosphere."*

And *"It Takes a Tough Man to Make a Tender Chicken."*

308

2. ACTIVE VERBS AND A POSITIVE ATTITUDE.
Good copy should be written in the active voice.

It should *move.*

In most cases, you should write in a positive, and assertive manner. Upbeat.

Every sentence with a passive verb should be examined critically.*

So should every sentence that contains a negative.

In "comparison advertising" and certain types of positioning, it may be necessary to be negative.

Certainly, you can still be positive when you're being negative. Particularly if you're a bit po-mo.

But remember, Avis said, "We Try Harder."
And "We're Only #2."

They didn't say, "We're not #1."

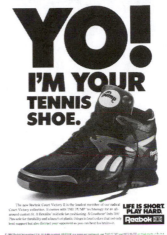

An Upbeat Attitude Can Help Make Products More Desirable. *We've shown this ad before, but it's worth looking at again. See what the attitude does. You just know you're going to have fun in these nifty new shoes from Reebok.*

A Good Slogan Should Make a Good Button.

Active verbs and a positive attitude.

* DID YOU CATCH THAT?
That sentence should probably read, "Examine every sentence with a passive verb." Or, better yet, "Get rid of every passive verb."

*"Make it simple
Make it memorable.
Make it inviting to look at.
Make it fun to read."*

Leo Burnett

**CONSTRUCTION
& JUXTAPOSITION.**
Note the use of parallel construction and juxtaposition to build strength and interest.
Bad/Good. Fish/Pig/Rose.

Drink like a fish.
Eat like a pig
Smell like a rose.

3. PARALLEL CONSTRUCTION.

Good copy is well built.

Your sentence structure should be consistent.

Your phrasing should be consistent.

Verbs should generally be in the same tense.

Pronouns should be kept under control.

Is it first person plural (we), second person (you), or third (he, she, they)?

Be consistent. Consistency creates clarity.

The structure of your thinking will be reinforced by the strength of structured writing.

The classic ad below builds power with a series of sentences using parallel construction.

There are lots of examples:

"Better Things for Better Living."

"The Quality Goes in Before the Name Goes On."

"It's a Good Time for the Great Taste."

"What You Want is What You Get."

Many memorable sentences and many memorable ads use parallel construction.

So should you.

Parallel construction builds the case and makes this ad work harder.

I laughed.
I cried.
I remodeled
my bathroom.

FREE. Call **1-800-524-9797**, ext. 751. A 32-page bathroom guidebook from American Standard overflowing with amazing facts, ideas and inspiration. For your copy, call or send this coupon to: American Standard, P.O. Box 90318, Richmond VA 23230-9031. *American Standard*

NAME _____

ADDRESS _____

CITY _____ STATE _____ ZIP _____ PHONE _____

When are you planning to start your project? _____ within 3 months _____ within 6 months _____ after 6 months

EASY TO READ. EASY TO UNDERSTAND.

The ad above accomplishes a lot with clear simple writing that connects with some emotional truths.

The first truth is that reading about your bathroom is probably pretty dull. Wink. Wink. Nudge. Nudge.

So this headline is actually a bit of a put-on.

But wait. You just read the whole thing (parallel construction pulled you through it), you smiled and sort of agreed with the writer, who probably cried about the current state of his or her bathroom.

See how the rhythm of the thing carried you into the sale? So that you ended up a lot more involved thinking about it than you'd planned.

So, did you fill out the coupon? Well, if this ad was really about you – someone due to remodel a bathroom, it sure made you think about it.

And, of course, there's always the 800#. In bold.

CLEAR CONSTRUCTION. CLEAR COMMUNICATION.

Not only is there a powerful visual demonstration (a hand on the cooktop), but the simplicity of the sentences makes it easy to understand this ad.

I don't know how an induction cook-top works (do you?), but easy-to-read writing makes me think I can.

And the parallel construction of the two headlines is the key.

This is the maid of fair renown
Who scrubs the floors of Spotless Town.
To find a speck when she is through
Would take a pair of specs or two,
And her employment isn't slow.
For she employs

SAPOLIO

The early epics of civilization were poems – so were many early ads.

Says Phoebe Snow.
About to go
Upon a trip
To Buffalo:
"My gown stays white
From morn till night
Upon the Road
of Anthracite"

Lackawanna
Railroad

SEN-SEN

CONFECTION

5¢

BREATH TAKING
REFRESHMENT

Dandy Candy
Keep It Handy

Reg. Trade Marks

JEEPERS CREEPERS, WHERE'D YOU GET YOUR BEEPERS?

4. ALLITERATION, ASSONANCE, AND RHYME.

Good copy sounds good.

You should make use of the phonetic characteristics of the words you use.

Alliteration – is the similarity of the first letter or sound of words, usually consonants.

For example, "Let It Be Lowenbrau" used a rhythmic double alliteration of the *L* and the *b* in "Lowenbrau."

This creates a distinctive theme that could be used by no other beer.

Assonance – is subtler. It relates to the internal similarity of words, usually vowels. "Invest in Karastan," has both assonance *and* alliteration.

Do you see which is which?

Rhyme.

Finally, rhyme has its reason.

A rhyme is memorable.

The early epics of civilization were poems for a very simple reason – they were easier to remember.

It was an oral tradition – poems could be passed along and remembered in a way prose could not.

For this same reason, a well-turned rhyme can nail your message in people's memories.

From   "Winston Tastes Good
         Like a Cigarette Should."
    (Sorry, I don't smoke, but it's in there.)

To   "Plop Plop Fizz Fizz
        Oh What a Relief It Is!"

The power of the poem is proven.
And it keeps your copy movin'.

Rhyming can make ordinary messages more fun and more interesting. Think about it.

None of the topics in these ads is that unique – a new nail polish, a bank loan, a fashion show, a cruise, an iced coffee, and a sauce that doesn't drip.

Yet, by using a strong and memorable rhyme, these messages get our attention – and they're easy to remember.

RHYME TIME!

"Rhyming forces recognition of words. You also establish a rhythm, and that tends to make kids want to go on.

If you break the rhythm, a child feels unfulfilled."

Dr. Seuss

"Dare to Compare"

NAUGHTY BUT NICE.

When this line was first proposed by copywriter Shirley Polykoff, the men in the room were troubled. Wouldn't women take it the wrong way? The provocative (for the time) line was one of the critical elements to Clairol's success.

TIMES CHANGE.

Once upon a time, people wouldn't think about talking about products this way. Then again, once upon a time, there was no such thing as a sports bra.

Double and Triple Meanings added extra power to this '60s ad for a Black "Anti-Machine" candidate in Chicago.

5. PUNS, DOUBLE MEANINGS, AND WORD PLAY.

Good copy is clever. Sometimes.

When these devices work, they can make your copy richer and more interesting.

And they're fun to write.

But, BEWARE!

When they don't work, they're confusing.

Worse yet, you're giving the reader an excuse to not take you seriously.

Puns are fun, and double meanings feel twice as nice, but don't be clever at the expense of clarity.

The pun is *not* the lowest form of humor.

The lowest form of humor is a smart-ass ad that wastes the client's money.

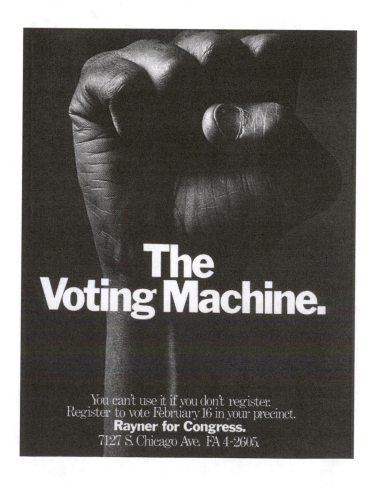

Mud and Guts. NISSAN

Outdoor is a great place for a play on words. People see it more than once.

HAIR TODAY.

Look at the fun you can have with some stock art, bright writing, and smart art direction. This campaign for a local hair salon won national awards.

A bad haircut is no laughing matter.
7 South 8th for Hair

A bad haircut can be a real nightmare.
7 South 8th for Hair

A bad haircut can make anyone look dumb.
7 South 8th for Hair

A bad haircut is a crying shame.
7 South 8th for Hair

This Week, We're Going Out On A Limb.
Pier 1 Imports

CLEVER BUT CLEAR.

The copywriter and art director made an ad for holiday ornaments at Pier 1 clever and appealing without sacrificing clarity. You see it. You get it.

A hard man is good to find.
SOLOFLEX
Weightlifting. Pure and Simple.

Ads like this helped build the Soloflex image. But infomercials sold them.

PUNS, DOUBLE-MEANINGS, AND WORD PLAY.

When they work well, they speak for themselves.

Take another look at the campaign on the left. Visual puns, using stock art of famous faces, give this hair stylist a distinct and inviting personality.

There was a clear strong strategic approach. They dramatized the Problem– a bad haircut – in a charming way.

The writer and art director earned a few national awards as well. – freelance work that paid off big.

315

TWO OUT OF THREE AIN'T BAD.

SAM SCALI
Inducted into the Art Director's
Hall of Fame, 1984

ED McCABE
Inducted into the Copy Hall of Fame,
1974

MARVIN SLOVES

All of us at Scali, McCabe, Sloves would like to congratulate Sam Scali on his induction into the Art Director's Hall of Fame.

We're very proud.

We're also proud of the fact that Sam is not alone. He joins his partner, Ed McCabe, who entered the Copy Hall of Fame in 1974.

And that makes Scali, McCabe, Sloves something very rare indeed: an advertising agency with two founding partners in the Hall of Fame.

Both of these men are advertising legends for good reason. Together, they have created some of the most renowned advertising of all time.

If you're interested in talking to a great art director or a great copywriter about your advertising, Sam and Ed aren't hard to find. They still come to work every day.

Or, if you'd like to talk to the person who does most of the talking for Sam and Ed, call Marvin.

There is, unfortunately, no such thing as a Management Hall of Fame.

But Marvin Sloves is a great reason for creating one.

SCALI, McCABE, SLOVES, INC.

800 Third Avenue, New York, N.Y. 10022 (212) 421-2050 Offices in: Houston, Melbourne, Montreal, Toronto, London, Düsseldorf, Mexico City

6. GOOD COPY VS. GOOD GRAMMAR.

In general, good copy is good English.

Copywriters are allowed three exceptions to the general rules of good grammar:

1. Sentence Fragments.

For effect and brevity, sentence fragments can often make copy better.

And clearer.

Overuse will create a choppy effect.

Like this.

Sentence fragments can strengthen and shorten your copy with no loss of communication.

2. Beginning a Sentence with a Conjunction.

Because we often write one-sentence paragraphs.

And because we often have more than one thing to say.

Or for some other reason. . .

The use of conjunctions or connectors at the beginning of sentences is acceptable.

But don't overdo it.

3. Ungrammatical Usage.

As Will Rogers said. . .

"A lot of people who don't say ain't ain't eatin."

English is a wonderfully flexible language.

New words and usages emerge constantly.

When used for effect, slang and/or bad grammar is permissible. Sometimes, it's desirable.

Contemporary copy should reflect contemporary usage, realizing that an ad targeted at teenagers might not please high-school English teachers. But this should be done with care.

Writers have a responsibility to treat our language with respect. After all, we make our living with it.

NOW WHAT?

After you've done all that, what do you do?

You do it again. That's *Re-Writin'*.

THINK DIFFERENT

Technically, the line should read Think Different*ly*.

But it wouldn't be as good.

First, it's not how people talk.

Second, the strategy for this campaign is to be *different*.

And, conforming to stuffy rules of grammar is, sorry to say, one of the things that makes the point.

The history of advertising is littered with English teachers' nightmares.

For years, there was a slogan "Winston Tastes Good, Like a Cigarette Should."

"Like a cigarette ought to" is better English – but not better advertising.

Then again, selling fewer cigarettes probably would have been a good thing.

DOUBLE MEANINGS.

Here, a common phrase does double duty as a headline that sort of says – assuming that we're thanking the cereal boxes, or maybe the people at Post Cereal – that the cereals are full of goodness.

Again, it's kind of questionable English – not exactly clear what is being said – but it's clear to us in a moment. And that's the point.

& ReWritin'

Be careful! That's Chivas Regal!

Bad poets borrow.
Great poets steal.
Copy by Tom McElligott

I was working on the
proof of one of my poems
all the morning,
and took out a comma.
In the afternoon
I put it back again.

Oscar Wilde

Q. How many account execs
does it take to change a
light bulb?

A. I'll get back to you on that.

HOW DO YOU REWRITE RIGHT?

Chances are, you've little experience with the amount of editing and rewriting practiced by copywriters.

But a few new habits can help get you started.

THE MORE THE BETTER.

Tom McElligott's been known to write 200 headlines before getting the one he likes.

How many did you write?

Did you look at them with a critical eye?

Then did you write a few more?

The first simple rule seems to be that the more you write, the better the final results seem to be.

TIGHTEN YOUR WRITIN'.

Next habit. Solid structure.

Does your ad have a beginning, middle, and end?

Did you "tell 'em what you're gonna tell 'em"?

Is it clear to the casual reader?

With many good ads, a casual glance will tell you what the ad is about at the same time you want to know more. You shouldn't have to dig. Dig?

Most openings are overwritten. (After all, you were just getting warmed up when you wrote it.)

You must condense and distill.

You must be interesting, involving, and informative. *Immediately!* Not eventually.

Get the most meaning into the fewest words.

Create a rhythm and try to hold to it.

As you move through the middle, think strategy.

Is there a reason to buy this product?

Do you help people connect with the brand?

Which sentences and phrases deliver the Support most clearly and persuasively?

Build on those. Cut the rest.

The end of your ad should wrap the package.

With a ribbon.

Reward the Reader. Ask for the Order.

Tell 'em what you told 'em.

DO IT AGAIN.

So far, so good. You've been tough, but fair.

Congratulations.

But it's not enough to be tough.

You gotta be brutal.

VISUALIZE YOUR COPY.

You need another new habit.

Visualizing your printed copy.

Not words on a page, but type in an ad.

As you write body copy, you should begin to have an idea of how your finished copy should look.

CHARACTER COUNT.

As you develop the layout, work with the art director to generate a rough "character count."

Here's how:

First, select the desired *type size.*

Type size is measured in "points."

This book is in 13 point type, "automatic" leading on this program, makes each line about 15.6 points.

This is 16 point. This is 12 point. This is 9 point. (Pretty small.)

Now look at the layout. Count the average number of letters on an average line and the number of lines.

A little math, and you've got your character count.

Set the margins on your word-processing program to the number of characters in each line and you'll start to see how your copy will fit.

Better yet, put the actual point-size on your screen – so you can really see what you're writing.

REQUIRED READING:

The Elements of Style by Strunk & White. Read this book.

Their Table of Contents provides a handy checklist and guide.

You should pay particular attention to sections on style and composition.

Rules like the following should become either memorized or instinctive:

• Choose a suitable design. Hold to it.
• Make the paragraph the unit of composition.
• Use the active voice.
• Put statements in positive form.
• Use definite, specific, concrete language.
• Omit needless words.
• Express coordinate ideas in similar form.
• Keep related words together.
• In summaries, keep to one tense.
• Place the emphatic words of a sentence at the end.
• Place yourself in the background.
• Write in a way that comes naturally.
• Write with nouns and verbs.
• Revise and rewrite.
• Do not overwrite.
• Do not overstate.
• Avoid the use of qualifiers.
• Do not affect a breezy manner.
• Use orthodox spelling.
• Do not explain too much.
• Do not construct awkward adverbs.
• Avoid fancy words.
• Be clear.
• And – use a dash to set off an abrupt break or interruption and to announce a… summary.

The book is a lesson in itself.

Every copywriter should own one.

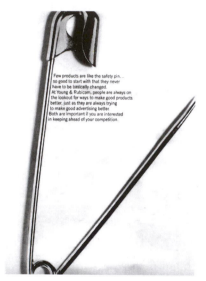

Few products are like the safety pin...
so good to start with that they never
have to be basically changed.
At Young & Rubicam, people are always on
the lookout for ways to make good products
better, just as they are always trying
to make good advertising better.
Both are important if you are interested
in keeping ahead of your competition.

PLAY IT SAFE.

You just wrote it.

Sure, it's perfect.

Look again – bet you can make it even more perfect.

The more you learn to polish your writing – which, when you get down to it, is simply re-writing – the better you'll be.

Another good thing will happen.

You will stop being so reluctant to rewrite your work.

You'll have taught yourself that doing it one more time makes it better.

Of course, you will have a brand new problem.

Knowing when to stop.

& ReWritin'...

IT'S POSSIBLE TO WRITE good copy to almost any length. Long or short.

Most beginning writers overwrite.

Except for the ones who underwrite.

That's why this next habit is so important.

FORGET WHO WROTE IT.

If you're going to become a good rewriter... *forget who wrote it!!!*

You must become as objective as possible about your own work.

We fall in love with our own words (I do it all the time), and failure to be objective and tough-minded in the rewriting stage can be your downfall.

Even though you wrote every one of those wonderful words, that doesn't mean someone else wants to read them all.

Even though it was tough to write it the first time, you can still make it better the second time.

And the third.

Try to look at your words through someone else's eyes. It's the start of really teaching yourself to write for others.

COPYWRITERS WHO MAKE THE CUT KNOW HOW TO CUT COPY.

Here's a thought from Bill Bernbach: *"You must have inventiveness, but it must be disciplined. Everything you write, everything on a page, every word, every graphic symbol, every shadow, should further the message you're trying to convey."*

He's right. Rewrite.

And though you love to write, the rest of the world doesn't have time to fall in love with every word.

Someone has to cut the copy.

Let it be you.

As a final bit of cruelty, take a look at the part you like best, the part you really didn't want to cut.

It's often a piece of "business" or *"schtick"** used for extra entertainment, interest, or attention.

Your piece of "business" may be:

• A joke in the headline paid off in the body copy
• A joke in a TV commercial that's set up at the front and paid off at the back**
• A running gag in a vignette sequence
• Humorous background action in a TV spot
• A clever turn of phrase
• Etcetera

Remember, the objective of your ad's "business" is to help your client's business.

Bernbach observed, *"Creativity that doesn't reinforce the proposition in an ad or commercial isn't creative, it's* disruptive."

So take a look at your ad one more time.

Is it as strong and persuasive as you can make it?

How will it help your client's business?

Ask yourself these questions now. Someone else will surely ask them later.

If you can answer these questions satisfactorily, you're in business.

Though taste and writing habits may vary, these are the underlying principles of good copywriting style: *Readin', Writin', Rhythm, 'n ReWritin'.*

Review your work and your work habits.
And never stop.
Learn to cut your copy!
Be your own toughest critic.
Shorter *is* better.
Less verbal. More *visual.*

In conclusion…

write tight.

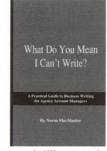

WE REPEAT.

Here's a little book we publish for business writing.

Pick up a copy. Couldn't hurt.

It's all about how to write those business documents – like the memo that provides support for your brilliant creative idea.

A Warning.

Business writing is different.

At a certain point in my career I found myself writing positioning memos and field marketing guides. The pay was good, but my wife noted that my writing had changed a bit.

She was right. I had to consciously shift gears to get back in the other groove.

Good News.

The good news is if you're good at writing creative, you're often pretty good at writing documents like positioning memos. And the pay is good.

So pick up a copy – just in case.

And next time somebody needs solid writing to support your idea – hey, it might be you.

*

In the '60s, the Yiddish vaudeville term *schtick* was commonly used by copywriters. (Groucho Marx's cigar and eyebrow wiggle were his *schtick.*)

In advertising, *schtick* refers to a wide range of devices, both good and bad.

**

The final clever line at the end was also sometimes known as the *clitchik.*

Typing & Typography

To improve your print writing,
widen the margins and narrow the
measure on your computer's word-
processing program.

Too many copywriters write with
narrow margins and wide lines.

That may be fine for letters,
novels, and term papers.

But it's <u>not</u> the way to write copy.

A column of advertising copy is
usually 30 to 50 characters wide.

(40 is a good place to start.)

You'll notice that many of your
sentences break in the middle of
important phrases.

As you rewrite your copy, <u>adjust</u>
the words and phrases so that copy
"breaks" naturally.

If possible, "lines should be broken
the way they are spoken."

If the layout is in process, your
art director can give you an estimated character count.

To create readable copy, you must
make your copy relate to the page.

And to get it right, you need to
work with the art director.

It's a team sport, remember?

Historical Note: *This is part of a* <u>*typewriter!*</u> *These machines were still being used when this book was first written.*

TYPE & LAYOUT
by Colin Wheildon.

We really really like this book. In fact, I think I've purchased two dozen. I give them to writers and art directors.

Wheildon is an Australian art director who has spent a good bit of time studying readability.

Introduction by David Ogilvy.

Get this book. Read it. Use it.

Exercises:

1. RESET THE MEASURE ON YOUR WORD-PROCESSING PROGRAM TO BETWEEN 30 AND 50 CHARACTERS.

2. READ A TYPE BOOK.

3. PICK UP A MAGAZINE YOU CAN SPARE. TEAR IT APART.
PICK THE TYPOGRAPHY YOU LIKE BEST. PICK THE ADS THAT ARE EASIEST TO READ. PICK THE MOST INTERESTING. PICK THE THREE WORST, TYPOGRAPHICALLY.

4. PREPARE A PRESENTATION ON THE TYPOGRAPHY THAT YOU LIKE THE BEST.

Ready to write? Good.
You've got a lot of op-
portunities coming up – to
put principles to work – in
print.

Effective Surprise! *That's what you want*
to create on behalf of your brand.

Print Principles

THERE SEEMS TO BE A SHORTAGE of good print copywriters in this electronic media age.

Yet, print is the easiest medium to master.

It's relatively simple to produce.

There's a lot of it that needs doing.

And, it holds still.

Some books focus on types of headlines, or types of appeals. This book focuses on types of print *ads*.

Headlines and appeals will vary due to strategy and circumstance, but the underlying *structure* of print ads has remained fairly constant.

As far as this book is concerned, there are six basic types of print ad structures:

1. One-Liners & Banners
2. News (Including Demos)
3. The Spiral
4. The Story
5. The Sermon
6. The Outline

And, of course, combinations of these.

Some may think there are more than six types and some may think there are fewer. (For example, ads that work and ads that don't.)

But you'll find this approach quite comprehensive.

You should try to become familiar with these types of ads and be able to write them as needed.

Remember, every good ad has a *structure*.

And there's more than one way to write one.

A. One-Liners & Banners

IT'S THE ESSENCE of the message.

One simple statement that says it all.

This is generally the best way to start writing on a project. And the most challenging.

Whether it's a theme line, headline, poster, outdoor board, or caption, this is the test of great copywriting.

Remember, let the visual do as much of the work.

The Double at Work. *Turning around a familiar phrase freshens the message.*

The Two-Liner. *Sometimes your One-Liner needs an answer.*

Classic.
This One-Liner by Hall of Fame copywriter Ed McCabe positioned the Horn & Hardart restaurants.
The theme?
"It's not fancy. But it's good."

Face It. *Faces can say a lot about the benefits of your product and the personality of your brand.*

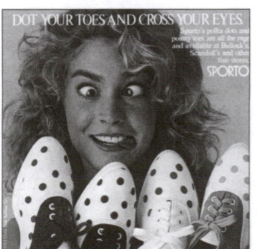

We Love This Ad.
"Dot Your Toes and Cross Your Eyes." We can't read the copy. We don't care. Do you?
The writer and the art director (and the model) teamed up to capture the spirit of these Sporto shoes.

BURMA-SHAVE.

Before there were banner ads, there was Burma-Shave.

A BEARD

It was shaving cream. But more important than that, they had an advertising campaign that was uniquely memorable

THAT'S ROUGH

– as long as you were in the habit of driving down country roads between 1925 and 1963.

AND OVERGROWN

Typically, six consecutive small billboards would be posted along the edge of highways, spaced so they could be read consecutively by motorists driving by. The last sign was the name of the product.

IS BETTER THAN

You can see how it works.

The idea didn't survive the shift to an Interstate Highway system – the media buy worked best on smaller highways.

A CHAPERONE

As we migrate to the Information Highway, it might be time to try it again. See if you can make it work for some of your current products.

Burma-Shave

GOODYEAR HITS THE INFORMATION HIGHWAY.

On a roll with award-winning banner ads in various sizes.

They advertise tire sales and help you find a Goodyear Dealer.

Simple and hard-working. With and without the blimp.

BANNERS.

You see them all the time – animated outdoor boards on your computer screen.

Now they're getting super-sized.

There are also three new types:

Fixed Panel. These look like part of the panel and scroll up and down.

XXL Box. You can turn pages inside them.

Pushdown. This opens up to display a larger ad. This seems like a good idea; the message stays out of the way unless someone is interested.

But, whatever format you use, there is something more important – creating a message that someone would actually want to open.

That's the real challenge of the Banner Ad.

It's one thing to do a clever "one-liner" print ad that amuses as you turn the page, or that catches your eye for a moment on a billboard as you drive by.

But it's tough to motivate a click through.

Naturally, it's going to help if you're advertising something that people are interested in, but, even so, we take a pass on a lot of things in which we have marginal interest.

Let's think about how we can improve on banner ads as we do this next set of exercises.

TV COMMERCIAL
SPECIAL FINANCING
FIND A RETAILER

GOODYEAR.
Get there

LEAVE ROOM FOR THE MOUSE. Successful interactivity demands involvement. As they say, "when designing a mousetrap, leave room for the mouse."

Here, CP+B has a little fun and lets you play with the Rabbit.

Type a word and something fun happens. Breed. Jump. Hop. Honk. Etc.

The key is building an engaging narrative that promotes the brand and invites involvement.

_____ **like a Rabbit.**

(Write on the line to play with the Rabbit)

submit →

 Breed your own rabbit

✕ CLOSE

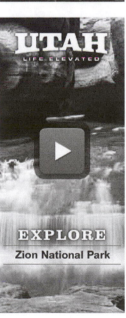

OUTSIDE THE BOX. Click on the arrow and an office worker "escapes" his box and explores the wide-open beauty of Utah.

Extra dimensionality and entertainment result from taking the standard designs of the web and adding a dimension of humor and narrative.

It's all more involving when you can add story value.

327

CARAMEL KNOWLEDGE

Famous Faces make you look good. It's one way brands get famous.

FACE VALUE.

People look at faces.

This is a powerful and natural human instinct.

We almost can't help ourselves.

There's a simple, basic reason – we look back at ads that look at us. It's instinctive.

Got a great face? You're on your way to a great ad.

We repeat. People look at faces – famous or otherwise.

PEOPLE OR PRODUCT? OR BOTH?

There's no rule. Great advertising has been done with people, and great advertising has been done with "product as hero," like the ad below.

But there's one thing both kinds of ads have in common – the visuals do such a strong job, you don't have to say a lot.

You look. You like it.

Be careful! That's Chivas Regal!

ONE OF THE DRAB HOMEBODIES
WHO READS McCALL'S.

A face is like a work of art.
It deserves a great frame.

Looking for an Edge? One easy answer is to get "edgy" looking people.

The European Tradition. *Posters have always been a more important medium. Here, a bilingual play on words for longtime advertiser Perrier.*

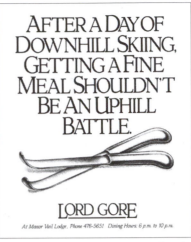

Double-Meaning Visuals. *Remember the Horn and Hardart ad two pages back? Here's an upscale version for a restaurant near a ski resort.*

The American Tradition. *Point of Purchase – like bank posters. Never miss an opportunity to build your brand.*

Get 'Em Quick! *With writing and visuals that communicate instantly.*

Strong visuals *make copy stronger.*

Simple ideas *work best.*

Produce Posters. How can you sell more fruits or vegetables at the point of sale?

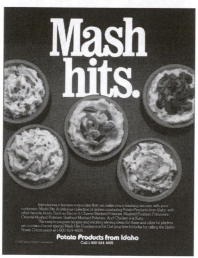

News Flash:
You Have an Agency

CONGRATULATIONS!

Here are your four clients:

1. DENTAL FLOSS. Johnson & Johnson or a brand you invent. (Background on next page.)

The Benefit. Flossing removes plaque from teeth and prevents gum disease.

The Problem. Unpleasant and inconvenient.

The Target. People with teeth (30+).

2. A FRUIT OR VEGETABLE. Pick your own. Advertise them generically ("carrots"), or give them a brand name ("UpDoc Carrots").

You should probably do a little background research on your chosen fruit or vegetable.

The Objective. Increase consumption.

First Assignment. In-store poster.

3. A SERVICE. You may choose either:

Individual professional – accountant, doctor, etc.

Service organization – health, financial, etc.

Other service jobs – babysitters, barbers, bartenders – maybe a unique service company (lawn care).

First Assignment. Bus bench back.

4. AN EXISTING BRAND.

Pick a product you can buy in a store.

Buy it. Use it. Write ads for it.

List: Objective, Benefit, Target, and Problem.

First Assignment. Do in-store poster or "shelf talker." Can it be an outdoor board, too?

5. BE SURE TO WRITE A STRATEGY FOR EACH.

Use a consistent Strategy format.

#23: One-Liners & Banners

NOW, let's do some writing…

6. WRITE A THEME AND A ONE-LINER FOR EACH OF YOUR CLIENTS.

Stick to the Strategy. Think Target.

Banner Bonus: Write and Design (simply) a Banner Ad that encourages involvement with each of your "clients."

7. WRITE A FEW MORE.

Remember, the more you have to choose from, the better your final selection will be.

Banner Bonus: Now try involving your client in a more amusing and light-hearted way

8. WRITE VISUALLY!

You've probably been writing a lot of words.

Most of the ads you've seen in this chapter have had a strong visual.

Try to think of the visual first. Find it or draw it.

Look at it. Think.

See what happens.

Banner Bonus: Sketch an involving visual for a banner for each product. It can be a game, limited animation, whatever. Then, after you've done the visual, write some words.

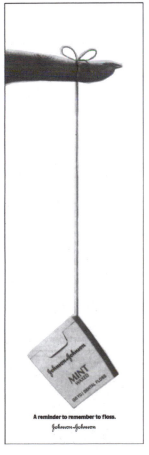

A reminder to remember to floss.
Johnson-Johnson

BACKGROUND: Dental Floss.

Flossing removes plaque (a constantly forming thin, sticky, colorless film containing harmful bacteria) and food particles from between teeth and under the gumline – where a toothbrush can't reach.

Tooth decay and periodontal disease often start in these areas.

How to Floss.

1. Break off about 18 inches of floss and wind most of it around one of your middle fingers.

2. Wind remaining floss around the same finger of the opposite hand. This finger will "take up" floss as it's used.

3. Hold tightly between thumbs and forefingers, about an inch of floss between them. No slack. Use a gentle sawing motion. Guide floss between teeth. Never "snap" floss into gums.

4. When floss reaches the gumline, gently slide it into the space between the gum and the tooth.

5. Hold floss tightly against the tooth. Gently scrape the side of the tooth, moving the floss away from the gum.

6. Repeat. Don't forget the back side of your last tooth.

Flossing Hints.

• Establish a regular pattern and time.

• Think of your mouth as having four sections. Floss half the upper teeth, then the other half. Do the same for your lower teeth.

• If you don't have good finger dexterity, you may find a commercial floss holder helpful.

• Ask your dentist for advice.

• Most children cannot floss their own teeth until about age 10. Even then, flossing should be supervised.

• Improper flossing may injure gums. Be gentle.

• Your gums may bleed and be sore the first five or six days. As plaque breaks up and bacteria are removed, your gums will heal and bleeding will stop.

• Flossing can improve your breath – as it removes the bacteria in plaque.

Continuity, Frequency, Loyalty. Promotions like this one, where Pepsi drinkers save and redeem points for branded products and other prizes, can be successful for certain "badge" brands. This type of program depends on a product that is used frequently. Do any of your brands have the potential for a loyalty program?

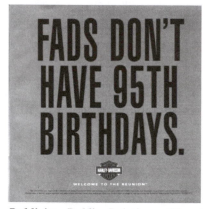

Publicity, Public Relations, Direct Marketing, and Event Marketing. Here, Harley-Davidson turns their 95th Anniversary into a Big Event – with lots of PR, direct marketing involving their current customers, and an event that's newsworthy. When it's a strong brand and a strong idea, it can all work together.

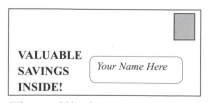

What would it take to get you to open the envelope? Think about it. And now start paying attention to the mail you get.

#24: Congratulations! Your Agency Just Grew

SUDDENLY your ad agency has been asked to perform additional marketing services functions – everything, in fact, in The MarCom Matrix.

You really don't have the experience, but your agency needs the extra income and you don't want a competitor providing the service. So you say yes.

You might want to skip ahead to sections that talk about these specific areas, but, like so many things these days, your client isn't giving you much time.

So, here's what you have to do:

1. CREATE PROMOTIONAL EVENTS.

Do it for each of your brands.

The objective is to increase (promote) sales.

First, think about the behavior that will do that. Then develop a theme for your promotion that provides a call to action for that behavior.

For example, your theme could go on a display, a T-shirt, button, bumper sticker, or coupon ad.

If possible, try to build some brand equity with your promotion – all in one to five words.

2. PUBLICITY AND PUBLIC RELATIONS.

All of your clients want to be in the news. How will you do it?

Think of a tactic (there's a list on the opposite page). Write a lead sentence for a press release that goes with that tactic.

If you want to think about this some more, read the tactics list again and skip ahead to Chapter Nineteen.

3. DIRECT MARKETING.

Each of your clients has two lists. One of current customers and another of people very much like their current customers.

All they need right now is a headline (a one-liner?) to put on the outside of their envelopes.

Can you do it?

5. EVENT MARKETING.

Well, can you turn any of your ideas into an event?

In a pinch, you can try a Grand Opening or an Anniversary. But work to develop something that really connects with your brand.

And don't forget "cause marketing." Maybe there's a program, like Children's Miracle Network or a local sports team, where you can connect your brand with an existing event or series of events.

6. NEW MEDIA.

OK, each of your clients probably needs a website. But they probably have different needs.

Here's what you have to do.

A. Name the .com site – assume that their name has already been taken or is being used for something else, like corporate communications.

B. State the basic objective. In one simple, easy-to-understand sentence, state the basic purpose of each of your clients' websites.

HELPFUL HINT.

Remember the Domino's example from the end of Chapter Four? You might want to take another look if you don't remember (it's on p. 134).

That example shows you how you can develop one basic idea through all these forms of Marketing Communications.

HERE ARE THE MOST POPULAR TYPES OF MARKETING PUBLIC RELATIONS TACTICS:

Here are thought-starters – A to Z – from Thomas L. Harris, co-founder of Golin-Harris:

Awards – for example, "Best-Dressed" for a fashion marketer.

Books – like Campbell's recipes.

Contests – an opportunity for more product involvement – like a Bake-Off.

Demonstrations – can you present product "demos" in an interesting way?

Events – yours or someone else's.

Festivals – ditto.

Grand Openings – Great for retailers. Remodeling? It's a Grand Re-Opening!

Holidays – can you tie-in with a day (or month or week) or create your own?

Interviews – do you have a spokesperson who can make media appearances?

"Junkets" – is there a reason to bring the press to you? A fancy press tour?

Key Issues – can your brand connect with or support an issue or worthy cause?

Luncheons – feed 'em and pitch 'em.

Museums & Memorabilia – does your brand have a history? Publicize it.

Newsletters – these can double as direct mail to a variety of "publics."

Official Endorsements – does someone famous like your brand? Could they?

Product Placement – can put your brand in a movie or TV show.

Questionnaires – do a survey. Then, publicize the results. Think about it.

Radio – "Trade for Mention" contests.

Sampling – look for opportunities

"Thons" – marathons, walkathons, etc. link brands to worthy causes.

Underwriting – sponsorship of events

Vehicles – cars, trucks, hot-air balloons.

"VNR" – this stands for Video News Release. We'll talk about these later.

Weeks – like a holiday, only longer.

eXpert Columns – written by real (or invented) spokespersons.

Youth Programs – kids, teens, babies.

"Zone" Programs – target local areas.

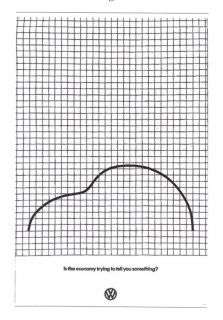

Or buy a Volkswagen.

Volkswagen Used the News. Bill Bernbach believed advertising should be "sociological," in tune with current events, reinforcing the feeling that the product was also in touch with the times. Above, an ad that tied into a gas shortage. Below, an ad that commented on a dismal economic picture. VW was even able to turn bad news into good news.

Is the economy trying to tell you something?

B. News &

It's ugly, but it gets you there.

PEOPLE READ PRINT for new information.

An ad that seems to contain worthwhile new information is more likely to be read.

New information is usually a good reason to run an ad, whether it's a new product or new price. Yet, most retailers have sales, new products and/or product improvements.

The copywriter's challenge is to make product news more than the same old story.

The day after man landed on the moon, an ad appeared with a photo of the moon lander.

The ad was from good old Volkswagen and it said simply, "It's ugly, but it gets you there."

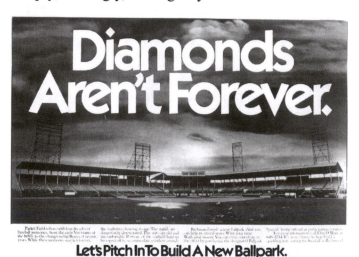

Diamonds Aren't Forever.

Let's Pitch In To Build A New Ballpark.

The Home Field Advantage. When you can connect with something of local importance, your message also gains in importance.

Keeping It New

With all the options that new media provides, and the general shortening of attention spans, keeping messages fresh is a full-time job.

Let's review some of the ways we can do this.

- Connect your brand with the news – like the VW examples.
- Connect your brand with contemporary trends and culture – this is used by a lot of brands, particularly those that connect with youth culture and fashion.

Some, like Benneton, have had some luck connecting with controversy. CP+B (remember their "brief?") looks for "social tension."

OK, here's another way to keep it new.

Howard Gossage's "J-Trick"

That's what I call it. Instead of the usual create-the-whole-campaign approach which is pretty much an industry standard, Howard would create a campaign that would generate its own news.

He used a "journalistic" approach.

How'd he do that? Good question.

First, he'd make some sort of announcement – often it was a contest, but it might be something else – a plan to color tire air, a weird premium offer (like Beethoven sweat shirts for a classical radio station and Rainier Ale).

Ad #2 would be about the reaction to ad #1 – and, to some extent, the ad would feel like reporting the news. The contest winner. The response to the weird offer. Etcetera.

Then, he'd look for something else to validate the response. In two instances, he created books that contained the responses to his ads.

Can You Make Your Advertising Make News? *Above, a British glue creates a series of messages that stick in your memory. Below, a carpet store connects a news story (a Russian border dispute), with their products to freshen the message for their carpet sale.*

SOCIAL TENSION

An early adopter of controversy as a strategic differentiator, Benneton's "United Colors of Benneton" campaign highlights topics such as racial diversity to make a fashion statement by making a social statement.

MAKING NEWS & MAKING IT FLY.

Gossage was hired by *Scientific American* to increase their advertising lineage.

Research showed that their readers took a lot of airplane trips.

So, without being very direct about it, he developed a campaign that would get them airline advertising.

Any increase would be dramatic, since they had none.

He announced the *Scientific American* Paper Airplane contest, using his journalistic and opportunistic instincts and the pseudo-scientific observation that the newly developed SSTs looked a bit like paper airplanes.

The first ad was a media sensation.

It ran only once in the *New Yorker* and *New York Times*, but it was covered on the nightly news and numerous other print media. For free.

By the end of the first day, *Scientific American* had two airline accounts.

The second ad, in typical Gossage fashion, advertised the judging of the contest and that was it. Except, of course,

THE GREAT INTERNATIONAL PAPER AIRPLANE BOOK

for the best-selling book that resulted. It's still available on Amazon – over 30 years later.

Dear Miss Afflerbach, which was the collected responses to Eagle Shirt ads (co-authored by the client), and *The Great International Paper Airplane Book*, which is probably still available.

Howard did this trick when all you had was ads and coupons – with all the interactive tools available in New Media, he would have had fun.

So now let's talk about New Media Extensions to "keep it new."

KEEPING IT NEW IN NEW MEDIA. The first guideline I'd use is another of Howard Gossage's favorite quotes, "*when designing a mousetrap, leave room for the mouse.*"

What that means is we can't just fill up a corner of the messaging with what we want to say.

We need to find some way to involve the person on the other side of the page… or the computer screen. How do we do this?

Blogs, for example, invite additional comment. Games invite their own kind of involvement. Getting valuable stuff for free? It still works.

Hey, you're smart, and you've probably spent more time online than I have. Have a few ideas.

We'll add them to the next exercise. If you want to share them with me – copywork@aol.com.

How much news is there in a car payment? A writer and art director teamed up to turn an ordinary monthly payment into some breakthrough advertising.

336

Demonstration Makes It News

Try to find a way to demonstrate your advantage.

Got something to say? *Show it!*

As far as this book is concerned, anything that demonstrates something is called a "Demo."

There are different kinds of Demos:

- There are *side-by-side* demos.
- There are *product usage* demos.
- There are *problem* demos.
- And more, as we will demonstrate.

The Claim. *Each of these ads seems to demonstrate by making a claim in a dramatic fashion. Above, a simple fact becomes more powerful with strong art direction and writing. Below,* the media itself *serves as the demonstration.*

Advertise Your Advantage. *Here's a side-by-side demo for house paint. Again,* visual reinforcement. *Saying it is fine. Showing it is better.*

This ad will self destruct in 5 minutes.

The life span of this ad is directly proportionate to your attention span for this page. But an ad in the Yellow Pages puts your name at peoples fingertips day and night, 365 days a year, in 96% of all homes and businesses.

Which goes to show that the secret to long-living advertising may not be so much a function of what you say, or how you say it, but where you say it.

The Yellow Pages. They never stop selling.

Pacific Northwest Bell

Dramatize the Problem. Dramatize the Benefit. *It's sort of a "before and after" demo for a small piece of exercise equipment. The choice of media space — a nice wide horizontal format — helped dramatize the message. Want to do a good Demo? It's all in knowing how to handle it.*

"Rams move to St.Louis; pick up new receiver."

Hello.
Southwestern Bell Telephone

New Information. *A new pro football team coming to town provides an opportunity for St. Louis advertisers.*

Irony and Sarcasm. They're not always appropriate, but under the right circumstances, with the right message, they can be very powerful.

Danger Brings Drama. With the right words, even a quiet photograph can be dramatic and dangerous.

THE "GOOD DEED" DEMO.

When you're demonstrating for someone else's good, you generally generate a positive attitude.

You demonstrate that you're the "Good Guy."

When you demonstrate for a worthy cause, the result can be extremely powerful – and you can generate some of the same feelings with something as simple as baby clothes.

What's more, links to new media can add movement and more to your demonstration.

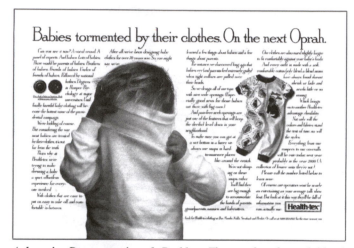

A charming Demonstration of a Problem. The actual product – children's clothes – isn't that unique. Nor are the benefits dramatic – reinforced knees and clothes you can get on and off more easily. Here, charming visual demonstration adds drama in a humorous way.

TURN OLD NEWS INTO NEW NEWS.

When you can make something old feel like something new, that's effective surprise.

This classic tourism ad takes centuries-old product features and makes them fresh.

ANTICIPATE THE NEWS.

Avis is ready for the winner of a tennis tournament – whoever that winner is.

TURNING BAD NEWS INTO OPPORTUNITY.

Here, Jif makes the best of a difficult situation – telling consumers that their brand is safe. Very straightforward. Not a time to be cute or clever.

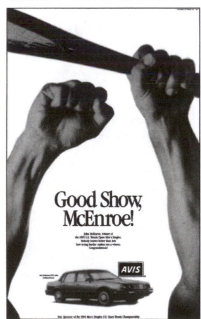

NEWS ADDS VALUE.

Ads like this also help the brand leverage the value of sponsorship. You know they were a sponsor, even if you didn't watch the event.

*Some News Doesn't Last. But if it's part
of a long-term campaign, it can still do a
good job of building the brand.*

This week, the teams driven
to be number one
are driving Number One.

*Ads that Connect with the News. First,
Hertz leverages Super Bowl sponsorship
with a "salute" ad that congratulates
Hertz for being Number One as much as it
salutes the two top teams. And, of course,
Hertz had two more ads ready, so that the
day after the Super Bowl…*

HOW LONG CAN NEWS BE NEW?
Legally, you can only say "new" for six months,
but this ad for Maxwell House Coffee ran for over
two years. How'd they do that?

Note how the writer generated a feeling of news
and excitement with a rational copy story, yet
never used the word "new."

This is very much a Hopkins-style ad.

Guess who did it? (Answer: Ogilvy's agency.)

By the way, do you know who first used the phrase,
"Good to the Last Drop"? Teddy Roosevelt!

Now let's see if we can make news in a more
modern setting.

#25: Make it News

1. MAKE "NEWS" FOR EACH OF YOUR FOUR PRODUCTS (FROM ASSIGNMENT 11).

Write at least one ad for each product:

A. At least one should feature *product news.*

B. At least one should use a *demo.*

What kind of Demo is it?

C. One should relate to a *current event.*

2. FOR ONE OF YOUR PRODUCTS, CREATE THREE DIFFERENT DEMOS.

Describe them in a short paragraph or try to *visualize* them with a sketch and a caption.

EXTRA! EXTRA!
READ ALL ABOUT IT!

3. NEWS STORY.

Grab a news story from this week's news.

Then, figure out a way to turn it into an ad for some product involved in or related to the news story. (It doesn't have to be one of your current products, but if it is, that's even better.)

4. TESTIMONIAL.

Create a unique *testimonial* using a famous personality of your choice.

5. PRICE NEWS.

Write a *sale* or *coupon* ad for one of your products. Make it feel exciting.

6. GOOD DEED DEMO.

Do a *"Good Deed"* Demo.

Use a current client or, if necessary, select another product, service, or worthy cause that you can "tie-in" with your client.

… this ad ran. With News that reinforced their long-term brand position. Now, Hertz further leveraged their Super Bowl sponsorship with a "salute" to the #1 team. And, of course, this further reinforced their #1 position.

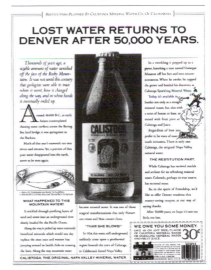

Late-breaking Product News. Here, a humorous attitude combined with a lot of product facts, creates news over a simple product introduction – California bottled water now available in Denver.

Shoes in the News. *Can you find a way to dramatize your product's benefits in the real world? And then, do an ad that tells the world about it.*

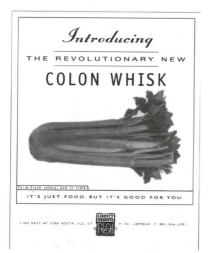

Vegetables Are Good for You. *This isn't exactly news – even if there's a new study that proves it. Think about it. How are you going to get people to eat their vegetables?*

#26: Wanted: More News

IT DOESN'T STOP. Your client is so pleased with your ad agency's work that he has… guess what?

Right. More work.

Now, we need to work a little harder to develop work that's even more newsworthy.

Here are a few more things you need to do:

1. CREATE A REALLY GREAT BILLBOARD.

One of your brands has secured the main billboard in town. It's big. And everyone sees it.

What are you going to do with that billboard?

And then, how can you leverage that billboard into something special? To help get you thinking, or should we say, "to help you use your noodle," here's a little integrated event Campbell's put together.

2. GOOD NEWS. A NEW STUDY SHOWS THAT YOUR VEGETABLE (OR FRUIT) _____.

Fill in the blank with a health benefit.

How will you dramatize this great news?

The budget will let you do a news release, a newspaper ad, and a local sports celebrity has agreed to pose with your vegetable or fruit.

Create a photo opportunity.

3. WANTED! A NEWSWORTHY PROMOTION.

Your clients just went to an all-day seminar. In the morning, they heard a speaker talk about how promotions can increase sales.

And, in the afternoon, they heard another speaker talk about how Marketing Public Relations (MPR) can generate lots of free publicity.

Now they want you to do it.

Create a promotional theme, write an ad that feels like "news," indicate at least three possible MPR ideas (don't forget to look at that MPR list on page 333), and write the "lead" for your press release.

4. YOW! YOUR SERVICE NEEDS A NEW DIRECT MARKETING CAMPAIGN. FAST AND CHEAP!

Suddenly, the budget can't afford those nice letters and envelopes, but they can afford postcards.

Create a cool postcard with an offer that will bring in new customers from the nearby area.

5. AN INVITATION TO EVENT MARKETING.

Two of your clients need to do booths for a trade show. Write a theme.

They're each having a very nice cocktail party on the first night of the convention (Monday). Write and design a cool invitation that will go to their best customers. (If you need more information on the convention, look up the trade group this client might belong to and find out about their convention. It's usually listed on their website.)

6. NEW MEDIA NEWS. AN E-MAIL PRESS RELEASE.

I know, I know, we all hate "Spam." But you can write an e-mail that people will click on.

What will you say in the message box?

How will you make your e-mail interesting.

And, where will readers go when they click to find out more – or do something cool.

How About a Cool Postcard for Your Service? That's one of the most cost-effective ways to send your message through the mail. But, of course, there better be a good offer on the back of the postcard, too.

The Trade and the Sales Force. A brand like Lee knows that they're a big part of successful marketing. Which is the most important secondary target for your product? For example, with dental floss, it would be dentists and dental hygienists.

343

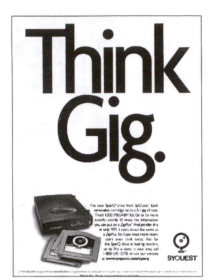

THE HEADLINE SAYS IT ALL.
And, at the same time, it makes you want to know more. Basically, the copy repeats the premise in the headline.

If it's long copy, it keeps building, using good writing and strong Support to hold your interest.

A SPIRAL OFTEN STARTS WITH AN INTERESTING VISUAL.
Then, they follow it up with interesting copy. On the right, similar visuals dramatize the subject matter – the copy gets quickly to the point.

In one case, a health care provider wants to help you "stand up to osteoporosis."

In the other, a furniture retailer – features prices on orthopedic furniture "that won't break your back."

Bright writing. Front to back.

Even the media buy – a long skinny ad – helps reinforce the subject matter.

C. The Spiral

THIS COPY FORMAT expands the information as it goes along. It says it. Then it says it at greater length.

The Spiral is very flexible – from headline to end-line, the story is stated and restated.

This approach is based on traditional newswriting principles. Reporters never knew where the editor would cut the story.

Copywriters never know when you'll stop reading.

The key is to repeat yourself without seeming to repeat yourself.

First, your headline makes the point, and then the copy makes the point again.

And then you sum it up.

But you need to keep adding something new – to keep it interesting.

This section was a Spiral.

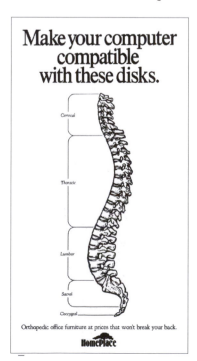

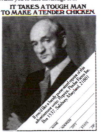

SAYING THE SAME THING OVER AND OVER AND OVER DOESN'T HAVE TO BE BORING.

Frank Perdue's agency helped him be interesting about chickens.

When you get right down to it, you get the point of the ad with the headline. Buy Perdue Chickens – Don't Get "Plucked."

But it keeps on going.

They tell you about this.

They tell you about that.

Guess what? They have good chickens – and they're a good value.

And maybe you learned something.

If so, good. Part of the point of the ad was that Frank Perdue had a lot to say about chickens.

And you got that point – whether you read the ad or not.

Bright, insightful writing can make the point and still make you want to read more. Here, a lovely ad for a jeweler.

SOMETIMES SAYING IT ONCE IS ENOUGH.

Here, a local hospital uses a bus card to announce a new service – or, rather, the return of something that doctors don't do much any more.

You see it. You get it. Take one.

The Counterfeit Mailbag.

The secret thoughts of an entire country were carried in leather bags exactly like this one. Except this one, a copy, isn't under lock and key in a museum. It's for sale.

I borrowed an original from a friend, a retired mailman who, like thousands before him, was kind enough to test it out, for years, on the tree-lined streets of small towns everywhere. Before you were born.

The test was successful; even though discontinued, it can't be improved upon. It's simply perfect as a device for carrying important ideas and feelings back and forth. And the same as with those old and scarce and beautiful mailbags, people will look forward to seeing what you've got inside.

The Counterfeit Mailbag. Containing one vast unzippered pocket, and another zippered. Shoulder strap and handle.

Size: 15" long x 7" wide x 12-1/2" tall. Strong, soft leather that will only get better. A beauty.

Price: $275.

How to take care of the Mailbag.

The first scratch will kill you, but in fact, it's the first step in the right direction: patina.

So the sooner it gets scratched, nicked, bumped, dug, hit, squeezed, dropped, bent, folded and rained on, the better. Really.

When you receive your mailbag, it's so fiercely new looking I'm almost ashamed of it. But there's no choice. It would cost too much to pre-age each mailbag before sending it out to a customer. (Antiques cost more than new, for a reason.)

Here's my recipe for "accelerating" the aging process. First, spend one day (the day you get it) the way it is. Brand new. Then, the next day, scratch it all over with your fingernails. Lightly. This will horrify you, at first. Then, spray-mist it with plain water, lightly. Let it dry. The scratches will lose their rawness. They will look old. Repeat this treatment as often as you can stand to: once a week for 5 weeks. Then once a year. (Clean mailbag with plain water only. Not petrochemicals, not oils, not detergents, not mystery solvents, not leather "cremes." It will do just fine with plain water and will outlast both of us.)

CATALOG COPY.

Here's a place where you need spirals by the pound.

Every ad has to entice the reader, explain the product, and ask for the order.

This page is from T*he Peterman Catalog*, which was quite successful for many years. Then it wasn't.

It's a tough business.

Next time you get a catalog in the mail, take a closer look.

You may learn something.

You may even buy something.

#27: Spiral

START SOMEWHERE INTERESTING and go where you should go. That's all there is to it.

First, figure out where to start. Then let 'er spin.

Believe it or not, the prunes have more fiber than the cereal.

If you've been eating bran cereal to get your daily fiber, we have a little suggestion.

The tasty California prune. Because three prunes actually have even more dietary fiber than this entire bowl of bran flakes.*

The fact is, prunes have more fiber per serving than almost any food you can name.

And if you add prunes to your cereal, you won't just be getting more fiber. You'll be getting different kinds of fiber.

Which is important. Because many nutritionists suggest that wheat fiber and fruit fiber is a healthy combination.

Besides, there's one more thing prunes can do for bran cereal. They can make it taste delicious.

*1/2 cup of 40% bran flakes.

Prunes. The high fiber fruit.

1. WHAT'S INTERESTING?

Pick one of your products and start with something a reader might find interesting – the Benefit, the Product, the Problem. Whatever. Like prunes being high in fiber.

Now, write a headline. Think target.

2. WRITE SOME COPY. THINK STRATEGY.

Next, write some body copy. It's easy. Really.

Your headline might focus on one part of the Strategy, and your copy flow will spiral through the important parts of your message.

3. MAKE A CHECKLIST.

After you write your ad, look at the way you spiraled through your Strategy.

Here's an example:

Part of Ad	Part of Strategy
Visual	√ Consumer Benefit
Headline	√ Product Benefit
SubHead	√ Support/Reason Why
Copy Flow	√ Consumer Benefit
	√ Product Benefit
Theme	√ Consumer Benefit.

Do it once, just for fun.

Spiraling through your Strategy will become instinct. Common sense will guide your Structure.

In a very natural way, you'll develop an underlying sense of sequence and structure. The key – just do it.

D. The Story

ONCE UPON A TIME, this was a common format.

Many early print ads were stories, such as Caples' famous "They All Laughed."

Product stories, testimonials, and case histories are types of ads that may take a Story approach.

Here, good writing is good storytelling.

FACT OR FICTION.

Whatever story you decide to tell, try to search for the inherent drama in your product and the people who use it. (Remember the Capo d'astro bar?)

With luck, you'll find a story worth telling.

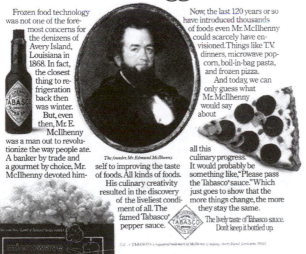

Every brand has a story.

WAKING UP
(A True Hotel Story)

The client wanted to party.
So you didn't get back to your room until after 1:00 in the morning.
You called the desk clerk to set up a 6:00 a.m. wake-up call, then crashed.
Only five hours of sleep before the big presentation.
You would have liked more.
And you got it.
Because nobody called to wake you up.
Except your boss, at 7:55:
"Chuck, where are you? We're all in the lobby waiting.
The meeting starts in five minutes."
Somehow you got through it.
Nobody seemed to notice the little piece of toilet paper you stuck on your neck where you cut yourself shaving.
Nobody said anything about the way you tied your tie, with the back part an inch lower than the front.
And nobody could possibly have realized what the inside of your mouth felt like because you had no time to brush your teeth.
But you did.
Oh yes, you did.
There's only one thing to do.
Go to the hotel that knows how to take care of business.

NEXT TIME RAMADA
1-800-2-RAMADA

TELL US A STORY.

Set the scene and establish characters.

Establish dramatic conflict, bring in your hero (usually the product or service), and then pay it off.

Here's an "on the road" story, one that every business traveler can relate to.

In this ad, you can read yourself into the story. And maybe, just maybe, "next time," you'll try Ramada.

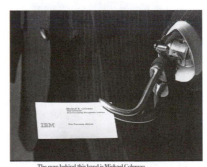

The man behind this hand is Michael Coleman.
The company behind this man is IBM.
There's a story behind both of them.
After the Marines and Vietnam, Coleman earned his MBA and began selling computers for IBM. Promotion followed promotion, and he now teaches our customers how to get the most out of their computers.
His success doesn't surprise us. People with disabilities keep proving that they are as capable as other workers. As reliable. As ambitious. And just as likely to succeed.
At IBM the proof is everywhere, in every part of our business.
The same is true at other companies.
Yet, some people just won't believe that the disabled can do the job.
It has to make you wonder who's handicapped.
And who isn't. **IBM**

This powerful visual *tells a story all by it-self. And it says a lot about the company.*

347

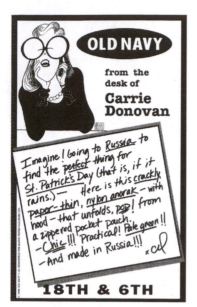
WHAT'S THE STORY?

We all like "the dish."

Here, gossip tells the story.

It's slightly Po-Mo. Even though you know that "it's just advertising," it's kind of fun to read. Who knows, you might want a light-weight Russian anorak.

Below, there's nothing like life and death to give a story a bit of drama.

THE SATURN STORY.

When GM first built the Saturn division, they wanted a brand that appealed to people who were purchasing smaller foreign-made cars.

It couldn't feel like a GM brand. So, without being dishonest, they had to create "A Different Kind of Car Company."

So they focused on people as well as cars. The people who made the car (in Spring Hill, TN), and the people who bought the car.

Saturn's agency developed some very distinctive brand advertising based on these stories.

The ads and the strategy were excellent. Wish the cars had been better.

SUCCESS STORY. Today, stories like this would never get through the legal department.

They were done before TV, but they still feel like TV commercials.

A comic book approach, can be an effective way to tell your story.

Credibility might suffer, but you'll get great readership.

One other thing…

"3 cakes of yeast a day?"
YUCHH!

TIPS FOR BETTER STORYTELLING:

- Paint images.
- Use concrete words.
- Create suspense. Try starting with a provocative sentence or a provocative question.
- Use words that sing. As George Lois says, *"words that bristle with visual imagery."*
- Try using children and/or animals. Cute never hurts.
- Practice. Remember, people remember stories.

SITES.
Check out the Milk site (gotmilk.com). The Goodby agency has always been good at story-telling. Here, they've taken various aspects of the brand – even the history of their advertising – and wrapped them in an engaging story. If you're a brand, chances are you have a story – even if it's a bit of company history – and your website is a perfect place to tell that story.

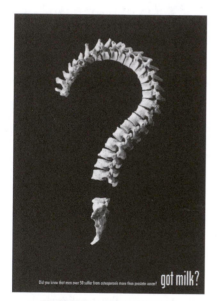

FINDING A NEW STORY.
Check out the Milk site (gotmilk.com). Goodby & Silverstein understands the power of story. And they know how to find new stories to build their brand.

Here, the importance of milk for strong bones.

NEW MEDIA – NEW NARRATIVES.

There are three kinds of story being generated on New Media – blogs, games, and sometimes sites.

Blogs are, in their own way, a narrative. Now it's not clear to me how much of a blog you can generate about a branded product, even a hip one like Nike. But, if you had some sort of sponsored blog by Nike or some other athletic brand, and it contained stories by athletes or training tips in a narrative format, that might work. The blog is a new narrative form and we'll be seeing more interesting work. (By the way, I so don't get Twitter, feel free to explain it to me.)

Games have a plot. Sometimes it's a simple one, sometimes more complicated. For the most part, brands get to sponsor these things, or have the logo bouncing around – that's fine as far as it goes. However, if you can find a way to get a more involving narrative built up that legitimately involves your brand, you may have a good idea. We'll burn a few brain cells on that in the Exercises.

Search. At present, Google is the "killer app" on the 'Net. SEO (Search Engine Optimization) is one of the major strategies. And, of course, after you've accomplished that, you have to be able to optimize that first response when they go to your site.

The first question to ask is, "What's the good word?" Then, "What's next?"

Social. We're all connected, and that's kind of enjoyable. But is there an e-commerce strategy imbedded in all of that connecting? As this book was being written, this was a topic on the minds of many. If you can figure out an appropriate way to make this pay for advertisers and marketers, you may have a very successful career.

#28: Store Story

This assignment can be a lot of fun.

The "Store Story" helps you go from writing ads to thinking about all the things it takes to make a business work.

1. WRITE A STORY FOR EACH OF YOUR PRODUCTS.

Try for a range of Story types: product stories, testimonials, case histories, fact and fiction.

Even a comic book.

Generally, you'll want it to be a story about how your product solved a problem – but try to look for fresh ways to tell your Story.

2. THE STORE STORY.

The engaging ad for Banana Republic is an excellent example of what we're talking about.

A. Create Your Store. You can create one from your imagination or pick your favorite shop (and maybe use this assignment to pitch some freelance). Here's a handy checklist:

Store name.

What need does it fill in the market?

What products will you sell?

What services will you offer?

Who is your target customer?

(Don't forget the location.)

B. Write an Introductory Ad.

Tell the story of why you started your store.

C. Write a Product Story Ad.

It should be a good ad for your store as well as a good ad about the product.

D. Write a Customer Story Ad.

(Probably a case history or testimonial.)

E. Write a "Why We're Having a Sale" Ad.

Name the sale. Any other promotional ideas?

Before there were health clubs, there were Charles Atlas ads in comic books. Can you imagine how many young boys could "read themselves into the story?"

351

PIER PRESSURE.

A store like Pier 1 has to keep generating traffic. That means they have to keep on generating reasons for customers to come visit. It's a tough job.

It means short-term retail action combined with long-term image building.

CAN YOU BELIEVE THIS STORY?
It's how Banana Republic got started. Really!

Which just goes to show you. However your story starts, you can never be sure how it ends.

The moral of this story is the Store Story assignment is one of our favorites. Because it gets you thinking about how to put a business together.

That's our story. And we're sticking to it.

E. The Sermon

WHEN ASKED HOW HE WROTE HIS SERMONS, the preacher replied,

"First I tell 'em what I'm going to tell 'em.
"Then I tell 'em. Then I tell 'em what I told 'em."

That's pretty good advice for a copywriter.

In the Sermon, the writer acts as an authority, not merely informing, but instructing.

Sermons are often written in the *"corporate we."* It personifies the corporation and builds a "one to one" dialogue with the reader.

Many successful advertising themes use this same "we" device. (We believe, we care, etc.)

You don't have to preach.

Sometimes, you're just a good friend.

To write a good Sermon, you must feel you have something worth saying.

For example, Volvos keep you safe.

And then tell your story with conviction. Amen.

Avis is only No. 2 in rent a cars. So why go with us?

We try harder.
(When you're not the biggest, you have to.)

We just can't afford dirty ash-trays. Or half-empty gas tanks. Or worn wipers. Or unwashed cars. Or low tires. Or anything less than seat-adjusters that adjust. Heaters that heat. Defrosters that defrost.

Obviously, the thing we try hardest for is just to be nice. To start you out right with a new car, like a lively, super-torque Ford, and a pleasant smile. To know, say, where you get a good pastrami sandwich in Duluth. Why?

Because we can't afford to take you for granted.
Go with us next time.
The line at our counter is shorter.

SERVICE SERMONS.

Are you in the business of delivering service or quality products? Then you might want to deliver Sermons on:

- Reliability
- Caring about customers
- Your corporate philosophy
- Commitment to doing a good job

Above, a Sermon from Avis.

Below, two Sermons from Volvo.

The Early Volvo Position was durability with a strong economic argument. The position steadily evolved to safety, which appealed to families and women. It was a natural shift from the durability position.

VOLVO
A car you can believe in.

IMAGINATION AT WORK.

Jeff Immelt, GE Chairman and CEO has this to say, "*For GE, imagination at work is more than a slogan or a tagline. It is a reason for being.*"

It's an expression of their business strategy. And it feels like a mission.

Here, they advertise their search for business opportunity by extending the delivery of their medical technology.

WHOLE GRAINS AT WORK.

Smart writing activates the product and the company.

GRAB THE TREND.

Bill Bernbach noted that there was strength in being "sociological."

Three current mega-concerns are "Green," "Health," and "The Economy."

See how three smart marketers connect with these issues. Each campaign has a bit of a sermon embedded in it, but, by tapping into contemporary concerns, they're not "preachy."

The best sermons don't feel like sermons.

Each uses a broad theme that hits the right cultural note with clear strategic focus:

Example: GE.

An early adopter of a "green strategy," at least for a big company, is GE – a company that got big by being smart.

Today, GE Divisions put up windmills and make energy-efficient kitchen appliances.

Example: Kashi.

"Seven Whole Grains on a Mission" taps into the cultural vibe of better and more natural foods.

It's a simple product story that adds value with attitude that connects with its target. They convey a health benefit without making an overt claim.

Example: Walmart.

Today, saving money is both smart and necessary. Walmart connects their low-cost offerings to higher values: like living better and being energy smart.

As they say, "Save Money. Live Better."

We lose
too many customers
this way.

Till death us do part.

THE MOBIL STRATEGY.

A classic piece of business thinking. *"We sell gas and oil for a living, and we want everyone to be a potential customer."*

It may be beautiful to die for love in a poem.

But it's ugly and stupid to die for love in a car.

Yet how many times have you seen (or been) a couple more interested in passion than in passing? Too involved with living to worry about dying?

As a nation, we are allowing our young to be buried in tons of steel. And not only the reckless lovers—the just plain nice kids as well.

Everyone is alarmed about it. No one really knows what to do. And automobile accidents, believe it or not, continue to be the leading cause of death among young people between 15 and 24 years of age.

Parents are alarmed and hand over the keys to the car anyway.

Insurance companies are alarmed and charge enormous rates which deter no one.

Even statisticians (who don't alarm easily) are alarmed enough to tell us that by 1970, 14,450 young adults will die in cars each year.

(Just to put those 14,450 young lives in perspective, that is about 4 times the number of young lives we have lost so far in Viet Nam.)

Is it for this that we spent our dimes and dollars to all but wipe out polio? Is it for this that medical science conquered diphtheria and smallpox?

What kind of society is it that keeps its youngsters alive only long enough to sacrifice them on the highway?

Yet that is exactly what's happening. And it's incredible.

Young people should be the best drivers, not the worst.

They have the sharper eyes, the steadier nerves, the quicker reflexes. They probably even have the better understanding of how a car works.

So why?

Are they too dense to learn? Too smart to obey the obvious rules? Too sure of themselves? Too *un*-sure? Or simply too young and immature?

How can we get them to be old enough to be wise enough before it's too late?

One way is by insisting on better driver training programs in school. Or *after* school. Or after work. Or during summers.

By having stricter licensing requirements. By rewarding the good drivers instead of merely punishing the bad ones. By having uniform national driving laws (which don't exist today). By having radio and TV and the press deal more with the problem. By getting *you* to be less complacent.

Above all, by setting a decent example ourselves.

Nobody can stop young people from driving. And nobody should. Quite the contrary. The more exposed they become to sound driving techniques, the better they're going to be. (Doctors and lawyers "practice;" why not drivers?)

We at Mobil are not preachers or teachers. We sell gasoline and oil for a living and we want everyone to be a potential customer.

If not today, tomorrow. And we want everyone, young and old, to have his fair share of tomorrows. **Mobil**

We want you to live.

Are you going to your folks for Christmas?
Or are they coming to you?

Drive carefully. We want you to live.
Mobil.

A POWERFUL AD. A POWERFUL CAMPAIGN. When this ad ran, one radio announcer was so moved that he read the whole ad to his audience.

Word for word. During drive time.

This campaign for Mobil from DDB set a new standard for taking the high ground.

SEASON'S GREETINGS.

A little grim, but the holiday season has some of the highest accident rates.

So, again, the advertising has a strong reason for being.

A SERMON CAN TALK ABOUT CORPORATE PHILOSOPHY.

This can be serious business

The ad on the right was done by Zenith, which was, at the time, a leading US TV manufacturer. Japanese TVs were taking over the market, and this ad threw down the gauntlet.

While the ad was viewed as a success, Zenith finally went under – and, last time we looked, the brand name had been purchased by a Korean Company.

Techniques and Tactics.

Often, a philosophical point is made with a *symbolic visual.*

Here, a bold American worker with arms folded and a challenging look made the point.

The reader is usually asked to think about something he or she may not have thought of – such as an aspect of *product quality* – or *corporate commitment.*

Print is often used to state the case.

Often, hard facts are used as Support for an abstract concept – tangibles as Support for intangibles.

If the company is serious about this sort of thing, the program is usually coordinated with the involvement of a high-level PR firm.

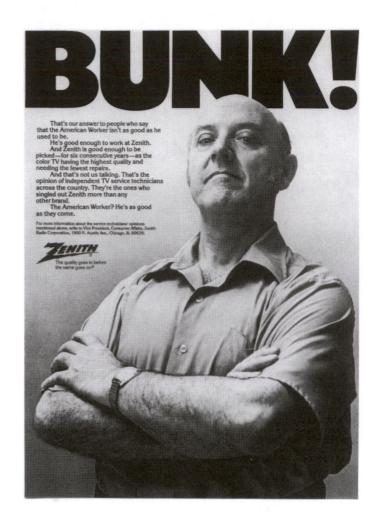

A SERMON CAN PRESENT A NEW WAY OF THINKING.

A Sermon is supposed to make you think.

A Sermon is supposed to make you feel good about the advertiser – and good about yourself.

That's why we consider ads like this to have certain Sermon-like qualities.

"Training Wheels for the Feet." There's a nice little bit of philosophy that intrigues your mind.

And there's a "we care about your little one's little feet" attitude that elevates the advertiser and the product.

Product facts and philosophy.

In a Sermon, they work together to support the argument – and make us believers.

#29: The Sermon

1. WRITE A SERMON FOR EACH PRODUCT.

   A. At least one should feature a **symbolic visual.**

   B. At least one should be a **poster.**

   C. At least one should feature a **new way of thinking** about the product.

   D. At least one should feature the **corporate philosophy** of your brand.

If you're having trouble moving up or planning your career, attend one of our seminars. With the proper footing, there's no telling how far you'll climb. **Working Opportunities For Women. 647-9961.**

**DO ADVERTISING
THAT DOES GOOD.**

Bill Bernbach said a lot of things we should think about. Like this…

"All of us who professionally use the mass media are the shapers of society.

We can vulgarize that society.

We can brutalize it.

Or we can help lift it onto a higher level." It's something to think about.

One way we can add to the "uplift" is to seek out worthwhile advertising opportunities. Sure, they don't pay as much as the fat and sugar-laden products that are too much with us.

But there's another bigger payoff – feeling good about the work you do.

Free Lance!
FIND A WORTHY CAUSE TO WORK FOR.

Pick something you care about. Write an ad about it.

   You might even try to see if you can get an assignment writing for them.

THE RIGHT AD AT THE RIGHT TIME.

Our bus company, the CTA, was being forced into a fare increase.

   It was a small account at the agency I worked for. At the time, I was working with Dave Kennedy, the future half of Wieden + Kennedy.

   We thought that maybe we could help. So we did a tiny ad campaign. It was this newspaper ad and bus cards with a tear-off pad.

   As you can see, the headline wasn't subtle, the copy made a pretty good point, and the coupon gave you a choice – you could check off YELL or SCREAM. Or both, I guess.

   Anyway, the next week when the CTA went to pick up their mail (stamps were only three cents), the Post Office said, "That will be $7000 please." What? The bus card coupons were postage paid, and they'd put up a bunch of them, but nobody dreamed that we'd get that kind of return.

   When the dust settled, 200,000 coupons had been sent in.

   I don't believe it myself, but that's what they told me.

   One newspaper ran an editorial headlined "Yell and Scream."

   And, as the CTA was sorting the coupons by legislative district, the Illinois State Legislature decided to save them the trouble. They voted the CTA a subsidy. Our little ad campaign made the difference.

   Do it right, and you can do some good.

HERE'S A GOOD EXAMPLE.

Even though you can't read the copy in this small ad, you know what the whole ad's about just by looking at it.

It's going to give you a number of good reasons to shop at Pier 1.

You can also read the bits of copy next to the items that interest you – without having to read the whole ad.

And, if you happen to be in a shopping mood, you just might read the whole thing.

> *"To encourage the feeling of accessibility, we often stick coupons or other response forms in ads.*
>
> *It is not so important whether they really send in the coupons, as long as they feel they can.*
>
> *A visible invitation to respond, whether it is used or not, adds another bit of believability to the characterization."*
>
> **Howard Gossage**

F. Outlines, Websites, Catalogs, & More

LONG COPY ADS with large amounts of information are often Outlines.

So are short ads that list key facts.

Brochures and catalogs are usually developed from Outlines, as well. And now we have websites.

SUBHEADS TELL THE STORY.

A quick reading of subheads or website tabs provides navigation information.

A variety of type "color" – **boldface,** *italics,* and • bullets can create additional interest. (But not all in the same sentence, please.)

Small illustrations and captions add appropriate visual information (by the way, more people read captions than body copy).

OPENING SECTIONS & HOME PAGES.

This part lays out your story, with emphasis on *why it's in the reader's interest* to read the whole thing.

It's often handled with **A Boldface Subhead** that summarizes the whole ad.

Home pages have the same function – but it's a bit more complex. Now you have to be interesting while giving clear navigation information.

THE CLOSING SECTION – AN INVITATION TO ACTION.

Reward the reader. He or she has invested time and effort. Offer an opportunity to do something.

On a website, it seems easy – after all, we can "click here" for something to happen, but as we all know that's easier said than done.

Give some thought to classic direct response

techniques – get an easy click – something free – before you try for an actual purchase.

Try tactics like**:**

• Asking for a brochure, helpful guide, or "free evaluation"

• Receiving a free gift or sample

• Or just coming in for a visit – store or website

Research indicates that effective requests for action can have a dramatic effect on results.

And a good way to start is… *make an Outline!*

Don't Forget the Captions! *They're read more often than body copy. Every time you have a visual, think of a good thing to say. Or vice versa. Every time you have a good thing to say, visualize it.*

3 KINDS OF OUTLINES.

Here are three major types of Outlines:

Rational/Long Copy.

With a "considered purchase," one that involves a significant expenditure and where there is some "risk" in making a bad decision, an ad that presents all the reasons makes sense.

Think of The FCB Grid. The rational/ high involvement quadrant (upper left) has many of these types of products.

The Andersen Window ad at the left provides a lot of reasons, and even tells you how to find out more.

For a certain kind of product, this is a smart approach.

The Visual Outline.

This type of outline can do many things.

Expand on a simple topic. The bank ad on the left does this. Hey, it's a loan. But they use visual variety to involve you and maybe give you an idea for a loan that you hadn't had before.

Make a complex topic interesting.

A good Visual Outline can help us work through technical reasons why.

Make an old topic new. The ad for MedCenters on page 362, the one with the big cigarette butt, tells the same old story in a new way.

Show a lot of stuff. The Dodge minivan has a lot of features. The visual outline with captions on page 362 tells that story in an easy-to-understand way.

The "How-To" Ad.

This is a great all-purpose opening that "tells 'em what you're going to tell 'em" and draws in the reader who wants to know more.

Often, each section is reinforced with a small visual as well as a subhead.

Act Now! Turn the Page…

Read an outstanding "How-To" from International Paper done by Ogilvy.

Reproduced full size – part of a great campaign.

How to write clearly

By Edward T. Thompson

Editor-in-Chief, Reader's Digest

International Paper asked Edward T. Thompson to share some of what he has learned in nineteen years with Reader's Digest, a magazine famous for making complicated subjects understandable to millions of readers.

If you are afraid to write, don't be.

If you think you've got to string together big fancy words and high-flying phrases, forget it.

To write well, unless you aspire to be a professional poet or novelist, you only need to get your ideas across simply and clearly.

It's not easy. But it *is* easier than you might imagine.

There are only three basic requirements:

First, you must *want* to write clearly. And I believe you really do, if you've stayed this far with me.

Second, you must be willing to *work hard*. Thinking means work—and that's what it takes to do anything well.

Third, you must know and follow some *basic guidelines*.

If, while you're writing for clarity, some lovely, dramatic or inspired phrases or sentences come to you, fine. Put them in.

But then with cold, objective eyes and mind ask yourself: "Do they detract from clarity?" If they do, grit your teeth and cut the frills.

Follow some basic guidelines

I can't give you a complete list of "dos and don'ts" for every writing problem you'll ever face.

But I can give you some fundamental guidelines that cover the most common problems.

1. Outline what you want to say.

I know that sounds grade-schoolish. But you can't write clearly until, *before you start*, you know where you will stop.

Ironically, that's even a problem in writing an outline (i.e., knowing the ending before you begin).

So try this method:

• On 3"x 5" cards, write—one point to a card—all the points you need to make.

• Divide the cards into piles—one pile for each group of points *closely related* to each other. (If you were describing an automobile, you'd put all the points about mileage in one pile, all the points about safety in another, and so on.)

• Arrange your piles of points in a sequence. Which are most important and should be given first or saved for last? Which must you present before others in order to make the others understandable?

• Now, *within* each pile, do the same thing—arrange the *points* in logical, understandable order.

There you have your outline, needing only an introduction and conclusion.

This is a practical way to outline. It's also flexible. You can add, delete or change the location of points easily.

2. Start where your readers are.

How much do they know about the subject? Don't write to a level higher than your readers' knowledge of it.

CAUTION: Forget that old—and wrong—advice about writing to a 12-year-old mentality. That's insulting. But do remember that your prime purpose is to *explain* something, not prove that you're smarter than your readers.

3. Avoid jargon.

Don't use words, expressions, phrases known only to people with specific knowledge or interests.

Example: A scientist, using scientific jargon, wrote, "The biota exhibited a one hundred percent mortality response." He could have written: "All the fish died."

4. Use familiar combinations of words.

A speech writer for President Franklin D. Roosevelt wrote, "We are endeavoring to construct a more inclusive society." F.D.R. changed it to, "We're going to make a country in which no one is left out."

CAUTION: By familiar combinations of words, I do *not* mean incorrect grammar. *That* can be *un*clear. Example: John's father says he can't go out Friday. (Who can't go out? John or his father?)

5. Use "first-degree" words.

These words immediately bring an image to your mind. Other words must be "translated" through the first-degree word before you see

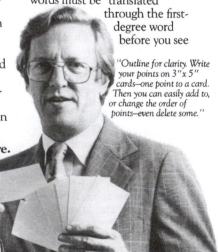

"Outline for clarity. Write your points on 3"x 5" cards—one point to a card. Then you can easily add to, or change the order of points—even delete some."

360

"Grit your teeth and cut the frills. That's one of the suggestions I offer here to help you write clearly. They cover the most common problems. And they're all easy to follow."

the image. Those are second/third-degree words.

First-degree words	Second/third-degree words
face	visage, countenance
stay	abide, remain, reside
book	volume, tome, publication

First-degree words are usually the most precise words, too.

6. Stick to the point.

Your outline— which was more work in the beginning—now saves you work. Because now you can ask about any sentence you write: "Does it relate to a point in the outline? If it doesn't, should I add it to the outline? If not, I'm getting off the track." Then, full steam ahead—on the main line.

7. Be as brief as possible.

Whatever you write, shortening—*condensing*—almost always makes it tighter, straighter, easier to read and understand.

Condensing, as *Reader's Digest* does it, is in large part artistry. But it involves techniques that anyone can learn and use.

• *Present your points in logical ABC order:* Here again, your outline should save you work because, if you did it right, your points already stand in logical ABC order—A makes B understandable, B makes C understandable and so on. To write in a straight line is to say something clearly in the fewest possible words.

• *Don't waste words telling people what they already know:* Notice how we edited this: "Have you ever

wondered how banks rate you as a credit risk? ~~You know, of course, that it's some combination of facts about your income, your job, and so on. But actually, M~~any banks have a scoring system...."

• *Cut out excess evidence and unnecessary anecdotes:* Usually, one fact or example (at most, two) will support a point. More just belabor it. And while writing about some-

Writing clearly means avoiding jargon. Why didn't he just say: "All the fish died!"

thing may remind you of a good story, ask yourself: "Does it *really help* to tell the story, or does it slow me down?"

(Many people think *Reader's Digest* articles are filled with anecdotes. Actually, we use them sparingly and usually for one of two reasons: either the subject is so dry it needs some "humanity" to give it life; or the subject is so hard to grasp, it needs anecdotes to help readers understand. If the subject is both lively and easy to grasp, we move right along.)

• *Look for the most common word wasters:* windy phrases.

Windy phrases	Cut to...
at the present time	now
in the event of	if
in the majority of instances	usually

• *Look for passive verbs you can make active:* Invariably, this produces a shorter sentence. "The cherry tree *was* chopped down by George Washington." (Passive verb and nine words.) "George Washington *chopped* down the cherry tree." (Active verb and seven words.)

• *Look for positive/negative sections from which you can cut the negative:* See how we did it here: "The answer ~~does not rest with carelessness or incompetence. It lies largely in~~ having enough people to do the job."

• Finally, to write more clearly by saying it in fewer words: when you've finished, stop.

Edward T. Thompson

LET ME COUNT THE WAYS.

Here's a fun way to make multiple points.

Often, a product's superiority is an accumulation of minor advantages.

Try to combine this accumulation into one strong benefit statement.

Above, Purina convinces you that they have a better way to worm your dog.

Below, MedCenter Health Plan tells you how you can live longer.

How Can You Not Read This Ad? It looks interesting. It has fun visuals. And it has information with a benefit – live longer.

Outlines Can Make Products Interesting.
You see intriguing things. And you need to read.

#30: Outline/ Brochure/Website

1. PREPARE OUTLINES FOR EACH PRODUCT.

Each Outline should include:

A. Headline

B. Subheads

C. Visual(s) and appropriate captions

D. Introductory and **closing** copy

E. Offer or other response behavior.

2. TURN OUTLINES INTO BROCHURES.

3. NOW TURN THEM INTO A WEBSITE.

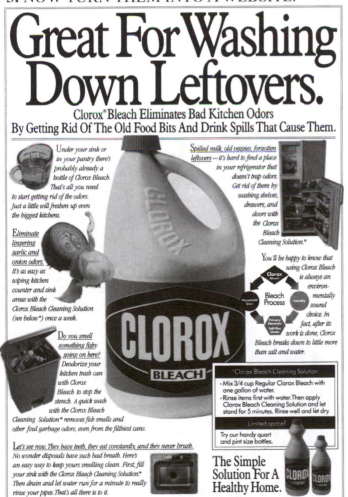

CA WEBPICKS.

One of the best ways to stay up to date on terrific work in Web Design is through the pages – and website – of *Communication Arts Magazine* – better known as "*CA.*"

They have a subsite called "WebPicks," which features the best current work.

Here are a few from a recent visit.

**Huntington Library.
"Beautiful Science."**

A wealth of information related to breakthroughs in science in a uniquely accessible framework.

A Kicking Shoe site.

It isn't just Nike. Here, Foot Locker features Puma's Archive Collection – "Foot Locker Unlocked."
footlockerunlocked.com/pumaarchive/

Games? Oh Boy!

Here, Hasbro gives new excitement to their classic board game, Risk – a nice combination of humor and manly violence.
hasbro.com/risk/flash_world.cfm

Don't just sit there, Subscribe.

As you start out in the business, *CA* is a great way to keep in touch with the best work. You should be reading every issue.

Fortunately, there's a Student Subscription rate. www.commarts.com

WHAT ABOUT HEADLINES?

As advertised, we didn't spend much time on "How to Write a Headline."

Once you understand what the communication is supposed to do, a good copywriter should be able to write a good headline. So can a lot of art directors.

What's a Good Headline?

Well, I guess a good headline is:

- Dramatic.
- Involving.
- Interesting.
- Informative.

Hey, it should be at least one of these.

With luck, it will be all of them.

Many prefer the benefit to be in the headline. That's hard to argue.

Some say the headline should *"relate to the reader."*

Nothing wrong with that, either.

Whatever. Just so it works.

It can be a question, a statement, an announcement, a quote (like the famous Rolls-Royce headline), a title, or just the name of the product.

How do you write a headline?

Easy. Write a lot of them.

Then, pick the one you like best.

Sometimes it's short and sweet.

Sometimes it isn't.

Sometimes unselected headlines make good subheads or body copy.

Sometimes they become the headlines for follow-up ads in the campaign.

And sometimes you save 'em for later, because you never know…

Generally, a good headline should give a sense of what the ad is all about.

And, usually, other people say…

"Hey, that's a good headline!"

I guess that's how you know.

#31: Wrap-Up

1. FIND EXAMPLES OF:

   A. One-Liner

   B. News

   C. Spiral

   D. Story

   E. Sermon

   F. Outline

2. FIND THREE EXAMPLES THAT DON'T FIT.
What **combinations** were used?

3. PREPARE A PRESENTATION OF YOUR PRINT.
Select and organize the print work you've done.
Which ads worked best?
Which formats were you best at?
Which areas need work?

Before You Send Another Business Letter, Check The Margins.

REMEMBER…

Good print ads are involving.

They tell you. And they sell you.

Remember what Gossage said… *"People read what interests them. Sometimes it's an ad."*

364

Finally...

*"There's no rule that there are
six types of print ads."*

It's been a way to teach you the *structure* of print ads and help you develop some range.

We hope the lessons covered in this section will help you become a better copywriter.

But nobody can do it for you.

In addition, you really have to be aware of the increasing importance of visual communication and the entire range of new media formats.

That's where it's headed. Logos, posters, comic books, and nonlinear design on your computer screen may be the print of the future. Deal with it.

Keep asking yourself whether you're saying what people should really be *seeing*.

And don't forget the captions.

Now, we're going to shift gears a bit.

In the next section, we're going to talk about *writing* what people will be *hearing*.

Time to tune into radio.

WHAT'S THE COMBINATION?

Of course, many ads are combinations.

This one is a Good Deed Demo and a Sermon – a fairly common combination.

The life insurance company makes the point that lack of exercise is more likely to kill us than the electric chair.

**SERMON OR OUTLINE
OR SPIRAL?**

Who cares. It's a nice ad for baby clothes.

The point of this section is not to get you to categorize ads that have already been done, but to help you get a handle on the basic types of print advertising solutions available to you.

And I bet we've done that.

Next time you're faced with an advertising problem, you'll have a better understanding of the different ways you can solve that problem with a terrific piece of print. Right?

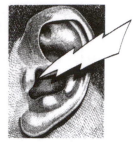

*"It's not a microphone.
It's an ear."*

Robert Sarnoff, founder of NBC

"People don't remember radio as a source of information because they do not consciously listen to it. Rather, they bathe in it and sit in it."

Tony Schwartz

"One of the most fruitful uses of radio, from an advertiser's standpoint, is narrow-casting *– rather than broadcasting."*

Tony Schwartz

OTHER KINDS OF CREATIVITY.
Pep Boys wanted to reach buyers at their time of greatest need – during nasty weather. The agency asked station managers to report weather conditions – they then ran ads at appropriate times. Sales went up 55% to 92% in those markets.

"Sounding."

"When you're working on the ear, you're working on sound. And once sound penetrates the ear, then you're working on the emotions of people.

Now, do I have to say *something to stir the emotions – or shall I* sound *something to stir the emotions?*

Certain words require to be sounded, *not said. 'What's new... whatsnew?'*

The second "Whatsnew" is slurred, but acceptable because it sounds *right.*

In commercial copy, there are certain words, certain phrases, that are not to be said, but sounded."

Bob Marcato, Announcer

366

Sound Advice for Radio

RADIO IS THE **THEATER OF THE MIND**.
It's an inside game.
It plays between the ears.
While print relates to the *reader,* radio relates to the *listener.* For about 60 seconds.

TIGHTER TARGET AUDIENCES.
Target audiences are smaller and more defined: Age, sex, and music preference are examples.
Radio offers distinct timing and geographic advantages. Like drive time. AM and PM.
Other types of targeting, such as ethnic group, are more easily accomplished on radio.
Use this information to make your person-to-person communication more personal.

THREE KINDS OF RADIO COMMERCIALS.
There are three kinds of radio commercials:
**• The Pitch • The Situation • The Song
Combinations** create variations.

1. THE PITCH.
It's simply an Announcer (ANNCR) talking to you. Your two basic tools are: the announcer's voice and your words. Add anything else you want.
For example, sound effects (SFX).

2. THE SITUATION.
You create an event, a small drama that places your product in a situation of your own creation.
It's often comedic, and limited only by your own imagination.

3. THE SONG.

Radio was made for music.

Music can give your words new dimension.

One of the most satisfying experiences you may have as a copywriter is to help create a memorable piece of advertising music.

People don't hum the announcer.
Steve Karmen
Jingle Writer

COMBINATIONS.

The three types of radio commercials can be combined.

The major types of combinations are:

• Beds • Donuts • Tags • Vignettes

Music and rhythm find their way into the secret places of the soul.
Plato

The Bed.

This is a Pitch with a Song in the background.

The Song might move to the foreground – usually to sing the theme.

The announcer talks, the music creates a mood and sometimes reinforces copy points.

The Donut.

This is a Song with a hole in it.

It's a Pitch in the middle of a Song.

It begins with a Song. Then the announcer pitches the product. This seems to make everybody feel like singing… so they usually do.

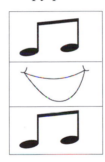

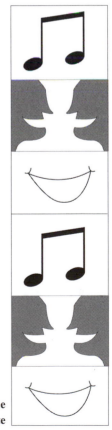

The Tag.

The Tag is a Pitch at the end of a Song.

Usually the announcer (often the local announcer) tells you where to get the product or provides other information – such as a special promotion.

The Vignette.

The Vignette is a flexible format that uses *all three* types – in any sequence.

You'll hear short Situations, and bits and pieces of the Pitch often held together in a Song.

These cost more and can be harder to produce, but, done right, can make quite an impact.

The Vignette

367

Radio Structure:
Context, Content & Conclusion

IT'S SIMPLE. Beginning. Middle. End. In radio, it's helpful to think of *Context, Content,* and *Conclusion.*

Got it? Context. Content. Conclusion.

Let's see how they work with the three basic types of radio commercials:

THE PITCH.

In the Pitch, you establish Context at the beginning. You may work to establish the brand theme or the Selling Idea, or, often, you establish the Problem.

You also work to establish a relationship with the listener, with tempo, tone of voice, and attitude.

The middle moves to Content: information, reasons for buying. And so on.

The end is the **Conclusion**:

Stating the theme. Wrapping up the sale.

Providing purchase information.

Encouraging the listener to *act.*

In the Pitch on the left, a second, softer announcer track (usually with more echo) provides an answer to the main announcer. In this case, the phrase "Hear Here" (or is it "Here Here"?) is the device.

THE SITUATION.

The Situation has some structural similarities .

The Context at the beginning of a Situation is usually *place* and *personality*.

Who is speaking? *Where? What's* the Problem?

The Content in the middle of a Situation usually builds through *dramatic interaction.*

The Conclusion is often some sort of *payoff*… a punch line, a problem solved.

It's simple. Beginning. Middle. End.

Context. Content. Conclusion. Got it?

SITUATION COMEDY TEAMS. Often, you'll find the same two characters in new situations.

Often, the commercials were written by the performers. Some famous radio comedy teams were: **Bob & Ray** (you may be more familiar with Bob Elliot's son, Chris), **Stiller & Meara** (you're more familiar with their son, Ben), and the legendary **Dick & Bert**.

Dick Orkin and Bert Berdis, both creative radio superstars, now work separately.

Orkin's "Radio Ranch and Home for Wayward Cowboys" demo tape should be heard by every writer. Their website is www.radio-ranch.com.

Bert Berdis, a former agency creative director, is now at his own Bert Berdis & Co.

Collaboration. A good way to create situations.

If you're working on a radio project and find another writer who has a sense of humor you appreciate, you might want to give it a try.

The techniques are similar to the improvisational techniques used by comedy groups like Second City, where you take a premise and try to create a scene.

Watch some of those types of shows and try to apply those techniques to creating a Situation for your next radio project. Who knows?

You might be the next great Situation Comedy Team.

THE SITUATION
Molson Golden "Fridge" :60 Radio

For Molson Golden, the same two characters would find themselves in new situations, usually involving his obsession with Molson Golden. She reacts.

Note the rhythm of the language – some of it may look funny written, but it's how people speak. Here goes…

SFX: Doorbell
HER: Hang on.
HIM: Hello?
HER: Hello.
HIM: Hi, I'm your neighbor, next door neighbor.
HER: Yeah.
HIM: I missed you when you moved in, I guess.
HER: Really?
HIM: I wanted to explain about that shelf in your refrigerator.
HER: The shelf? Oh, you mean the bottom shelf. The one with the whole case of Molson Golden. Boy, what a great surprise that was moving in.
HIM: It was my Molson Golden, my Molson Golden.
HER: Your Molson Golden.
HIM: Yeah, I had an arrangement with the person who lived here before you.
HER: Oh yeah?
HIM: I sort of rented one shelf in her 'fridge.
HER: You don't have a refrigerator?
HIM: Yeah, I'm a photographer. Mine's full of film, and I needed someplace to keep my Molson Golden.
HER: Oh yeah, I see.
HIM: Cool, clear, smooth. I'm sure you understand.
HER: Yeah, I love it. It was terrific.
HIM: It was terrific.
HER: Uh-huh.
HIM: What do you mean *was?*
VO: Molson Golden, from North America's oldest brewer of beer and ale. The #1 import from Canada. Molson makes it golden.
HER: It really was a shame you missed the party.
HIM: I feel like I was there in spirit.
VO: Martlet Importing Co., New York.

THE SONG
Popeyes Famous Fried Chicken:
"Dr. John" :60 Radio

This Song was written with New Orleans rock star Dr. John.

It captures the spicy personality of Popeyes – a spicy Cajun-style fried chicken.

There is an Intro, a first verse, a chorus, a second verse, another chorus, and a special ending, which in musical terms is called a coda.

In other versions, verses and choruses were "dipped" and an announcer added to present promotional offers.

A music-only version of the melody line was recorded to replace the singers, so the feeling and melody of the song was maintained.

A shorter version of the same song was used for TV.

MUSIC INTRO (Piano Lick)
Girls: Dr. John for Popeyes!

VERSE 1.
Dr. John: I was raised on Cajun Cookin', that New Orleans cuisine.
Girls: Oo.
Dr. John: And the folks at Popeyes Chicken… well they know just what I mean. Help me, Girls!

CHORUS:
ALL: Love that Chicken from Popeyes.
Dr. John: You'll dig the way it's fried.
ALL: Love that Chicken from Popeyes.
Dr. John: Feels so good inside.

VERSE 2.
Dr. John: That New Orleans spice is *Oh so nice,* a scandalicious taste bud sin. So crunchy and spicy and juicy my Lucy, grab a piece and bite right in. Hey!

CHORUS:
ALL: Love that Chicken from Popeyes.
Dr. John: The best you ever tried.
ALL: Love that Chicken from Popeyes.
Dr. John: Your taste buds will be tantalized.

CODA:
Dr. John: And once you savor that eye-poppin' flavor, you'll say, this is some *serious* chicken!

(BUTTON)

THE SONG.

The Beginning of the Song is also called the Introduction or Intro.

In this section you establish musical Context – establishing tempo and musical attitude.

You may also use the Verse – the first one, to establish your context.

Then, you develop what you started. Content.

It may be a verse, it may be a chorus, or, today, it may move into a less-traditional musical structure.

Originally, advertising songs were sort of like show tunes – they may have been in many different styles, but they moved the plot along as well as made music. Today, unless you're purposefully corny, that may not work as well.

Give 'Em the Hook.

The End is usually the Chorus, which usually features your theme as the "Hook" in your Song.

While one hates to make rules, if you're going to work in this area, your Song better have a good "hook."

There should be a memorable musical phrase.

In pop music this is known as "the hook."

In advertising music, they try for the same thing. Only. . .

Music is very flexible. You may start with your Hook, establishing your theme at the beginning, or you might just repeat the Hook throughout.

So your Conclusion could also be your Context and Content. Confusing? Not if it sounds right.

Some musical forms, such as the blues, can be thought of as verse and chorus combined.

The list goes on. Whatever you do, it should have Structure. On the left is an example – a Song written with New Orleans' rock star Dr. John to capture the spicy personality of Popeyes Fried Chicken.

STRUCTURE: BEDS, DONUTS & TAGS. The most common type of radio commercial is a Combination of the three basic types of radio commercials. Each has structure.

In the Bed, a Song is the background for a Pitch. A major concern is matching the structure of the Song with the pace of the Pitch.

For example, the words and musical mood should match. The tempo and attitude should match.

Another technique is to start with announcer only and bring in the music as you introduce the product.

In the Donut, the structure of the Song is usually already written for you. The usual concern is making your Pitch match the size of the "Donut hole" and the attitude of the Song.

You may want to write your Pitch copy to refer to the lead in lyrics. For example. . .

Dr. John (SINGS):
　　'Cause Popeyes does it right.
LOCAL ANNCR:
　　That's right. Spiced right and priced right.
Donut Varieties.

There are a few. There's the Double Donut, with two holes, the Donut + Tag, with an additional Tag section. (The example at the right is a Double Donut with a Tag.)

There's something I like to use which involves *alternating* copy and singing...

ANNCR: Archway Cookies are made with good food.
SINGERS: Archway Cookies. . .
ANNCR: Like oatmeal, apples, dates. . .
SINGERS: The Good Food Cookie.

Finally, there's the Tag – the open place at the end of many radio commercials.

It's a smart way for retailers to use radio.

TWO DONUTS + A TAG.
Here's a commercial designed for local restaurants. It takes the "Against" position – positioning this local restaurant against fast food chains.

The Song is in a funky musical style – right for a place that serves ribs.

There are two Donuts and a Tag.

"Take a Break from the Chains" :60

MUSIC INTRO (One bar)
VOCAL: Take a Break from the Chains! (Take a break) Those uniform uniforms, it's all the same.

Those clever commercials and advertising claims. (Come On)

Take a Break from the Chains.
(Take a Break from the Chains).

ANNCR [DONUT ONE]:
At Jim & Johnny's in Oak Park, you get good food made in a real kitchen, instead of some assembly line.

Hey, a lot of places may cook up more food, but nobody cooks up better.

Real folks, real food, and real good.

Special dishes like Johnny's famous barbecued back ribs – best in town. Take a break from the chains at Jim & Johnny's, on Lake Street, in the heart of Oak Park.
VOCAL: Take a Break from the Chains (Take a Break) Those uniform uniforms, it's all the same...
ANNCR [DONUT 2]: This week, try Jim & Johnny's barbecue special.
VOCAL: Come on (Come On), Take a Break from the Chains!
ANNCR. TAG: At Jim & Johnny's on Lake Street, in Oak Park.

See how this works? The Song establishes the Selling Idea. The first Donut gives you the idea of the restaurant.

Then, the second Donut delivers a promotional message.

The Tag repeats and reminds you where the restaurant is located. 371

HOW TO PLAY TAG.

Some things you can do with tags:

- **Special Promotions** – you can change them quickly and add extra energy to your image.
- **Local address information.**
- **Local phone numbers.**
- **Announcements** – Happy Birthday to employees and customers, or anything that adds the personal touch.
- **Community Involvement** – use your local tag to increase local involvement.

VIGNETTE:

Golden Bear – "Where." :60

Here's a nice little example of vignette structure – a short song, the musical question "where?" punctuated by little situations.

SONG: Where . . .

GUY: Where can I find really good tasting food... I mean all across the menu?

SONG: Where...

GAL: Where can I get anything from a light salad to a great steak on my lunch hour... and still have time left for a little shopping?

SONG: Where...

GUY #2: Where can I get great breakfasts, you know really fantastic pancakes, perfect eggs and an endless cup of coffee or tea anytime of the day or night?

SONG: Where...

GUY #3: Where can I get a Senior Citizen's Discount on any regular menu item, from a sandwich to a meal?

SONG: Where...

GAL#2: Where can I afford to take the entire family and satisfy everyone's appetite?

SONG: Where... at Golden Bear.

ANNCR: At Golden Bear Family Restaurants you can choose what you like and be confident you'll like what you choose. Because we take extra care to bring you delicious wholesome food every day.

Whether it's breakfast, a sandwich, a whole meal, or one of our exciting specials, and you know why? Because what's really special at Golden Bear is *you.*

SONG: You can choose what you like; you'll like what you choose.

Where... at Golden Bear!

Address and offer information helps your spot work harder in the retail environment of radio.

So give those Tags a little extra effort.

LOCAL ANNCR: I'll repeat that. Give those Tags extra effort... starting *today!*

THE VIGNETTE.

In the Vignette, you can interweave all the different elements of radio. Here's a Vignette 60:

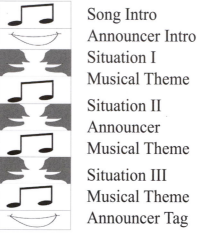

Song Intro	Beginning
Announcer Intro	
Situation I	
Musical Theme	
Situation II	Middle
Announcer	
Musical Theme	
Situation III	End
Musical Theme	
Announcer Tag	

HEY! YOU DON'T TALK LIKE YOU WRITE.

You're used to reading what you write.

With radio, you have to *listen* to what you write.

You may even need – um – new punctuation.

Tony Schwartz notes, *"If we use normal punctuation marks in written copy, it will be very difficult for someone to* sound *the words. Commas, semicolons, etc., are designed for the written word... There is a clear need for a system of oral punctuation marks that will indicate what people do when they speak...*

Spoken words that make complete sense when heard are incongruous when transcribed with written punctuation marks."

...AND MORE STRUCTURE.

Now let's examine two more bits of structure:

The *horizontal* dimension – Time & Tempo.

The *vertical* dimension – Sound.

Time & Tempo

THINK OF RADIO as a *horizontal time line* sixty seconds in length. That's *Time.*

Now think of the pace at which you move along that line. That's *Tempo.*

TIME & TEMPO – THE PITCH.

For example, the Pitch. The tempo of your announcer's delivery can be a distinctive part of your commercial.

Readin', Writin', and *Rhythm.* Remember?

Hear how extra emphasis can be used for effect.

Pauses. . . can add. . . **importance**. . . to key ideas.

Use *repetition* of certain words or phrases to tie your script together. Because *repetition* works to build both rhythm and emphasis.

The parallel construction inherent in *repetition* can help you build a solid rhythmic script.

Repetition can help people keep track of what you're saying. Need we say it again?

How many words? That's up to you.

Depending on the tempo of the announcer, you can have almost as many words as you wish.

The real question is – *what's the right rhythm to deliver your message to the listener?*

Mood and attitude also affect tempo.

Your attitude can be tough and competitive. . . or. . . relaxed and friendly.

You can build excitement by pushing the tempo. Or you can add importance by moving more slowly.

Tempo is one of the major ways you can make your Pitch distinctive. And memorable.

TIME & TEMPO – THE SITUATION.

The Situation also has tempo.

The entire sixty seconds should have form.

Context. Content. Conclusion… bah-da-boom.

PERFECT PITCH. Here's a pitch that Tony Schwartz designed to recruit new sales people for Bamberger's Department Stores.

Before writing the commercial, some of Bamberger's best employees were interviewed, asked why they chose Bamberger's as a place to work, and what they liked about their job.

They were also asked what radio stations they listened to.

Here's part of the spot.

ANNCR: Well, what are you doing with yourself now that the kids are all grown up and gone?

Wouldn't it be fun to go out and meet new people, maybe even start working again? You've got a lot to contribute.

And an extra paycheck could go a long way.

You know, there's a new department store opening in September at the Lehigh Valley Mall. Bamberger's.

And they really do need people like you. People who like to shop and who like to help other people shop.

And Bamberger's will have so many different work schedules — mornings, afternoons, evenings, full time, part time, weekdays, Saturdays — and they'll have employee discounts and nice benefits, too.

You know, Bamberger's really appreciates people like you, people who care and try.

So you probably won't stay at your starting salary very long...

Guess what? *Exactly the right kind of people showed up at Bamberger's – looking for jobs!*

"THE STRAW MAN."
Steve Steinberg, who taught radio at The Portfolio Center, suggests developing an imaginary competitor for your product – a "Straw Man."

You dramatize your advantage as you create a humorous situation. Here, Dick Orkin sells Breakfast at McDonald's as a waiter at "Chateau Le Foof."

McDonald's "Chateau LeFoof." :60

SFX: Bell
Waiter: Good morning, Mr. and Mrs. Whifflebottom.
Whifflebottoms: Good morning.
Waiter: Enjoying your stay at Chateau Le Foof?
Whifflebottoms: Quite.
Waiter: I assume you'll be joining us for breakfast.
Whifflebottoms: Breakfast?
Waiter: Yes, one boiled egg covered with poached salmon bits and set on a slice of dry toast all for the very reasonable price of seventeen dollars and forty- nine cents.
Mrs. Whifflebottom: No, no, we'll be going to McDonald's.
Waiter: McDonald's?
Mrs. Whifflebottom: They have a breakfast special for ninety-nine cents.
Waiter: Ninety-nine cents?
Mrs. Whifflebottom: Two farm fresh eggs scrambled in creamery butter, a toasted English Muffin, and crispy crunchy hash brown potatoes…
SFX: Feet exit
Waiter: I see, well have a good day then… Ah! Mr. HodNoggin!
HodNoggin: Morning.
Waiter: You'll be enjoying our delicious breakfast special?
HodNoggin: Breakfast special?
Waiter: Yes, an enormous boiled egg, smothered in a sea of poached salmon bits and set on a massive slice of dry toast all for only twelve dollars and forty- nine cents.
HodNoggin: No!
Waiter: Nine dollars and seventeen…
HodNoggin: No!
Waiter: Four dollars…

(Continued on next page.)

Beginning. Middle. End.

You need to feel the overall structure of your spot.

In the beginning, you must establish the Situation, introduce your characters, and perhaps the Problem.

You may wish to introduce the product. Context.

Then, you move to the middle where the product is a key part of the drama. Content.

And the end, with product as hero. Conclusion.

The tempo of all this action will also affect the mood and attitude. The spot on this page, done by Dick Orkin's Radio Ranch has the speed and tempo of an old-time farce.

Dramatic structure and comedic timing are key –here, a fast-moving situation with people stepping on each other's lines.

Or. . . perhaps a bit more laid back. . . warm and intimate conversation with background music reinforcing the mood.

The right tempo will give your Situation a sense of itself. At the right tempo, it will feel right.

TIME & TEMPO – THE SONG.
For the Song, tempo is also critical.

An average pop song lasts about three minutes.

Naturally, you can't stuff a whole song's worth of words and music into sixty seconds. Don't try.

Don't overwrite.

Don't rush the tempo of your commercial.

Don't try to squeeze in a few extra lyrics or a little more copy.

Find the tempo that's right for the mood and attitude you wish to convey. And stick to it.

Make your copy fit the tempo.

And to help you do a better job, let's talk about *natural rhythm.*

Natural Rhythm

ONE OF THE BASIC PRINCIPLES of writing for the ear is… "natural rhythm."

What is it? First, it's self-explanatory.

It means your writing and phrasing is built with the natural rhythm of the words you use.

Let's start by examining the natural rhythm of words and phrases.

For example, the word "emphasis."

Think of three notes in an even tempo.

Now, say the word "emphasis." The first note, the first syllable has extra *em*phasis.

Three notes with an accent on *one*.

"Emphasis" is a waltz. *Em*-pha-sis.

One - two - three.

Naturally, this varies with each word and with each combination of words.

Consider "serendipity" and "different."

Seren*dip*ity – two even notes, then three faster ones, with the "dip" accented.*

One-two-*three* and four. Ser-en-*dip*-i-ty.

For the word "different" you have a choice of two different natural rhythms.

*Diff*er*ent* – two fast notes and a slower note.

One and *two. Diff*-er-*ent.*

Or… two notes with the accent on the first.

Diff-rent. *One,* two.

There's more than one natural rhythm.

Phrases have rhythm, too.

The phrase "one of the best" has a few possible natural rhythms.

You can emphasize *"one"* to create the phrase *"One* of the best…" *One,* two, and three.

Or, you can emphasize *"best"* to create the phrase "One of the *best*…" One, two, and *three*.

HodNoggin: No! I'll be having scrambled eggs, an English Muffin and hash browns at McDonald's.

Waiter: Ah! Very good! (softly) You supercilious twit.

Mrs. McFarfel: Good Morning!

Waiter: Ah! Mrs. McFarfel, you'll be having breakfast here?

Mrs. McFarfel: No, I… But I…

Waiter: I've locked all the doors… You won't be going to McDonald's!

Mrs. McFarfel: Help! Help!

SFX: Clatter, yelling & commotion (continues underneath).

ANNCR: The incredible ninety-nine cent Breakfast Special – at participating McDonald's.

FIND YOUR RHYTHM…
The Motel 6 Campaign.

Once upon a time, copywriter David Fowler, enjoyed listening to radio personality Tom Bodett on National Public Radio.

Then he was assigned a radio project for Motel 6. It was the perfect match – a folksy, no-frills radio personality that was a perfect fit for the no-frills product – Motel 6.

He wrote copy that fit Bodett's rhythm – from the opening, *"Hi, Tom Bodett here for Motel 6,"* to the final *"We'll leave the light on for you."*

It could happen to you.

Keep listening.

UP BEATS & DOWN BEATS.

When counting musical beats, the *down beat* is the number of the beat (one - two - three-four, etc.) beginning with one.

The *up beat,* the in-between beat, is indicated as "<u>and</u>."

Thus, "One - two - three - four" indicates four down beats.

"One <u>and</u> two <u>and</u> three <u>and</u> four <u>and</u>…" indicates up beats as well.

You will find copy works well when some of your emphasis words hit on down beats.

And you will find that if you think of your copy rhythmically and match it to the music, it will fit more naturally.

SOUND: THE "VERTICAL" DIMENSION.

Radio is an acoustic environment.

You don't see it. You hear it.

You don't just write it, you shape it.

For example echo and sound effects can create differently sized space.

The tone of your announcer, the vocal characteristics of actors, and music... they all play a part in shaping the *vertical dimension* of sound.

Sound – The Pitch.

Even a single voice in the Pitch has vertical range. Even your copy goes up and down.

Inflections and intensity add additional dimension. Each sentence has an arc. You'll feel a rhythm as thoughts and words go up and down.

Each component of voice recording – presence, echo, equalization, and the voice tone itself – can help you build distinctiveness with a single voice.

Finally, an announcer should do more than read your words – he should "sound" them. (See opposite page.)

Sound – The Situation.

The vertical component of sound can be quite important.

For example, the voices in a Situation should have *tonal contrast*.

Unique voices will help establish your characters quickly and clearly. Dick Orkin's distinctive voice has been one of the key factors in his success.

Background noise and sound effects can also help you "set the stage" and shape your acoustic environment.

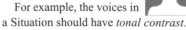

(Continued on next page.)

Or, you can string the words together into a four syllable adjective. "Oneofthebest."

When writing for music, you'll discover even more rhythmic potential, because music offers even more rhythmic options.

As you become more aware of the natural rhythm of words, you'll find your writing improving.

You'll find natural rhythmic emphasis will merge into your message and strengthen your writing.

Naturally.

AN EXAMPLE FOR YOU.

Look at Steve Karmen's natural rhythm:

> ***This Bud's for you!***
> *For working hard all day*
> *just like you always do.*
> ***So here's to you!***
> *You know it isn't only what you say,*
> *it's what you do.*
> ***This Bud's for you!***
> *For all you do, the King of Beers*
> *is comin' through.*
> ***This Bud's for you!***
> *You know there's no one else*
> *that does it quite the way you do.*
> ***For all you do – This Bud's for you!***

SOUND CONCLUSIONS.

And that's what radio is all about:

Pitches, Situations, Songs,
and **Combinations.**
Time and Tempo...
Natural Rhythm...
Sound.
And, of course, it all has **Structure.**
Beginning. Middle. End.
Context. Content. Conclusion.
Sound advice for radio.

#32: Radio Review

FOR YOUR RADIO ASSIGNMENT, you have your choice of four products. Or more:

- **A Fruit or Vegetable.** Use the one you used in your print assignment.
- **A New Product.** Invent a new product that *solves a problem.* Describe it and name it.
- **A Beverage.** Pick a popular beverage.
- **A Restaurant.** Pick one of your favorite local restaurants. Pick up a menu.
- **Write a Strategy and Theme for Each.**

1. THE PITCH.

A. Write a "Hot" Script.
Announcer and SFX (sound effects) only.
Thirty seconds. Lots of words. Good rhythm.
How many words?

B. Write a "Cool" Script.
Announcer and SFX only. :60.
Pauses… deliberate drama.
How many words?

2. THE SITUATION.

A. Describe three or four situations based on your **new product.**
What are the Situations and characters?

B. Write Two Situations.
Use the same characters in both Situations.

C. Want to make your commercial "funnier?"
Read the next chapter. *Quick!*

3. THE SONG.
Take your **beverage.**

A. Write three possible "Hooks."

B. Indicate alternate rhythmic treatments of each with <u>underlines</u>.

SOUND (CONT.)
Sound – The Song.
Your final result will be better if you understand various vertical elements:

The Low End, bass drum and bass guitar, reinforces the basic tempo, rhythmic pattern, and the "root" of the chord progression.

The Middle Range is the center of your sound – melody and harmony.

This is the area where clutter can occur. Try to maintain acoustic "space" in the overall sound for your message.

Helpful Hints for the Middle Range:

- As Grammy-winner Quincy Jones notes, *"you don't put the instruments in the same sonic strata as the voice. You have to put instruments above and under, but let the lead voice make its statement uncluttered and clear."*
- When writing announcer copy to an existing music track, try to find a tone and tempo that "fits" the music.

The High End of your music track may offer additional opportunities:

- Distinctive percussion effects, some of which might reinforce copy points.
- Symphonic strings to give the track more size and an expensive sound.

Remember... **the voice that carries your message, whether singer or announcer, should have its own space; the music should surround and reinforce... not interfere.** Sound advice.

GoodHabits:

Here are a few habits that can help you develop your radio writing skills:

1. Read your scripts aloud.
Leave time for pauses and SFX.

2. <u>Underline</u> words you wish emphasized and indicate pauses… in your written script.

This can help your talent better understand how to read your scripts.

3. Familiarize yourself with some local audio studios. What equipment do they have available? Do they have sound effects and a music library?

4. Listen to the tapes of voice talent. Local and national.

5. Learn to announce. Don't be shy, you can do it.

6. Listen to jingle house sample reels.

7. Familiarize yourself with some of the local musical talent.

8. Who does the jingles you like best? Track down their sample reels.

9. Listen to the demo tapes of radio specialists: Chuck Blore, Ken Nordine, Dick Orkin, and Bert Berdis.

10. Listen to some old Stan Freburg recordings.

11. Finally, start producing some of your scripts in demo form.

Use friends at work as actors.

This can help you develop your production skills as well as writing skills.

C. Write a Song using an introductory verse, a chorus, a second verse, a closing chorus, and a coda. Tap your foot. How long is your song?

D. Write a Song with an alternate structure – most beginning writers write songs that are too long. Hint: Try for two-line verses.

4. WRITE SOME COMMERCIALS FOR YOUR LOCAL RESTAURANT.

A. What ways can you localize your spot?

B. What times or special occasions can you use?

C. What special items or promotions will you feature?

D. Write two commercials. Announcer only.

E. Do an *Announcer Testimonial.* Assume the radio announcer has been to the restaurant and liked it.

Sample Radio Format.

```
Client Name
"Commercial Title"
Commercial Length: 60"
Version/Date (optional)
```

ANNCR:	Writing radio's quite simple, really. Indicate who's talking on the left. And write it on the right. I'm the Announcer, but you can call me "ANNCR."
SFX:	DOOR OPENS
MAN I:	Hey, just dropped in to remind you…
ANNCR:	Of what?
MAN I:	…that in radio, people interrupt each other a lot.
ANNCR:	You mean like in…
MAN I:	…like in real life. Okay, cue the jingle.
MUSIC:	MUSIC UP
VOCAL:	Radio! Radio! Listen to the Radio! (MUSIC UNDER)
ANNCR:	That's right, <u>listen</u> to the radio…
MAN I:	And be sure to read your script at a nice pace.
ANNCR:	Naturally.
MAN I:	(TALKS FAST) Not so fast that you have to rush and sound like you're late for something…
ANNCR:	…and trying to get in every copy point.
MAN I:	(SLOWLY) And not so slowly that… uh… more music?
VOCAL:	(MUSIC UP) Your words are going to glisten Every time you listen to the R-A-D-I-O!
LOCAL TAG:	(10" – MUSIC UNDER)
ANNCR:	Write it right and the next radio commercial for an advertiser near you may be yours. Call 1-800-RADIO. Void where prohibited.

MUSIC BUTTON

Yo! MoPo-Mo!

PO-MO MAKES SENSE on a lot of radio stations.

In every market, there's a whole sector of the listening audience that's a bit mo' po-mo in their response to advertising messages.

Clubs, clothing stores, restaurants, and all those other businesses that want your business… they may need to go a bit po-mo. So…

Let's think about how po-mo works in radio.

IRONY AND AN IRREVERENT ATTITUDE. How do you do irony in audio? Some of this will depend on your voice casting.

So, one of the things you'll have to do is find voices that can deliver that attitude for you.

One of those voices might even be your own.

Check out local comedians at the improv.

If we sell, we might also need to make fun of the fact that we're selling. It has to hit the right note.

Nike had corny jingle singers croon, "Hey There, Holiday Shoppers." Smart po-mo.

YOU UNDERSTAND WHAT WE MEAN – EVEN IF IT'S DIFFERENT FROM WHAT WE SAY. Po-mo works as subtext.

On the surface you're saying one thing, but you're really saying another. Yes? No?

The traditional structural things we talked about still apply… only there's another underlying structure – sort of the opposite.

Many marketers who sell to the youth market get this, but many others won't. So you may have a bit of an educational job to do.

PO-MO PITCH/SONG.
Mr. Pickled Pig's Feet Eater :60
Compare this spot to the classic "This Bud's for You" on page 274. This send-up of all the "real hero" beer commercials, with overly dramatic music and sarcastic copy, is an award-winning Bud Light radio campaign called "Real American Heroes."

DRUM OPENING/MUSIC UNDER:
ANNCR: Bud Light presents Real American Heroes.
SINGER: Real American Heroes…
ANNCR: Today, we salute you, Mr. Pickled Pig's Feet Eater.
SINGER: Mr. Pickled Pig's Feet Eater!
ANNCR: Ignoring all you know about pigs and where they live and what they step in, you look at their pickled paws and say, "Yummy!"
SINGER: Lookin' tasty…
ANNCR: Craving only the most daring meal, you pass up the cow tongue, skate by the head cheese, dismiss the Rocky Mountain Oysters.
CHORUS: Rocky Mountain Oysters
ANNCR: But a pig's foot soaked in pickle juice, now that's good eatin'.
SINGER: Save me a pickle…
ANNCR: So crack open an ice-cold Bud Light, Mr. Pickled Pig's Feet Eater (SFX: CAN OPEN), because it takes guts to eat those feet.
SINGER: Thank you, Mr. Pickled Pig's Feet Eater!
ANNCR: Bud Light Beer, Anheuser Busch, St. Louis Missouri.

NIKE I.E. CASUAL SHOES
"Feelings" :60

WOMAN: (To the tune of the song "Feelings" – Off-key) Feelings, nothing more than feelings, trying to forget my feelings of love. Feelings… Whoa, Whoa Whoa… Feelings… Whoa, Whoa Whoa … Feelings… Whoa, Whoa Whoa… Second Verse. Feelings, nothing more than feelings, you should try the feelings of I.E. Shoes with Nike Air. Tear drops rolling down on your face vanish with the feelings of I.E. Shoes with Nike Air… Whoa Whoa… Feelings, try them on for thirty days, if you don't love the feeling just bring them back to the store.
ANNCR: I.E. Shoes with Nike Air, the second best feeling in the world… Whoa, Whoa.

Okay, now this was a Song.

Only this would probably not be the way to sell me comfortable shoes – or maybe it would. People of all ages pretty much hate "Feelings."

The irony and irreverent attitude still manages to convey the core message – the shoes feel good on your feet.

Without making a big deal of it, they also throw in a promotional incentive – try them free for 30 days, if you don't like them, bring them back. Whoa, Whoa.

HE MAKES YOU SOUND GOOD.
One of the MidWest's radio experts is Jeff Hedquist.

Located near the bustling metropolis of Fairfield, Iowa, he delivers first-rate radio scripts and production.

Better yet, he's glad to give you some of his good advice for free.

Just go to hedquist.com and you'll find free articles, a newsletter, and, of course, a lot of good radio examples to listen to.

THE RIGHT EMOTION FOR THE PROBLEM.
Want your eyes lasered? Goofy won't work.

Unwanted facial hair, credit problems, a public service spot…

The tone might be a bit po-mo. Or not.

How about apartment rentals and car loans?

Figure out how to tune the emotional dimension – so people break into your message.

"NEW SCHOOL JINGLES."
Notice a lot of old rock 'n' roll in commercials?

One of the best ways to connect with a target is playing music he or she listened to as a young teen.

So all those songs you listened to a few years ago will show up again when it's time to sell you Buicks.

Songs send much different signals than jingles. They work nostalgically and subliminally. They create an emotional environment.

Jingles are overt, emphatic, and predictable.

We now have what Rick Lyon of Rick Lyon Music refers to as "new school jingles." Bob Seger singing *Like a Rock* for Chevy and Steve Miller singing *Fly Like an Eagle* for the Post Office.

"New School Jingles" add their emotional content to a brand's message. One of the first was Nike introducing a new shoe with the Beatles' *Revolution*.

LISTEN AND LEARN.
Po-mo or no, you need to find lots of good radio to listen to. Sad to say, there probably isn't a ton playing on your local station.

Check out the radio specialty houses.

We've reprinted a few of their names here.

Consider working with one of them. They know what they're doing, and they can teach you a lot. If you listen.

Radio Production

SOME USEFUL THOUGHTS on producing radio:

1. Own a Stopwatch. Whether it's a feature on your digital watch or a big old clicker like your track coach used to use, you need one as part of your life.

2. Have your first copy cuts ready before you go to your recording session. Then, get ready to cut it some more. Really good voices sometimes need a bit more time to work with the words. Sound effects may last longer than you think. And you may find you need an extra pause to make a point.

3. Find a terrific audio production engineer. As soon as you can, find the best one you can and become friends for life. Look for someone with:

- **Good technical skills.** Not everyone has them.
- **A good sense of humor.** Is it funny? How do we make it funny? Where do we find that sound effect? Look for a good comedic collaborator.
- **Good judgement.** Again, you'll often be alone in the studio with this person. You often need at least one other set of ears you can trust.

4. Build your own talent pool. Get to know the voices in your market. There will be some good ones. If you hear a local spot with a voice you like, track him or her down. Then, as you write, you may be already hearing things in your mind. Many of the best radio production teams use a lot of the same people.

5. Listen to your mix on a small speaker. Hey, it sounds great on that big system. But in the real world, people are going to be hearing it in their cars, with the volume turned way lower than you have it in the studio. Most studios have a "worst case" audio set-up. Listen to that mix on that small speaker.

If it's still right – congratulations. Nice spot.

If not, aren't you glad you knew before you took it back to play it for your boss and the client?

"I SAW IT ON THE RADIO."

AN AD FROM THE RAB.
The RAB is the Radio Advertising Bureau. This is the group that's concerned with, you guessed it, radio advertising.

The ad above, with the pipe-smoking trout, makes the point that you can do some very imaginative things on radio that you can't do anywhere else.

The RAB sponsors the Mercury Awards, with a nice big prize for the best radio commercial of the year.

Their website has lots of resources for people who want to write radio spots, including sample scripts and background information for various business categories. So, if you were doing work for a travel agency, they'd be able to give you some background on the travel agency business and even some sample scripts – for thought-starters.

Almost every radio station belongs to the RAB – and their website is www. rab.com.

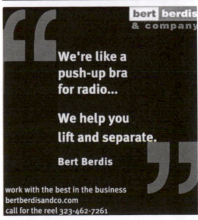

"People like to smile, they like to laugh. No great psychology here... Increasingly today, we have to create a message with some entertainment value, some surprise, so we reward people for paying attention rather than just clicking the remote or turning the page."

Bob Scarpelli, Chmn. DDB Chicago (Agency for Bud's "Whassup")

Fun with Puns. *Humor gives this small space ad a bright, friendly personality – making classical music sound inviting.*

Brand Character. *Actor Jim Varney leveraged some local gas company spots into a commercial empire. His comedic spokesperson talking to an off-camera "Vern," saying, "KnoWhutImean?" was virtually franchised to advertisers around the country. And this turned into a career that featured some feature films. Sadly, Varney died of lung cancer. Not funny. Know what I mean?*

HA!
A Quick Course in Comedy

WHAT'S FUNNY? I'm not sure either.

A mathematician who analyzed jokes called it "The Disaster Effect."

If it were true, it would be a disaster.

But it ain't. So you laugh.

If it really did rain cats and dogs.

If you really had a banana in your ear.

The quick gasp. The slight pause between the punch line and the laugh.

These are all reactions to "The Disaster."

It isn't true, but it *is* funny. Sometimes.

Sometimes the truth is funny, too.

This is humor based on *humanity*.

The conditions we've all experienced:
- Growing up
- The first date
- School, friends, work

The characters we all know:
- The Braggart
- The Cheapskate
- The Good Ol' Boy
- The Jewish Mother (or Italian, or whatever)

We know them. We "get it."

I BRAKE FOR VERN. *KnoWhutImean?*

These are devices generally used to create humor:

1. The Double Meaning
2. Exaggeration
3. Incongruity
4. Humanity

Let's take them one at a time.

AH = ART
AHA = IDEA
HAHA = HUMOR

Something to think about.

DOUBLE MEANING. DOUBLE MEANING.
One thing means more than one thing.

Buns/fat… evil/weevil. Get it? Of course you do.

When double meanings work, you build in extra interest and entertainment. On the double.

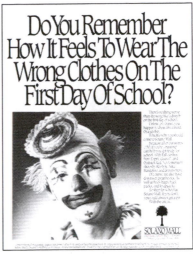

Exaggeration and Humanity. *They work together to make a point about back-to-school clothes. The exaggeration gets your attention, and then the humanity (remembering how you felt) makes the necessary emotional connection.*

Funny Car. *The Volkswagen personality is built into its ads as well as its design. The brand is clever and happy with itself, even though it has limitations in power and size. Quick, clever headlines – usually with a double meaning – drive home the brand's uniqueness and make you feel that the car itself is just a bit smarter than other cars.*

Original.   Chunky.

Sex Can Be Fun. *Here, advertisers add interest to their products by dialing up the sexual references. Another issue, taste. How do these ads strike you?*

Exaggerate the Difference. *Here, something as simple as a new variety of spaghetti sauce is made new and clever by creating a visual exaggeration.*

Who's the Humor For? *The ad above was done some time ago. On some levels, it feels a little dated. Yet, the target, a woman who wants a certain type of product, gets the humor – and the point. Below, we see a somewhat different angle at work – for anglers.*

EXAGGERATION FOR EFFECT.

Jimmy Durante was born with exaggerated looks. He said, *"If you're gonna have a nose, have a nose!"*

We have to create it.

Exaggerated characters, visuals, and situations can create comedy.

Overstatement and understatement are two other ways to use exaggeration. Most of the things we advertise are part of everyday life and, often, if we don't add something, our messages will be dull.

Exaggeration can add drama, interest, and entertainment to those messages.

Totally.

Find the Wow! *It's just lobsters at a Grand Opening. But look what happens when you add humorous drama and a bit of exaggeration. It makes the Grand Opening a little grander.*

384

[Send for Your Free Starter Kit Today!]

WINE COLLECTING TAKES UP LESS SPACE THAN ANTIQUE CARS, IS QUIETER THAN HI-FI, AND TASTES BETTER THAN STAMPS

People always say that every man ought to have a hobby but they never mention the real reason, which is: it's the only way he can be alone at home.

Most men, therefore, will choose a hobby that is so bulky, messy, noisy, or boring that no one can bear to be near him; a high price to pay for solitude.

The wise man will forsake these self-tortures and take up wine collecting. It works just as well, no one will bother him: A) children do not drink and so are not interested; B) women love to have wine at the table, but they feel, quite rightly, that

the collecting of wine is, like hunting, man's work. And so it is.

Wine collecting has one magnificent advantage over other hobbies: you can drink it. Also, it is neither expensive nor complicated to start. One may begin with two or three different reds and two or three whites; but which ones? To help you we will be happy to send you the labels of all thirteen Paul Masson table wines (plus a description of the delicious differences of each) to give you a collector's feel right away. Write: Paul Masson Vineyards, Dept. Y-1, Saratoga, California.

INCONGRUITY.

A favorite commercial began, *"Honey, let's take the penguin for a walk."* Humor creates a higher logic as it makes surprising new connections.

Above, with a curious juxtaposition, Howard Gossage encourages us to take up wine collecting.

Cows encourage us to eat chicken. And we are asked to "leave a light on" for criminals.

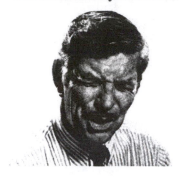

"You'd have a headache, too, if someone folded your forehead."

...because relieving a headache should be as easy as getting one.

Incongruity Can Get Attention. Here, an experimental newspaper ad uses the fold in the middle of the paper to make you think about a headache remedy.

Can Death Be Funny? Yes. This chapter features ads for food, insecticide, fishing, and seat belts, which involve the actual or potential demise of someone or something. In each ad, that "disaster" is part of the structure of the humor. It's also worth mentioning that humor often contains another "d" word. Danger. Funny isn't funny to everybody.

For example, eating meat offends many vegetarians. But cows telling you to eat chickens at Chick-fil-A is sort of funny. At least I think so. Do you?

BUCKLE YOUR SAFETY BELT.

The Human Condition. We forget to buckle up, we like to fish, and kids do the darnedest things. We recognize this in ourselves, and in that recognition is the strength of this kind of humor.

"Mikey." This famous commercial for Life cereal has lasted for years. Why? First, the instant recognizability of the situation with characters we all know. Second, the warmth and likability of the characters gives it staying power.

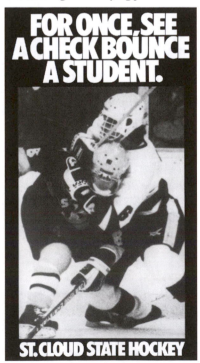

FOR ONCE, SEE A CHECK BOUNCE A STUDENT.

ST. CLOUD STATE HOCKEY

Made you look. Made you laugh.

THIS WOMAN HAS A SERIOUS SLEEP DISORDER.

HER HUSBAND.

HUMANITY.

The first three devices are *external*.

Humanity is *internal*.

Often, the reaction is not a big laugh, but a small smile and the warm feeling of recognition.

The more you like people, the better you will be able to create this type of humor.

The easy way to use humor is to make fun *of* people. (Careful that you don't find yourself making fun of the same people you're trying to sell.)

Try to have fun *with* people. The ad above will resonate with a woman who is kept awake by her husband's health-threatening snoring.

But the key is to let them be in on the joke. Get it?

Well, that's how to be funny. I think.

When developing advertising humor, try to let it emerge from the product or product use situation.

Just as Leo Burnett sought the inherent drama of a product, you should seek the "inherent humor."

"Touching that truthful chord is at the root of all great humor."
Sharon Kirk

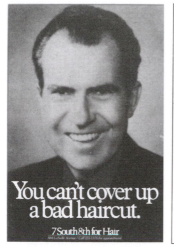

IRONY & IRREVERENCE.

Above, a barbershop leverages a political scandal (that photo is Richard Nixon, who, as president, was involved in a "cover-up") to sell haircuts, while the Episcopal Church makes a serious point with humor.

Sarcastic humor is a part of our lives and a part of advertising. It's even a bit po-mo.

Often, a more serious point is being made.

This effect can be accomplished using all of the devices we've already discussed – double meanings, exaggeration, and incongruity.

What about humanity? Well, sort of… but since the point being made – such as in the Virgin ad – is often a bit on the nasty side, don't expect a warm toasty feeling.

But if you do it right, your ad *will* have more impact.

HISTORICAL HYSTERIA.

A bit of history can be fun. You can use the past to make a comment on the present.

Each of these ads connects something from the past with a contemporary tone, and the result is interesting and humorous communication.

Juxtaposition and contrast of major and trivial facts is Incongruity that gives this humorous headline impact and drama.

Historical Figures representing certain values or characteristics are Exaggerations that can communicate quickly.

The same picture hangs in tiny lake-bottom post offices.

Our murderers row: Wanted since 1936. From left to right, It's Fat Rap, Husky Jerk, CountDown, Original, and Jointed.

Humanization. We can also humanize things that aren't human. Like animals. Above, the humanization of game fish adds humor and story value to a fishing tackle ad. Below, "...Sparky opted in-stead for a quiet dinner at home."

Her invitation intrigued him, but Sparky opted instead for a quiet dinner at home.

The best-tasting Dog Chow ever. Dogs don't know it has real meat and bone meat. Or who do agree. Or 43 nutrients. They really know how good it tastes. Purina Dog Chow brand dog food. It's on complete.

All You Add Is ♥

Sure mom, McDonald's sounds great.

The "Sure mom," ad and the one for someone "mediocre" are good examples.

You get the humor in the restaurant ad, and they don't have to make some competitive claim.

SAYING THE OPPOSITE. What happens when you "get it?"

You understand the double meaning. The irony.

You're amused by exaggeration. So even though it isn't true, you don't argue the point, but agree with the tangential truth. Ha Ha.

Are you a **MiSERABLE WENCH?** *Would you like to be?*

Now you can turn a bad hair day into an asset. Make pitted skin, poor demeanor and foul mouth work for you. We need miserable wenches and pretty maidens for The Pirates of Penzance. Open auditions will be Saturday and Sunday, March 23 & 24 at the UT Music Building East, Chorus Room 2.106 (Sat. 12-4, Sun.

1:30-4:30 p.m.) Bring sheet music from a Broadway show or opera, and resume and headshot if available. Be prepared to dance a bit. This popular musical comedy will run June 21 until July 7, 1996. For more information, please call the Gilbert & Sullivan Society of Austin at 472-4772 or 345-5950.

The "mediocre" ad makes its own connection.

In fact, they probably wouldn't want to talk to anyone who was dim enough to take them literally.

Likewise, someone who gets the "miserable wench" joke has the right attitude to perform in a Gilbert & Sullivan revival in a "wench" outfit.

Likewise, if you get the "Lemon" joke, you might feel OK with a VW.

Lemon.

Humor makes an interesting connection.

When we "get it," we connect with others who also "get it."

The connection is deeper with the people you want to talk to, and the message is much more powerful.

Fun with Money. *Here, American Express has the strategic objective of encouraging card use for everyday purchases. They have Jerry Seinfeld use his AmEx card for groceries, gas, and yadda yadda yadda.*

THE STRATEGIC USE OF HUMOR.

You already use humor strategically.

Your current use is for social strategy. To break the ice, to seem like a nicer person, or even to use humor as a hostile act. Think about it – "making fun" of someone may not be a friendly act.

By the same token, that's how advertising uses humor. We might want to "make fun" of the competition – like they do in those Daffy's ads.

We might want to use self-deprecating humor to make an AmEx credit card seem less ritzy and the *Village Voice* more fun-loving. See? It's strategy.

FOR EXAMPLE. . .

Let's say you're working on a lemon scented cleaning product. Here's what you could do:

• Work **double meanings** off the lemon characteristic – like "Lemon-aid."

• Create an **exaggerated** cleaning situation or an exaggerated "clean freak" type of character.

• Create a **human** and **humorous** situation where cleaning is important. Like your Mom is coming to visit your apartment…

• Juxtapose a straightforward message within some sort of **incongruous** situation.

Irony, of course, would be optional.

Fruits and Vegetables Can Be Fun.
Humor has a lot of use when you're trying to add interest to something that people have seen a million times before. Here are two examples.

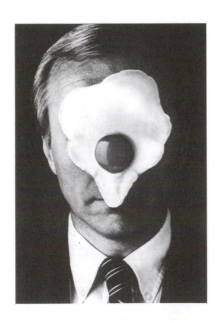

#33: That's Funny
Pick a product. Any product. Have fun.

1. CREATING HUMOROUS DEVICES.
Make your fruit or vegetable funny.

2. CREATING MORE HUMOROUS DEVICES.
Take a look at your "client list." See if you can jot down humorous ideas based on:
A. The Product
B. Product Features
C. Product-Use or Problem/Solution
D. A "Straw Man"
Remember the "ladder" from the strategy section? Look at the ladder (Attribute/Feature/Product Benefit/Consumer Benefit/Value) and see if you can find a place where you can make things funny.

3. WORD PLAY.
Write a silly limerick or a "Burma-Shave" poem for your product. (Note: Burma-Shave had little sequential signs which you read as you drove by. *"In this world/of toil and sin/the head grows bald/ but not the chin/Burma-Shave."*)
A short poem, please – 2 to 4 lines.

4. INCONGRUITY.
A. Think of a visual that features an incongruous juxtaposition featuring your product and write a straight headline. See what happens.
B. Do an ad with a gorilla in it. Or a banana.

5. CHARACTER STUDY.
A. Develop a comedic character related to some aspect of the brand, product, or usage.
B. Develop a character based on "The Problem."

6. WRITE A HEADLINE FOR THIS VISUAL.
"Egg on your face." Get it? Any product.

TV.

MORE THAN CHANNELS HAVE CHANGED. Once, creating and producing television was an expensive and complicated process involving all manner of specialized suppliers. Today, add an HD video camera and you've probably got enough to do a simple spot on your desktop.

Technology has changed – it's more affordable and more accessible to everyone.

Access has changed – not only are there more channels, but YouTube and similar sites provide access to virtually everyone with a video.

We've changed – you've grown up watching a wide variety of TV. As a result, your visual literacy and sophistication is already quite remarkable.

You've seen a lot. You know this stuff. Whether or not you know all the technical terms, you "get it."

TRUE STORY.
My daughter was certainly familiar with video production while she was growing up.

She'd been to shoots and edits and pretty much knew the drill – not that we'd talked about it much.

Still, when she showed up with one of her first music videos – "Fly Girl" done for an on-the-rise singer named Queen Latifah – I was impressed.

She'd shot everything you needed for a good edit – cutaways, overlays, master shots – it was a solid piece of work.

The video even won an award. Good job, Jessica. I asked her. "*How did you know to do all that?*" She answered simply, "*It just sort of made sense.*"

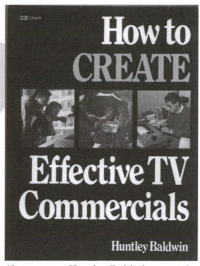

40 years ago, Huntley Baldwin wrote the first edition of this book, *How to Create Effective TV Commercials*, a solid look at how we did TV spots back then

40 years later, his son, Hunt Baldwin, is co-writing a TV series about the ad business – *Trust Me*. Evolution marches on.

TECHNOLOGY FOR EVERYONE.
Once, producing television was expensive – now all have access to the technology.

Moviemaking is all about having the right connections.

APPLE & FINAL CUT.
You'll probably want to start out on the easier Apple programs, like iMovie, which gives you nice basic capabilities, but, sooner or later, you (or a good friend who bought all the equipment) will want to move up to a more robust program, like Final Cut Pro.

That's the basic technology now available to create your own video.

There are other platforms, and things are evolving nicely, but while once you could wait a few years before diving in, this is now an area where you need to be developing familiarity. You might not become a video editor, but you should know what's involved.

Good advice. If it makes sense, it probably does.

If it doesn't make sense, well, either it doesn't or you'll be needing special effects.

ONE THING HASN'T CHANGED.
With all those changes going on, it's interesting to know that one thing about television really hasn't changed much at all – Formats.

The formats of television commercials, news shows, sitcoms, promotional announcements, etc… they're still pretty much the same.

In fact, that's one of the reasons you laugh at those fake TV commercials you see on *Saturday Night Live* – you get the format.

When they show the funny product instead of the serious product, everybody gets the joke.

Because everybody gets the format.

So, here's how we're going to organize this section.

• **The Basics** – Some principles of effective video that are worth covering, including some initial points on production – not to mention a bit of Good News/Bad News.

• **Formats** – we'll cover the six most common. Naturally, there are variations and combinations.

• **TV Production** – some words to the wise, including…

   • **Your First TV Spots** – things to consider that might be helpful.

   • **Vocabulary** – terms you really should know.

OK, lights, camera, action.

The Basics

First, *TV is visual*.

This may seem like stating the obvious, but it's a huge shift for a writer and a big shift from print.

You must learn to communicate with pictures. Words are not enough. What's more, the words and pictures need to connect. In fact, the visuals should tell the story.

A good television commercial should communicate *with the sound turned off!* What will we see?

Second, *TV moves*.

Again, that probably seems obvious, but it's a new way of writing. So think about it.

What *movement* will occur as you move from the beginning to the middle to the end? What will you write as you move along that visual path?

Finally, remember: *people aren't paying much attention.* You are. The client is. They aren't.

You must be perfectly clear, and, at the same time, you must be intriguing or interesting.

This is a slightly Zen concept – you have to pay a lot of attention to create something that works with people who aren't paying much attention at all.

So…

Think *visually*.

Think of how your commercial *moves*.

And you really need to be clear, because *people aren't paying attention.*

Now, here are some of the other things you need to keep in mind:

- Audio/Visual Integration
- Beginning/Middle/End
- Clarity
- Understanding Production

Let's take them one by one.

THE POWER OF STORY.

One of the many things they do well at Goodby, Silverstein is create TV spots that tell stories.

Here, they tell us a story about Cracker Jack. It takes the old "prize inside" story to a new level using an "experimental extra extra large size" as the narrative device.

Stock boys try to stock it.

Families take the extra large size home and can't get it in the garage. Oops.

And, finally, a little girl finds a prize inside her Cracker Jack – a pony! (Smile.)

They take a product (Cracker Jack) and a feature (prize inside) that everyone is familiar with and make it fresh and entertaining by creating a brand-new thirty-second story with the product as the hero.

How Do You Invite the Eye? *TV is a visual medium. Your opening frames are like the headline to a print ad.*

Visuals. Demos. Talking Persons. Slice of Life. "Punchy," is part of an audio-visual mnemonic *for Hawaiian Punch. They use a number of stylistic devices to serve up a single memorable message.*

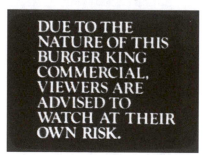

DUE TO THE NATURE OF THIS BURGER KING COMMERCIAL, VIEWERS ARE ADVISED TO WATCH AT THEIR OWN RISK.

Words and Pictures. You plan them in pre-production. *You produce those pictures during* production. *And you put them all together in* post-production.

AUDIO/VISUAL INTEGRATION.

Basically, you need to say what you show and show what you say.

The two dimensions – audio and video – need to relate in a meaningful way, though it can be an unusual juxtaposition.

For example, classical music and cars bumping into each other in slow motion.

The two work together – even though it is a bit of a surprise.

Another point about audio and visual, you're working with four dimensions. Not two. Each of these dimensions – audio and visual – actually has two sub-dimensions.

Your visual dimension has words and pictures. You can show something – and you can super-impose words. Don't overdo it, but you can do two things visually. Pictures. Words.

Audio – same thing. You have the words you say, and you have the surrounding sound: music, sound effects, and the attitude of the words you say. Words. Sound.

A low, rough, male voice or a soft, female voice can communicate very different things – even when the words are the same.

Music and sound add further range. If you sing it instead of say it, that's something else again.

But whatever you show, whatever you say, what's happening on the screen and what's happening on the soundtrack, need to be connected in a meaningful way.

394

BEGINNING/MIDDLE/END

Good communication has a simple structure.

That's particularly true for shorter pieces, like TV commercials and music videos.

Personally, I find it helpful to first envision the ending. That's right…

To begin, think of the end.

What is it exactly you wish to accomplish? What are the final thoughts you want the viewer to remember?

Well, it's a pretty good guess that one of those things is… the brand.

Another good guess is you'll want to communicate your Selling Idea.

You may have another job or two to do, too – a shift in attitude, a persuasive bit of support, or an overall emotional connection.

Whatever it is, it should be clear and simple.

With that final impression in mind, you're ready to begin at the beginning.

#1. THE BEGINNING.

For openers, you need an Opening Section.

It should, literally, "open the window."

It should provide the viewer with information about what's going on. Context.

You must begin your commercial so it's *easy* for people to understand.

You want to be interesting, but not confusing.

That's what you *should* do.

Here are three things you *shouldn't* do:

1. Don't overwrite. Don't overdo it.

You need to establish things quickly. Many commercials are overwritten and too complicated in the opening section. This creates time problems that last for the rest of the commercial.

The Final Frame. The Brand. The Theme. The Call to Action.

Direct Marketers know what they want you to do. Call this number.

Open the Door.

Say Hello.

Welcome to Miller Time. *It's a bar. It's a beer. It's perfectly clear.*

Intriguing. Involving. Intimate. *With the music of "Me and Mrs. Jones" playing in the background, Nike used this extreme close-up to get us interested in one of their athletes, Marion Jones.*

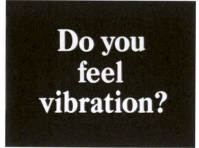

A provocative question *can help generate relevant interest for Goodyear Auto Centers.*

Too much time, too many words, or too much establishing "business" creates a burden that can make the remainder of your commercial less effective.

Tell 'em what you're going to tell 'em. Quickly.

Better yet, show 'em. They should get it in a glance.

2. Don't be confusing.

Huh? While there is always pressure to be clever and original, an idea that took a long time to think up may take a long time for the viewer to understand.

"Huh?" doesn't cut it. Remember, nobody's paying as much attention as you are.

Tell 'em what you're going to tell 'em. Clearly.

Better yet, show 'em.

3. Don't be irrelevant.

Many commercials are *uninteresting.* Why?

It's a function of your message not being *relevant* or *meaningful* to the viewer.

Consumers don't care how many meetings and rewrites it took you to sell the spot.

They're considering whether to change the channel, get a beer, or go to the bathroom.

And, like you, they've seen a few commercials.

You need to figure out what's interesting to *them* – not to you. That's the trick.

You can be intriguing – that's fine the first time – but it needs to pay off for the viewer.

Tell 'em something that's interesting to *them.*

So...

You must be clear.

Quickly.

With *interest.*

That's for openers.

#2. THE MIDDLE.

The middle section is often where you provide Support – the reasons, rational or emotional, for buying the product. Here's where you make the sale.

In my view, the basic question you must answer is "What sort of Support?"

How do you make your case to the consumer?

Even though that support might be an emotional connection, you have to do more than entertain.

You have to provide something that will help persuade the customer to select your product in preference to the competition.

Sometimes it's easy.

Sometimes you have just what you need:
• A convincing demonstration.
• Strong visuals.
• Great music.
• A meaningful emotional connection.

Sometimes it's tough.

You may have too much or not enough:
• No dramatic difference.
• A complicated message.
• A hard-to-visualize benefit.
• A low-interest product category.

Whether it's easy or tough, the middle of your commercial should relate to your Strategy – how are you connecting your target with your brand?

How are you better than the competition?

That connection will probably be a key part of the strategy. If it's a meaningful connection (interesting and relevant to the target), it should work.

Whether it's something in your Support section, something important to your target customer, or something that's just plain memorable, it should help you get where you're going.

Strategies are synergistic – so is good TV.

Driven to Keep Your Interest. *With no "hot" new models, Nissan brought back their "Z" car heritage in this engaging commercial starring a real doll – Barbie. They built the brand image while they were building new cars.*

Featured Personality. *Look who said "Hello." In this commercial, the GE Dishwasher really speaks for itself...*

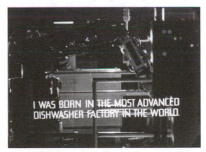

dramatizing how "smart" it is in a clever spot with no spoken copy! Computer sounds and subtitles do the job.

As feature after feature is clearly and interestingly demonstrated, they really do "Bring Good Things to Life."

THE PLAIN, SHORT STORY OF GOOD ADVERTISING.

The style of this classic piece by Fairfax Cone is a bit dated. But the message is still fresh and appropriate. We put it here, because he reminds us to be clear.

Advertising is the business, or the art, if you please, of telling someone something that should be important to him. It is a substitute for talking to someone.

It is the primary requirement of advertising to be clear – clear as to exactly what the proposition is.

If it isn't clear – and clear at a glance or a whisper – few people will take the time or the effort to try to figure it out.

The second essential of advertising is that what must be clear must also be important.

The proposition must have value.

Third, the proposition (the promise) that is both clear and important must also have a personal appeal.

It should be beamed at its logical prospects; no one else matters.

Fourth, the distinction in good advertising expresses the personality of the advertisers; for a promise is only as good as its maker.

Finally, a good advertisement demands action. It asks for an order.

It exacts a mental pledge.

All together these things define a desirable advertisement as one that will command attention but never be offensive. Remember –

Reasonable, but never dull.
Original, but never self-conscious.
Imaginative, but never misleading.

And, because of what it is and what it is not, a properly prepared advertisement will always be convincing and it will make people act.

This, incidentally, is all that I know about advertising.

Fairfax Cone
Foote Cone & Belding

#3. THE END.

Now we finish where we began.

At the destination you first imagined.

In addition to providing necessary information, the end of your commercial should reward the viewer. Better yet, the whole commercial is rewarding and worth watching again.

Whether it's a well-turned phrase, a great visual, a memorable musical theme, a warm, friendly feeling, or a punch line… tie the ribbon.

Visually and verbally.

You must say it *and* show it.

Clearly, meaningfully, and *memorably.*

So your message stays with the viewer after the commercial has faded to black.

Remember, the objective of your commercial is to get people to prefer your product to the *competition* – the mission your commercial must accomplish.

And that's The End, my friend.

THE NEED FOR CLARITY.

With all you've gone through to create your spot, this may seem redundant, but it needs mention.

In fact, I have to remind myself regularly.

Your TV spot needs to be perfectly clear.

Sure, you can be funky, hip, informative, sophisticated, or silly. But… *you must be clear.*

Are we clear about this?

The viewer will not give your commercial anywhere near the same attention that you, your boss, the account executive, or the client gave it.

Beware. This lack of clarity may not be clear to you, your boss or the people you work with. (They have the same high interest level that you do.)

Another problem is that things that are important to people who make commercials are often not meaningful to people who watch them.

This may not be clear when you're in the thirteenth meeting and the seventeenth rewrite.

Are you being clear?

Will your audience "get it?"

And don't be afraid to say it again.

That's right, don't be afraid to say it again.

PRODUCTION INTRODUCTION:

Over time, you'll probably become experienced at producing television.

That experience will be a result of doing a lot of things right, and – sad to say – seeing things go wrong along the way.

First. *You learn by doing*.

The ad industry has a rich history of expensive TV production screw-ups. Evaluating TV before it's produced is a risky proposition at best.

Variables like production budget, acting, video quality, music track, and all the other things that go into "putting it in the can" make a pretty good list of all the things that can go wrong.

There have been low-budget triumphs, big-budget busts – and everything in between.

But… that's kind of how it works.

Some of you will be quick studies with a rapid learning curve and others… well, all I can say is try to not make the same mistake twice.

Second. *First time work looks like first time work.*

Unless you really know how to light and shoot and edit, even fairly cool student stuff usually isn't very polished – not quite up to the quality of a local used car spot. Was that really your ambition?

And, is someone really going to hire you based on something a notch above home movies?

Then again, you've got to start somewhere and nobody said it was going to be easy.

PRODUCTION ON THE RUN.

Chevy's "Fresh Mex" spots were "done fresh today." The result is pretty nuts.

"This commercial was made today." That's how it begins. Funky, hand-drawn supers in hot colors give the video a fresh feel.

They try to add a bit of visual proof, and make some point about the freshness of the food at Chevy's

And, without all the fast food cliches you've seen a million times, they drive home the point – Fresh Mex!

The Production Challenge.

Get up early. Shoot it. Edit it. Run it.

And then… think of what you're going to do tomorrow.

Fortunately, not every day.

To be continued… Nike kept us involved by inviting us to view different endings to the commercial on a special website.

Final Frames should leave us with the right strategic thought about the brand.

Focus – Front to Back. Here, TBWA\ Chiat\Day stays focused on a single proposition. "We treat you like a person. Not a prescription."

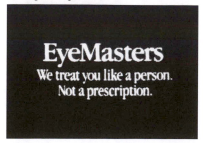

But, hey, you've gotta start somewhere.

We're going to work to give you the context and the tools to make good decisions at the beginning of your video career.

By the way, if you're already at an agency, you might be surprised at how much of this advice will also work for you.

Chances are, you've got a small budget, limited resources, and Ridley Scott and Joe Pytka are busy.*

Finally, get ready to make a serious time commitment.

Video production will suck up incredible amounts of your time, energy, and resources (including money).

Yeah, you can do it. But wait until you see all the time and effort it takes.

If you're looking for a job, the amount of time you'll spend prepping, producing, and finishing a single spot compared to how you could spend that time preparing a book with lots of ads and scripts.

Given limited resources, it might be a bad idea, particularly if you're trying to do it on your own.

Then again, more and more programs are having students produce spots as part of a course. Good. Work hard. Do your best.

And realize that one purpose of these courses is to provide a safe place for you to make your mistakes – and learn further lessons from the mistakes made by your fellow beginners.

The well-known feature director Ridley Scott started out doing TV spots (he did Apple's "1984" among others). Joe Pytka is still a top TV commercial director.

Ready?

OK, almost time to start thinking about your TV commercial.

To begin… start at the finish.

We'll say it again, start at the finish.

First, concentrate on *the final impression* of your commercial. Imagine the destination.

Many writers spend too much time thinking about the beginning of a commercial.

They worry about gags, situations, openings, attention-getting devices, and the like.

Start at the finish. Where are you going?

You should first concentrate on the final impression of your commercial.

Try to have this clearly in mind before you start to write your commercial.

What do you want people to *see?*

What do you want them to *feel?*

What do you want them to *think?*

What do you want them to *learn?*

What do you want them to *do?*

To create the path…

> first imagine the destination.

THE FINAL FRAME.

Think about how it's all going to end.

Often, the final frame is as simple as your brand's logo and your theme – maybe there's a nice payoff visual, too.

As you begin, keep that final frame in mind.

Okay, now let's look at some formats to help you get there.

The Final Impression. Have it clearly in mind – otherwise you'll be half-baked.

THE POWER OF ONE IDEA.

Maalox takes the generic problem of an upset stomach and generates ownership with a single, memorable idea, "The Maalox Moment."

The problem is dramatized and paid-off with the simple memorable slogan.

One goal is to break into the consumer vocabulary with a catch-phrase that dramatizes the need for the brand.

The advertising stays focused on this one simple, powerful idea.

It's even integrated into a consumer response program. If you have a Maalox moment, write: Maalox Moments, P.O. Box 8388, Philadelphia, PA 19101.

TV Formats

ONE PROBLEM FOR COPYWRITERS just starting in TV is a narrow repertoire, a lack of familiarity with the range of executional solutions available.

The objective of the next section is to help you become familiar with the range of TV commercial formats available to you. Naturally, creating categories creates room for debate.

But as far as this book is concerned, these are the six major types of television commercials:

A. **Slice** (short for slice-of-life)

B. **The Talking Person**

C. **The Demo**

D. **The Visual**

E. **Graphic Collage**

And of course. . .

F **Combinations.**

We think you'll find these broad categories pretty comprehensive. We'll cover the range of options available in a useful and memorable way.

Let's take a look...

Slice of Life.

The Talking Person.

The Demo.

The Visual.

Graphic Collage.

TV SCRIPT FORMAT

PRODUCT NAME:
"TITLE"
LENGTH:

VIDEO INSTRUCTIONS IN ALL CAPITAL LETTERS, SINGLE SPACED.	**AUDIO:** Copy indicated in upper and lower case. Double spaced.
SUPER: THEME.	**ANNCR:(VO)** Theme.

A. Slice

SOME OF THE BEST COMMERCIALS, as well as some of the worst, are "slice of life."

Comedy commercials, such as those for Alka-Seltzer and Volkswagen are Slice.

One of Volkswagen's best slice of life spots was at a funeral. You can see it on the next page.

The touching dramas of Hallmark and FedEx's surreal dramatizations are also Slice.

So are many "McDonald's Moments."

Short pieces of Slice strung together, usually with music, create the Vignette.

How do you start slicing?

Imagine a situation where the product plays an integral and important part. Then write it down.

That's easy. The hard part is making it special. Situations, characterizations, and dialogue.

Any way you slice it, you have to make Slice come alive to make it "slice of life."

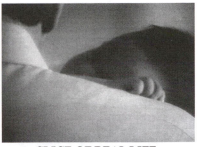

SLICE OF REAL LIFE.
Copywriter Bill Heater was working on a pitch for the John Hancock account. Research showed that people only thought about insurance when undergoing some major life change.

The first spot was videotaped in his home and co-starred his infant daughter, Jenny Katherine. Copy went like this…

"I love you little Jenny Katherine.

I want to tell you something very, very important. Daddy got a raise.

That means I can buy you a sandbox, sliding board. What do you think?

Think we should put some of it away? What do you know about the stock market?

I love you little Jenny Katherine.

Guess what, Daddy got a raise."

Guess what? Daddy won the account.

"Real Life, Real Answers" grabbed little slices of life – of people in the middle of some important life change –and connected them with John Hancock.

A Slice of History. This classic spot from Goodby has a collector of all things Aaron Burr, making a peanut butter sandwich. Suddenly, a radio quiz show calls with a question – and the answer is… Aaron Burr! But since there is no milk to go with the sandwich, he cannot say the answer clearly. Tragedy! And a life lesson for us all. Got Milk?

BITS OF SLICE = THE VIGNETTE.
The first Vignette commercial was probably Dick Greene's "Tummies!" for Alka-Seltzer, with great music and a great theme – "No matter what shape your stomach's in."

This classic DDB spot begins with a parade of very large automobiles.

Male Voice Over: I, Maxwell E. Snavely, being of sound mind and body, do bequeath the following:

To my wife Rose, who spent money like there was no tomorrow, I leave $100 and a calendar.

To my son Rodney, who spent every dime I ever gave him on fancy cars and fast women, I leave $50... in dimes.

How to Slice

Imagine a situation where your product plays an important part. That's the key.

The opening section should usually establish your situation. Scene and characters.

The middle section builds your sale.

It may be problem/solution, it may be a sequence of happy vignettes... whatever.

The key is that you slice your situation so that it's easy and interesting for the viewer to understand.

And it should be a situation that works toward selling the product, whether it's facts or feelings.

The closing section is the payoff.

At the end, we know why we should buy.

In the best slice of life, we can relate to the product and the situation in our own life – even if we need a sense of humor to do it.

Look at this classic Volkswagen commercial.

In the opening, we see that it's a funeral.

It's clear. It's interesting. And the "Last Will" voice over makes it both humorous and profound.

In the middle, we see a sequence of spendthrifts in big cars (get it) getting their just reward.

Then in the closing sequence, we see the virtue of owning a VW – with quite a payoff!

To my business partner, Jules, whose motto was "spend spend spend" I leave nothing, nothing, nothing.

Finally, to my nephew, Harold, who oft time said: "A penny saved is a penny earned."

And who also oft time said: "Gee, Uncle Max, it sure pays to own a Volkswagen..."
I leave my entire fortune of one hundred billion dollars.

PNI – THE SECRET OF SLICE.

Years ago, I worked with a lot of smart people in the Research department at Leo Burnett. And, since P&G was a major client, we looked at a lot of Slice commercials.

Some worked better than others.

After a while, they figured out one of the big reasons – and developed a way to measure it. They called it "PNI" or Product Narrative Integration.

The better the product was integrated into the plot/narrative of the story, the better the commercial was in a whole range of factors – persuasion, memorability, effectiveness – call it what you want.

Why is that? Well, first human beings are pretty good at remembering stories.

As little children, that's how we learned. Stories filled our days, with a bedtime bonus.

So, as we tell our stories, the better we make the product an important part of the story, the more effective it will be as a commercial message.

For example, how the lack of milk caused a problem in "Got Milk?"

How the lack of a credit report caused a problem in the FreeCreditReport.com commercials.

THE NATURE OF BREAKTHROUGH.

It's very common to hear inspirational messages on how we need "breakthrough" communications. I agree. We need to repeat this point.

The real nature of effective breakthrough is when people "break in" to your message.

The breakthrough happens when people say to themselves, "*yeah, I really need a glass of milk with a cookie or a peanut butter sandwich.*" Or a young guy says, "*hm, I better get a credit check before I make a big move, in case there's something I don't know.*"

**BAD CAR. BAD JOB.
GOOD SLICE OF LIFE.**
The musical spots for FreeCreditReport.com may not be great music, but it's pretty good advertising. Not only does each individual spot make its point, but, like a sitcom, you see the players make their way through a variety of comedic situations.

IT'S ALIVE!
It's a big world – full of variety and possibility. How do you find the most powerful connections? Tony Schwartz has a suggestion:

"An advertiser's research should deeply explore the actual experiences people have with products in real-life situations, and structure stimuli in the commercials in such a way that the real-life experience will be evoked by the product when the consumer encounters it in a store."

ESTABLISHING SHOT
We see we're at a Laundromat.

REACTION SHOT
Garth sees something… or someone.

PRODUCT SHOT
Kim Basinger and All-Temperature Cheer.

TWO SHOT
Garth and Kim meet and talk.

FUNNY BIT
He's had his laundry drying for two hours.

BEFORE/AFTER
Not exactly what you'd see in a laundry spot, but, hey, it's *Wayne's World 2*.

THE CHEER STORY.

On the right, a slice from my life.

I'd been in the business about four years and had never done a "slice of life" commercial.

I'd won awards and had this kind of snobbish attitude toward this popular format used by marketers such as P&G.

So there I was, at Leo Burnett working on P&G. I was in charge of a detergent brand that was pretty much dead in the water – Cheer – with ads that people didn't seem to like much – there was a rumor that someone in Texas had shot the TV when one of their spots was on.

Anyway… there I was and I had to write a Slice commercial for All-Temperature Cheer. I was only able to think of one experience – learning how to do my own laundry when I went away to college.

But it was real. And it worked.

It changed Cheer from a no-growth brand to a solid #2 in a very competitive category.

As the brand started growing, we did research. Older women remembered going through a similar experience, or, if their children were young, they thought they would one day.

The spot wasn't just about Cheer – it was about them! We also realized that, when you create a little slice of life on the television (just like a sitcom), it begins to exist on its own. So we did two more.

In one, he meets a girl at a Laundromat.

And, on the left, a slice of something else. A few years later, *Wayne's World 2* did their own version. Garth meets Kim Basinger in a laundromat – and there's the box of All-Temperature Cheer.

Hey, you never know.

SFX: *(Door opens, light goes on)*
Mom: *Okay now Harold, when you go away to college, you'll have to wash all your crazy clothes.*

Harold: *I thought you just put 'em in the machine and...*
Mom: *There's more to laundry than that. Today's clothes have changed.*

Mom: *Look at these things... new fabrics, new colors, you've got to use the right temperatures.*
Harold: *Sure, Ma...*

Mom: *See this tag...*
Harold: *Sure, you sewed them on all my clothes...*

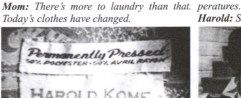

Mom: *No, this one. Permanent press. Wash it in warm water.*

Mom: *This crazy thing is a bright color, and I don't want to see it all faded. Use cold water.*

Harold: *When do I use hot water?*
Mom: *With these Harold, white things.*

Harold: *I need three detergents?*
Mom: *No, Harold...*

Mom: *...three temperatures, one detergent – All-Temperature Cheer.*

Mom: *It's specially made to really clean in all those temperatures.*

Mom: *Hot, warm, or cold. Use All-Temperature Cheer.*

Mom: *Fill it evenly... don't stuff!*

Harold: *Hey, Mom, it did work in all temperatures, this shirt looks groovy.*
Mom: *You're a good son, Harold.*

ANNCR (VO): *All-Temperature Cheer. For the way you wash now.*

Mom: *All-Temp-a-Cheer, Harold!*

B. The Talking Person

THE TALKING PERSON is, simply put, the *personification* of your message.

It's your selling message. In person.

Ask yourself. Who is this person?

A celebrity? A distinctive character?

An enthusiastic consumer? The client? Or maybe a duck?

How do you add dramatic dimension?

The right visual environment.

The right props.

The right words.

It's important to add *visual* information to the *verbal* information your Talking Person provides.

Don't feel limited to only one person, either.

Dialogue can add additional dramatic interest.

The Talking Person can be part of a Slice commercial, such as the continuing character dramas of P&G and others.

How do you get started? Easy.

Think of what you want to say.

Then, think of the perfect person to say it.

It may be some*one* or some*thing* that represents the inherent drama of your brand, like Leo's "critters." Finally, add appropriate *visuals*.

It walks. It talks. It's advertising with *personality!*

A Real Person. The founder of Wendy's projected the spirit of the brand.

Squeezing Out a Selling Idea. Hate him or love him, Mr. Whipple is the vehicle for delivering the memorable selling line, "Please Don't Squeeze the Charmin."

Who Needs to Talk? The character of Charlie Chaplin's "Little Tramp" was the perfect vehicle to introduce IBM's line of PCs. At the time, a big success.

PROBLEM/SOLUTION.

"Problem/Solution advertising is as old as advertising itself, simply because the basic function of many products is to solve people's problems.

But avoid the temptation to make the commercial all problem; the solution is what you are selling."

Luis Bassat
European Creative Director

Product Presenter. For years, Josie the Plumber sold Comet Cleanser in a Slice/Demo.

Remember, the Talking Person doesn't have to be a real person. Charlie the Tuna, Morris the Cat, and Tony the Tiger are all excellent Talking "Persons."

Celebrities can work, particularly if they bring some unique characteristic that connects with your brand.

BUTKUS: I tell ya, trying to get cultured isn't easy. We just went to the opera, and didn't understand a word.

BUBBA: Yeah. That big guy in those tights sure could sing.
BUTKUS: Well, at least we still drink a very civilized beer. Lite Beer from Miller. Lite tastes great.
BUBBA: But us impresarios drink it because it's less filling.
BUTKUS: We can't afford to get filled up. Tomorrow night we're going to the ballet.
SMITH: Yeah, sure hope they do it in English.

Your Talking Person can even be part of a Slice commercial – or present a unique Demo.

Simply put, it's the Selling Idea. In person.

Or how about two?

TWO TALKING PERSONS ADD DRAMA.

Two Talking Persons add dialogue.

It's sort of like Slice, but different.

They talk to the customer and each other.

On the left, some Lite comedy from Miller – a pioneer in getting good advertising performances from athletes.

Today, we see it all the time, back then it was groundbreaking.

A Po-Mo Logo. Jack, of the well-known Jack-in-the-Box sign, was brought back from the junk heap and turned into a hip, though not particularly well-spoken spokesperson for the brand – about what you'd expect from someone whose head is an overgrown Ping-Pong ball.

An Entertaining Way of Delivering the Strategy. American Express wanted to communicate an ordinary idea – use your American Express card for everyday purchases. Clever spots featuring comedian Jerry Seinfeld kept you watching while they made their point.

ANNCR (VO): Lite Beer from Miller. Everything you always wanted in a beer. And less.

The Maytag Repairman.
He's lonely because Maytag's are dependable. Inherent drama at work.

ANACIN "COAL MINER."

(An actor who talks like a hard-working coal miner gives Anacin's story extra impact.)

MINER: Tell ya what, you go down a half-mile shaft... It's dark... Damp... 'bout

12 million ton o' rock on top ya. An' ya getcha a headache. Wheeh!

Buddy, ya better have ya some Anacin. Yessir!

ANNCR: Anacin. More medicine than any regular strength pain reliever.
MINER: More medicine, 'at's good. But what's better is not havin' no more headache down in the hole.

He's Lying. It's Joe Isuzu, the lying car salesman for Isuzu. Outrageous lies. Hilarious commercials. Not sure they worked. But everybody remembered them. And... he's back!!!

TALKING PEOPLE, PRODUCTS, AND PROBLEMS. Can you make your strategy talk?

Who/what would be the best vehicle to deliver your Selling Idea? Answer that and you're on the way to finding your Talking Person.

For example, McCulloch Chainsaws found the perfect spokesperson – unique, humorous, and qualified as an expert in the category – Barney the Beaver!

MCCULLOCH 10" TV

BARNEY: You've got power. Sharp teeth. Even a chain brake. Next to a guy like me, you've got everything.
ANNCR: See the feature-loaded McCulloch 310 at your McCulloch dealer.

The same thing happened with the people at AFLAC. Not much vocabulary – but what he knew was just... ducky.

Famous People are Real People, Too. Here, Jane Seymour in her real-life role as a mother speaks for Gerber Baby Food, and Steve Ballmar, in his real-life role as President of Microsoft and "FOB" (Friend of Bill), delivers his message.

Walmart knows the power real people can bring to advertising. Here, a satisfied customer endorses their batteries.

THE TESTIMONIAL.

Real people out there like your product and they'll tell you why. See what they say. (By the way, actors can act like real people, too.) And, let's face it, we're all a lot more like the admiring people in those testimonial spots than the actors.

Television can be a window on reality. Open it.

One of the strengths of testimonials is simple but obvious – the people in these ads are the most like your customers – so it's easy for your customers to identify with the people in the ads. And, if those people like your brand, well maybe I might like your brand, too.

And that makes it easy to make your point. Looking for an idea? Talk to people who use the product – and really like the product. Testimonials can be a strong place to start.

The Maysles Brothers have been experts at this type of commercial. On the left are some of their thoughts.

Number one in a series: How to produce commercials that are credible and creative—some thoughts from the Maysles.

Reprinted from **BACK STAGE**

On The Art Of Real People Commercials
Seven Easy Rules

Real people commercials? No scripts and no actors? But how can you be sure it will work? How do you handle the freedom? In our business, the same questions come up again and again. How do we avoid those boring old testimonials? Is there a method to our magic? We think so. After sixteen successful years of real people experience, these seven rules seem to sum it all up:

1 Know your strategy.
Remember—no client's strategy exists without extensive research. Keep the key points in mind and you'll know when to guide and—better yet—when to follow.

2 It's all in the casting.
When selecting real people, choose subjects who express themselves openly—and make sure they're people you like. Without the right people, your commercial is dead.

3 Produce small.
Put your subjects at ease by keeping their environment familiar; artificial settings, large crowds and huge amounts of equipment can intimidate anyone.

4 Guide, never push.
Treat your subjects like friends, and they'll return the favor: they'll come through with more substance and style than any script ever promised.

5 Stay spontaneous.
Every situation has more than one response—so give your subjects the freedom to come up with their own. Spontaneity equals believability.

6 Be patient.
Patience inspires confidence—and a confident subject is sure to give you the good stuff. Use time as your ally.

7 Keep it real.
Don't edit the life out of your spot once it's shot—leave room for the humor, the little comments and gestures that keep the real in a real people commercial.

Once you follow these rules, producing a real people commercial is easy. Easier still is to produce it with us. For us, you see, these rules aren't really rules. They're a natural expression of our work—and that's the art of real people commercials.

MAYSLES FILMS, INC.

THE MASTERS OF REAL PEOPLE COMMERCIALS

C. The Demo

TELEVISION IS UNIQUELY SUITED for visual demonstration. Consider. How can your product be demonstrated visually? Demonstrate. Dramatically.

There are many types of Demo:

SIDE-BY-SIDE.

The traditional Side-by-Side, compares your product with another.

Guy on porch eating pizza...

BEFORE/AFTER.

The Before/After dramatizes both the Problem and the benefit. And, if you think about it, Subway's Jared is kind of a demo.

Guy on porch eating pizza...

with lots of Tabasco Sauce.

Before *Vlasic's New Big Pickle Slices.*   **After** *Vlasic's New Big Pickle Slices.*

PRODUCT PERFORMANCE.

The Performance Demo is another related type of Demo. It dramatizes how well your product works.

For example, Timex Torture Tests. "Timex takes a licking and keeps on ticking."

Mosquito bites guy, flies away...

IN-USE & NEW-USE.

The In-use Demo shows how the product is used and how the product works. That's how a lot of infomercials work.

The New-use Demo shows people new ways to use the product. Like a recipe or serving idea.

And remember...

Demos can be real or symbolic.

...and explodes.

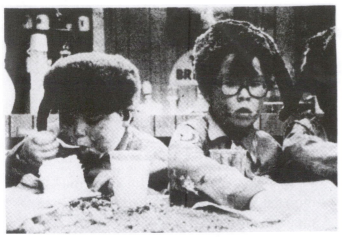

"Torture Tests"

YOU CAN DRAMATIZE product performance by dramatizing the Problem – or you can dramatize the product usage Situation.

Above, a humorous "torture test" for Mr. Big Paper Towels.

A graphic representation of a new product technology or a humorous overstatement – each, in its own way, is a demo.

Demos can be based on:
- Test Results
- Sales Figures
- Popularity
- Uniqueness
- Whatever…

Visual Demonstration is the key.

Don't just say it.
Show it.
Demonstrate.
Dramatically.

TIMEX TORTURE TESTS.
For years, Timex had demonstrated the durability of their inexpensive watches with visually dramatic demos – like this one with baseball star Mickey Mantle.

Then, as market opportunities appeared they were able to grow into areas like watches for kids with an already established reputation as a durable brand.

THE DOLLAR TEST.
Our spokesperson searches for something he can get for a dollar. At McDonald's he achieves success.

THE CHEER DEMO.
On the left is a demo first done at a P&G sales meeting. The technical staff wanted to show the ability of Cheer's formula to remove stains in cold water.

As Leo Burnett, Cheer's agency, was looking to develop a new campaign, they came up with a graphic recreation of that sales meeting demo – with a comic actor doing the demo accompanied by music.

The result was interesting, powerful, and very effective. Variations of this demo format ran for years.

Incidentally, the actor, Jobe Cerny, is also the voice of the Pillsbury Doughboy.

413

MCDONALD'S SUED TO STOP THIS BURGER KING SPOT.

Here, the little girl who grew up to be Buffy the Vampire Slayer compares McDonald's and Burger King beef patties.

ANNCR (VO): A very, very big message for grown ups.

LITTLE GIRL: Do I look 20% smaller to you? I must to McDonald's. When I order a regular burger at McDonald's,

GIRL: they make it with 20% less meat than Burger King. Unbelievable!

GIRL: Luckily, I know a perfect way to show McDonald's how I feel.
I go to Burger King.
SINGERS: Aren't You Hungry for Burger King Now?

P.S. Yes, that's Sarah Michelle Gellar in an early role as Big Mac slayer.

DEMOS THAT BECOME BRAND ICONS.

Good demos are clear – and they keep on going.
   The Energizer Bunny keeps on going (durability).
   Animated Scrubbing Bubbles visualize the cleaning process.

THE DEMO THAT ISN'T THERE.

We begin with a Chicago snowstorm. We see the cars of Chicago Bulls buried under snow. Then we pan to an empty space – Michael Jordan's Chevy Blazer is gone – dramatizing the problem and solution.

Water-filled balloons at a high school reunion dramatize bladder control problems with humor.

THIS CLASSIC SPOT DEMONSTRATES *DRAMATICALLY!*

 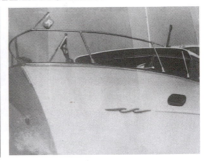

(Music Up)
ANNCR: *(VO) Watch closely... you're about to see something you've never...*

... seen before. Here comes Fuji Film

with color pictures so true to life...

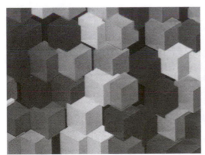 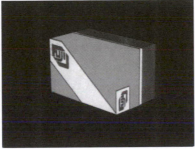 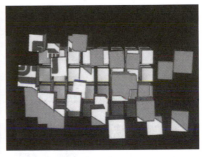

it's a real breakthrough.

Fuji Film.

Fuji's advanced technology has developed a precise color balance.

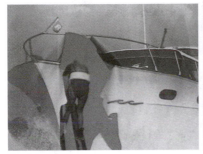  

The better the color balance,

the truer the picture.

Consistently brighter... clearer.

With Fuji, seeing is believing. So see for yourself.

Get Fuji Film. And get the true picture.

(MUSIC OUT)

WE LIKE GEICO.

They show how much variety you can wrap around a single-minded strategy.

Basically, they deliver the same "save money" message, but they serve it up with good humor, so we don't get bored.

Above, their relatively new "visualization of the benefit," which, of course, is the money you'd save.

Below, a name/mnemonic critter – a gecko – sounds like GEICO – which has gradually grown into a charming and useful character.

STATE FARM.

Here's Keith Reinhard's story on how he came up with this classic commercial:

"State Farm complained, 'You can't see insurance, so the logo is critical. But it's not big enough and it doesn't stay on the screen long enough.'

My solution?

Sixty solid seconds of logo!

I used the familiar State Farm bumper sticker to create a simple visual metaphor for the auto accident, then the full restoration of the logo to represent the car's like-new condition.

Simple? You bet.

But that simple spot won me my first Clio for State Farm.

Simplicity is the essence of unforgettable advertising."

That spot helped Keith drive his career all the way to Chairman of DDB.

And he's a good egg.

D. The Visual

TELEVISION IS A VISUAL MEDIUM.

Imagination begins with images.

How can you create interesting imagery for your brand? How can you *visualize* the benefit?

Or the problem?

How can you show what you say?

Remember, your audience can move, too.

You can fly them through space, so they see the Big Picture. You can shrink them, so small things seem larger. Just imagine. See?

Here, an egg on wheels gets put back together again by State Farm – a metaphor for car insurance. See?

STATE FARM "EGG."

ANNCR (VO): Handle with care. That's what...

this familiar emblem really says. And you'll get one like it when you insure your car with State Farm – the biggest car insurance company there is.

Then wherever you drive, whether your need for claim service is large or small...

You'll have a friend nearby to handle everything with care. See your State Farm Mutual insurance agent

soon and have your car marked for careful handling. You'll be surprised at how little it costs...

probably less than you're shelling out now. **THEME:** *"And like a good neighbor, State Farm is there."*

The product itself can be visualized very dramatically. Logos and other product graphics can reinforce your selling message.

Many brands use visual mnemonics to make themselves memorable.

Many image campaigns rely on visual impact and unique, memorable imagery.

Consider…

What is your product's visual "world?"

Study the images associated with your product.

Try to create new combinations – new relationships – that's where you may discover the Visual.

Visuals are an international language. Beauty. Smiles. Art. Fashion. Children.

Remember, the world *is* shrinking.

The visual speaks to everyone.

Show what you say. See?

VISUALIZE CONCEPTS.
Here, a complicated concept is made simple.

If everyone knew your house was for sale, you wouldn't need a broker.

With a humorous visualization, Century 21 makes this concept both easy-to-understand and important – if you're thinking of selling your home.

VISUALIZE PROBLEMS.
What did you have for breakfast?

Kellogg's Nutri-Grain Breakfast Bars visualize the problem of "too many donuts" in a humorous and relevant way, as people "wear" their breakfasts.

Here, a donut around the waist causes a problem on the subway.

COLOR.
As mentioned earlier, color can be used as a core Selling Idea. Very visual.

Dockers dramatized the subtle colors of Dockers pants – brown, grey, khaki.

Levi's used obvious music – blues – in concert with filmed tone poems that celebrated casual and contemporary fun in Levi's. When these spots hit, they were some of the coolest things on TV.

HOW NOW, BROWN?
Today, the Martin Agency leverages the brown of UPS into a powerful brand message, "What Can Brown Do for You?"

DRINKING AND DRIVING CAN KILL A FRIENDSHIP

Powerful Message – Simple Graphic.
This TV commercial from the Ad Council is an example of public service advertising at its very best.

Visual Gags. *Traditionally, the Yellow Pages has inspired great visualizations and great advertising. After all, it's the book that has everything in it. This recent award-winning campaign presents visual puns. In the one above, a squad of Marines performs various dances – Rock Drills.*
The theme line – "If it's out there, it's in here."

"I NEVER MET A METAPHOR I DIDN'T LIKE."
A few more examples: On the upper right, a tragic toast visualizes an important message. Michelin's babies dramatically symbolize the importance of safe tires. The Michelin Man delivers brand recognition.

The Gerbil Wheel *symbolizes dull, ordinary cars, which makes this red Kia Soul exciting in contrast.*

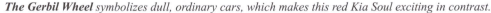

The Eye of The Artist

VISUAL IMAGINATION can bring new dimension to your story. When the artist's eye looks at ordinary objects, they are no longer ordinary.

Here surrealism approaches perfume, beverages, and even Wendy's hamburgers – with the weird comic vision of director Joe Sedelmeier, who did "Where's the Beef?" and early FedEx.

The strange sequence on your right dramatizes waiting for a burger at a "non-Wendy's."

It's advertising, and, in a curious way, it's also art. Surreal art.

Just as Renaissance nobility and merchants commissioned portraits, modern corporations can be patrons of the arts in their advertising.

And the quality of the art itself communicates much about the quality of the advertiser.

One way or another.

THE SURREAL VISION.
With today's technology, if we can imagine it, we can create it. Above, French perfume.

Below, an Italian beverage.

419

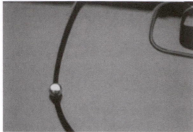

KEEP IT STRONG AND SIMPLE.
Even an expensive and complicated product like Lexus (made by Toyota) can be dramatized with a simple Demo.

A rolling steel ball dramatized their engineering and workmanship.

Advertising can create new context.

Nissan quickly recreated Lexus' Demo using one of their less expensive models.

From steel ball to hard ball.

#34: TV Workout 1

PICK THREE PRODUCTS. They can be from previous exercises or new ones. We'll assume you already have a Strategy and theme.

The objective of this assignment is to help you develop range and flexibility in using TV formats.

Naturally, your ideas won't be of equal quality. Some TV approaches will be a better "fit."

Don't worry – just try to do the full range of approaches for each product.

1. PRODUCT #1_____.
   A. Develop a **Visual.**
   Write a 10" TV spot.
   B. Develop three **Talking Person** ideas.
   Write a 30" spot using the best idea.
   C. Write a **Slice** 30".
   Single situation or Vignette.
   D. Do a **Demo** 15".
   What kind of demo is it?

2. PRODUCT #2_____.
   Same as above.

3. PRODUCT #3_____.
   Same as above.

4. START A TV NOTEBOOK.

Have it sitting near where you watch most of your TV. When you see a spot you like, make a note – brand, production comment, etc.

Then, track it down on the Internet. These days, a lot of the major work is easy to find on the Internet.

Get in the habit. Note the spots you like and why. Become a student of good TV.

E. Graphic Collage

This type of commercial has two key differences.

1. "TRACK-DRIVEN" VIDEO.

This type of commercial tends to be "track-driven." The audio portion (copy and music) is often done first – the video (and the edit) develops from that.

Most music videos are done this way, and this has influenced the way commercials are now done.

In addition, today's audience is able to process video information at a much faster rate and is used to the non-linear nature of track-driven edits.

2. EXISTING VIDEO IMAGERY.

Instead of creating a commercial from scratch, the production process often involves using a number of existing images.

Footage is often reused – such as "hero" product shots. In many cases, such as local auto dealer spots, preproduced material is provided.

Often, part of the job is "picking up the pieces." Some elements you may have to work with:

- Logos and graphics.
- Existing footage.
- Existing music.
- Other elements from previous commercials.
- Other miscellaneous materials including: slides, photos, ads, news footage, and anything else that's lying around and seems to be paid for.

Many local commercials are put together this way, and a surprising number of national ones.

The reediting of other people's footage with new audio tracks is also used in presentations and pitches – in what has come to be affectionately known as the "Rip-o-Matic" or "Steal-O-Matic."

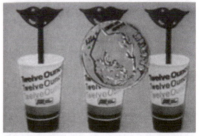

Pick-Up Art Can Be Convenient.
AM-PM advertises hot dogs, drinks, and low prices with a collection of images in the "pick-up" animation style used by Monty Python's Flying Circus.

TECHNICAL PRODUCTS
TECHNICAL PRODUCTION.

One way to communicate the technical excellence of products like computers and printers with TV that's a production tour de force.

That's the thinking behind the excellent work Goodby Silverstein does for H-P.

First, their printers ink wonderful photos in time to the tune of *Picture Book* by the Kinks. The song lyrics add story value to this high-tech tour de force.

First, with one person, Francois.

Then, with a group of people showing all the possibilities of an H-P printer.

For H-P computers, they stay high-tech, but personal activities tell the story. In this commercial, Serena Williams.

Theme – The Computer is Personal Again.

Simple or Complex

A GRAPHIC COLLAGE can be as simple as inter-cutting between film and titles.

Titles and supers add an intellectual counter-point to the message and give it new meaning.

Or a Graphic Collage can be rich and complex.

On the left, state of the art H-P.

Below, advertising developed by Wieden + Kennedy for Black Star Beer, which features a montage of "historical" advertising footage for a beer that never existed before.

It was "Po-Mo with a budget." The brand-new ads featured ironic (and very funny) send-ups of old-time beer advertising cliches.

THE ONLY PLACE IN THE WORLD.

Where you can see the Black Star Beer campaign is the AdBuzz Theater at www.adbuzz.com.

Mature viewers only.

It's in the Edit

YOU MAY START WITH WRITING, but you finish with editing – and all the other techniques of "post-production."

A strong music track, great graphics, a good editor, and your own imagination can combine to create a rich video tapestry.

In general, the better the material your start with, the better the edit you end up with.

"HEROES" AND "STOCK."
Many major advertisers have large libraries of produced footage which are cut into new commercials or used to produce additional spots.

For example, many food and beverage marketers already have "hero" shots of beverage pours.

There are also services that provide "stock footage." Need a wheat field? A rocket? A sunset? Chances are, someone has shot it already.

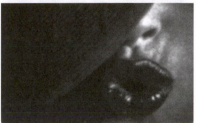

The Layered Look. Now you can stack video images in layers, similar to the way they constructed old-time animation with cels – only now it's with computers.

Grids and Graphics *can make it happen.*

GRAPHIC ELEMENTS.

In today's visually-driven video communication, you will often find a need for strong, simple graphic elements: Logos, slogans, promotional themes, and combinations.

These are often prepared separately, and sometimes given additional preparation, like some sort of introductory animation, or a glow around the logo, or a build as the theme is introduced.

Sometimes, as with Intel, there is also an audio logo along with the video logo.

"Talk to Chuck" is used in print as well as television.

The $5 Footlong campaign combines a number of elements – the $5 hand, the footlong graphic, which is also repeated by amateur actors, and the Subway logo with an additional advertising theme. Complicated, but since it's shown and not said, we get it right away.

"Supers" & Titles

"SUPER" IS SHORT FOR "super-imposition." It's what you say on screen. Titles are either supers used at the beginning of a spot or full-screen supers that may be used anywhere.

Though TV is driven more by the visuals than the words, there can be important opportunities to let the strength of the words move the video along.

In addition, supers and titles cost much much less than most other forms of video.

Usually, they can be done on a computer or the character generator at the editing house – which is part of their computerized editing set-up.

But remember, the screen isn't like the printed page, you have to limit your words.

The Slogo.

Sometimes a slogan can be turned into a logo-like element. These usually come in handy.

Titles and Appetite Appeal. These were the ingredients for this simple but effective execution in Burger King's "Aren't You Hungry?" campaign.

424

F. Combinations.

MANY TELEVISION COMMERCIALS are combinations and variations of these commercial types. Here are some examples:

SLICE / DEMO / DONUTS.

It's very common to use Slice to establish the problem your product solves.

Then, you stick a Demo in the middle.

Finally, a little Slice of happy ending.

TALKING PERSON/ DEMO/DONUTS.

Another common structure is to use a Talking Person with a Demo in the middle.

ETCETERA.

Talking Persons emerge in Slice commercials. Visuals, such as mnemonics, are often put in Slice commercials.

Sometimes it's cool. Sometimes it's corny.

Think of "Punchy." A cartoon Talking Person, with a memorable line of copy: "How would you like a nice Hawaiian Punch?"

And then… well it's not exactly a Demo, but you sure do remember it – that's why they call it a mnemonic.

And, of course, the Energizer Bunny has their pink Visual/Demo/Mnemonic appearing within other familiar formats – even another Demo, like this fake commercial for a sinus remedy.

LOOK FOR NEW COMBINATIONS.

Remember, these formats are not designed to limit your imagination, rather to give your imagination some useful reference points.

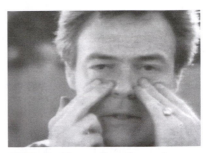

GIRL: *Daddy, smell my flowers!*
DAD: *Ohh, my sinuses.*

SPOKESMAN: *When sinus trouble strikes, reach for Nasitene. Only Nasitene has fast-acting muchinol.*

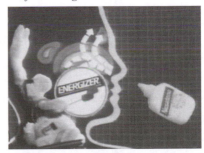

Watch as nasal passages open…
(Energizer Bunny walks past chart…

…and walks past spokesman.)
ANNCR: (VO) *…still going. Nothing outlasts the Energizer. They keep going and going and going…*

Solving the Problem

Here's the commercial that solved the problem for Band-Aid that was described on pages 212 and 214.

It's a Talking Person with a Demo in the middle.

Can you think of any other approaches that might work?

What if you had to extend the campaign?

Who is the target? What other ways to reach this target come to mind?

BOY: Wanna see the cut under my BAND-AID bandage?

Mommy said keep it covered and it'll be all better faster. Wanna see it?

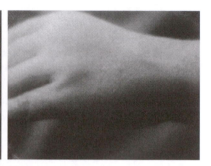
Hey

Where'd my cut go?

ANNCR V/O: Only Johnson & Johnson has proven...

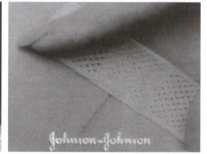
that BAND-AID Brand heals cuts faster.

Up to twice as fast as uncovered cuts.

BOY: It was here. Honest, I mean it.

ANNCR V/O: Cuts covered with BAND-AID Brand are proven to heal up to twice as fast. Only from Johnson & Johnson.

#35: TV Workout 2

Let's try some Combinations.

    You may use ideas from previous exercises.
Or new ones.

1. TAKE ANY TWO IDEAS FROM
THE PREVIOUS ASSIGNMENT.
Combine them into a TV spot.
What kind of combination is it?

2. DEVELOP A MNEMONIC.
Write a :30 Slice commercial using it.

3. COMBINE A TESTIMONIAL WITH A DEMO.
Write sample "testimonial" comments.
How would you produce it?

4. CREATE A COMMERCIAL FROM ONE OF
YOUR FAVORITE PRINT ADS.
What format(s) did you use?

Collage + Mnemonic. This spot for Agree uses basic visual tools – beauty shots and product visuals – cut to a strong rock music track. There's a simple mnemonic for the "Turn Up The Volume" Selling Idea – an Agree logo on the Volume knob of a stereo. It's a nice contemporary way of stating the benefit.

Slice, Visual, Demo, Even Real Spots! The Energizer Bunny keeps going through a range of commercials – most of them imitation versions of formats we're familiar with – two women talking about coffee, soap in a shower, and even a real commercial for Purina Cat Chow, then owned by the same company that owned Energizer Batteries. The fake brand names were fun, too. Trés Cafe, Nasitene, Alarm, and my favorite – wine from Chateau Marmoset.

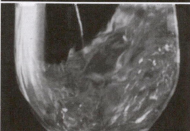

TV Production

COPYWRITING IS A CRAFT. So is producing TV.

Like so many things in our business, it's something you learn by doing. It's not easy.

Even something as simple as opening a bottle and pouring can be expensive and complicated if you want to do it well.

Your best initial resource is people who've done it already: producers, directors, editors, and other more experienced writers and art directors.

Another good resource is sample reels – from commercial production houses and award shows.

Study them. How were the commercials you liked constructed? What worked? What didn't?

Hang out. Watch. Learn.

Finally, do "animatics."

Animatics are rough versions of TV commercials. Originally, they were storyboards put on videotape with a sound track, but new technology is providing other ways to do that.

Producing animatics for research or presentation can teach you important principles of producing and editing TV commercials. It's particularly good training for producing soundtracks.

Producing TV *is* easier said than done.

But the only way to learn is to do it.

In this section, we'll cover:

• **The Three Stages of Production** – pre-production, production, and post-production.

• **"The Winking Dog Syndrome"** – early production problems, and how to recognize them.

• **Bonus: Your First TV Production** – some early words to the wise – and a few ideas. Hope they help.

428

Production Values

THAT'S WHAT WE TRY TO PUT ON THE SCREEN. All the things – small and large – that are involved in producing television, they all add up to production values.

You should be thinking about production values every step of the way. Because you can add to them every step of the way.

THE TIME/MONEY/QUALITY TRIANGLE. This is an age-old "truth" that can help you today.

You can't have all three. (Unless you're very lucky.)

Need it fast? Well, it will cost more. The more you rush, the more you pay – and the more risk that the quality of your final result will suffer.

Got limited money? Well, in general, the more time you can spend, the more you can save. Though, of course, time is money, too.

Got no time and no money? Well, even if you're smart and lucky, the quality probably won't be all you'd wish.

Then there's quality. A strange factor. You know that you want the commercial for the expensive sports car to look terrific. But if the spot for the bargain store looks like they spent too much, you might be suspicious that it isn't quite a bargain. Then again, if it's too cheesy, you might not want to go.

We'll start with these two thoughts:

• You want the quality of the final product to be appropriate for the job you're trying to do.

• In general, the more time and attention you can spend on the front end, in *pre-production,* the better the overall production will go.

Let's keep this in mind as we work our way through the three stages of production.

Production Trip. *The "spontaneous" documentary feel of this Nissan SUV commercial took advance planning: travel for equipment, crew, and talent; local permits; and getting film back for processing.*

PRE-PRODUCTION NOTES.

When you send a board out for bid, you need Pre-Production Notes.

In some ways, this piece of paper is as important as your script. The bid will be built on a combination of your script (and board) and the "Pre-Pro Notes."

Your notes should contain things like:

Deliverables. What do you want? Film delivered to you or the completed spot?

If you'll be handling the editing and post-production somewhere else, you only want a bid for producing the film.

This is also a good place for describing the kind of spot you want. Bright and light-hearted. Modern and cutting-edge.

Sets/Location. Where do you want to do this? In a studio or on the coast of France. Location and set issues will be a critical part of the bid.

Talent. This will help guide those in charge of arranging the casting session.

It will also be critical for how much this commercial may cost in residuals. One principle? Three? Extras? (If they react to the product, they're principles.)

Props & Misc. Who provides product? What other things will be needed?

Special Effects/Post-Production/ Misc. Music? Sound effects? Pre-score or post-score? Computer effects?

Let 'em know what else is going on.

You'll get better, smarter bids. And if someone has a problem remembering what was asked for and promised, you've got your Pre-Pro Notes.

Great Casting helps make the humor work for "Got Milk." He just ate a peanut butter sandwich and can't answer a trivia question because he don't "Got Milk."

Pre-Production, Production, Post-Production

THERE ARE THREE CRITICAL STAGES in the production of every TV commercial. Each one can "make or break" your spot.

PRE-PRODUCTION. PART ONE.

Pre-production is pretty much what you think it is – it's all the things you do before you produce.

Here are some of the critical things you do:

Bids and Budgets.

How much will it cost? It's a critical question – with a lot of variables. Do you get a cute puppy from the shelter or the best animal trainer in Hollywood?

And just in case you think getting the best you can find will solve all your problems, don't. A friend had an absolute disastrous shoot with Lassie. Go figure.

Basically, you have to identify all of the cost items and get production bids from the suppliers that you think are right for the job.

Casting and Talent.

Sometimes the production house handles some of this, but it's a critical agency decision – often, the client is involved in final approval.

There are often additional cost issues involved.

A dozen union actors on-camera could cost your client a bundle. Sometimes it's enough to move the shoot overseas. If your script has a lot of people in it, that's another thing that will be discussed.

Legal Clearance.

You may be adjusting your script due to concerns raised by the client legal department.

And, most important, choosing your…

Production Suppliers.

The major types of suppliers you'll be selecting are:

• **Production House.** This company will be responsible for the film and video. Their services may or may not include post-production.

This supplier could be a major film production company with well-known directors or a local cable station – or anything in-between.

• **Audio or Music House.** If music or special audio effects are a part of your production, you'll want to get these specialists involved. In some cases, music production may have been a part of the initial presentation to the client. If you're using an already existing piece of music, you may be negotiating for music rights as well.

• **Post-Production.** This is primarily editing and finishing, but it may include some sort of special effects. For example, if your commercial combines live action and specialized animation, you may be choosing one company to produce the film and then another to create special effects on that film.

PRE-PRODUCTION: PART TWO.

Once your major suppliers have been chosen, it's time to put them to work. Here are some of the things you'll be looking at:

Schedules and Logistics.

It's rolling now. You'll see when things have to be done. Even though you may have hired the company for the director, you'll begin to appreciate what a good producer can do.

Approvals.

Talent needs to be approved. Locations. "If we pick this location, there will be an extra hour of travel. And that will cost…"

"Now that the bid's approved, we'll need the first third…" And so on.

**THINGS YOU SHOULDN'T DO
IN PRE-PRODUCTION:**

I'm sure there's a longer list than this, but these were the ones I could think of:

Bidding Too Many Companies.

Bidding takes time. If you let a job out for bid with more than four, you're abusing the relationship.

If you can't make up your mind, talk to people with more experience to get a handle on who you should be bidding.

Bidding too many companies short-term can hurt your reputation long-term.

Bidding the Wrong Companies.

Pay attention. If it's comedy, pick a production house that knows how to do it – with the right casting, direction, and film techniques.

If it's specialized table top, with motion control and familiarity with the right kind of specialists, like prop-builders and food stylists, get those companies.

Try to focus on the right companies for this particular job. Try to avoid a political situation, where some people have to be bid for the wrong reasons.

If you do get in that situation, I have no advice for you. It happened to me once, and all I can tell you is that honesty was not the best policy.

The only reason it wasn't a disaster is that the production company knew that they weren't right for the job and showed some class and turned it down.

Don't count on this happening for you.

Unrequested Bids.

What if they want to bid anyway?

Well, sometimes it's hard to stop that sort of thing, but what will you do when that company comes in with the low, low bid and you don't want to use them?

See the problem?

You need a gatekeeper, and you need to be able to say, "*No, not this time.*"

Even if you really mean, "*Never!*"

Producing Too Fast.

Time pressures keep getting worse.

Sometimes there is an air date that can't be changed. So I'm not telling you to go slow. But I will say this…

(Continued on next page.)

THINGS YOU SHOULDN'T (CONT.)

• **Try to build in as much lead time as you can.** Remember the TMQ triangle.

• **Hold on to your "turn-a-round time."** Try to build it into the schedule.

• **Build in a "weather day."** Or don't shoot outside.

• **15% "Contingency."** Things happen. Budget for it. Tell your client that it's responsible business practice. It is.

• **Compare Bids.** Did they miss anything? If there's something too low, up that item to where it ought to be – then make them live with their bid.

• **Have a procedure for overages.** They're going to happen – even if your procedure is "no overages," make sure it's spelled out ahead of time.

• **Tell 'em what you want.** Don't over-direct, but be clear as you know how to be about what you want out of the production. Don't get carried away by the bells and whistles and nice treatment (they're making money off you, of course they're going to treat you nice). When it's all done, they're gone, the checks are cashed, and your reputation is riding on the job.

• **It's in the details.** Prep. Prep. Prep. Props. Talent. Location. Shot list.

• **Stay on top of it.** *During pre-pro, everything is important.*

Prep Your Props. *These custom street signs help make this commercial work.*

Props and Misc.

Stylists and "PAs" (production assistants) will be doing things and asking questions you may not have thought of, like "What color napkins do you want?"

You may need to arrange for boxes of product, or uniforms of a certain size, or logos, or trucks, or who-knows-what to be shipped to arrive in plenty of time.

You start to realize: There are a lot of things to do. And any one of them could cause a huge problem!

One more thing. Pre-production is over.

You are now in production.

PRODUCTION. STAGE ONE.

You're still prepping, but now the meter is starting to run at a good clip. (You'll see in the bid what everyone is getting per hour and per day.)

Some of what they're doing, they do all the time (book the caterers, book the lighting package, book the crew). So no big deal.

And some of this is brand new. (Get a dozen hardware store owners to show up at the shoot, get little souvenir clap boards with their names on them done up, and put an extra PA on to make sure everyone gets there from the airport. Oh yeah, and what about make-up and wardrobe?)

The thing that you realize about production is that *you're doing something that has never been done before.* Sure, plenty of TV commercials have been done before. *But not this one!*

You start to realize all the things that can go wrong.

Suddenly, here comes that well-intentioned last-minute comment from the client based on your revision because of the comment from legal.

Everyone is rushing around, as efficiently as they can to see that everything shows up at the right place at the right time. In the middle of all of this, here is my advice on *the one thing you must do…*

SHOT LIST AND SCHEDULE.

You need to get a shot list. You must do this.

Look at the board. Look at the script.

Try to see the final edit in your head.

What shots will you need to put this together?

First, what are all the shots that you'd like to have to put this together? Establishing shot. Close-up. Reaction shot. Product shot. Etcetera.

Second, what is the minimum you'll need to be able to deliver the spot you promised – instead of having to consider a new career so early in life.

This is serious. What are the shots?

When during the day will these shots be done.

You have a right to expect a shot list from your director. The director needs to put it down and tell you what he or she will do and when it will be done.

During the day to come, you will certainly focus on making sure each shot is as good as it can be, but you also must focus on getting it all "in the can."

(Yeah, it's often video now, so it's not really "in the can," but old phrases die hard.)

A Word of Warning.

Directors particularly like great establishing shots which they usually do at the beginning of the day.

In general, they'll do the widest stuff first and the tightest stuff (like the final product shots) last.

That's good, you get the whole thing lit and then you break it down as you move in closer.

But… if too much of the day is going into that shot, you may have a problem. That's why you need to *insist* on a shot list and schedule – this is the production company's guarantee of what they will do and when they will do it.

It is also, frankly, a bit of protection if things go awry. But we don't want protection, we want a great spot.

Here's how you can help make it happen.

Wide Shot

Medium Shot

Two Shot

Close Up Shot

Here are some of the shots and angles that you need to edit a spot. This simple Slice spot for Apple – two men in an office trying to set up a computer – needs a number of different "set-ups" to create an interesting spot. We don't realize how many different angles get used to put together a simple spot – until we have to do one ourselves!

Check Out the Shot List for this commercial for Lee Jeans...

Dad sits down...

...pops the button on his jeans...

...which shoots past the kids...

...ricochets off the goldfish bowl...

...and shoots past Dad, who's joined the kids, knocking the painting askew.

PRODUCTION. THE SHOOT!

First, your day often starts very early.

Often, the set has to be lit. Though much of the prepping has already been done, the lighting crew and equipment are usually hired for the shoot day.

Here's where the shot list and schedule come in.

People should tell you when they will be shooting – this will vary according to the needs of the shoot – and the budget.

Get there early – before you have to – and find somewhere to be in view but out of the way – let them do their job.

The director will have much on his or her mind. If there is "synch-sound," one of your major concerns will be how the lines are read. Try to have as much of this as possible worked out beforehand. Let the talent know the reading you like; let the director know the reading and attitude you want.

There's probably no avoiding a bit of comment from you when they're finally shooting, but the more you can get those thoughts and opinions into their heads beforehand, the happier you'll be.

Production Protocol.

There will probably be a number of folks from the agency and client. That's normal.

But there's one rule during the shoot.

Only one person talks to the director. It may be you. It may be the producer. But it's one person.

You can't have a bunch of people and a bunch of opinions adding distraction.

Fortunately, these days, you can all sit in front of the monitor, see what's going "in the can," and get that one point of view pulled together.

You get to have a point of view. You get to have it the way you (or the client) wants it. *But only one person talks to the director.*

"IT'S A WRAP." OR IS IT?

"Wrap" (not rap) means the shoot is "wrapped up."

That means you got everything you wanted to get.

The means you were paying attention to the shoot, the director was paying attention to you, the talent was performing, and the crew was doing their job.

If everything went smoothly, or as smooth as it ever goes, you may actually be done on time.

But if it didn't go smoothly, or perhaps you were pretty ambitious and the production company agreed, even though they might have known they wouldn't get it done on time, you may be dealing with…

Overtime.

Overtime is expensive. There may be a bit of it in the budget already. It may also be time to use a bit of that contingency we mentioned (don't use it all up now, there's still a long road ahead).

You don't want overtime, but you may be dealing with it – like it or not.

If things look like they might go that way, get the account exec and the client ready with whatever they feel the proper response is. (You'll already have a clue during lunch, when you compare your proposed shooting schedule with the actual schedule. A client that will not pay overtime might motivate the production company to get a move on.)

What I'm saying is, stay alert and anticipate.

Fortune favors the prepared mind.

Ultimately, you get what you need.

It's a wrap – and the beginning of post-production.

THE POST-PRODUCTION PATH.

Basically, the post-production consists of stringing together and synchronizing all the audio and visual elements and assembling them into one final spot.

But there's more to it than that.

It's a marvelous combination of art and technology.

AUDIO ELEMENTS:

There are four kinds.

Direct Voice (Synch).

Dialogue (and sound) recorded with the video. It is synchronized – and it's called "synch" for short. If you lose synchronization, things are "out of synch."

Voice Tracks.

Audio elements like announcer copy. Usually recorded later at an audio studio.

Music Tracks.

These are usually done separately by a music house. They are often two separate audio elements – the music track itself and the vocals. Today, tracks are usually done in stereo, though it is a "compatible" stereo, without the amount of separation you'd find in a record.

Pre-scoring and Post-scoring.

Pre-scoring is doing the track before you do the video, then "cut to the track." *Post-scoring* involves doing the music after the video.

Sound Effects.

Most audio studios have libraries of standard effects – like screeching car brakes.

Other times, you may have to create something.

That process is called "sound design."

VIDEO ELEMENTS.

These may start with the film or video that you shot, but there are many other sources for video.

Animation and Computer Animation.

This is a whole different way of generating video. In the case of film and tape, you shoot what exists. In the case of animation and computer animation, you are creating something that has never existed before.

Film and Video.

In addition to what you shoot, you may end up dealing with "library footage."

For example, hero product shots or other pieces from previous commercials. You may also find yourself looking for "stock footage." Why go to the volcano when you can pick up some film already shot?

Other Graphic Elements.

Logos and photos are just two examples. Today, these can be treated and restored, and even animated.

BOB EBEL IS GREAT WITH KIDS.
Here's a frame from one of the classic spots he directed for Oscar Mayer.

When you work with a specialist, you need to let him do his job. So, you need to make sure the director knows what you're looking for, and then let the director do it. After all, that's why you hired the director in the first place.

HOW'D THEY DO THAT?
Here, production and post-production works together. A dancer leaps into the air, and we see her suspended in mid-air as we circle around. Very Matrix.

This effect was the result of setting up synchronized cameras around the dancers and grabbing the shot at just the right time. Then, taking all of the shots from the individual cameras, and intercutting them at just the right point in the master shot. Get it?

The producers of this commercial for The Gap really had to have it together every step of the way – from pre-production, through production, to post-production.

Once post-production was exclusive territory, using complicated film-editing equipment, processing, and difficult-to-implement optical effects.

Today, computerized editing equipment and programs, like Avid and Final Cut Pro, make the process much more accessible.

On some levels, almost anyone can do it. But the best in each specialty still command (and deserve) top rates and are much in demand.

In the beginning, you can become familiar with the basic post-production process on your computer or the video facility at your agency or school.

Is it complicated? Sure. But it's simple, too.

The analogy would be food and cooking.

The better the recipe (concept), the better the ingredients (audio and video), and the better the cook (director, editor, audio engineer, and you), the better the final result. Bon appetit.

In the sidebar, we've covered the elements you'll be working with. Now let's put them together.

POST-PRODUCTION. ASSEMBLY.
Editors are technological artisans. They use technology, but the best of them do it with art.

As you edit, you'll see that subtle timings of just a frame or two (video goes at 30 frames a second, film at 24 frames a second) can make a difference.

You may be tempted (or forced) to do some of this yourself, but, if possible, spend as much time as you can with those who are already accomplished. You'll learn a lot about what it takes to put a spot together.

Simple or complex. You may have something that is simplicity itself. In that case, try to make it as clear and clean as possible.

If it's complex – with lots of layers, graphics, and effects, both video and audio – you'll see how much can be done. Not only that, it's fun.

The $50,000 editing system. Now 98% off.

Final Cut Pro 3

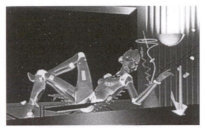

IMAGINE THAT.
A shiny computer-generated robot with the voice of Kathleen Turner tells the world about the advantages of tin cans.

A straightforward message becomes new and exciting.

Nike Knows Music. This "Bo Knows" commercial, with multi-sport athlete Bo Jackson, was cut to a track by Bo Diddley.

Was it clever compositing that produced these video visuals for IBM, or did they just build a real big desk and file cabinet? If you do it right, no one will know.

It's truly amazing to see the flexibility and possibility that technology has opened up for all of us.

But, again, the more you can spend time with truly accomplished editors and audio engineers, the better your work will be and the better you will be.

Audio Mix and Sound Design. While the audio and video are ultimately put together, they're usually treated separately, with specialists in each area.

One of the new fields in audio is "sound design." This utilizes all available audio tools: music, sound effects, and computer generated sounds, to assemble the ultimate audio track. Try to find the reels of some good sound designers and hear the added level of impact and interest good audio can produce.

Video Assembly. The edit you see on the Avid has to be finished. Usually, this involves going back to the original visual source material and assembling a final spot using the highest quality video image (Avid edits are usually done with lower quality video that is derived from your originals).

Often, assembly and "rendering" can take many hours. In addition, this is the time that final tweaks like color correction (making the logo greener) can be made. All I can say is keep paying attention.

"The Winking Dog Syndrome"

MORE PRODUCTION PROBLEMS:
Winking Dogs aren't the only examples. Here are a few others. Some happen on the shoot, and others happen as you're getting ready to produce your spot.

Rubber Pencil.
The board shows angles and proportions that don't exist and can't be shot.

Too Many Words.
The ever-popular 33-second script. Twenty pounds in a ten pound bag. And nobody's able to make the cut. The result? Blahblahblah.

Making Fun of the Customer.
Gee, everyone laughed at the casting session. Is your target ugly idiots who act goofy and like to be laughed at?

"Let's Do It Both Ways."
This is a major symptom of the dreaded "Ad-Man's Disease." Too much film – too few decisions. Now you get to edit.

"The Spinach in the Trombone."
My term for last-minute ideas that seem clever at the time, but look strange, stupid, or simply inappropriate after the film is shot.

There's a great example in the movie *Nothing in Common.* Granny's going away on a long trip. They decide to have her say "goodbye" to her cat. Watch the reaction of the Creative Director, played by Tom Hanks.

LET ME TELL YOU A STORY. When I first started at JWT Chicago, I paid attention to everything that went into production. And I paid attention to what came back. The dog food spots were often disappointing.

They weren't as good as the storyboards.

Then I looked at the storyboards again. The dogs were smiling in anticipation, laughing. . . *winking!*

In the finished spots, the dogs were. . . dogs.

The Winking Dog Syndrome is still with us, perhaps not as obvious, but that makes it harder to catch.

Consider… will everything in the frame show up in the shot in the same proportion? Or, does your board have a slight case of "rubber pencil?"

Does the storyboard show the time it takes to get from one frame to another? Or, is there a lot of copy in one frame with not much happening – and then frames with a lot of action and not much copy?

Will real actors smile as broadly as those storyboard cartoons? Get the idea?

They say every dog has his day – just so it isn't the day they shoot your commercial.

Watch out for Winking Dogs.

Their bite is worse than their bark.

Your First TV Spots

THINGS WILL GO BETTER if you work within your capabilities – the capabilities of your equipment, your talent, your resources, and your budget.

Sure, we want you to hit the heights and win at The One Show. But we also want you to come through for that first client who trusts you.

And, even if it's a student project, trust me that you will get a better grade if you look like you knew what you were doing – instead of getting that sad but kindly smile and the encouraging "nice try" comment when what you did really didn't work very well.

With that in mind, here are some approaches that could serve you well. We call it…

STUPID CAMERA TRICKS.

Shoot some testimonials.

You'll probably want what they call a "three-quarter" shot – not straight into the camera, but off-axis. Try to get the lighting nice, and you might want to get a strong simple background – perhaps with the brand colors.

Or, if you've got interesting background action – like tires being changed, or a busy office, do that.

Be careful with the sound! You don't want background music going on. You'd be surprised at how loud that couple at the next table can be – at exactly the wrong time. Use a "lavolier" mike if you can.

I've found that it helps to give the testimonial people a few run-throughs – film them all and have someone taking notes, if possible.

Tell them it'll be "like playing catch." They'll respond to your question. Repeat the sequence and, usually, the second or third run-through you'll get the good takes. But don't forget to film the rehearsal – sometimes the first take is the only good one.

Bonus:

This a bonus section. If you take my advice and things go wrong, hey, I gave it to you for free, what do you expect?

Goofy Angles. Goofy Testimonials. *Here, Snapple goes a bit po-mo with Wendy the Snapple receptionist and testimonials based on customer letters.*

Nothing like a stupid mascot outfit for a bit of entertaining video and good brand identification at this "training session."

And Wendy visits a Snapple family with lots of corny reality. Goofy and corny is OK if we're all in on the gag.

A Convenient Camera Angle (in a convenience store, of course) sets up this little drama where a Coke delivery man tries to grab a Pepsi and knocks over the whole display case.

ANNCR: (VO) *If a year of civilization has taken its toll, we recommend one week at Club Med...*

Time Moves Ahead. The Camera Stays Still. Here, we see the gradual tanning and relaxation of a guy enjoying and evolving on a Club Med vacation.

A Nice Payoff for Club Med without spending a ton of money – unless, of course, you wanted the production trip.

If there's a particularly good line (nice language, nice phrasing), you might consider asking them to turn to the camera and deliver that line. Cut the best of 'em together, add a front and your theme line, and, chances are, you've got a spot.

Lock down the camera.

Get a wide angle – maybe like a security camera – and see if you can make it happen that way.

Get a medium angle – then cut or dissolve in sequence and make your point that way.

Can you do it in one take?

Did you see the movie *Angel Eyes?*

Look at the opening scene – one long take.

Doing it in one take will be interesting enough that it will go past the rough spots. Maybe.

Move the camera.

OK, maybe you can't do it all in one take, but if you can get the lines delivered to the camera as you're moving, and you've got good movement on the front and end of each scene for "cut points," you might be able to have something nice

Can you do it on the move? Look at *West Wing*.

Many of the new video cameras have a "SteadiCam" feature that will let you move around without the camera shaking all over the place – though you still have to be smooth and good.

By the way, don't forget to settle down a bit when you need to make a serious selling point. I'll repeat that. Don't forget to settle down a bit when you need to make a serious selling point.

Cut to the music.

Get a strong music track and cut to the beat.

To do this, you need to generate as much good video source material as you can – you'll be amazed at how many scenes and shots you'll use up with aggressive cutting. You'll need a good editor.

Supers over static shots.

Design a shot that's fairly empty, or has action in just a part of the frame, and deliver your message with supers and a voiceover.

Lock it down. Speed it up.

Lock down the camera in front of a place where there's good action – whether it's the weather (cool clouds rolling past), or people going in and out, or working, or building something – then, if you can rig a "speed up" editing sequence (hopefully not frame by frame), you could have something interesting. Or not. Then you find out you've wasted a day.

Look Ma, no camera!

Or, you could try a few things that hardly use any video at all. For example, the SouthWest Airlines commercial at the right uses…

Title Cards and Stock Footage.

Many retail concepts that depend on price information can work well with… the price information.

Stoopid Animation.

Use old-fashioned art cards, graffiti, ransom notes for supers, or some other funky graphic style.

Maybe with a bit of very limited animation.

Have fun with the sound track.

It could be very hip.

Switcher Fest.

The gizmos on the editing equipment that make all those effects are called switchers. Learn what they do and use them to build your spot.

Take basic graphics, art, supers, and logos and try to build something interesting.

Even a simple piece of video can be manipulated in a number of interesting ways. Have the editor or video technician show you the possibilities.

The Art of Being Artless. *A TV spot for the price of a TV dinner.*

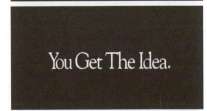

Supers and Stock Footage *do the job.*

HOW MANY TIMES WILL WE USE "WHASSUP?"
An independent low-budget film was the inspiration for Budweiser's "Whassup?" commercials. So, it can happen.

FIRST TIME TV PRODUCTION.
Lesson #1 – if you're not rich, you'd better be smart.

HOW CHEAP CAN YOU DO IT?
Motel 6 used a black screen to make the point that all rooms are the same when you're sleeping.

Small budget commercials can have big impact – and they'll know it's because of you, not the budget.

For reservations call
505-891-6161

Remember, *you're the added value.*

Pick up some "Pick-up Footage."

Remember, the better the ingredients, the better the final dish. See what you can cook up.

Anything from the polished shots provided by car dealers, to stock film (you can find stock houses that provide film as well as photographs), to old home movies and "funniest home video" clips.

All of the Above.

It's a new world. You have opportunities and possibilities that never existed before.

Become familiar with the production process, develop good habits from pre-pro all the way through post-production and who knows what you can create?

#36: TV Workout 3

1. PRODUCTION INVENTORY.
   Write a quick summary of production resources that are available to you – video and audio.

2. REAL WORLD EXERCISE.
   Write the *cheapest* commercial that you can think of. 30 seconds. Any product.

3. ONE-TAKE EXERCISE.
   Write, design, and choreograph a spot you could shoot in one take for a local restaurant or bar.

4. REAL WORLD EXERCISE [#]2.
   Write the *second cheapest* commercial you can think of. 30 seconds. Plus two 10 second spots.

5. BUILD YOUR BOOK EXERCISE.
   OK, write a commercial based on one of your print ads using one of the techniques suggested in this section. 30 seconds. Plus two 10s.

442

TV Terminology:

Note: Video technology is changing rapidly, with new formats and new capabilities at every stage of the production process. These terms are accurate, but underlying technology may change.

ANNCR: Abbreviation for Announcer.

ANNCR: (VO) or **ANNCR (VO):** Announcer, Voiceover

A-ROLL: The first roll of a multi-element edit or mix. Video or audio.

ASPECT RATIO: This is a major new concern. It is the ratio between horizontal and vertical for the image. With all the new formats, stay alert!

BG: Abbreviation for background, as in **(MUSIC BG).**

B-ROLL: secondary footage that adds meaning to a sequence or disguises the elimination of unwanted content. Sometimes referred to as a cutaway.

Color Correction: Adjusting colors or contrast to produce either the truest color rendition, or to create a special or artistic effect.

CU: Abbreviation for close up.

DAILIES: The film from the day's shoot.

ECU: Extreme Close Up.

FADE (IN or Out): In audio, to reduce or increase volume. In video, it usually means **FADE up from black or out TO BLACK.**

FX: Abbreviation for effects – sound effects / special effects / video effects.

MATTE: Originally a film process which combined filmed images by cutting mattes to match the shape. Today it can be done electronically. Often used as a verb.

MCU: Medium Close Up.

MIX: The combining of audio elements in a soundtrack.

MORTISE: Area, usually geometric, containing a second image. Also used as verb.

MOS: Film shot without sound.

NEGATIVE: The original film stock is usually negative.

NEGATIVE TRANSFER: Turning the film negative into a positive video image.

OFF-LINE: Inexpensive editing to prepare the edit using lower resolution files for greater efficiency preparing rough and final edits

ON-LINE: Expensive editing – final assembly and optical effects at the highest quality for Broadcast or replication.

ROUGH CUT: Usually an early cut or the Editor's first cut.

Raw Footage: all of the original images from the film or video camera prior to any editing.

SFX: Sound Effects.

SUPER: To superimpose. As in "Super the Title on the end shot."

SYNCH: The synchronization of audio and video. "In-synch" and "out-of-synch."

Transitions: Means of going from one shot or scene to another. Transitions include but are not limited to cuts, dissolves, wipes, page peels, and zooms.

TWO-SHOT : A shot with both characters in it.

WIDE SHOT or **LONG SHOT**: A scene shot from a distance.

Onwards.

THIS IS A SHORT SECTION.

We're pretty much done.

There's already enough here to think about.

But we've got a few things left.

Short and sweet.

We'll talk about campaigns. Briefly.

We'll talk about duh future – without being very specific, since our crystal ball is out for repairs.

Finally, as a going away gift, we'll give you one of the all-time classic pieces on developing a "voice" for your client.

It's Chris Wall's classic piece on Apple.

Then it's Glossary, Index, and out.

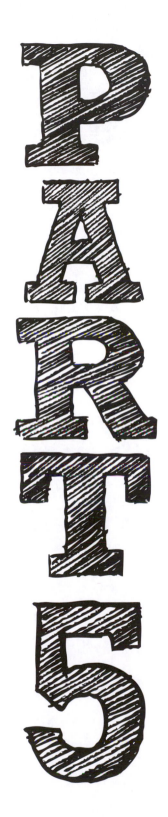

PART 5

Campaigns

THE STARBUCK.

This little piece of guerrilla media anchored early Starbucks introductions.

It was a coupon for free coffee handed out with great abandon when a local Starbucks opened up.

EVOLUTIONARY ICON.

The GEICO Gecko was just one stage of a strategy based on "15 minutes could save you 15%." They kept focused and reacted intelligently, learning as they went.

APPLE'S MEDIA VEHICLE.

Steve Jobs provides extra PR punch for virtually every Apple introduction.

He knows how to make news.

As a result, Apple has strong Marketing PR for virtually every important product introduction.

MANY BOOKS have been written on how to put an advertising or MarCom campaign together.

We're going to keep it to one page – and one chart.

Take another look at The MarCom Matrix. It's a simple representation of the ways you can implement your campaign with marketing communication. Learn how to make the most of it.

Think back to all the things we've said about this kind of communication being receiver-driven.

Throw in a consumer insight or two, find out how much money you have to work with, and you should be able to figure it out.

WHEN ALL YOU'VE GOT IS A HAMMER…
Be careful. Advertising is a great way to go through a lot of money – fast.

All too often, the first time out merely teaches you something you didn't know. Don't make your first ads an expensive lesson.

And don't necessarily think "advertising first."

As they say, "When all you have is a hammer, every problem looks like a nail."

Bring a full toolbox.

"COME BIG OR STAY HOME."
My mother-in-law had some advice that is particularly appropriate for today's entirely too crowded media world.

To make an impact, you have to "Come big."

If you don't have it yet, "stay home."

Keep working until you've got it.

You only get one first chance.

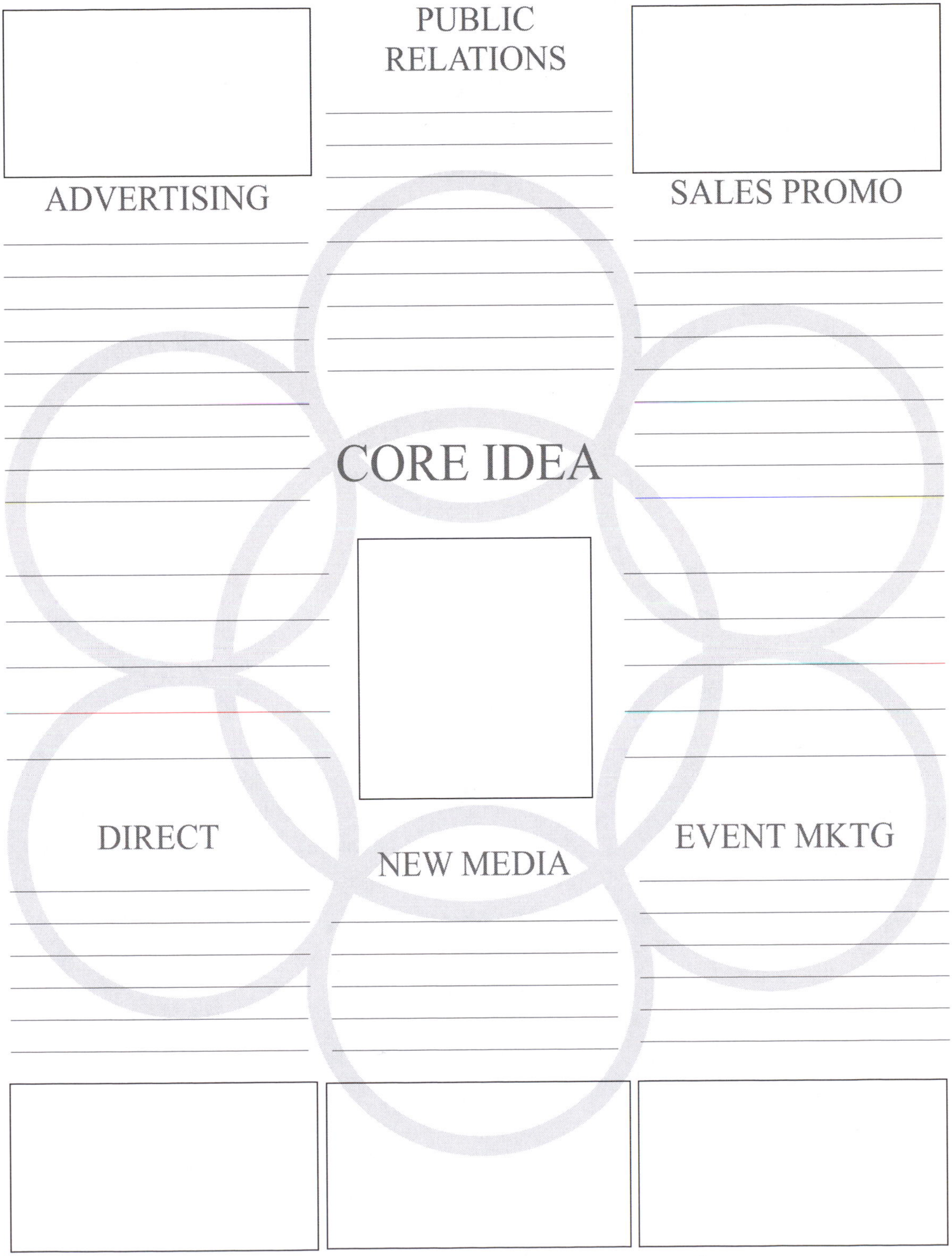

PUBLIC
RELATIONS

ADVERTISING

SALES PROMO

CORE IDEA

DIRECT

NEW MEDIA

EVENT MKTG

NOTE: a pdf of this and other worksheets is available in the CAFÉ section of adbuzz.com

Duh Future

QUATERNARY ECONOMIC ACTIVITY.

It's easy to end with upbeat inspiration like, "when you love what you do, you'll never work a day." But that isn't always how our working life works out.

So here's a useful final concept – think of it as a going away present.

Quaternary Economic Activity. Huh?

Okay, quickly, here's a brief economic history of civilization.

Primary Economic Activity.

The lives of ordinary people changed thousands of years ago with the coming of the Agricultural Revolution.

By settling down to grow crops, lives and civilizations changed.

We had cities and bread. And beer.

There were also wars and what we like to think of as the steady march of progress – but the lives of ordinary people didn't really change all that much until a few hundred years ago.

Secondary Economic Activity.

We had the Industrial Revolution.

With mass-produced cloth and furniture, and mass transportation, the lives of ordinary people received a major upgrade.

The wheels of progress turned faster and there was greater abundance.

So far so good.

Tertiary Economic Activity.

Midway through the 20th Century, we had another form of economic activity become important – services.

This is tertiary economic activity.

This growth of information and technology is powering more improvement in the lives of a lot of people – worldwide.

(Continued on next page.)

AS I WAS FIGURING OUT how to end this book, I picked up *A Whole New Mind: Moving from the Information Age to the Conceptual Age.*

Here's how it starts…

"The last few decades have belonged to a certain kind of person with a certain kind of mind – computer programmers who could crank code, lawyers who could craft contracts, MBAs who could crunch numbers. But the keys to the kingdom are changing hands.

The future belongs to a very different kind of person with a very different kind of mind – creators and empathizers, pattern recognizers, and meaning makers.

These people – artists, inventors, designers, storytellers, caregivers, consolers, big picture thinkers – will now reap society's richest rewards and share its greatest joys."

Hey, works for me.

Whether the picture this author paints is quite so rosy (his name is Daniel Pink, so there might be a little of that), the basic point is probably valid.

The Information Age has certainly created a lot of information – up to our eyeballs.

What do we do with it?

Creating something useful and beautiful and memorable out of all that data – well that's a creative task.

So it just might be that, if you decide to work in a creative field, you've got your work cut out for you. It's what we call "an abundance of opportunity."

LESSONS LEARNED? WE WISH.

Recent years have demonstrated that putting too much trust in financial formulas and people who think they know all the answers is not always a winning strategy.

We also know that when times are tough, one of the best ways to win is to imagine a better future.

So that's where we'll leave it.

My crystal ball? Sorry, it's out for repairs.

All I can offer is a mirror on the past and what I hope is still true – that inspiration and hard work (aka perspiration) tend to make a winning formula.

We're counting on you to imagine that better future – and make it come true.

A LITTLE MORE GOOD NEWS.

We live in a country that seems to know how to handle revolutions. We usually come out the other end in better shape than when we started.

So, as this evolutionary revolution builds up a head of steam, I'm thinking that all the stuff we've been talking about for the last 450 or so pages is going to come in handy.

Just can't tell you which stuff – or when.

It's going to be different, that's for sure.

For me, it was years before I was able to create the music and video I envisioned.

For you, it's waiting on your desktop. Go for it.

That's it. We could add a few more pages and kill a few more trees, but why? You've got what I've got that's useful. The rest is up to you.

Use what Kenichi Ohmae calls *"that ultimate non-linear thinking tool, the human brain."*

OK, one more thing…

Give your gift.

QUATERNARY (CONT.).

Alvin Toffler speaks to this change in a very interesting book called *The Third Wave*, and you might want to read a copy in your spare time. If you have any.

So, what's next?

Quaternary Economic Activity.

Simply put, this is economic activity done for its own sake.

A worthy cause, a friend's music group, a concert, an art project, there is a wide range of activities that use up time and resources and produce a payoff.

Only, in many cases, the payoff is personal satisfaction.

These activities can make your life richer, and they can enrich the lives of people around you.

So, what's the point?

The point is that your working life may be about doing things that other people want you to do – not all that wonderful.

It'll be a job. No big news there.

But the larger truth is, in this interesting world we live in, there is a lot of opportunity for quaternary economic activity.

You might not get paid in cash.

You might not quit your day job.

But there's a payoff just the same – and your life will be the richer for it.

Hold that thought.

NOTE: You can see me share this and other "Thoughts for the Day" in the CAFÉ section of www.adbuzz.com.

When working on Apple, you are following in the footsteps of many wise, talented, and creative people. They also got massive headaches.

This piece was written by Chris Wall when he was at BBDO/LA.

It provides an excellent view of what it takes to develop a long-term stance and tone of voice for a brand.

It is reprinted with his permission and our apologies – we really had to cut it down. Sorry. But, as Chris says, "*write copy to fit the layout*."

The good news is, we kept the insights.

Unlike the rest of the book, this article was set in "Apple Garamond." That's Garamond condensed 80%.

After Apple, Chris went to Ogilvy, working with Steve Hayden on IBM, so if you see some IBM stuff that seems a little Apple-like, well, you'll know why.

This was written in 1991, as the early version of Windows was being introduced – the technical comparisons are now out-of-date. And how do we explain to you who Leona Helmsley was?

"Do you want to spend the rest of your life selling sugared water or do you want a chance to change the world?"

– *Steve Jobs to John Sculley, 1983*

"You're hired. Here. This is due tomorrow."

– *Steve Hayden to you, date unknown*

The Communicator's Guide to Success and Survival.
by Chris Wall, BBDO/LA

Preface.

It's the best of times.

It's the worst of times. It's Apple.

Seldom in your career as a communicator will you have the opportunity to work with products that are so good and so clearly different in vision from their competitors.

Never again will you have the chance to work so many hours on so many tasks that are so vaguely defined, that can change at the drop of an offhand remark by an industry pundit; where your clients applaud your great work on Monday and tell you on Tuesday that you were totally off the mark.

Working on Apple is like trying to nail Jell-O to a bulletin board – like driving on a freeway where the posted maximum is 75 and the posted minimum is 85.

1 Apple year = 5 human years = 35 dog years.

Working on Apple, you will have the chance to make your career, win major awards, and make a real contribution to the success of a Fortune 100 company. You will also have the opportunity to destroy your personal relationships, raise your blood pressure, and take advantage of those psychology benefits in the health insurance.

The good news is, Apple will do incredibly exciting advertising, take calculated risks, and give you the chance to do the unexpected.

The bad news is, they will change the assignment on you, they will change the assignment on you again, and quickly dismiss great advertising if it doesn't say exactly what they believe it should say in exactly the way they think it should be said.

Apple exists in an industry where monumental change takes place overnight.

Where the life of even a successful product can be less than a year.

Don't expect a lot of time to develop your ideas. (They develop entire products in a matter of months, so it's not unreasonable for them to expect you to do an ad in a week or two.) The faster you can develop your communications, the quicker you can adapt to change, the greater success you will enjoy.

The purpose of this guide is to give you a little perspective on Apple communications and help you understand the basic ingredients that go into any successful Apple ad.

I. The Apple Voice.

The very best Apple communications have one of the most distinctive voices in all of business communications.

It sounds a whole lot like Steve Hayden in a good mood.*

It isn't easy to pick up the Apple Voice.

The Apple Voice has three basically different moods that you need to understand. All three can be found occasionally in a single piece.

*The Apple Voice can be funny, serious, hopeful, glib, wise, practical, but can never, ever sound like Leona Helmsley.***

1. The Hopeful, Optimistic Apple.

This voice is serious, intelligent, and human. It has the quality Steve calls *ponderosity*. It has a profound quality and relates the way Apple builds products to the ambitions and aspirations of our readers and viewers.

It espouses that one person with the right tools and a great idea can accomplish anything, and that people working together with the right tools can change the world and make dreams come true.

---

* Steve was head of BBDO/LA and a long-time Apple creative force, beginning at Chiat/Day, Apple's first agency.
** Leona Helmsley ran some New York hotels. Their ads featured Leona. She was a b----. But that wasn't why she went to jail.

This is not b---s---. The people at Apple believe this. The people who have written really great Apple communications believe it.

If you have a point you want to make and you can make it with this voice, it is almost impossible to go wrong.

It makes people feel good about Apple. It gets test scores that are off the charts.

Best of all, it truly reflects the spirit of Apple people and the products they make.

This voice belongs to Apple, and you are its custodian. This is the voice you will use if you're working on an education ad. For an example of this voice, see *Industrial Revelation, MacWorld, I'm Different,* and most education print ads.

An Apple computer is a basic, practical tool for just about any human being. But most people don't realize all the things an Apple Computer can do.

2. The Practical Apple.

This voice wants you to know why the particularly bright engineers at Apple build computers the way they do. How those computers work. And why the way they work is better than the way other computers work.

This is the voice that easily relates complex technology to real-world benefits.

It works very well in business ads, new product ads, and in product television spots.

Examples of the Practical Apple can be found in *Manuals,* most of the product TV spots, *Testing 1-2-3, Testing 4-5-6,* and the original Macintosh introduction insert.

3. The Radical Apple.

This is the nitroglycerin of Apple communications.

Funny, flip, roguishly smart, and confident that we have a better way of working. The best thing about this voice is that it attracts lots of attention. It is fun to read and watch. And it has a certain charm in a world of bland, predictable corporate communications.

The worst thing about it is that it is taken as arrogant and condescending.

Without this voice, Apple would never have created perhaps the single most successful ad of the last decade – *1984.*

Don't be afraid to use this voice.

It's a good idea to handle the Radical Apple Voice with care.

Just use it with care.

Examples where it has worked well include the print ads *Just what the world needs...* and *Welcome IBM. Seriously.* And the TV spots *Testing 1-2-3, Testing 4-5-6,* and *1984.*

Where it backfired was the *Lemmings* TV commercial and *The Berlin Wall* print ad.

II. The Apple Advantage Points.
The Evidence for Any Argument.

In 1989, a lot of people spent a lot of time defining the Apple Advantage Points (also known as the "points of light"). These points serve as the outline for the body copy of any Apple ad thusly:

1. Powerful technology that is easy to use.

Although this point wasn't discovered until 1989, it's really the basic idea behind Apple since the days in the garage.

Macintosh – with its simple, graphic interface – made the personal computer useful to millions of people who couldn't or wouldn't invest the time to learn the peculiar syntax personal computers had borrowed from their mainframe cousins.

Everything about Macintosh was designed around a real-world metaphor – the desktop. Instead of you having to adapt to the way the computer works, the people who designed Macintosh adapted it to the way that you work.

This was a revolutionary concept.

Ultimately, it is this philosophy that continues to distinguish Macintosh from other computers and Apple from other computer companies.

Each subsequent version of Macintosh has increased the power and sophistication of its technology enormously with only a small increase in complexity to the user.

2. Thousands of programs that work together.

Prior to the arrival of Macintosh, every computer program worked differently, according to the whims of its author.

The command to save a document in one program could be the command to erase a document in another – even though you were using the same machine.

On a Macintosh, programs are consistent, and they work together. Although there are thousands of Macintosh programs, there is only one way to print, open, save, or close a document. You can copy information from one program and paste it into almost any other program, so you never have to do the same work twice.

3. Built-in networking.

At its most basic level, Apple makes it easy to connect a Macintosh to other computers so you can share information, send electronic mail, etc.

You can use a very sophisticated, complex network without a lot of training.

This gets back to Apple Advantage #2; networking software works exactly like all other Macintosh software.

4. Growth without disruption.

In the DOS world, each subsequent iteration of the operating system has required users to get new versions of their applications. Or, a new version of a program would be incompatible with previous versions and would have entirely new commands. This is disruption.

In the Macintosh world, it's much simpler. The Mac interface is basically the same today as it was in 1984. New features have been added, improvements have been made, but the basic way of working is still the same.

The basic benefit of this is that you can add new features and capabilities as Apple improves the system software – quickly, easily, inexpensively, without enormous interruptions in your business.

1. Powerful technology that is easy to use.
2. Built-in networking.
3. Thousands of applications that work together.
4. Growth w/o disruption.
5. Cool graphics help impress potential dates.

If you have trouble remembering the Apple Advantage Points, just write them down on a small piece of paper. If you think of any new points, be sure to include them.

III. The Basic Reader Perspectives.

Every Apple ad is written to one of two perspectives.

1. The User Perspective.

People who use computers want to know what's in a Macintosh computer for them. You can talk to them with any Apple Voice that is appropriate.

They care about the emotional appeal of Apple as well as the practical. The User Perspective is in the Chiat/Day spot *Basketball* and more practically focused spots like *Macintosh Office* and *Manuals.*

2. The Management Perspective.

These guys don't care about the hopeful, optimistic Apple. Spare them anything remotely philosophical unless, of course, you relate it to a practical benefit. The benefit to them is that people use Apple computers more and get more done with them with less training. *Testing 1-2-3* is a particularly successful example of this perspective.

IV. Three Ways to Explain the Advantages of a Macintosh.

When it's all said and done, you've got three choices:

1. Product.

Explain how a Macintosh works. Demonstrate point by point why it does what it does and how that differs from other computers. Show it. Explain it. Demonstrate it. This is your basic new product ad.

2. Task.

Explain why a Macintosh is a better way to accomplish any particular task. For example, Macintosh is a better way to work with numbers not only because it has great spreadsheet programs (any computer has them) but because it's easy to learn and set up (so you spend more time working and less time learning); because all the programs work together; because it makes it easy to work with other people. And so on.

3. People.

Explain innovative ways real people are actually using Macintosh.

V. The Basic Arguments Against Macintosh (Circa 1991).

(NOTE: This is a discussion of the counter-arguments to the following four "Arguments Against Macintosh:"

1. It's not affordable. 2. It's not compatible.
3. It doesn't connect. 4. No applications.

Many normal, well-groomed people are confused by the technical aspects of buying a personal computer. It is our job to help them.

VI. Art Directors Who Write, Writers Who Art Direct.

You are inheriting a unique tradition of advertising.

Apple ads are frequently better written and more interesting than the articles in the magazine in which they appear.

It is your responsibility to maintain that tradition.

Any copywriter good enough to get a job working on Apple knows the basic cliches of copywriting. Lots of fragments for emphasis. Clever word plays and jokes.

Quite simply, the use of phrases like "quite simply."

Use them to help make your points. But don't kid yourself into thinking these little devices are a substitute for hard facts, insightful analysis, and passionate reasoning.

Detail is everything. Apple ads have achieved no small measure of notoriety among copywriters for the bright, amusing quips in the legal copy. At first blush, they seem to just be one of the more charming manifestations of the Radical Apple Voice. But they tell the reader something very important: that everything in an Apple ad is written to be read and enjoyed, that Apple, as a corporation, pays attention to the smallest detail.

I'm a copywriter, so this has mostly focused on writing.

Art directors are also responsible for good writing. They should read the copy and, if it isn't as good as they think it can be, they should say so.

Much of the print work of the late 1980s was influenced by the clean, dramatic Apple look. As an art director on Apple, you are following in the steps of the best: Lee Clow, Yvonne Smith, Houman Pirdavari, and Brent Thomas, to name a few.

It never hurts to study their work and measure yours against it.

Don't fall into the trap of changing the Apple look just for the sake of change.

Every time someone played around with the "Apple look" to "make it better" we have come away with something far less satisfying than we had before. I know, because I've fallen into this trap.

Apple ads should be beautiful and consistent. The best Apple ads of 1983 bear a striking resemblance to the best of 1986, which look a lot like the best of 1989.

It's wonderful to win an award for an ad. It's far better to win two awards: one for the great individual ad and one for the great campaign.

Art direction is just as important as great writing. Maybe more so.

The beauty of Apple ads isn't just "an art problem." Copywriters are responsible, too. That means you should do things like write copy to fit the layout.

Don't present a layout with half as much room as you need and wind up with an ugly ad filled with eensie-weensie type.

This sound obvious. But it's amazing how often a really good concept winds up weak and unsatisfying because the members of the team don't work together.

VII. Apple. Where the Future Is Tomorrow, Every Day.

The next decade is going to be at least as exciting as the last – technologies are going to come together very quickly – computer, telephone, television, fiber optics, cellular, photocopy, laser printing, maybe more.

Imagine a Macintosh with a television, cellular telephone, and VCR built into it, small enough to fit on your desk. Or in your briefcase.

I'm not letting you in on anything confidential, you can see most of the pieces today at any MacWorld Exposition. It's just a matter of time – and not much, at that – before someone will pull it all together for you, eventually at a reasonable price.

In the next few years, it's important that we help Apple win not just market share, but mind share. We must expand and redefine what " $\bullet$ " stands for that is consistent with our "computers for people" heritage.

We must protect those values and attitudes, and we must find new ways to express them as others clamor to jump on our bandwagon.

If we do, if we continue to make Apple communications relevant, dynamic, and innovative, we will help Apple become one of the first great global brands of the 21st Century.

Chris Wall/BBD$\bullet$/January 1991

Doing a really good job on
Apple advertising for a few years
has helped many copywriters and art directors
have long, rewarding, highly paid careers.
Making it possible for them to indulge in
exotic, expensive, utterly pointless hobbies
like collecting ancient pottery or
everything ever made by the Franklin Mint.

Glossary:

Advertising and marketing has its own vocabulary – here are some common words and acronyms, and their generally accepted meanings in the industry.

A

AAAA: The "4 A's." American Association of Advertising Agencies.

AAF: American Advertising Federation.

"A" Counties: Larger urban counties.

A & B Roll: The use of two rolls of film or videotape to achieve some sort of **wipe** or **dissolve** between the two. Now done electronically.

Account Executive: The person who is in charge of running a piece of business (the account) at an advertising agency.

ADDY: Advertising award given by local ad clubs/regional advertising groups through the American Advertising Federation.

ADI: Area of Dominant Influence. Market definition based on TV viewing.

AEF: Advertising Educational Foundation.

AFM: American Federation of Musicians. The musician's union.

AFTRA: American Federation of Theater and Radio Artists. Performance union for talent appearing on audio or videotape.

Animatic: Rough commercial, usually a storyboard laid off onto videotape and the frames matched to a rough soundtrack. An animatic which uses photos is also called a "photomatic." An animatic which uses pieces of other commercials is commonly known as a "steal-o-matic" or "rip-o-matic."

Aspect Ratio: Horizontal/vertical proportion of video image, i.e. width to height. The two most common aspect ratios in broadcast TV are 4:3 and 16:9.

Attention: An initial objective of an advertisement.

Attitude: The feelings people have towards a product or service.

Audio Mix: Combining or "mixing" audio elements to produce final soundtrack.

A/V: Audio Visual Presentation. Once exclusively slides with an audio track, this now refers to a number of formats, with PowerPoint currently dominant.

Avid: Commonly used video editing system.

B

"B" Counties: Smaller urban and suburban counties.

Bait and Switch: Illegal practice of baiting customers with a low-price on goods which they are then unable to buy or discouraged from buying.

Bells and Whistles: Usually special video effects. Or extras in general.

Benefit: In advertising, this is usually short for "consumer benefit," the positive result the consumer receives from use of the product or service.

Bite: A short segment of audio.

Bleed: When the "live" area of an ad, such as the photograph, "bleeds" off the page. A non-bleed ad has a white border around it.

"Blooper Soap": Description of overdone reading of copy. It refers to an old comedy tape in which the announcer ends up shouting every single word of the phrase "Blooper Soap Is Real Good!"

Boilerplate: Standard legal copy, often used on coupons.

Bold Face: Type style that is darker and heavier than the regular "reader" face.

Broadside: One page promotional flyer, folded for mailing.

"Buckeye": Description of crude, obvious approach (except in Ohio).

• **Bullet Points:** Way of listing multiple points in presentations or print ads.

Burke: A type of "day-after recall" research supplied by Burke Research in Cincinnati and used by P&G and other package goods marketers. It is often used as a verb. To "Burke" something. Or "it won't Burke."

Business to Business: Advertising of products and services from one business to another (as opposed to consumer advertising). "B to B."

C

CA: *Communication Arts* – an important industry magazine focusing on design and art direction.

Call-Outs: Small captions next to items or features in an ad.

"C & D" Counties: Predominantly small town and rural counties.

ChromaKey: Way of "Matting in" backgrounds by shooting foreground actors against a Chromakey blue or green. On film, the technique used is "UltiMatte."

Clearance: Procedure of submitting scripts or storyboards to TV networks for approval before they are shot. Also "Network Clearance."

CLIOS: Advertising industry award competition. There are many.

CMYK: 1. Color printing derived from four color plates: cyan, magenta, yellow, and black (K). 2. A magazine featuring the best in student creative work.

Color correction: Technical process of altering color values of film or videotape.

Comp: A "tight" or comprehensive layout, including type.

Compression/Compression Ratio: Basically, a reduction in the size of the data to save space or transmission time. The greater the compression ratio, the greater the potential quality loss

Contingency: Part of production budget (10-15%) set aside for unknowns.

Copy: The words in an ad. (Of course, this word has other meanings as well.)

Copy/Contact: Dual job. An account executive/copywriter who works directly with the client. Once common on small or specialized industrial accounts.

© **Copyright:** The exclusive right to a publication, literary, dramatic, musical, or artistic work. The copyright to an ad is generally owned by the advertiser, and a copyright symbol plus the year of publication must appear on the ad.

Cut: Going from one scene to another with no intervening effects.
May be used as a noun ("nice cut") or a verb ("It doesn't cut").

D

Dailies: Film that was shot that day. One usually views dailies the day after they were shot. Also used to refer to all the film from the shoot.

Demo: 1. A demonstration in a TV commercial. 2. A rough version of a jingle submitted by a music house. 3. A sample tape submitted by a film house. 4. Short for "demographic profile."

Demo Rates: Lower rates which apply to the production of music demos. If the music is approved, there may be additional money due.

Demographics: Statistical data about target consumers, i.e., age, income, family size.

Dissolve: Fading from one scene to another.

Dog & Pony Show: A big presentation for a client or prospective client.

Dominance: Often an objective in many areas of advertising.
In media – dominant space or schedule. In business – dominant share.

Donut: TV or radio spot with a "hole" in the middle for local or promotional use.

DTP: Desktop publishing.

Dub: 1. A copy of an audiotape or videotape. 2. To substitute a new voice track.
(A voice replacement may also be called an "overdub.")

Dummy: Mock-up or layout of brochure or other multipage piece.

Dupe: Copy. Same as **dub.** Can be noun or verb.

E

Echo: Audio effect which gives the voice and acoustic space more size.

Effects: Term referring to a wide range of audio and visual (optical) techniques.

Electronic Pre-Press: The process of preparing print files for final printed production.

Empty Suit: Executive who adds little.

Emulsion: The part of the film that holds the image. It's on one side.

EQ: Sound equalization or re-adjustment.

Eye Camera: Research device used many years ago, which measured the dilation of the pupil when a person looked at an ad. It is being used again – occasionally.

Eyebrow: A small pre-head at the top of a print ad.

F

FCC: Federal Communications Commission.

FDA: Food and Drug Administration.

Fill: Lighting used to "fill in" dark areas.

Final Cut: 1. Final edit on a production job. 2. Popular Apple-based editing software.

Focus Group: Research technique where 6 –12 consumers discuss product and/or advertising. Often observed from behind a one-way mirror.

Four Color: Full color printing derived from 4 separate plates. Usually called CMYK: cyan, magenta, yellow, and black (K).

FPS: Frames per second. Film is 24 fps. Videotape is 30 fps.

Frame Count: Numerical record of the number of frames in a commercial or a part of a commercial. Often used for animation or music scoring.

Frequency: Media statistic measuring the number of times various percentages of an audience see a commercial.

FSI: Free Standing Insert. Media vehicle for delivering coupons in newspapers.

FTC: Federal Trade Commission.

FX: Common abbreviation for **effects** in scripts. Sound or video.

G

Generation: A measure of how far removed a dub is from the (analog) master. The master is first generation. The dub is second generation. A dub of that is third generation. There is a gradual diminution of quality – which varies. This has become less critical as we've moved to digital.

GRP: Gross Rating Points. A way of buying and measuring media based on the cumulative number of ratings points (usually Nielsen ratings).

H

Headline: The words that make the initial connection in an advertisement.

Hook: The part of a song (or jingle) that "hooks" your memory.

Hype: Generally negative statement describing empty claims and enthusiastic selling with no substance. Sometimes used as a verb meaning add excitement or energy, e.g., "hype-up the product shot."

I

IAB: Interactive Advertising Bureau – industry group for new media advertising.

ID: A short commercial message. Usually 10 seconds. . . or less.

Image: 1. Result of factors that add up to how people think and feel about a product. 2. Adjective used to describe advertising that is more attitudinal than factual.

Impact: 1. Initial attention-getting. 2. Lasting result of attention-getting and memory.

Inherent Drama: Advertising philosophy of Leo Burnett. He believed it could be found in every product or service.

ips: Inches per second. Audiotape speed. Faster speed = better quality. Less relevant with digital.

J

Jive: Slang for phony, empty, trying to be hip but not.

Jump Cut: Type of edit where continuity is sacrificed for effect.

K

Keyline: Final assembly of type and art for print. Also called **paste-up**. Now done digitally.

L

Layout: Graphic representation of an ad. Can be rough or tight.

Lead Time: Amount of time needed to complete a job.

Leading: The amount of space between lines of copy. Pronounced *ledding*. (Typesetters used to put bits of lead between lines of type.)

Leakage: In recording, occurs when extraneous sound "leaks" into the microphone.

Left Hand Side: Scene and action description in a TV script.

Library Music: Pre-recorded music used for a fee. Also known as **stock music** or **needle drop.**

Local Tag: A part of the commercial, usually at the end, with no pre-recorded announcer. Local station announcers then read appropriate local **tag** copy.

Locator Copy: Address information in a tag.

Logo: Identifying graphic treatment or device for product or service. Short for "logotype."

M

"Marionette Effect": Actors become phony – saying words they would never say.

Master: Usually refers to first generation video assembly or audio mix.

Matte: Film or video effect where one image is overlaid onto another. A matte is used to block out the underlying image.

Maven: Yiddish word for "expert."

Mnemonic: Memory device usually used to register product name or benefit.

Mortise: A cut-out area in which a second image appears. Also used as a verb ("Mortise in a product shot").

Multing: Repeating vocal or instrumental parts on additional tracks to create the sound of a larger group. Short for multitracking.

N

NAB: 1. National Association of Broadcasters. 2. Newspaper Advertising Bureau.

NAD: National Advertising Division of the National Advertising Review Council. A self-regulatory body which reviews advertising.

NARB: National Advertising Review Board. Reviews decisions of NAD.

Needle Drop: Also known as **library music** or **stock music.** Originally, you paid each time you dropped the needle on the record.

Nielsen: Refers to data from A. C. Nielsen Company. Usually refers to TV viewership, but may refer to retail sales, or even box office results.

Negative: The film in the camera is negative film.

Negative Transfer: Process of putting film negative onto a positive videotape image.

Nine Wheel Logic: Type of support that seems to prove a point, even though it doesn't.

O

Objective: The mission or goal of an advertising or marketing program.

Off-Line: A type of tape editing that is free-standing.

On-Line: Tape editing where all elements and effects can be used.

Opticals: Various visual effects (dissolves, supers, etc.) performed during the final part of the post-production process.

Out-of-home: Any ads which appear outside the home (e.g., bar posters, stadium signs).

Outdoor: Advertising which appears outside. Also **out-of-home.**

P

4Ps: Shorthand formula for basics of marketing: Product, Price, Place (distribution), Promotion.

Paste Up: Same as **keyline.** Now this is done electronically.

Penetration: The depth or degree of presence felt, usually expressed as percentage. Examples: Market penetration (% distribution) Media penetration (% of target).

PDQ: Pretty darn quick. A rush job.

"Permission to Believe": Concept credited to Leo Burnett. It allows the audience to go along with your message. This may be real, though minor ("peas picked in the moonlight") or totally made up (Keebler Cookies "made by elves").

P.I.: Per Inquiry. Type of advertising, usually television, in which the media is compensated depending on the number of orders or inquiries.

POP: Point-of-Purchase. Also called "POS," Point-of-Sale.

Portfolio: Folder containing samples of writer's, artist's, photographer's, or model's work. Also known as the "book."

Post-production: Activities which occur after production, i.e., editing, mixing, optical work, and final assembly. Also called "Post-pro."

Post-scoring: Writing the music *after* the film is edited to match or reinforce visual timings and cues in the edit.

Pre-production: Activities necessary to get ready for production. "Pre-pro."

Production: The actual filming or recording of a commercial.

Psychographics: Psychological description of target consumer, e.g., nurturing mother, adventurous, sensate, etc.

Q

Qualitative: The non-numerical aspects of a situation – i.e., attitudes, "image," and types of research – which give a "feel" but are not statistically accurate. For example, **focus groups.**

Quantitative: Numerical data. Market share, customer demographics, etc.
These are "hard" research numbers from large sample research.

R

RGB: Colors on a screen – derived from: red, green, and blue. Remember, the radiant image you see on a screen will not look the same as reflective art on a page.

® Registration Mark: Indicates name or logo is legally registered and owned.

Reach: The percentage of an audience reached by a media buy.

Reason Why: Facts which support consumer benefit or product performance.

Right Hand Side: Voice script broken out for reading.

Rough: Anything in rough form: layout, mix, edit, etc. Sometimes spelled "ruff."

Rough Cut: The initial edit of a film or tape without optical effects.
In the days of film editing, splices and other marks of assembly are visible.

Rough Mix: Early mix of audio elements.

S

SAG: Screen Actor's Guild. Performers' union for actors in filmed commercials.

Sales Promotion: Use of incentive to stimulate purchase behavior.

Schtick: Yiddish vaudeville term for a piece of "business."
For example, Groucho Marx's cigar and eyebrows were his *schtick*.

Scratch Track: Rough version of music or audio track.

SFX: Sound Effects. Sometimes used as an abbreviation for Special Effects.

Share: Percentage of market held by a brand.

Share of Voice: Percent of ad weight held by brand in product category.

Side Light: Lighting that comes predominantly from the side.

Side by Side: Type of comparison commercial or Demo.

Slogan: Phrase used to advertise a product. Usually the theme of an ad campaign.
Many products have numerous slogans, some quite old.

Slogo: Slang. A combination of slogan and logo.

Small Space: Print advertising utilizing small-sized media spaces.

SMPTE: A standard electronic time code used in video editing. SMPTE stands for Society of Motion Picture and Television Engineers, the professional group which established the code. Also known as **Time Code.**

Spec: 1. Short for "Specifications." 2. Short for "Speculative" – work done to get new business, usually with no payment from the prospect.

Spread: An ad covering two pages. A full page spread uses two full pages. A horizontal spread uses two horizontal half pages.

SRDS: Standard Rate and Data Service. Publishes media rates – primarily magazines.

Stock Music: Pre-recorded music which can be used for sound tracks for a small licensing fee. Also known as **library music** or **needle drop.**

Stop Motion: Animation created by images or objects moved and filmed frame-by-frame. A form of stop motion using clay is called "Clay-Mation."

SubMaster: Master without certain elements, usually supers (video submaster) or announcer (audio submaster) which will be used in the final version or versions.

Super. Words "super-imposed" over the picture. Also used as verb (to super-impose words over the picture).

T

Table Tent: Point-of-purchase signage that sits on a restaurant table or bar-top.

Tag: Copy, often localized, used at the end of the commercial.
Usually used to supply purchasing information – offer details, address, etc..

Target Audience: The audience to whom you are aiming your media message.

Target Market: Group of people in the marketplace who are best prospects for your product. Also "target consumer," "target customer," or just "target."

TBD: To Be Determined.

Telemarketing: Marketing done via phone. Can be "inbound" or "outbound."

Time-Code: Numerical code, such as SMPTE, used to indicate frame of videotape.

™ Trademark: Symbol used to distinguish a product, usually protected by law and indicated by a ™ symbol. Any word, symbol name, or device used to identify goods and distinguish them from those sold by others.

Transit: Advertising associated with mass transit.
Bus cards inside busses, the outsides of busses, and kiosks at bus stops.

Turnaround (Time): Time necessary to implement revisions.
Usually integrated into a production or approval schedule.

Turn-key: An event that includes all materials required so that the program is easy to implement, i.e., you just "turn the key."

TV Safe: Area of TV screen for clear title read.

Typo: Typographical error.

U

UltiMatte: A matte of the film image is generated along with the negative.

UltiMatte Blue: The background color on which UltiMatte is shot.

UPC: Universal Product Code. Those bar stripes on packages.

USP: Unique Selling Proposition. (For complete definition, see page 34.)

V

VALS: Research which emphasizes Values and LifeStyles.

VCR: Video Cassette Recorder.

VFX: Video Effects.

VHS: Popular 1/2" video format.

Video Assist: Video Hook-up on a film camera that shows what's filmed.

Videotape: Tape used to record video. Used in many formats. Common formats *were* 1", 3/4", and 1/2" (BetaCam). DV (Digital Video) is now used widely.

VO: Voice Over.

W

Wipe: Graphic video effect which provides a transition from one scene to another. Examples: Clock Wipe, Flip Wipe, and Page Wipe.

Work for Hire: Unless otherwise specified, creative work that is paid for is the property of the person or company that pays for it, not the creator. The work is regarded as "work for hire."

X-Y-Z

X-Acto™: Type of razor-blade knife used in mount rooms.

YUPPY: Name for Young Upscale Professional. Also YUPPIE. This sort of nicknaming of target markets and consumers is fairly common.

Zap: Change channels.

Zoom: Film or tape production term, to move in or out on subject – usually with a "Zoom" lens. Used as noun or verb ("Zoom in on the product").

Some Numbers . . .

SOME AUDIO AND VIDEO NUMBERS.

Audio Tape Speed is measured in inches per second – "ips."

With the shift to digital audio and CDs, this is much less relevant, but in case it ever comes up.

30 ips was used for highest quality audio mastering. **15 ips** was used in most professional audio studios. **1$^{7/8}$ ips** is the usual speed of audio cassettes.

Film Speed: Film is normally 24 frames per second.

Tape Speed: Videotape plays at 30 frames per second.

Time code matches up with this speed. For example, 01:04:03:22 indicates one hour, four minutes, three seconds, and 22 frames.

30" (or **:30**) **TV Commercial:** About 29 seconds, with fade up and fade to black.

30" (or **:30**) **Radio Commercial:** 30 seconds in length.

60" (or **:60**) **Radio Commercial:** One full minute.

10" (or **:10**) **ID:** About 9 seconds – if you push it, 9.5.

Billboard: From 3 to 8 seconds of audio. Usually used with a still photo or graphic.

PRINT NUMBERS.

Agate Line: Unit of print space – 1 column inch wide by 1/14".

There are 14 lines to 1 inch.

Column: Different newspapers may have different column widths.

Point: Type size. There are 72 points to 1 inch.

Index:

EARLY ACKNOWLEDGEMENTS:
THIS BOOK IS THE RESULT of many lessons from agency professionals and clients. Thanks for your help and experience. (You know who you are.)

A few people are entitled to specific thanks:

H. J. and **Babette K. Bendinger** who taught me that life is a team sport.

Dave Berger and **Norm Brown** of FCB for help on early versions and **The FCB Library** for valuable assistance. **The Leo Burnett Company** for a terrific four year education. **Howard Cutler** and "Adopt a School." **Ken Jones** and **Jim Gilmore** of MSU, and the late **Prof. Larry Baricevic** of St. Louis University.

Cynthia Burns, formerly of the Kellogg School at Northwestern, and **Paul Geisler** of Kimberly-Clark, for help and assistance in the Strategy section.

Apple Computer (particularly Rich Binell), for their support of a strategy seminar that resulted in great improvements, and **Chris Wall,** formerly of BBDO/LA, for his wonderful piece on Apple.

Norm Grey (formerly of **The Portfolio Center,** now head of **The Creative Circus**), for hosting a week to class-test and work on the New (2nd) Edition.

Roy Sandstrom for type and cover design.

Harant Soghigian and **"Sam" Macuga,** agency professionals dedicated to quality. Thanks for the use of 8 Quince Street on Nantucket, where the initial version of this book was written…

To **Alan Quarry** for the Canadian translation.

Much thanks to **Kevin Heubusch** for industrial-strength proofing and to **Last Minute 'Lizabeth** for coming through once again.

To **The Copy Workshop Crew,** for going above and beyond every day…

…and most of all… **Lorelei.**

Acknowledgements:

IT'S HARD TO READ the label when you're inside the bottle. As we finished this book, I was finally able to take a look at what we've done.

Clearly, I need to thank two people – **Howard Gossage** and **Marshall McLuhan**.

In a time of complexity and revolutionary change, they offer us a simple perspective.

It's the media evolution, stupid.

THE SUPPORTING CAST.

That said, a few more need to be thanked.

Dan Wieden, son of an ad man, who was early to the new rules of the game.

Jeff Goodby, who knew, perhaps before any of us, that Howard's story was going to be at the heart of it.

And **Alex Bogusky**, next generation of a designing family, who saw that it was time for our industry to get over its fear of controversy and head into the eye of the storm.

BUT WAIT… THERE'S MORE.

A few others helped make it happen.

Dave Kennedy. I listened. I remembered. Thanks.

George Burrows, who brought Jeff and I together over a well-chosen bottle of wine.

Stephanie McLuhan, who stayed at our offices and left us her father's legacy.

Rich Binell, working copywriter, still hanging ten on the waves of change. He reminds us that even in the middle of a revolution, there's time for fatherhood, fishing, and friendship.

—Bruce Bendinger

BOOKS FROM THE COPY WORKSHOP

adbuzz.com | 773-871-1179 | FAX 773-281-4643 | thecopyworkshop@aol.com

INFORMATION

DESCRIPTION

Advertising & The Business of Brands:
Media Revolution Edition.
by Bendinger, Altman, Avery, Barnes, et. al

600 pages, $80.00

ISBN# 978-1-887229-38-8

It's a revolution! A Media Revolution! Twelve of the top professors in ad education team up to create an up-to-date introduction. If you want to learn how the ad business really works, how it's meeting the challenge, and where you can get started, this is the book. Want to know more? Visit the Study Hall at adbuzz.com and try your hard at the Practice Tests

Strategic Media Decisions, 2nd Ed.:
Understanding The Business End Of The Advertising Business
by Marian Azzaro, w. Carla Lloyd, Mary Alice Shaver, Dan Binder, Robb Clawson, and Olaf Werder
556 pages, $67.50

ISBN# 978-1-887229-33-3

Welcome to the $300 billion business of media. Learn how it works from some of media's top professors and top professionals. This is a book in touch with today - packed with genuine substance and contemporary best practices in a clear, easy-to-read format.
FREE WORKBOOK. A student workbook is available on the MediaBuzz Web site, which also features additional material and information.

The New Account Manager, 2nd Ed.:
by Don Dickinson

414 pages, $47.50

ISBN# 978-1-887229-37-1

A smart book about one of the most challenging jobs in business - account management.
Use as a core text for a management course, or as a supplement for your student agency.
The 2nd Edition includes a new chapter on Account Management in the Era of IMC, featuring contributions from top professionals in a variety of fields.

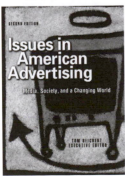

Issues in American Advertising:
Media, Society, and a Changing World
by Tom Reichert, et al.

328 pages, $45.00

ISBN# 978-1-887229-35-7

Professor Tom Reichert felt he needed a small supplement for his large intro class – one that exposed beginning students to a few of today's important issues. It was reader-friendly and contemporary. Then we decided to turn it into a full-blown advertising and society text – with contributions from top people in each area. 18 timely topics written for a student audience.

BOOKS FROM **THE COPY WORKSHOP**

adbuzz.com | 773-871-1179 | FAX 773-281-4643 | thecopyworkshop@aol.com

INFORMATION

DESCRIPTION

The Book of Gossage
by Howard Luck Gossage
Introduction by Jeff Goodby, w.
Stan Freberg, Kim Rotzoll, John
Steinbeck, and Tom Wolfe.

2nd Edition -
Includes the Disc
of Gossage. 400
pages. $50.00

ISBN# 978-1-887229-28-9

This is a book about and by *"The
Socrates of San Francisco,"* Howard
Gossage, the copywriter who introduced the world to Marshall McLuhan, helped start Friends of the Earth
and brought interactivity to his unique
brand of advertising.
He was 30 years ahead of his time, so
the world may be ready.
The Second Edition also features
The Disc of Gossage - packed with
extras; a radio address, an ad gallery,
and more.

How To Succeed In Advertising When All You Have Is Talent
by Laurence Minsky

480 pages, $47.50

ISBN# 978-1-887229-20-3

From the Beetle to the Mini. From "Eat
Mor Chikin" to the AFLAC Duck. From
"Think Different" to "Got Milk." This
completely revised and expanded 2nd
edition includes life lessons from 18 of
advertising's most important talents.

Readings in Account Planning
Edited by Hart Weichselbaum

328 pages, $47.50

ISBN# 978-1-887229-36-4

As Head of Planning for the Richards
Group and one of the founders of the
US Account Planning Group, Hart
Weichselbaum has been one of the
key players in the growing profession
of account planning. He has selected
some of the best articles in the field
for this outstanding collection.

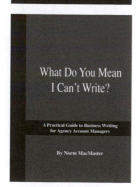

What Do You Mean I Can't Write?
*A Practical Guide To Business
Writing For Agency Account
managers*
by Norm MacMaster

74 pages, $11.75

ISBN # 978-1-887229-29-6

Years ago, top ad agency executive
Norm MacMaster wrote a guide for
beginning account executives.
It became legendary - with copies
handed down from generation to generation. With the author's permission,
we bring this underground classic to
light - clear and practical, it provides
beginners with the information they
need to do the job.